Introduction to

Logic and
Critical Thinking

Introduction to
Logic and
Critical Thinking

Merrilee H. Salmon
University of Pittsburgh

Under the general editorship of Robert J. Fogelin
Dartmouth College

HBJ

Harcourt Brace Jovanovich, Publishers
San Diego   New York   Chicago   Washington, D.C.   Atlanta
London   Sydney   Toronto

For WBH and AHH

ISBN: 0-15-543060-2
Library of Congress Catalog Card Number: 83-82440

Printed in the United States of America

Preface

This book is designed to help students who are beginning college to acquire a deeper understanding of the relationships between logic and language and to increase their skills in critical thinking. Students must be equipped with these skills if they are to be able to recognize situations in which unsupported assertions require justification, to analyze and assess the arguments they encounter in everyday life, and to formulate and present cogent arguments of their own.

Motivation for achieving these goals is provided by means of a variety of examples and exercises that show the usefulness of critical-thinking skills in everyday life. Students are asked to analyze exactly what claims are being made in various contexts and to determine whether reasons are given or should be given to support the claims they are asked to accept. Once assertions that require support have been distinguished from arguments (in which reasons are given for claims), three categories of argument types are distinguished: deductive arguments, inductive arguments, and fallacies. Standards for evaluating various types of arguments are presented. Many examples and exercises focus on the reconstruction of arguments in ordinary language.

A special feature of this text is the careful analysis of inductive reasoning prior to the treatment of deductive arguments. Several reasons can be given for this reversal of what has become the standard order in introductory texts.

- Inductive reasoning based on samples, arguments from analogy, statistical syllogisms, and arguments that attempt to establish causal connections have already been encountered frequently by students in their roles as consumers, citizens, and problem-solvers. Interesting real-life examples can be used to illustrate and explain the standards for evaluating these pervasive forms of argument.
- In their examination of familiar types of inductive reasoning, students gradually gain sensitivity to the structural features of arguments and to such important logical distinctions as the difference between universal and statistical generalizations. They are thus better able to appreciate the value of the more formal treatment of deductive reasoning that follows the analysis of inductive arguments.
- When inductive arguments are presented in this way, students are less likely to be left with the impression that only deductive arguments are really effective and that inductive reasoning is an inferior alternative to be relied on when nothing better is available.

After 16 years of teaching introductory logic courses to small groups of students and to large lecture groups with the assistance of teaching fellows, I am convinced of the value of treating induction before deduction. However, the text is designed so that it can be used by instructors who prefer the more usual order. Chapters 1, 2, 6, 8 (followed by the Appendix), 9, and 10 may be followed by Chapters 3, 4, 5, 7, and 11.

Another unusual feature of this text is its treatment of fallacies. After a brief general account of fallacies is presented in Chapter 2, particular types of fallacies are addressed throughout the text within the context of analyzing the correct forms of inductive and deductive arguments that various fallacies resemble. In addition, some theoretical background is supplied to show that fallacious reasoning frequently involves systematic types of error. One example is the belief that causes must somehow *resemble* their effects; another is the common tendency to overlook solid statistical data when presented with some particularly vivid information that conflicts with the data. Such errors are not the result of carelessness, individual psychological quirks, or an intent to deceive. This approach to fallacies fosters a deeper understanding of correct as well as incorrect forms of reasoning.

The language used in the text is as simple and direct as possible. Technical vocabulary is introduced only when it is required and is redefined in Review sections at the end of each chapter. Formal methods are employed when they are useful for clarification, and even those students who begin the course with an aversion to formalization ("math anxiety") can usually master these methods with little difficulty. Instructors who wish to minimize attention to formal methods can omit the material on probabilities (Chapter 5 and Section VI of Chapter 7), the formal proof method in the Appendix, and Section VII on logic and computers in Chapter 8 without loss of continuity.

All of the material in the text can be covered comfortably in a semester course that meets four times a week. If the course is fast-paced, most of the material can be covered in a semester course that meets three times a week. Fewer hours of class time may require more selective coverage, but the chapters and sections are designed so that this can be done easily. For example, Chapter 5, Section VI of Chapter 7, Section VII of Chapter 8, and the Appendix may be omitted. If time is short, Section IV on Venn diagrams in Chapter 9 may also be omitted, inasmuch as an alternative set of rules is presented for evaluating syllogistic arguments.

Over the years of teaching logic and thinking about how it should be taught, I have received much help from those who were my teachers, teaching assistants, and students. Although they cannot all be named, it is a pleasure to acknowledge their contributions. Special thanks go to Robert Fogelin at Dartmouth College, and to the reviewers, who offered valuable criticisms of a draft of this text: Donald Anderson, Los Angeles Pierce College; Paul Bassen, California State University, Hayward; Charles Chastain, University of Illinois at Chicago Circle; Allan S. Gnagy, University of Kansas; Russell Kahl, San Francisco State University; Walter H. O'Briant, University of Georgia; Elliott R. Sober, University of Wisconsin; Eric Stiffler, Western Illinois University; and Robert Wengert, University of Illinois at Champaign-Urbana. Bill McLane of Harcourt Brace Jovanovich provided expert advice and editorial assistance for which I am most grateful.

Finally, my deepest thanks go to my husband, Wesley C. Salmon, for his logical expertise, generous advice, and staunch support.

Merrilee H. Salmon

Contents

C H A P T E R   4

Causal Arguments   91

C H A P T E R   8

Arguments in Which Validity Depends on Connections Among Sentences

201

C H A P T E R 11

Paying Special Attention to the Language of Arguments: Definitions

295

A P P E N D I X

Proof Method for Truth-Functional Logic

315

INTRODUCTION TO ARGUMENTS

I. INTRODUCTION

"Don't believe everything you hear!" is advice that you have probably received, and given to others, more than once. That advice is not just a warning against liars. It is also encouragement to seek evidence for claims and to judge them in light of that evidence. Gathering evidence and determining whether it supports or undermines questionable claims are two aspects of *critical thinking.*

Critical thinking also involves paying careful attention to what we hear and read so that we can extract the meaning and respond appropriately. In some cases, it would be silly to ask for evidence. A remark about splendid—or foul—weather is usually just a conversation opener; asking for evidence in such circumstances could be done jokingly, but not seriously. Seeking evidence is not ordinarily a suitable response to songs or poetry, or to simple requests, such as "Please pass the salt." We would not ask for evidence when someone claims that her favorite flavor of ice cream is chocolate. Being able to recognize situations in which requests for *evidence* are appropriate is an important part of critical thinking.

We use language primarily to communicate with one another, but communication takes many forms. We sometimes engage in small talk just to "stay in touch" with others. We express our feelings of joy, sorrow, sympathy, anger, hope, and fear in language. We ask questions, give directions, make requests and give commands. We also use language to convey information.

Questions about evidence primarily arise when we use language to transmit information. We should be concerned with evidence whenever it is important to know whether or not what we read or hear about various states of affairs is true.

The context, or situation, in which information is offered influences the degree of evidence that is required. If a stranger tells me there is a fire in the office building where I'm working, I won't bother to acquire much evidence; I will get out as soon as possible. If that same person tells me a building where I used to work burned today, I will turn on my radio or go out for a newspaper to check the story before I accept what I have been told.

There is more at stake than a desire to be well-informed in not wanting to accept falsehoods as true. We *act* on the basis of our beliefs, and many of these actions have serious consequences for our own and our society's well-being.

At one time or another, you have probably thought critically about advertising claims that promise quick and easy weight loss or guarantee to teach techniques that will make you irresistible to members of the opposite sex. If you are like most people, you distrust politicians' claims about their proposed accomplishments in office. You probably wouldn't buy a car from a used-car salesman just because you were told that it had been owned by a little old lady who drove it only on Sundays.

It is more difficult to take a critical attitude toward claims made by your friends and by various "authorities," such as teachers, television newscasters, and newspaper reporters. However, it is often important to insist on evidence even in these contexts, especially when you intend to act on the information you receive from these sources. Many considerations apply to questions of the *quan-*

tity and the *quality* of evidence required to support a particular claim. In this text, we will consider these issues in some detail, but a few general remarks and examples will help to get us started.

Trustworthiness of your source of information is, of course, an important consideration. A trusted source, however, does not always override the need for further evidence. For example, if a friend tells you there is a special unadvertised sale of tapes and records at a nearby store, you may not want to check the story before trying to collect some bargains. The cost of acting on information that may be incorrect is not very great in this situation. But if a friend tells you that a certain powdered substance produces a feeling of euphoria and well-being when inhaled, with no unpleasant side effects, you—knowing the risks—will be wise to seek further evidence before trying the substance yourself. The amount of evidence you require before you act on a claim depends in part on the type of consequences for you, or others, if the claim turns out to be true or false.

If we are to take a critical attitude toward information presented to us, we must also understand the difference between *evidence* and other devices that are sometimes used to make us believe the things people want us to believe. Advertising techniques are notorious for successfully convincing people that information about advertised products is reliable. Sometimes evidence is presented to support the truth of advertising claims. Results of tests, such as washing dirty sweatsocks in two types of detergent and comparing the results, are reported in ads. An advertiser sometimes cites evidence gathered by "independent laboratories" to show that a product has all the virtues claimed for it.

In many advertisements, however, no evidence at all is presented. Instead, an ad may show beautiful, athletic, fashionably dressed people who are obviously having a wonderful time smoking the advertiser's cigarettes, or drinking the advertiser's brand of gin. In these cases, *psychological pressure* is used in place of evidence to try to convince us of the superiority of a product.

Threats, which may be either subtle or blunt, are another nonevidential way of getting people to believe things they are told. Political campaigns often play on the fears of voters by showing scenes of violence and proclaiming that the candidate will reduce crime in the streets. This shows some concern on the part of the candidate for the problem. Pictures or descriptions of violent crime, however, are obviously not *evidence* that the candidate has the ability to do anything about the situation. Nevertheless, such techniques are often effective in making people believe this is so.

It is not always wrong to use means other than evidence to convince people to believe claims. However, it is a serious intellectual mistake to fail to distinguish between nonevidential persuasion to support a claim and evidence to support a claim. This mistake is called *committing a fallacy.*

Exercises

Consider each of the following exercises (contexts are given in each case), and then answer these questions:

(1) What claims are presented?

(2) Is any evidence offered for the claims?

(3) Is it appropriate to seek evidence, or further evidence, under the circumstances?

(The first two exercises are answered for you. Do you agree with these answers?)

1. Taken from a nonfiction travel book, *Prospero's Cell*, by novelist Lawrence Durrell:

> Climb to Vigla in the time of cherries and look down. You will see that the island [Corcyra] lies against the mainland roughly in the form of a sickle. On the landward side you have a great bay, noble and serene, and almost completely landlocked. Northward the tip of the sickle almost touches Albania and here the troubled blue of the Ionian is sucked harshly between ribs of limestone and spits of sand. Kalamai fronts the Albanian foothills, and into it the water races as into a swimming pool; a milky ferocious green when the north wind curdles it.

This passage claims that from a given vantage point (Vigla) in summer (the time of cherries), you can see the sickle shape of the island. Durrell describes Corcyra's location with respect to surrounding geographical features, states, and towns. The language that is used in the description is very expressive (for example, "the troubled blue . . . is sucked harshly between ribs of limestone") and is designed to convey the feelings of both serenity and untamed beauty that the island has inspired in the author.

Durrell offers no evidence to support his claims. He does speak with the authority of one who has been there. There is no special reason to doubt the information he presents—he is not being paid to promote trips to Corcyra. If the reader is concerned with acquiring knowledge about faraway places, or plans to take a trip to the island, or simply enjoys the beauty of the author's language, no evidence is required. If, however, the reader requires precise knowledge of the terrain described, say to plan a military invasion of the area, further evidence is desirable.

2. An account of *Amanita verna*, a type of wild mushroom, taken from *The Mushroom Hunter's Field Guide,* a book by Professor A.H. Smith, a recognized expert on mushrooms:

> Edibility: Deadly poisonous. The symptoms are delayed, making applications of first aid almost useless. Never eat a white *Amanita*.

Here, information about the poisonous character of the *Amanita* and the difficulty of treating cases of such poisoning is presented, along with a directive not to eat any white *Amanita*. No evidence is provided, but the context of the situation—especially the credentials of the author—gives the reader good reason to accept the claims and to follow the expert's advice without additional evidence.

3. Taken from a story in a college newspaper, the *Arizona Daily Wildcat,* by Beverly Medlyn, a student reporter:

> A comparison of annual rates of four major insurance companies reveals that [the costs of] identical automobile insurance policies for college students vary by as much as $200. [The comparison, described later in the same story, consisted of telephone interviews with insurance agents from the four companies. The reporter inquired about rates for a 20-year-old male college student, who had no history of automobile accidents; automobile make, model, and year were specified in each case.] So it pays to shop around and research the various types of coverage in order to get the best deal.

4. Taken from a newspaper report by Associated Press Science Writer, Alton Blakeslee. (Your attention should be directed to the claims and evidence presented by the proponents of legalizing marijuana.)

> Proponents of legalizing [marijuana] are apparently growing in number. They argue that it is less dangerous than alcohol, which kills thousands of Americans each year. No one becomes physically addicted to pot, they say, and it doesn't kill anyone under its influence. Marijuana, they assert, is safer than smoking regular cigarettes.

5. Taken from a nonfiction book, *None Dare Call It Conspiracy,* by Gary Allen:

> In the Bolshevik Revolution we have some of the world's richest and most powerful men financing a movement which claims its very existence is based on the concept of stripping of their wealth men like the Rothschilds, Rockefellers, Schiffs, Warburgs, Morgans, Harrimans, and Milners. But obviously these men have no fear of international communism. It is only logical to assume that if they financed it and do not fear it, it must be because they control it.

6. Taken from a sports news show. A football player comments on whether college football players should be paid for playing ball:

> Football players should be paid because they work five or six hours a day, and have to play—work again—on Saturdays. It is just like a real job.

7. A description of a television commercial for a particular brand of travelers' checks:

> The scene shows a young American couple, on vacation in the Orient. The woman, who looks pained and worried, tells the man that she has lost her purse, which contains all their money, checks, and identification. He seems alarmed, and together they hurry to the tour director. After the tour director ascertains that their checks were the advertised brand, he assures them there is no need to worry, because they can get help at a nearby office.

8. From a newspaper column, "Let's Explore Your Mind," by Albert Edward Wiggam:

> *Why does it cost Dad more these days to send Daughter to college?*
> Changes in styles are responsible. When Matthew Vassar founded Vassar College in 1861, three nails were provided for each girl's clothing—one each for nightgown, day dress and Sunday frock. Nowadays, when a girl unpacks her trunks at college, she has far more feminine contraptions than a family of 10 daughters had 100 years ago. Poor Dad!

9. From a letter to the editor in a newspaper, regarding the Supreme Court decision disallowing school prayer:

> Communism has won its greatest victory. Communists do not pray in school. Americans will not pray in school.... Without the sincere planting of the seeds of prayer in all of our children, Catholic, Protestant, and Jewish, we are finished. Communism has won. It's just a matter of time.

10. From a *Chicago Daily News* story about the alleged decline of the institution of marriage:

> It is false to say that the institution of marriage is falling apart; it is true, I think, that people are demanding more of their marriage partners than they used to—which, in the long run, is a step forward despite the chaos it creates for our age. If marriage were *really* falling apart, divorced persons wouldn't be as eager as they are to find another partner as speedily as possible.

11. From *Maya Archaeologist,* by J. Eric S. Thompson. Thompson is discussing a piece of carved jade, found at an ancient Mayan site:

> On its back was a yellowish stain to which adhered a very small quantity of a sticky black material.... [O]n burning, it gave out a smell very like the unmistakable odor of burned rubber. The Maya burned rubber as an offering to the gods, not because of the smell, for one can't imagine anyone, human or divine, enjoying that, but, I think, because the black smoke evoked the black rain clouds under the old magical formula that like attracts like. Accordingly, it is reasonable to suppose that this little jade figure was placed on burning rubber in some sacrificial rite.

12. From *The Population Bomb,* by Dr. Paul R. Ehrlich. Lead poisoning is a serious illness. It causes mental and physical decay, and often leads to death:

> It is a sobering thought that overexposure to lead was probably a factor in the decline of the Roman Empire.... Romans lined their bronze cooking, eating, and wine storage vessels with lead. They thus avoided the obvious and unpleasant taste and symptoms of copper poisoning. They traded them for the pleasant flavor and more subtle poisoning associated with lead. Lead was also common in Roman life in the form of paints, and lead pipes were often used to carry water. Examination of the bones of upper-class Romans of the classical period shows high concentrations of lead—possibly one cause

of the famous decadence of Roman leadership. The lower classes lived more simply, drank less wine from lead-lined containers, and thus may have picked up far less lead.

13. From Shakespeare's *King Lear*. (Cordelia has been hanged; the lifeless body of his daughter is placed in Lear's arms.)

> *Lear:* She's gone for ever.
> I know when one is dead and when one lives;
> She's dead as earth. Lend me a looking glass;
> If that her breath will mist or stain the stone,
> Why then she lives.

14. From a United Press International newspaper story quoting Dr. L. Nelson Bell, moderator of the Presbyterian Church in the United States. (Discuss the claims made by Dr. Bell, not those made by the reporter.)

> "To deny the existence of Satan and the reality of evil spirits is to be more foolish than a soldier reconnoitering enemy territory without admitting that there is an enemy out there to do him harm."
> Acknowledging that the "unseen power" of evil spirits is a difficult concept for the modern mind, Dr. Bell added, "Electricity is also mysterious, but we do not question its existence or its power."
> "We can be sure electricity is real, because we can see and feel the things it accomplishes, such as lighting and cooling homes.
> "But if pain, hatred, war, suspicion, racism and other evils are manifestations of the devil's work, who is to say there is any lack of evidence in the modern world for his reality?"

II. ARGUMENTS

Evidence may be either verbal or physical. When you return damaged goods to a store to prove their condition before you collect a refund, you are presenting physical evidence to support your claim that the goods are damaged. Some situations—like requests for refunds—customarily require physical evidence. Remember all those detective stories which say that without a body there is no evidence a murder was committed?

In this text, we will be concerned primarily with *verbal evidence* to support the truth of claims. Verbal evidence may be presented in speech or in writing, and can include descriptions of physical evidence, since descriptions are formulated in words. The set of sentences consisting of the verbal evidence to support a claim together with the claim itself is called an *argument*. When we support claims by offering verbal evidence for them, we are *arguing* for our claims.

These uses of the terms "argument" and "arguing" are different from another use of the terms, which employs "argument" to refer to a dispute or disagreement and "arguing" to refer to the activity of engaging in verbal disagreement. The two uses are not entirely unrelated; when we are involved in a disagreement or dispute, we often try to show that our position is correct by stating evidence to support it. In dealing with problems of critical thinking, however, the word "argument" most commonly refers to a set of sentences related in such a way that some of the sentences purport to provide evidence to support one of the sentences, without any suggestion of dispute or disagreement.

Logic is the field of study concerned with analyzing arguments and appraising their correctness or incorrectness. The logician is interested in whether the alleged evidence in an argument would, if it were true, support the claim in question. Thus, logic is an important part of critical thinking.

In our study of arguments, it will be helpful to use special terms to refer to the separate parts of an argument. The sentences that state the evidence are called *premisses;* and the claim that is being argued for is called the *conclusion.* An argument may have any number of premisses, but it can have only one conclusion. In Exercise 6 of Section I, the argument that concluded college football players should be paid had two premisses: (1) Players have to work long hours; and (2) playing football is just like other real jobs.

The following argument has just one premiss:

> Abortion is the same as murder. Therefore, abortion is morally wrong.

Many arguments have more than two premisses. Darwin once said that his entire book, *The Origin of Species,* was just one long argument for a single conclusion: the truth of evolution.

A sentence acquires status as a premiss or a conclusion according to the role it plays in a given argument. The sentence "Abortion is the same as murder," which is the only premiss in the above argument, might be stated as the conclusion of a different argument in which someone tried to establish its truth. For example, the following argument has two premisses:

> Fetuses are persons. Any deliberate killing of a person is murder. Therefore, abortion is murder.

and its conclusion is the same sentence that served as a premiss in the earlier argument.

Of course, we could develop further arguments with new premisses to support either of the sentences that are the premisses of this argument. Although it is always possible to question the premisses of an argument—to ask for other arguments to support those premisses—this process stops in actual discussion when premisses are reached that can be agreed on as a starting point. Sometimes this happens quite quickly, especially when premisses state what easily can be observed as true. Other times, such as when the arguments concern the morality of abortion and the legalization of marijuana, it may take a long time to agree on premisses any less controversial than the proposed conclusions. Sometimes, disagreements are so deep that it may not be possible to agree on any mutually acceptable premisses.

Normally, the point of an argument is to establish the truth of its conclusion, which requires that (1) the premisses in the argument must themselves be true,* and (2) the premisses must provide the right type of support for the conclusion. Logic is concerned chiefly with the second point, namely, the relationship between the premisses and the conclusion. When we examine an argument in order to determine its *logical* strength, the question of whether the premisses are actually true is set aside in favor of answering whether the premisses *would* support the conclusion *if* they were true.

In a sense, critical thinking is broader in scope than logic, for in the former activity we must be concerned with whether the premisses are true and, perhaps, with the possibility of finding further arguments to support any questionable premisses. However, even when we are concerned with the truth of premisses, it is advisable to treat that question separately from whether the premisses, *if* true, would support the conclusion of a given argument.

Premisses and conclusions of arguments are usually stated in *declarative sentences.* These sentences are most commonly used in English to present information, or to "state the facts," and as such—in contrast to questions and commands—are either true or false.

Consider the following argument given by opponents of the legalization of marijuana:

> Marijuana should not be legalized because it is potentially dangerous and not enough is known about its long-term effects, and because use of marijuana leads to use of hard drugs.

The conclusion of this argument is the declarative sentence, "Marijuana should not be legalized." The three declarative sentences, conjoined in a complex sentence, that serve as premisses are: "it is potentially dangerous," "not enough is known about its long term effects," and "use of marijuana leads to use of hard drugs." Each of these sentences is a claim that might be either true or false. For the truth of the conclusion of the argument to be established, all of these premisses must be true *and* must provide good reasons for accepting the conclusion.

Although premisses and conclusions of arguments are usually declarative sentences, occasionally other types occur. The following argument, taken from *Our Mutual Friend,* by Charles Dickens, is presented by Gaffer, a river boatman, to a friend who has just helped him empty the pockets in clothing taken from a body they found floating in the Thames. Gaffer tries to convince his friend that this was not a robbery.

> And what if I had been accused of robbing a dead man, Gaffer?
> You COULDN'T do it.
> Couldn't you, Gaffer?
> No. Has a dead man any use for money? Is it possible for a dead man to have money? What world does a dead man belong to? T'other world. What world does money belong to? This world. How can money be a corpse's? Can a corpse own it, want it, spend it, claim it, miss it? Don't try to go confounding the rights and wrongs of things in that way.

*An exception to this requirement for true premisses occurs in a form of reasoning called *indirect argument,* which we will discuss in Chapter 2.

The premisses supporting the claim that dead men cannot be robbed are stated here in a series of questions. They are called *rhetorical questions* because it is assumed that only one answer can be given to them. Thus, these questions are similar to sentences that state facts and are unlike ordinary questions. Sometimes rhetorical questions are used to state the premisses or the conclusion of an argument in a dramatic fashion. If Gaffer had flatly said, "Money cannot be owned, wanted, spent, claimed, or missed by a corpse," the information conveyed would have been the same, but the interest and color displayed in his speech would have been quite different, and his argument may have seemed less persuasive.

III. RECOGNIZING ARGUMENTS

Before we can begin our detailed study of different types of arguments, we have to be able to recognize arguments as they occur in ordinary speech and writing. It would make no sense to accuse someone of presenting a weak argument for a case if no argument at all were being offered. The most we can reasonably do in such circumstances is to say that an argument *should* be given to support the claim.

Recognizing arguments is sometimes relatively easy because certain words in English, called *indicator words,* signal the presence of either premisses or conclusions of arguments. In several of the arguments presented already, the word "therefore" served to introduce conclusions. This is such a common use of the term in English that whenever "therefore" occurs we should be alert to the possibility that an argument is being presented—or at least is intended. Other terms often used to indicate the conclusion of an argument are "thus," "and so," "consequently," "necessarily," "hence," "it follows that," and "for that reason." Terms commonly used to indicate premisses are "because," "since," "for," and "for the reason that."

In the following the indicator words are underlined:

1. Taken from an ad paid for by the Mobil Corporation:

   Since private business is the most effective instrument of economic change, the government should utilize the resources of private business in its economic planning and decision making.

   Here, "private business is the most effective instrument of economic change" is the premiss. It purportedly supports the sentence that follows the comma. The premiss is signaled by the indicator word "since."

2. Taken from a newspaper story in support of equal pay for women office workers:

   Women office workers work just as hard as men office workers, and are just as productive. Therefore women office workers should receive the same pay as men in comparable positions.

Here, the indicator word "therefore" introduces the conclusion of the argument. The premiss is stated before the conclusion.

3. From a book, *The Vietnam War and the Right of Resistance,* by J. G. Murphy:

> Those who opposed the war by resistance to Selective Service may not fairly be charged with violating their moral obligation to obey the law of the land. <u>For</u> a condition of that obligation has been violated by government, and in so doing, government has forfeited its moral right to call upon citizens for obedience in this area.

In this argument, the conclusion is stated first and is followed by two supporting premisses, indicated by "for," which precedes them.

We cannot simply assume that an argument is present each time these special words occur, because they have other uses in English as well. "Since," for example, is sometimes used to indicate passage of time, as in "Since Harry has been away at college he has been receiving his hometown paper in the mail."

"Because" is frequently used to express a causal connection between two events, rather than to offer evidence that one of those events occurred. An example of this use of "because" occurs in the sentence "Richard Nixon resigned the presidency because a scandal resulted from the Watergate break-in and subsequent investigations." Here, no attempt is made to prove the truth of the claim that Nixon resigned. Instead, a cause is suggested for the well-known fact of his resignation.

It could be *argued* that Watergate was the cause of Nixon's resignation. Such an argument would state evidence that the Watergate events were *causally related* to the resignation. It might show that other suspected causes, such as Nixon's concern for national harmony, were not causally related to the resignation. Causal claims are not arguments, but they are sometimes premisses or conclusions of arguments.

Terms other than "because" are also used to indicate a causal connection between events. "For," "since," "thus," and "therefore" may all be used in this way. "Thus" is also sometimes used to introduce an example of some important point that a speaker or writer is trying to make. One example of this use of "thus" occurs in "Not all mammals give birth to live young. <u>Thus</u> the platypus is an egg-laying mammal."

It is helpful, when trying to decide whether an argument is present, to consider the context carefully and to ask

(i) Is the speaker or writer presenting evidence to support the truth of some claim?

(ii) Is the speaker or writer trying to explain why something happened when the fact that it did happen is not in question?

(iii) Is an example or illustration—rather than an argument—being presented?

Sometimes, particularly when the subject matter is unfamiliar, it is difficult to tell whether a causal claim or an argument is being presented. If, for example, someone were to tell me that the National College Athletic Association will soon rule that football players can be paid by colleges for playing ball because there has been so much pressure in favor of this move, I would not know whether this was an argument or a causal claim. Since I don't keep up with football news, I don't know what rulings have been made or are being contemplated.

It is an argument if I am being told that pressure for paying players is a *reason to believe* that the ruling will change. It is a causal claim if I am being told that the new rule that is going into effect is a result of pressure that was exerted. In many cases, we must ask questions, examine the context of the claim for clues, or make "educated guesses" about the intent of the person before we can decide whether a causal claim or an argument is being stated.

Another difficulty in recognizing arguments arises because very often they contain no words to indicate premises or conclusions. Here is such an argument, taken from a decision by the United States District Court of Appeals (District of Columbia; Bazelon, *Washington v. United States*):

> A judgment of acquittal by reason of insanity is appropriate only when a jury verdict of guilty would violate the law or the facts. We cannot say that this was the situation in Washington's case. The district court did not err in its refusal to enter a judgment of acquittal by reason of insanity.

The context (a decision by a court of appeals) is helpful in determining that an argument is being presented, because court rulings are supposed to be supported by reasons. The claim that the district court's judgment was not in error is stated in the last sentence of the passage, and the reasons for this claim (the premises) are given in the first two sentences. When examining a case like this, we should ask ourselves, (1) "What claim is being made?", and (2) "What evidence is offered to support it?" In this case, we can spot the conclusion if we know that it is the business of district courts of appeals to decide whether lower court rulings are correct. Without this background knowledge, it is sometimes difficult to decide whether a given sentence is intended to be a premiss or conclusion.

When no indicator words are present, it may be helpful to insert them (premiss indicators before suspected premises, and conclusion indicators before conclusions) to see whether or not the passage makes sense when it is reconstructed in this way. This method will not always work, because if we are very unclear about the context, we may be unable to see whether one way of constructing the passage makes more sense than another way. Assuming that the district court of appeals was ruling on whether the lower court was correct or not, if we inserted indicator words, the decision could read like this:

> Since a judgment of acquittal by reason of insanity is appropriate only when a jury verdict of guilty would violate the law or the facts and since we cannot say that this was the situation in Washington's case, therefore the district court did not err in its refusal to enter a judgment of acquittal by reason of insanity.

The meaning of the original passage is not changed when the indicator words are inserted; this supports our view that an argument is presented, and that we have identified its premises and conclusion correctly.

When we insert indicator words to mark the premises and conclusion of an argument, we must be sensitive to stylistic variations in the way arguments are presented in ordinary language. Frequently, for emphasis, the conclusion of an argument is stated before the premises, but it is stylistically awkward to begin an argument with "therefore." (In example 3 on page 11, the conclusion of the argument is stated first.) If we wish to insert indicator words and to have the passage retain correct English style, we sometimes have to re-order the sentences, putting the conclusion sentence last.

Exercises

In each of the following arguments, identify the premises and the conclusion. Remember that if no indicator words are present, first try to determine what is being argued for and then use the technique of inserting indicator words. Lastly, check to see whether or not the passage makes sense.

1. The earth is spherical in shape. For the night sky looks different in the northern and southern parts of the earth, and this would be so if the earth were spherical in shape.

—Aristotle, *Physics*

2. The human mind is not the same thing as the human brain. The human body, including the brain, is a material thing. The human mind is a spiritual thing. Nothing is both a material thing and a spiritual thing.

—Keith Campbell, *Body and Mind*

3. In England under the blasphemy laws it is illegal to express disbelief in the Christian religion. It is also illegal to teach what Christ taught on the subject of non-resistance . . . [W]hoever wishes to avoid being a criminal must profess to agree with Christ's teachings but must avoid saying what that teaching was.

—Bertrand Russell, *Skeptical Essays*

4. A coin has been tossed 12 times and has shown a "head" each time. The next time this coin is tossed, it will also show a "head."

5. All 70 students who ate dinner at the fraternity house on Friday became ill during the night. None of the students who live at the house but who didn't dine there that night became ill, so the illness must have been food poisoning caused by something served for dinner at the house on Friday.

6. Archaeology is truly an infant discipline. Its parent, anthropology, is scarcely a century old; as the child, it is even younger. Stratigraphic excavation was not done systematically until the early years of the twentieth century; carbon-14 dating is but 18 years old, and the corpus of anthropological theory upon which sound archaeology must rest has only become truly useful during the past 30 years.

—James Deetz, *Invitation to Archaeology*

7. Since there can be no talk of an independent ideology formulated by the working masses themselves in the process of their movement, the *only* choice is either bourgeois or socialist ideology. There is no middle course.... Hence to belittle the socialist ideology *in any way, to turn aside from it in the slightest degree* means to strengthen the bourgeois ideology.

—V.I. Lenin, *What Is to Be Done?*

8. Profits depend more and more on the efficient organization of work and on the 'self-discipline' of the workers rather than simply on speedups and other direct forms of increasing the exploitation of workers. The family is therefore important both to shoulder the burden of higher education, and to carry out the repressive socialization of children. The family must raise children who have internalized hierarchical social relations, who will discipline themselves and work efficiently without constant supervision.

—Peggy Morton, "A Woman's Work is Never
Done," *Leviathan* II

9. The year 1859 is perhaps the most important one in the history of biology to date. In that year Charles Darwin published his theory of evolution by natural selection, which has deeply affected not only biology, but other branches of human thought as well.

—L.C. Dunn and T.H. Dobshansky, *Heredity,
Race and Society*

10. In spite of the general's years, he evidently is a little vain of his person, and ambitious of conquests. I have observed him on Sunday in church eyeing the country girls most suspiciously; and have seen him leer upon them with a downright amorous look, even when he has been gallanting Lady Lilycraft with great ceremony through the churchyard.

—Washington Irving, *Bracebridge Hall*

IV. RECONSTRUCTING ARGUMENTS

In addition to lacking indicator words, arguments in English may fail to state some of the premises, or their conclusions. Moreover, they may occur in a context that includes language that is inessential to the argument itself. Once we recognize the presence of an argument, we frequently must reconstruct it by supplying missing parts and eliminating extraneous materials before we can evaluate its strength. We will consider the question of missing parts first.

1. Incompletely Stated Arguments

In ordinary language, arguments are often stated incompletely to avoid boring the listener or reader with information that is presumably obvious to all concerned.
     "John must have come up with the money to pay his overdue tuition bill, for he is graduating on Sunday " is an incomplete argument. The missing premiss is "No one with an unpaid tuition bill can be graduated from the university." Here, I have supplied a premiss that states "no one ... " because of my experience

with the inflexibility of university administrators on the matter of unpaid bills. Sentences like this premiss that state that *all* or *no* members of one class are members of another class are called *universal generalizations.*

"The Jones are wealthy, since they drive a new Cadillac" is another example of an argument with a missing—but presumably obvious—premiss ("most families who drive new Cadillacs are wealthy"). It is reasonable to ask whether the missing premiss is "All families who drive new Cadillacs are wealthy." "Most" is more likely to yield a true premiss than "all," since driving an expensive automobile is not an infallible mark of wealth. When we supply a missing premiss we want it to be true. Sentences like this premiss, which state that most members of one class are members of another class, are called *statistical generalizations.*

Frequently, missing premisses, like the two just supplied, are generalizations that are presumed to be well-known in the context of the argument. These generalizations connect the particular fact mentioned in the stated premiss with the conclusion. Generalizations state that two types of things are always or usually connected, or—in negative cases—that the two things are never or seldom connected.

Ordinarily, when a missing premiss is an obviously true generalization there is nothing wrong with omitting it. However, if we are particularly concerned with checking the correctness of an argument, we should see that the argument is stated as completely as possible. This means that we must occasionally spell out even what is obvious to everyone.

Another reason for searching out the intended or assumed, but unstated, premises in an argument is that some hidden premisses turn out, when exposed, not to be obviously acceptable. When this is the case, the argument may be weaker than at first we might have supposed. Consider the following two arguments, each of which depends on a general claim that is somewhat more questionable than those in the two examples just presented.

The first argument is taken from *Crime and the Criminal Law,* by Barbara Wootton, who for years was a magistrate in Great Britain and was also one of the first women members of Parliament.

> To punish people merely for what they have done would be unjust, for the forbidden act might have been an accident for which the person who did it cannot be held to blame.

The conclusion of Wootton's argument is that it would be unjust to punish people merely for what they have done (without taking into account their intentions as well as their actions). The reason she offers for this conclusion is that the forbidden act may have been a blameless accident. The unstated premiss, required to connect actions for which persons are not to blame with actions for which they should not be punished, is a general claim: Persons should not be punished for acts unless they deserve blame for those acts.

Is this general principle correct? Certainly in the British system of law, and in our own, actions committed with an evil intent or a "guilty mind" (*mens rea*) are distinguished from accidental actions. Most of us would agree that people should be *blamed* only for acts they intended to do, or at least were negligent in preventing. But both the American and British legal systems sometimes punish people for "accidental" acts, even when no blame is warranted.

These cases, called "cases of strict liability" by the law, include imposing parking fines, even when persons overpark through no fault of their own (a person might faint in a department store or be caught in an elevator between floors) and are not to blame for the circumstances that led to the overparking. Many considerations can be offered to justify strict liability laws. In the case of parking fines, strict liability is justified by appealing to the good use the city makes of the money collected from this source, the minor nuisance of paying a small fine even when the violator is not to blame, and the excessive court costs of allowing defenses for parking violations.

If we accept the principle of strict liability for some kinds of action, we cannot accept the general principle that connects punishment with blame in an unqualified way. The apparent conflict between strict liability and the principle that conduct should be punished only if it is blameworthy can be resolved by restricting the application of strict liability to *noncriminal* cases. Wootton's book, *Crime and the Criminal Law,* is clearly concerned with criminal justice, and her remarks can be taken to apply to this context. The principle connecting punishment with blameworthiness is well established in Anglo-American criminal law.

The second example is taken from *A Treatise of Human Nature* by David Hume:

> Since reason alone can never *produce* any action or give rise to volition [desire], I infer that the same faculty [i.e., reason] is incapable of *preventing* volition or of disputing the preference with any passion or emotion.

Hume, writing in the eighteenth century, was concerned with the nonrational aspect of human life—the area of feelings and emotion. One of his famous sayings is "Reason is and ought only to be the slave of the passions." Hume's words are less startling when we realize that "passions" in those days referred in a general way to human feelings, not specifically to sexual passion. Hume believed that human morality must be founded on the sort of goodness that human beings—with all their biological limitations, natural feelings, and sympathies—are able to achieve, rather than on some intellectual view of an ideal form of goodness.

In this argument for "natural morality," Hume's conclusion is "reason is incapable of preventing volition or of disputing the preference with any passion or emotion." The words "I infer that" indicate a conclusion is being drawn. Hume offers as evidence the claim that "reason" (the human intellect) cannot by itself produce or cause our desires and wishes. The hidden premiss in this argument seems to be the claim that a general connection exists between the lack of power to cause something and the lack of power to prevent that same thing:

> Nothing that is powerless to cause an activity or event of a certain sort is powerful enough to prevent that activity or event.

Does this premiss seem obviously true to you? A wall can stop a rolling ball, but it cannot set the ball in motion. Sometimes it seems to me that I can just look the wrong way at machines and *prevent* them from operating properly, but I certainly have no power to cause those same machines to function the way they should. I can prevent my watch from operating by dropping it into dishwater, but I am powerless to build a new watch or to repair a damaged one.

Perhaps we could restate or qualify Hume's missing premiss so that it appears more plausible. If, for example, Hume was referring not to individual human capacities but to what humans in general can do, the example concerning my watch is no longer applicable, because human beings can both produce and destroy watches. Can you think of a case in which humans in general have no power to cause or produce something but do have the power to prevent its operation?

When we are reconstructing arguments, as when we are determining whether an argument is being offered, careful attention to context—written, spoken, or implied—is crucial. If we intend to deal seriously with Hume's or Wootton's arguments, we must consider them in the larger context of these authors' works, and use whatever information we can gather to supply missing premisses. When we are engaged in a discussion with another person who presents an argument, we should ask questions to clarify any unstated premisses. When we are presenting arguments of our own, we should be sure they do not contain any hidden premisses that, if stated explicitly, would undermine our arguments.

When we are reconstructing arguments in situations that provide inadequate contextual information, we should supply the missing premisses that are the most plausible under the circumstances. This means that the missing premisses should have "the ring of truth." They should be premisses, that although they may not actually *be* true, at least are not known to be false or are not wildly unbelievable. The missing premisses should also be claims we could reasonably expect the proponent of the argument to accept.

Missing premisses of arguments are not always generalizations like those discussed in this section. However, we will postpone looking at other kinds of missing premisses until we examine specific types of arguments in a more detailed way.

Exercises

In each of the following examples, an unstated general claim is required to complete the premisses of the argument. Try to supply a plausible premiss to complete each argument. If the required missing premiss seems implausible, explain why.

1. Women office workers work just as hard as men office workers and are just as productive. Therefore, women office workers should receive the same pay as men in comparable positions.
2. Marijuana should not be legalized because it is potentially dangerous with respect to its long-term effects.
3. Marijuana should be legalized because it is no more dangerous than alcohol, which is already legal.

4. Marijuana should be legalized because the laws against it are not respected, and this breeds contempt for law in general.

5. Marijuana should not be legalized because it leads to the use of harder drugs, such as heroin.

6. Tomatoes will be expensive in late winter, since growers in Florida were hit by a hard freeze in December.

7. The boy who sits next to me in class doesn't have a home telephone, for he isn't listed in the telephone directory.

8. The governor doesn't have a private telephone, for there is no listing for his private phone in the telephone directory.

9. Prices are bound to drop soon, since they have been rising for a long time now.

10. You will pass the final exam in math, since you have passed all the earlier exams in the course.

11. Your tires should hold out for the coast-to-coast drive, since they have made it six times before without any trouble.

12. A head will show on the next toss of the coin, for the past six tosses have been heads.

2. Extracting the Essentials of an Argument From Its Surrounding Context

We will return to the problem of missing premisses in later chapters. Now we will turn to the question of sorting out the parts of an argument in contexts that contain sentences that are neither the premisses nor the conclusion of the argument.

Sometimes the additional material is background information inserted to tell us something about the quality of the evidence, how it was gathered, or why it is relevant to the conclusion. Consider the following passage, taken from *Sexual Politics* by Kate Millett:

> A witty experiment by Philip Goldberg proves what everyone knows, that having internalized the disesteem in which they are held, women despise both themselves and each other. This simple test consisted of asking women undergraduates to respond to the scholarship in an essay signed alternately by one John McKay and one Joan McKay. In making their assessments, the students generally agreed that John was a remarkable thinker, Joan an unimpressive mind. Yet the articles were identical; the reaction was dependent on the sex of the supposed author.

Our first clue that this passage contains an argument is the claim, presented in the opening sentence, that something is being proved. To prove a claim is to produce evidence that shows it is true. The conclusion of the argument (the sentence that is proved) is "having internalized the disesteem in which they are held, women despise both themselves and each other." The evidence for this conclusion is contained in the premiss: "the reaction [to the essays that were identical except for the sex of the supposed author] was dependent on the sex of the supposed author." Millett's premiss is in turn supported by (is a conclusion drawn from) the outcome of Goldberg's experiment:

> Women undergraduates evaluated identical essays, which differed only in the sexually distinctive names of the supposed authors, as being the work of a remarkable thinker when the supposed author was male, and an ordinary thinker when the supposed author was female.

Additional background information provided in Millett's passage assures us that the conclusion was something already widely known and that the experiment was witty. We are also told that the experiment was a simple test. None of this information is evidence to support the truth of the conclusion, but it does tell us something about the *quality* of the evidence presented and helps us to understand the author's point of view.

Here is another argument stated in a context that contains additional information. This example is taken from the syndicated newspaper column "How to Spot Rich People" by social commentator Andy Rooney:

> Another way to tell a rich person from a poor person is one I learned years ago when I worked for a morning news broadcast. We often had important people on it as guests and I began to notice one thing that the rich men had in common. They never wore overcoats.
>
> Nelson Rockefeller must have been on the show five times on different winter days and he never wore an overcoat or carried one. It was a long while before I realized he was so rich he didn't need one. He was never out in the cold because all he did was walk the ten feet from his chauffeur-driven limousine to the building and anyone can stand that much cold. For all I know Rockefeller didn't even own a raincoat or an umbrella. Most of the restaurants a rich person like him would eat in have canopies extended to the street.

The conclusion of Rooney's argument is "Rich men never wear overcoats." His premisses state that the sample of rich men he observed never wore overcoats. This evidence is strengthened by his suggestion concerning why rich men don't need overcoats. The rest of the passage contains information about how Rooney gathered his sample and humorous speculation about rich men's ability to dispense with raingear as well as overcoats.

Sometimes the context of an argument provides information that indicates something is true, while the argument itself attempts to establish that the situation is a good one or a bad one. In the following argument, philosopher Bertrand Russell, after telling us that rats behave a certain way toward food, argues that rats are sensible to do so.

> Rats will eat food that contains rat poison. But if, before eating, they were to subject their food to scientific analysis, they would die of hunger meanwhile, and so they are well advised to take the risk.

Frequently, examples that illustrate a point occur in the context of arguments. Such *illustrations* are not part of the argument, but they clarify points and aid understanding by making general ideas concrete. Patrick Devlin does this in the following passage from *The Enforcement of Morals*:

> *No society can do without intolerance, indignation, and disgust;* they are the forces behind the moral law, and indeed it can be argued that if they or something like them are not present, the feelings of society cannot be weighty enough to deprive the individual of freedom of choice. I suppose that there is hardly anyone nowadays who would not be disgusted by the thought of cruelty to animals.

Devlin supports his conclusion, which is italicized, with the premises that succeed it in the complex sentence. (His argument also depends on a premiss that is unstated here, but that Devlin tried to establish elsewhere in his book: Society cannot live without morals.) Devlin's concrete example of disgust is provided in the last sentence of the quoted passage.

In addition to background information and examples that serve to illustrate and clarify points, arguments often contain remarks that are intended to put the reader or listener in a *properly receptive frame of mind* to accept their conclusions. Such additional material might convey an atmosphere of humor, fear, seriousness, or any number of other moods. Millett does this, in the argument quoted earlier, when she tells us that Goldberg's experiment proves "what everyone knows." Such a remark may intimidate a reader who feels inclined to disagree with Millett, because it suggests that anyone who does not agree with her conclusion is disputing common wisdom. This tends to distract the reader from a critical examination of Millett's particular argument for that claim.

When we examine the support that the evidence provides for a conclusion, we should carefully separate any additional material from the actual evidence. The extra material may appeal to our emotions and discourage us from taking a close critical look at the central issue: Does the alleged evidence support the conclusion?

Sometimes arguments in ordinary language repeat—using slightly different wording—statements that already have been made in a premiss or in the conclusion of the argument. Quite often, a conclusion is stated at the beginning of a passage, followed by reasons for accepting that conclusion, followed by a restatement of the conclusion. When an argument is rather long and complicated, this is done merely for clarity and emphasis. Repetition is designed to ensure that the reader or listener does not fail to get the point. However, there are other motives behind repetition in some cases. As advertisers have taught us, repeated exposure to a claim can convince people that it is true, even when only flimsy evidence, or no evidence at all, has been offered. Consider the following passage, taken from *The Odd Woman,* a novel by George Gissing, and try to decide what use is served by repeating the conclusion at the end of the argument after stating it initially:

> It is the duty of every man, who has sufficient means, to maintain a wife. The life of an unmarried woman is a wretched one; every man who is able ought to save one of them from that fate.

Exercises

Each of the following passages contains at least one argument. For each argument, identify the premises and the conclusion, and discuss the role of any additional material in the passages.

1. Dear Readers: Here is the second part of Dr. George Ryan's testimony at a Senate Judiciary Subcommittee hearing on the human life bill. [The bill would make abortion, the Pill, and the intra-uterine contraceptive device illegal.]

Question: What economic effect would this bill have on those women?
Answer: Paradoxical. The president has promised to get government off our backs. This bill would not only LEAVE government on our backs, it would put government in our bedrooms. If this bill is passed and abortions are made illegal, it means at least another 700,000 babies will be born next year. A substantial percentage will be born to the poor and the very young—about two-thirds of whom will collect welfare.

Instead of a single cost of $125 for an abortion, we will pay $1,000 to $1,500 for a delivery, and at least $100,000 to support these welfare children until they reach maturity. This is a commitment of about 40 billion dollars each year.

Question: How did you come up with those figures?
Answer: Simple mathematics. I took the 1.4 million abortions [now being performed] a year—let's be conservative and say only half those women actually have babies. The other half would probably get illegal abortions or go out of the country to get one. But the remaining half are stuck—and probably poor. If two-thirds are on welfare, we are talking about 400,000 babies a year.

—Syndicated newspaper column by Ann Landers

2. In the past there has been much argument whether, in the strategy of inflation control, one should seek to come to grips with the level of demand or whether one should seek to deal with the wage-price spiral. . . . The proper answer is that both are important. Inflation could be controlled by a sufficiently heavy reduction in the level of demand. It could also be controlled with a less drastic reduction if something could be done to arrest the interreactions of wages and prices, or, to speak more precisely, of wages, profits, and prices.

—John Kenneth Galbraith, *The Affluent Society*

3. The public and its elected representatives are blessed with few issues so clearly defined, or with debates so easily divisible into right and wrong, as is the question of the Equal Rights Amendment.

The brevity and simple eloquence of the amendment (It might have been written by Hemingway, had he lived) deny the possibility that arcane shadings of interpretation could exist within its passages. There is no fine print, there are no subordinate clauses, subparagraphs, footnotes, nor any of the complex constructions of language and logic which lay most legislation open to disagreement.

There is only this: Equality of rights under the law shall not be denied or abridged by the United States or by any state on account of sex.

—Editorial, *Arizona Daily Star*

4. *Background information:* Discrimination—refusing to admit someone to a public place or business on grounds of race, sex, or religion—is against federal law. However, the law also respects the rights of people to associate privately with whomever they wish.

Last year [the national organization of Jaycees] voted to kick out the women members they had previously recruited. They even voted to kick out the chapters who wouldn't kick out the women they had previously invited. (Who says that chauvinists are chivalrous?)

But in Minnesota, the courts ruled that the Jaycees were actually operating as a public business. They were soliciting memberships, and open to anyone so long as that anyone was a male. So, this duly designated public business was forbidden to discriminate.

—Syndicated newspaper column by Ellen Goodman

5. Of course Stravinsky was right to describe a new piece of music as a new reality. He might also have described it as a new synthesis; for a new composition is just as much a new synthesis of contrasting elements as is a new scientific hypothesis. It is a bringing together of disparate sound sequences imagined by the composer, and is thus bound to reflect something of the composer's mental content.

—Anthony Storr, *The Psychodynamics of Creativity*

6. "Most people wear some sign and don't know what it's saying. Choose your sign according to your audience," Malloy said. . . . "A good dark suit, white shirt and conservative tie are a young man's best wardrobe friends, if he's applying for a white collar job in a big range of business and professional categories. They're authority symbols. It's that simple," he said.

—"Fashion," *Chicago Daily News*

7. An apparently progressive [evolutionary] advance may turn out ultimately to be a limitation. For instance, the insects successfully conquered the land by developing a method for breathing with the aid of fine air-tubes penetrating every tissue of the body. This constitutes an admirable mechanism so long as the creature remains small, but makes large size impossible. An insect as big as a rat just wouldn't work properly; actually no insect is bigger than a mouse. This limitation of total size naturally sets a limit to the size of the brain, and so to the number of cells in the brain, which in turn sets a low limit to the degree of intelligence and the flexibility of behavior. That is why insects are never very intelligent, but have to depend mainly on the marvelous but always rigid and limited behavior mechanisms we call instincts. This limitation of insect size is very lucky for us, because without it, man assuredly could never have evolved.

—Julian Huxley, *New Bottles for Old Wine*

8. "Of course—Mrs. Fairford gives the smartest little dinners in town. There was an account of one she gave last week in this morning's *Town Talk:* I guess it's right here among my clippings." Mrs. Heeny, swooping down on her bag, drew from it a handful of newspaper cuttings, which she spread on her ample lap and proceeded to sort with a moistened forefinger. "Here," she said, holding one of the slips at arm's length; and throwing back her head she read, in a slow unpunctuated chant: " 'Mrs. Henley Fairford gave another of her natty little dinners last Wednesday as usual it was smart small and exclusive and there was much gnashing of teeth among the left-outs as Madame Olga Loukowska gave some of her new steppe dances after dinner'—that's the French for new dance steps," Mrs. Heeny concluded, thrusting the documents back into her bag.

—Edith Wharton, *The Custom of the Country*

9. "A woman knows very well that all the talk about elevated subjects is just talk, but that what a man wants is her body and all that presents it in the most deceptive but alluring light; and she acts accordingly. If we only throw aside our familiarity with this indecency, which has become second nature to us, and look at the life of our upper

classes as it is, in all its shamelessness—why it is simply a brothel. . . . You don't agree? Allow me, I'll prove it," he said, interrupting me. "You say that the women of our society have other interests in life than prostitutes have, but I say no, and will prove it. If people differ in the aims of their lives, by the inner context of their lives, this difference will necessarily be reflected in externals and their externals will be different. But look at those unfortunate despised women and the highest society ladies: the same costumes, the same fashions, the same perfumes, the same exposure of arms, shoulders, and breasts, the same tight skirts over prominent bustles, the same passion for little stones, for costly glittering objects, the same amusements, dances, music, and singing. As the former employ all means to allure, so do these others."

> —Leo Tolstoy, "The Kreutzer Sonata"

10. Other physicists, notably Arthur Holly Compton at the University of Chicago, contended that the cosmic rays were particles. There was a way to investigate the question. If they were charged particles, they should be deflected by the earth's magnetic field as they approached the earth from outer space. Compton studied the measurements of cosmic radiation at various latitudes and found that it did indeed curve with the magnetic field: it was weakest near the magnetic equator and strongest near the poles, where the magnetic lines of force dipped down to the earth.

> —Isaac Asimov, *The Intelligent Man's Guide to the Physical Sciences*

V. REVIEW

The purpose of this chapter was to introduce you to the subject matter of *logic* and *critical thinking*. We have identified a number of skills that contribute to critical thinking:

1. Sensitivity to different uses of language.
2. The ability to recognize when evidence is required to support a claim.
3. Awareness of the distinction between the truth of sentences and the support they would provide for some other sentence *if* they were true.
4. The ability to recognize arguments, to identify their parts, to supply missing premisses that are unstated, and to separate the essential parts of an argument from the context in which it is stated.
5. The logical skill of evaluating an argument in terms of how well the premisses support the conclusion.

All of these critical-thinking skills are useful and important in our everyday lives. Our language reflects what is important in human culture, and, as with other vitally interesting aspects of human life, a special vocabulary has been developed for discussing issues in logic and critical thinking. Since some of this vocabulary may be new to you, it will be helpful to review the definitions of the most important terms:

Argument: A set of sentences related in such a way that some of the sentences purport to provide evidence for another sentence in the set.

Causal Claim: A sentence that states the cause of some event, as in "Rains caused heavy flooding in the suburbs last night."

Committing a Fallacy: Making the mistake of supposing evidence has been presented in support of a claim—or pretending that it has been—when some form of nonevidential persuasion has been used to try to achieve acceptance for a claim.

Conclusion: The sentence in an argument that is supposedly supported by the evidence.

Declarative Sentence: A sentence that asserts that something is the case (as opposed to a question, command, request, or exclamation). Declarative sentences may be either true or false.

Evidence: Support offered for some claim. This support may be physical evidence (as when damaged goods are presented to support the claim that they are defective) or it may be verbal evidence (some sentences are offered to support the truth of another sentence).

Indicator Words: English words commonly used to signal premisses or conclusions of arguments. Examples of premiss indicator words are "for," "since," "because," and "for the reason that." Examples of conclusion indicator words are "hence," "thus," "therefore," "and so," "it follows that," and "for that reason."

Logic: The study devoted to analyzing and evaluating arguments.

Premiss: A sentence that purports to state evidence in an argument.

Statistical Generalization: A sentence that states that some proportion of the members of one class are members of another class. Common forms of these sentences are: "Most _____ are _____," and "Most _____ are not _____." Statistical generalizations may also be expressed numerically, as in "x percent of _____ are _____."

Universal Generalization: A sentence that states that all or none of the members of one class are members of another class. Common forms of these sentences are "All _____ are _____" and "No _____ are _____."

These terms are the most important ones introduced in Chapter 1. We will be using them throughout our discussion. Two other terms that are a part of the standard vocabulary of logic and critical thinking are so often *misused* that they should be mentioned here.

Infer: To infer is to draw a conclusion on the basis of evidence. This is a mental activity that may be—but need not be—expressed in language.

For example, on the basis of the dark circles under my eyes, you may infer that I didn't get enough sleep last night, but you may be too considerate to mention that to me or to anyone else. However, if you *argue* that I didn't get enough sleep, you must *state* both the evidence (cite the dark circles) and the conclusion. Arguing, unlike inferring, is an activity that requires the use of language. When you *state* your reasons for drawing an inference—when you express in language the premisses and the conclusion—you transform the inference into an argument.

"Infer" is *incorrectly* used in the following sentence: "Your words infer that you disapprove of Mary Ann." Here, "infer" is confused with "imply," but the two terms are not interchangeable.

Imply: To imply is to provide a basis from which an inference may be drawn. Words, actions, looks, appearances may all "have implications"—that is, they may provide a basis for someone to infer something from them. It is also appropriate to speak of a person's implying something, through words, silence, looks, or some other feature. "Imply" also has another special meaning, in the context of deductive logic, which will be discussed later.

The best review of this type of subject matter is achieved by working further exercises. If you can complete the exercises in the following section successfully, you will know that you have mastered the material covered in Chapter 1. Some of these exercises are rather difficult, so do not be discouraged if they seem to require a lot of effort. Moreover, since these arguments are stated in ordinary language—which is not always as precise as we would like it to be—and since the selected passages are all taken out of broader contexts, different interpretations of a given passage are quite possible. In a given case, for example, it may not be entirely clear whether the author is providing an argument or a causal explanation or whether the author is providing just one argument or several. If a premiss seems to be missing, the most plausible missing premiss to supply may not be clearly identifiable. Whenever you think that more than one interpretation is plausible, mention this and give your reasons for each interpretation. If the skills of logic and critical thinking you are developing in this course are to be useful to you in the ordinary situations you encounter in everyday life, you must practice with examples taken from such contexts.

VI. EXERCISES

For each of the following passages:

(1) Indicate whether or not the passage contains an argument (or several arguments).

(2) Reconstruct any arguments: Write each premiss and conclusion as a separate sentence, and indicate which sentences are premisses and which sentences are conclusions.

(3) If the argument depends on a missing generalization as an implicit premiss, supply the generalization.

(4) Discuss any cases in which nonevidence, such as a threat, might be mistaken for evidential support.

(5) Indicate what role any additional material that is not part of the premisses or the conclusion plays in the passage.

1. Adam was led to sin by Eve and not Eve by Adam. Therefore it is just and right that woman accept as lord and master him whom she led to sin.

—Saint Ambrose

2. Men were thinking, writing, and creating, because women were pouring their energy into those men; women are not creating culture because they are preoccupied with love.

—Shulamith Firestone, *The Dialectic of Sex*

3. [Pennsylvania] could lose about $91 million in federal highway construction aid because lawmakers have blocked the start of an emission-inspection program for autos in Pittsburgh and Philadelphia.

Senator Eugene Scanlon, D-Allegheny, a leading emission-program critic, said last month he thought "the $91 million was worth it as a matter of principle."

He and his colleagues have maintained the federal government has no right to force a State Legislature to spend money for anything.

—*Pittsburgh Post-Gazette*

4. Pennsylvania may still have an out, if proposed clean-air-law revisions are enacted. [However, the Environmental Protection Agency] "feels the Clean Air Act as now written must be enforced because it is the rule of the land," Wassersug [EPA regional director] said.

—*Pittsburgh Post-Gazette*; (same story as in Exercise 3)

5. Hair analysis has been found to be a good test in screening large groups of people for exposure to toxic trace metals. It is not as widely used as blood analysis, but studies have shown that concentrations of lead, cadmium, arsenic, and mercury in hair provide a good record of exposure.

Also, since the metal grows out with the hair, lengthwise sections of hair can show the approximate time when a short, intense exposure occurred. . . .

Chromium is essential for the hormone insulin to work properly. Thus, in time, it may be that measurements of chromium in hair will be useful in identifying people with diabetes and in monitoring the course of the disease.

—Syndicated newspaper column
"Food for Thought" by Dr. Jean Mayer and
Jeanne Goldberg, R.D.

6. My suggestion for a wine to accompany chocolate desserts is different [from wines made from the muscat grape]. I prefer a rich, slightly sweet red wine. Indeed, it was a chocolate dessert that led me to change my mind about late-harvest zinfandels.

The proper use for those alcoholic, full-fruited wines with considerable residual sugar is with chocolate. The very strength of the wine cuts through the rich heaviness of the chocolate.

—Newspaper column "Wine" by Peter
Machamer, *Pittsburgh Post-Gazette*

7. Dear Ann: I am boiling over with the statement that the Air Force spends $12.6 million per year for private pet service by veterinarians. What nonsense!

Having put in 23 years in the armed forces, I happen to know that every base with a mess hall, in all branches of the Department of Defense, requires that all meat be inspected by veterinarians at the supply points. The meat is then distributed to the various units of the military. This is where the taxpayers' dollars go, and I'm sure you will agree it is a legitimate expenditure.

All services performed on privately owned animals must be paid for by the owners.

—Syndicated newspaper column by Ann Landers

8. The thought tends to wrap itself in a joke because in this way it recommends itself to our attention and can seem more significant and more valuable, but above all because this wrapping bribes our powers of criticism and confuses them. We are inclined to give the *thought* the benefit of what has pleased us in the form of the joke;

and we are no longer inclined to find anything wrong that has given us enjoyment and so spoil the source of the pleasure.

—Sigmund Freud, *Jokes and Their Relation to the Unconscious*

9. It is incontestable that sense perception plays a crucial role in the natural sciences. It serves as the sole means through which we can gather information about the world around us. Knowledge of general laws is posterior, in the empirical sciences, to knowledge of particular instances, and for the latter the evidence of the senses is required.

—Robert Swartz, *Perceiving, Sensing, and Knowing*

10. If a person is known to lie occasionally, it is not reasonable to accept something *simply* on the ground that he testifies to it. Similarly, once the senses have been discovered to be capable of deception, it is not reasonable to regard a belief as solid or permanent *merely* because it is based on sensory evidence. For it may turn out that the occasion on which the senses provided the evidence for the belief was one on which the senses were deceptive; and then, of course, the belief would have to be abandoned. Despite this, however, it may still be reasonable to regard some sensory beliefs as permanent and indubitable, if occasions on which the senses are absolutely reliable can be distinguished from those on which they are likely to deceive.

—Henry Frankfurt, *Demons, Dreamers, and Madmen*

11. Noting the diversity of Paraguayan languages, Dobrizhoffer comments: "Truly admirable is their varied structure, of which no rational person can suppose these stupid savages to have been the architects and inventors. Led by this consideration I have often affirmed that the variety and artful construction of languages should be reckoned among the other arguments to prove the existence of an eternal and omniscient God."

—Marvin Harris, *The Rise of Anthropological Theory*

12. If great art is a product of a great soul only a critic of spiritual stature can hope to recognize and appreciate artistic greatness when he sees it. To the trivial all things are trivial. A critic with limited powers of observation, a weak imagination, and a restricted scale of values must remain blind to artistic greatness and incapable of distinguishing artistic profundity from artistic triviality.

—T. M. Greene, *The Arts and the Art of Criticism*

13. Rules and regulations of the Securities and Exchange Commission compel the prospectus to dwell on all the problems and all the shortcomings the company faces in its competitive battle for survival and success. This is true, and since this is undoubtedly the first and last public occasion on which a company will stress the negative aspects of its situation, and since this is the point of entry for many new stockholders, the value (for investors) of reading the prospectus is enormous.

—*The Fine Art of Making Money in the Stock Market*

14. Poetry, indeed, cannot be translated, and therefore it is the poets who preserve languages; for we would not be at the trouble to learn a language when we can have all that is written in it just as well in translation. But, as we cannot have the beauties of poetry but in its original language, we learn it.

—Samuel Johnson

15. Encouragement of contempt for laws is more dangerous to society than occasional use of marijuana. Severe laws against marijuana do not discourage use of marijuana, but rather breed this contempt not only for drug laws, but for laws in general. Therefore severe laws against marijuana are more dangerous to society than the activity which they are designed to prevent.

—A. Blakeslee, "Should Marijuana Be Legalized?"
Associated Press

16. At this moment the King, who had been for some time busily writing in his notebook, called out "Silence!" and read out from his book, "Rule forty-two. All persons over one mile high to leave the courtroom."
"... that's not a regular rule; you inserted it just now."
"It's the oldest rule in the book," said the King.
"Then it ought to be number one," said Alice.

—Lewis Carroll, *Alice in Wonderland*

[Here, what is Alice's argument?]

17. Referring to the island of Corsica (note the rhetorical questions):

What can be found so bare, what so rugged all around as this rock? What more barren of provisions? What more rude as to its inhabitants? What in the very situation of the place more horrible? What in climate more intemperate? Yet there are more foreigners than natives here. So far then is a change of place from being disagreeable, that even this place hath brought some people away from their country.

—Seneca, *Ad Helviam de Consolatione,* quoted in
James Boswell, *Boswell on the Grand Tour*

18. Referring to a debate about whether humans have free will:

We were eating cold fruit-soup. The soup was served in a huge tureen. It was a beautiful piece of china, and Maria was particularly fond of it. She hated things being broken, even a Woolworth tumbler. The veranda was surrounded by large polished panels of glass. I got up, by now trembling with anger, and lifted the tureen up from the table. I said:
"Look, Maria, let us settle this problem in an empirical way, once and for all. If you continue to assert that I have a Free Will, you will thereby enrage me to the point when I cannot help smashing this tureen against the windowpane, for my actions are determined by your words. If you recognize that there is no such thing as a Free Will, the tureen will automatically be safe. But what is a tureen compared to the problem we are trying to settle?"
"It is my tureen," Maria said, watching my hands with anguish.
"I give you ten seconds to decide." I started counting—one-two-three, in a cold rage . . . . At the count of nine, Maria said:
"All right, you win, put it down."
"You admit that I have no Free Will?" I asked, to make quite sure.
"*You* certainly haven't."

—Arthur Koestler, *The Invisible Writing*

19. Because the . . . rules are designed to benefit all and because the punishments prescribed for their violation are publicized and the defenses respected, there is some

plausibility in the exaggerated claim that in choosing to do an act violative of the rules an individual has chosen to be punished.

—Herbert Morris, "Persons and Punishment,"
in *On Guilt and Innocence*

20. And although it is utterly true that God's existence is to be believed in because it is taught in the Holy Scriptures and, on the other hand, that the Holy Scriptures are to be believed because they have God as their source (because, since faith is a gift from God, the very same one who gives the grace that is necessary for believing the rest can also give us the grace to believe that he exists); nonetheless, this cannot be proposed to unbelievers because they would judge it to be a circle.

—René Descartes, "Letter to the Dean and Doctors
of the Faculty of Sacred Theology of Paris"

DEDUCTIVE ARGUMENTS, INDUCTIVE ARGUMENTS, AND FALLACIES

I. INTRODUCTION

In any argument, the premisses are intended to provide reasons for accepting the conclusion. Arguments can be classified in terms of whether their premisses provide (1) conclusive support, (2) partial support, or (3) only the appearance of support (that is, no real support at all). When we say that the premisses provide *conclusive support* for the conclusion, we mean that *if* the premisses of the argument were all true, it would be *impossible* for the conclusion of the argument to be false. Arguments that have this characteristic are called *deductive arguments.* When we say that the premisses of an argument provide *partial support* for the conclusion, we mean that *if* the premisses were true, they would give us good reasons—but not conclusive reasons—to accept the conclusion. That is to say, although the premisses, if true, provide some evidence to support the conclusion, the conclusion may still be false. Arguments of this type are called *inductive arguments.*

The third type of argument is hardly deserving of the title "argument." These arguments are commonly called *fallacies* or *fallacious arguments,* but "pseudo-argument," or "counterfeit argument," might be a more accurate name for them. In Chapter 1, we called the failure to distinguish between evidence for a claim and some other form of persuasion for that claim "committing a fallacy." We will use the term *fallacy* to refer to a set of sentences (all arguments are framed in language) in which some of the sentences are presented as if they provide evidence to support the conclusion, when, in fact, they are irrelevant to the conclusion and, even if they were true, would not provide a reason for accepting the conclusion.

In this chapter we will discuss each type of argument in a general way by considering examples of inductive and deductive arguments and learning to distinguish between them. It is important to be able to make this distinction because different standards for evaluating the correctness of arguments apply to the two types. Fallacious arguments sometimes mislead us into accepting a conclusion even though they lack evidence to support that conclusion. Often, they achieve this persuasive character because they bear a superficial resemblance to various types of inductive or deductive arguments. We will discuss some general characteristics of fallacious arguments here, but we will postpone a closer examination of particular fallacious forms until we are more familiar with the specific types of correct arguments that various fallacies resemble.

II. DEDUCTIVE ARGUMENTS

In a deductive argument, if the premisses are true, the conclusion must be true as well. This ability to guarantee the preservation of truth when moving from premisses to conclusion is the outstanding characteristic of deductive arguments, and it is obviously a valuable feature. How is the truth preserved? The answer, which points to a limitation on the powers of deductive reasoning, is that the conclusion of a deductive argument provides no new information that was not already present, at least implicitly, in the premisses. Thus, deductive arguments are *truth-preserving,* but they cannot extend factual knowledge.

To understand the features of deductive arguments, we must examine what is meant by "new information" and how information can be contained "at least implicitly" in the premisses of an argument. It will be convenient to discuss these issues in the context of some examples of deductive arguments.

To simplify matters, arguments in this book will often be written in a *standard form.* Each premiss will be listed on a separate line, and the conclusion, also listed on a line by itself, will be separated from the premisses by a solid line. When we use this device we do not have to indicate verbally which sentences are the premisses and which sentence is the conclusion of each argument.

The first argument that we will examine is as old as the first text in logic— about 2,300 years old! It is so commonly used in logic classes that you can hardly escape it, so you might as well be exposed to it now.

All men are mortal.
Socrates is a man.

Socrates is mortal.

The first premiss is a universal generalization. It contains the information that *all* members of one class, or type of thing (the class of men) are also members of another class (the class of mortals). The second premiss provides the information that the individual whose name is Socrates is a member of the class of men.

The conclusion of the argument combines the information contained separately in the two premisses but does not contain any additional information. It is fairly obvious in this example that there is, strictly speaking, no "new" information in the conclusion that was not already contained in the premisses. Neither premiss says explicitly (in just those words) what is in the conclusion, but the information in the conclusion is there in the premisses *implicitly.* Moreover, this is true not only for the simple argument in our example but also for every argument in which the conclusion follows deductively from its premisses.

If deductive arguments cannot give us any new information that was not already present in the premisses, what purpose do they serve? Why should you bother to state a conclusion if all of the information you need is already provided in the premisses? If all arguments were as simple as the above example there would be little reason to state conclusions. The mere mention of both of these premisses together would be sufficient for most people to "get the point" or "to put 2 and 2 together." Some arguments are actually presented without their conclusions. The premisses are stated, but the proponent of the argument omits the obvious conclusion for the same reason that obvious premisses are sometimes omitted. It is boring and occasionally condescending to dwell on the obvious.

Not all deductive arguments are simple, however, and sometimes the chain of reasoning that connects the premisses to the conclusion is long and complex.

When this is the case, although the conclusion contains no new information in the sense that it only selectively *recombines* information stated in the premises, nevertheless the conclusion may be novel in the sense that the audience to whom the argument is addressed may not have thought to combine the information in precisely that way, or may not have seen in what direction the premises would lead if they were combined in that way. Thus, we can say that although the conclusion of a deductive argument can contain no new information, it can put information together in ways that might not have occurred before and permit us to reach conclusions which are "new" from a psychological standpoint. Psychologically new conclusions sometimes surprise even the person who formulated the argument in the first place.

The following deductive argument reaches a conclusion that is apt to be psychologically new and surprising, even though it contains no new information. Smith presents the argument to his neighbor, Jones, who commutes from his suburban home to a job in the city, to convince Jones that he is spending three weeks of every year riding a commuter train.

> *Jones:* Three weeks a year—that's ridiculous!
> *Smith:* No, it's a simple matter of logic. You ride the train to and from work, one hour each way, five days a week, for a total of 49 weeks a year, allowing for your vacation and holidays. Using simple arithmetic, that comes to a total of 490 hours per year on the train. There are 24 hours in a day, and if you divide 490 by 24, you get 20 and 10/24 days. That's almost 21 days, or three weeks a year you spend on the train.
> *Jones:* Ouch.

The reasoning in this argument depends on the use of mathematics. Mathematical arguments are almost exclusively deductive in character. It is especially in our use of mathematics, including simple arithmetic calculations, that deductive arguments pervade our everyday lives. Balancing checkbooks, counting change, and setting up a budget all require deductive reasoning. Although you probably do not use geometry much in your everyday life now, if you studied it in high school, you were intensely involved in constructing and evaluating deductive arguments. You began the course in geometry with a set of first principles—axioms, postulates, and definitions—and then proceeded to derive theorems (conclusions!) on the basis of those first principles. This was an exercise in deductive reasoning, and some parts of it were subtle indeed. Even though you had all of the necessary premises in hand, it was not at all obvious in many cases how these premises could be combined to produce the theorem you were supposed to prove.

All other areas of mathematics, including those that, unlike geometry, are not formulated as axiomatic systems, essentially depend on deductive arguments. All mathematical *proofs* are deductive arguments. Furthermore, most people regard mathematical proofs as the purest form of deductive reasoning, because even the premises contain no information about what the real world is like. The mathematical principles that form the basis for mathematical proofs are themselves not now usually considered to contain factual information but rather to be true by definitions of the terms involved or to be true claims about abstract constructions of the human mind, such as numbers or geometric figures. This is what Bertrand Russell was referring to when he said "I fear that, to a mind of sufficient intellectual power, the whole of mathematics would appear trivial, as trivial as the statement that a four-footed animal is an animal" (*My Philosophical Development*).

Russell does not mean to say that all mathematics is trivial to *our* minds, for our intellectual powers are limited. When we *apply* mathematical reasoning to factual claims, as we did in the preceding example, in which the premises included the information that Jones spent two hours on the train each working day, the results may seem surprising—just as the results of a complicated mathematical proof may seem surprising. The point is that the use of mathematical calculations in an argument does not introduce any new *information* that goes beyond what is already stated in the premises.

Many arguments concerning ethics—in which the proponent attempts to show that an action is right or wrong or that a moral principle is acceptable or unacceptable—are deductive arguments. A standard way to establish that some kind of action is right (or wrong) is to show that all actions of that type are right (or wrong) because they fall into a broader class of right (or wrong) actions. The following argument provides an example:

> All deliberate killing of helpless persons is wrong.
> Euthanasia (mercy killing) is a deliberate killing of a helpless person.
> _____
> Euthanasia is wrong.

In this argument, as in all deductive arguments, *if* the premises are true, the conclusion must be true as well. The question of whether the premises *are* true (or acceptable, if one objects to regarding moral claims as true) is an important and interesting question, but the deductive character of the argument is independent of the answer to that question.

Other arguments commonly employed in ethics attempt to show that some moral principle is not acceptable because it would condone or permit actions that we consider to be immoral. This pattern of argument is somewhat more complicated than the last one, for it really contains an argument within a larger argument. The following example is an argument of this type:

(*First part*)

> Whatever is done as an expression of love is morally acceptable.
> Mrs. X, who believed her infant child's soul was possessed by demons that could be driven out only by beating, beat her infant child severely because she loved him.
> _____
> Mrs. X did something morally acceptable when she beat the child.

(*Second part*)

> The conclusion of the argument in the first part is obviously false.
> But that argument is deductive (if all its premisses are true, then its conclusion must be true as well).
> The second premiss states a fact about Mrs. X's behavior, and its truth is not in question.
>
> ---
>
> The first premiss is false. (It is not true that whatever is done as an expression of love is morally acceptable.)

This technique of demonstrating that a claim is false by taking it as a premiss and showing that it—alone or in combination with other premisses that are truthful and not in doubt—leads deductively to an obviously false conclusion is fairly common, not only in ethical arguments but in mathematics and many other fields as well. It may seem odd to regard a claim that we believe to be false as a premiss. Actually, this technique often is useful in the context of a dialogue, when a claim is put forth by one person and the other person tries to show that it is false. Consider the following dialogue:

He: You don't love me anymore.
She: Don't be silly. Suppose that I don't love you. If a woman doesn't love a man, she doesn't care what happens to him, she doesn't want to spend time with him, and she doesn't give him presents. But I do care what happens to you, I do want to spend time with you, and I do give you presents. So you see, I do love you.

This way of arguing is called *indirect proof.* We will look carefully at the logical structure of this form of deductive argument in later chapters.

One other feature of many arguments in ethics is worth mentioning here. It might seem that because there are exceptions to general principles of morality, these principles are statistical generalizations rather than universal generalizations. If moral principles were statistical generalizations, then the arguments in which they were premisses would be inductive rather than deductive. When we understand how exceptions are treated, however, we can see that moral principles are regarded as universal generalizations and that ethical arguments employing them are intended to be deductive.

For example, although the deliberate taking of human life is morally unacceptable in general, exceptions are recognized. If Jones deliberately kills Smith in self-defense, this act is not necessarily considered wrong. Such actions are permissible according to the general principle that allows killing in self-defense. The important point about such exceptions is that they too are governed by universally general principles, although these principles may be somewhat more limited in their application. Thus, to show that a particular killing was not a wrongful act even though it was deliberate, might involve showing that the circumstances surrounding the act require classifying it as a "killing in self-defense" rather than another sort of killing. Then according to the principle that killing in self-defense is morally justifiable, the act could be shown not to be wrong. When an apparent exception to some accepted moral principle is encountered, another deductive argument, based on a different acceptable general principle, will usually be employed to handle the exception.

Because in a deductive argument if the premises are true the conclusion *must* be true as well, certain words and phrases are often used in ordinary language to mark or note the strong support provided in these arguments. Words and phrases such as "must," "it must be the case that," "necessarily," "inevitably," "certainly," and "it can be deduced that" are frequently used to indicate that an argument is deductive. The terms "entail" and "imply," when used to refer to the connection between the premises and the conclusion of an argument, frequently indicate a deductive connection.

However, these terms may also be used when a conclusion is very strongly supported by evidence, but the argument is *not* deductive. The way to test whether or not an argument is deductive is to ask the question: Do the premises provide *conclusive* support for the conclusion of the argument? To answer this question for any except the simplest arguments, however, we need to know how to judge whether or not support is conclusive. We will concentrate on this point in later chapters. In the meantime, the clues provided here regarding the contexts in which deductive arguments are normally used and the special words used to indicate the presence of a deductive argument will provide some guidance.

Our task is complicated by the fact that arguments in ordinary language are often stated incompletely, so that it can be difficult to tell whether or not the missing premises make the argument deductive. Contextual clues for judging whether or not arguments are deductive are particularly helpful at this stage, because they help us to supply the appropriate type of missing premise. If a missing premise is to provide any real support for the conclusion, however, it should be no less plausible than the conclusion itself. If we ignore this caution about plausibility, we could transform *any* argument into a deductive argument with the addition of a premiss. (For example, the conclusion itself added to the premisses would make the argument deductive!)

Occasionally, people use terms like "necessarily" to bolster an argument—to make it look as if more support is present—when the support is considerably less than conclusive. This may be the case in the following argument, taken from an advertisement paid for by a large oil corporation:

> Because it is keyed so closely to the marketplace and so responsive to it, private business is *necessarily* the most effective instrument of [economic] change.

It is fairly easy to see that although the fact that private business is so closely tied to what people buy and sell may provide a *good* reason to believe that private business is the most effective instrument of economic change, it is hardly a *conclusive* reason to believe this. It is clearly possible that government, with all its powers (including the power to control the money supply, interest rates, taxes, import duties, and other aspects of the economy) may be a far more effective instrument of economic change than private business, even though private business is more closely tied to the marketplace. Of course, many large, private corporations, like the one that paid for this ad, would prefer that government refrain from using those powers and let a free market determine the state of the economy.

Another situation in which arguments are presented as deductive although the evidence is less than conclusive should be noted. Without wishing to detract at all from the logical powers of the master sleuth, Sherlock Holmes, we should realize that most of his so-called "deductions" are really inductive arguments. Consider the following passage from "A Scandal in Bohemia," in which Dr. Watson visits Holmes after a long absence. Although Watson hasn't told him so, Holmes figures out that Watson has returned to the practice of medicine.

> "And in practice again, I observe. You did not tell me that you intended to go into harness."
> "Then, how do you know?"
> "I see it, I deduce it. How do I know that you have been getting yourself very wet lately, and that you have a most clumsy and careless servant girl?"
> "My dear Holmes," said I, "this is too much. You would certainly have been burned [as a witch] had you lived a few centuries ago. It is true that I had a country walk on Thursday and came home in a dreadful mess; but, as I have changed my clothes, I can't imagine how you deduce it. As to Mary Jane, she is incorrigible, and my wife has given her notice; but there again I fail to see how you work it out."
> He chuckled to himself and rubbed his long nervous hands together.
> "It is simplicity itself," said he; "my eyes tell me that on the inside of your left shoe, just where the firelight strikes it, the leather is scored by six almost parallel cuts. Obviously they have been caused by someone who has very carelessly scraped round the edges of the sole in order to remove crusted mud from it. Hence, you see, my double deduction that you had been out in vile weather, and that you had a particularly malignant boot-slitting specimen of the London slavery. As to your practice, if a gentleman walks into my rooms smelling of iodoform, with a black mark of nitrate of silver upon his right forefinger, and a bulge in the side of his top hat to show where he has secreted his stethoscope, I must be dull indeed if I do not pronounce him to be an active member of the medical profession."

The fiendishly clever Holmes is right on all counts, as usual, *but* it is not *impossible* that Watson might have cleaned his own boots and that the signs of medical practice might have been the results of Watson helping out in an emergency rather than setting up his own practice. It may be possible to analyze arguments such as the ones Holmes gives here as *intended* deductive arguments in which a universally general premiss has been left unstated. In this case, however, such an approach is unlikely to work, because the required premisses, such as "Every pair of boots scored by cuts was cleaned by a clumsy servant," are no more plausible than the conclusion. Holmes's conclusion goes beyond the information he states in his premisses, and so his argument, although ingenious, is not deductive.

Before turning to inductive arguments, it should be emphasized that the way in which "deductive argument" is defined here rules out describing any argument as "deductive," regardless of whether or not its proponent intended it to be deductive, when its conclusion does not follow with certainty from its premisses. An argument may, of course, *purport* to be deductive, and fail to be so. The definition of "deductive" offered here is in accordance with the definition proposed in other, but not all, logic texts. The terminology is not uniform.

Sometimes "deductive argument" is defined as an argument in which the prem-isses purport to provide conclusive support for the conclusion. Arguments that fail to do so are called *invalid deductive arguments;* arguments that succeed are called *valid deductive arguments.* Thus, our term *deductive argument* is equiv-alent to *valid deductive argument* in the other terminology. Each way of defining the term has its advantages and disadvantages. The primary advantage of our definition is that it does not suggest that all inductive arguments are invalid deductive arguments solely because their premisses do not provide conclusive support for their conclusions. The structure and perspective of this textbook reflect the belief that it is better to recognize inductive arguments as a separate type of argument with a special role and value instead of viewing them as deduc-tive arguments that don't quite succeed.

Exercises

1. Find an example of a deductive argument—one that does not depend on any unstated premisses—in a source other than a logic textbook (a newspaper, book, magazine, etc.). Identify the premisses and the conclusion of the argument.
2. Which of the following claims are true?
   a. A deductive argument can have a false premiss.
   b. A deductive argument can have a false conclusion.
   c. A deductive argument can have all false premisses and a false conclusion.
   d. A deductive argument can have all false premisses and a true conclusion.
   e. A deductive argument can have all true premisses and a false conclusion.
   f. An argument can purport to be deductive without actually being deductive.
   g. Sometimes terms such as "necessarily" and "must" are used to introduce a conclusion that does not follow deductively from the premisses of an argument.
   h. If one of the premisses of an argument is repeated as its conclusion, then the argument is deductive.

III. INDUCTIVE ARGUMENTS

Arguments in which the premisses provide some support, but not conclusive support, for their conclusions are called *inductive arguments.* Thus, all of the premisses of an inductive argument can be true, and can support the conclu-sion, but the conclusion can still be false. Inductive arguments lack the definitive and the most valuable feature of deductive arguments—the ability to guarantee the preservation of truth. However, this apparent shortcoming is more than offset by a feature of inductive, but not deductive, arguments. Inductive arguments can extend our factual knowledge. Their conclusions contain new information that is not present, even implicitly, in the premisses of the arguments. Although the field of mathematics is well suited to the sole use of deductive reasoning, in all other fields of human endeavor—natural science, the social sciences, history, literary criticism, and the practical knowledge of everyday affairs—inductive inferences and arguments are indispensable.

Holmes's arguments that so impressed Dr. Watson in Section II, established the existence of a *causal connection* between two types of things or events, such as the connection between the bulge in Dr. Watson's top hat and his hiding a stethoscope in the hat. The following argument, which is the opening passage in Charles Darwin's *The Origin of Species,* is also causal.

> When we compare the individuals of the same variety or sub-variety of our older cultivated plants and animals, one of the first points which strikes us is, that they generally differ more from each other than do the individuals of any one species or variety in a state of nature. And if we reflect on the vast diversity of the plants and animals which have been cultivated, and which have varied during all ages under the most different climates and treatment, we are driven to conclude that this great variability is due to our domestic productions having been raised under conditions of life not so uniform as, and somewhat different from, those to which the parent species had been exposed under nature.

Darwin argues that great differences among individuals of the same species of domestic plants or animals (for example, think of the variety of dogs from Miniature Poodles to Great Danes)—which are much more noticeable than in wild species (for example, elephants)—are the result of humans breeding these plants and animals under a much greater variety of conditions than the conditions to which wild species are exposed. Humans have bred dogs for centuries in almost every part of the world—for sport, show, work, and a variety of other purposes. Elephants flourish in highly specialized environments in only two or three specific places, and there are only a couple of varieties of elephants.

Causal arguments are among the most frequently presented inductive arguments. We will look at them, as well as other types of inductive arguments, more closely in later chapters.

In addition to situations in which causal arguments are presented, arguments are typically inductive in several other contexts, which include:

1. Cases in which some claim about the future is made on the basis of what has happened in the past.

> That a stone will fall, that fire will burn, that the earth has solidity, we have observed a thousand and a thousand times; and when any new instance of this nature is presented, we draw without hesitation the accustomed inference.
> —David Hume, *Dialogues Concerning Natural Religion*

Philo, the speaker in this passage of the dialogue, does not actually state the obvious conclusion—that in the future stones will continue to fall; fire, to burn; the earth, to be solid—but his meaning is clear.

2. Cases in which some claim about the past is made on the basis of present evidence.

> Pollen grains, though microscopic, are preserved in peat bogs in a remarkable manner for hundreds and even thousands of years. Since the pollen of every plant has its own special form, it is possible with the microscope to establish what plants were growing at different points in time. The distinct layers in peat-bogs thus become, as it were, the pages of a great picture book illustrating the changing flora of the land through the ages.
> —P. V. Glob, *The Bog People*

Here, the pollen, which is observed in the present, provides the basis for reconstructing the types of vegetation that grew in prehistoric times. Historians, geologists, archaeologists—all who are concerned with knowledge of the past—use inductive reasoning in this way.

3. Cases in which a generalization is based on a sample of observations or experiments.

This is the type of inductive reasoning that is used by persons who conduct public opinion polls to determine who is a favorite political candidate or to learn about the public's attitude toward a particular piece of legislation. You have seen or heard such arguments, particularly in election years. Here is a different example of this form of reasoning, taken from a newspaper report about some recent research:

LOS ANGELES—Equal property splits in divorces make men richer and women substantially poorer, a California study has found, buttressing nationwide efforts to include a husband's earning potential in settlements.

The study of 3,000 divorces by a Stanford University researcher shows men improved their standard of living an average 42 percent in the first year after a divorce, while the living standard for women and children dropped 73 percent when income was compared to need.

—Jay Matthews, *The Washington Post*

In this passage, the reporter not only provides the conclusion and the evidence on which it is based, but also includes additional information about the effect the conclusion may have on future financial calculations for divorce settlements.

4. Cases that claim something about a particular case on the basis of what happens usually, or frequently, but not always.

The following passage, taken from Mark Twain's *Notebook,* is an amusing example of this common form of inductive argument:

At bottom I did not believe I had touched that man. The law of probabilities decreed me guiltless of his blood, for in all my small experience with guns I had never hit anything I had tried to hit. And I knew I had done my best to hit him.

5. Cases that claim that a particular kind of similarity holds on the basis of other known similarities between two types of things.

You often use this form of reasoning when you make the decision to buy a particular brand of merchandise on the basis of good performance by other items of the same brand. Similarities in materials, methods of manufacturing, and other product qualities provide evidence to support some further, as yet unobserved similarity (such as durability). This kind of reasoning also provides the focus for much of our medical research. Investigators observe the effects of various substances on experimental animals, which are similar to humans in certain respects, and conclude that those substances will affect humans in similar ways. Here is an example, taken from a newspaper article:

Marian C. Diamond, professor of anatomy at the University of California at Berkeley, warned recently that birth-control pills may inhibit development of the brain.

Dr. Diamond said that research reveals that female sex hormones contained in birth-control pills limit growth of the cerebral cortex, a part of the brain which regulates intelligence.

Dr. Diamond has been working with female rats into which she has injected a hormone equivalent to a birth-control pill. Such rats showed less growth of the cerbral cortex than rats not injected with the hormone.

—*Parade Magazine*

Recognizing contexts in which inductive arguments are appropriate will help us to determine whether a given argument is inductive or deductive, although, of course, the real test of an inductive argument is to ask: Do its premises provide some support, but not conclusive support, for the conclusion? For an argument to be inductive, the truth of the premises should make it *probable* or *likely* that the conclusion is true as well. As in deductive arguments, special terms point to the nature of the inductive link between the premises and the conclusion in an inductive argument. These terms include "probably," "usually," "tends to support," "likely," "very likely," and "almost always." When Mark Twain said "The law of *probabilities* decreed me guiltless," he indicated that his argument was inductive. The terms "may" or "might" are sometimes used to point to the tentative nature of an inductively drawn conclusion, as in Dr. Diamond's claim that "birth-control pills *may* inhibit development of the brain."

There is another important difference between deductive and inductive arguments. Whereas deductive support is an all-or-nothing affair (either the premises conclusively support the conclusion or they do not), premises in inductive arguments may provide varying degrees of support (from rather weak to very strong). The terms used to indicate presence of an inductive argument frequently provide information about the degree of strength of the argument as well. The terms "may," "might," and "possibly" are indicators of rather weak support; "almost always," "highly probable," and "highly likely" indicate strong support. The expressions "with practical certainty" or "with moral certainty" indicate that there is a very high degree of inductive support, that there is an overwhelming force of evidence—but this support still falls short of the *logical,* or *truth-preserving,* certainty demanded in deductive arguments. The phrase "beyond all reasonable doubt" is often used to indicate a strong inductive argument, but it is sometimes used to indicate a deductive argument as well.

Some arguments, particularly those used in science, combine inductive and deductive elements. For example, even before Louis Pasteur, the famous French scientist, applied his method of pasteurization to destroy harmful organisms in fresh milk, he suggested the process of gentle heating as a solution to the problem of wine souring during the aging process. Yeast cells, which are living organisms, are responsible for the fermentation necessary to make wine. Pasteur, however, noted with the aid of a microscope that there were several types of yeast, and he believed that some of them were responsible for souring in wine during the aging process. He reasoned that if all yeast cells in the wine were destroyed by gentle heating after the fermentation was completed, the wine could age without souring. His method worked and earned him the enthusiastic thanks of the wine industry in France.

The deductive part of Pasteur's argument is

> Yeast cells are the cause of souring in wine.
> Gentle heating destroys yeast cells.
> _____
> Gently heated wine does not sour.

Based on the success of Pasteur's experiment (heated wine did not sour), Pasteur *inductively* concluded that his belief about yeast causing the wine to sour was correct. This conclusion follows inductively, rather than deductively; although the yeast cells were killed by heating, it is *possible* that some other agent that also could be destroyed by heating was the causal factor in wine spoilage. Even though there is a deductive component to arguments of this type, their overall structure is inductive, because the conclusion about the cause does not follow with certainty from the premises concerning the success of the experiment. Arguments of this type, which are fundamental to scientific reasoning, will be examined more closely in Chapter 7.

Exercises

1. Find an example of an inductive argument in a newspaper, magazine, or other contemporary source. Reconstruct the argument in standard form (see page 32), and tell whether it falls into any of the categories described in this section.
2. Identify the premises and the conclusion of each of the following arguments. Classify each argument (as it is stated) as deductive or inductive. If you believe that an argument is *intended* to be deductive but fails to be (perhaps due to the omission of a universally general premise), discuss why you think the missing premise is any more plausible than the conclusion of the argument.
   a. The introduction of cooperative marketing into Europe greatly increased the prosperity of the farmers, so we may be confident that a similar system in the United States will greatly increase the prosperity of our farmers.
   b. Workers should vote for a program that will see that they get their fair share of the products of industry. Whenever taxes go up, prices go up; whenever prices go up, profits go up; and whenever profits go up, the workers get less than their fair share of the products of industry. So workers should vote for lower taxes.
   c. The last four Presidents of the United States have supported equality of races and civil liberties. But we do not have equality of races, and the erosion of our civil liberties continues. Therefore, Congress or some other force must be preventing our Presidents from bringing about the reforms they want.
   d. The *Farmers' Almanac,* which has an excellent record on such matters,

predicts that we are in for a hard winter this year. So there is going to be a tough winter ahead.

e. Arguments (e) and (f) are concerned with astrology.

> If a man's destiny is caused by the star under which he is born, then all men born under that star should have the same fortune. But masters and slaves and kings and beggars [whose fortunes differ greatly] are born under the same star at the same time. Thus, astrology—which claims that a man's destiny is caused by the star under which he is born—is surely false.
>
> —Pliny the Elder, *Natural History*

f. There are events which are foreknown by persons who have applied their observation to that end. Of this kind are tempests and gales of wind, produced by certain aspects of the Moon, or the fixed stars, towards the Sun, according to their several courses, and the approach of which is usually foreseen by mariners. . . .

 Since it is thus clearly practicable, by an accurate knowledge of the points above enumerated, to make predictions concerning the proper quality of the seasons, there also seems no impediment to the formation of similar prognostication concerning the destiny and disposition of every human being. For by the constitution of the Heavens, at the time of any individual's primary conformation, the general quality of that individual's temperament may be perceived . . . [and] an event dependent on one disposition of the Heavens will be advantageous to a particular temperament, and that resulting from another unfavorable and injurious. From these circumstances, and others of similar import, the possibility of foreknowledge is certainly evident.

> —Ptolemy's *Tetrabiblos,* quoted in Patrick
> Suppes, *A Probabilistic Theory of Causality*

g. Skin hue is neither a necessary nor a sufficient condition for being classified as black in our culture. That looking black is not in our culture a necessary condition for being black can be seen from the phenomenon of passing.* That it is not a sufficient condition can be seen from the book *Black Like Me,* by John Howard Griffin, where "looking black" is easily understood by the reader to be different from being black.

> —R. A. Wasserstrom, "Racism, Sexism, and Preferential
> Treatment," in *UCLA Law Journal,* 1977, 3:581–622

h. The real justification (perhaps a cynical one) for progressive taxation is that the wealthier receive more benefits from government and, therefore, ought to pay more. This may not be true in a strict accounting sense; the middle and upper classes don't use food stamps. But in this country, the essence of government is to preserve the social order. The well-off benefit from this far more than do the poor.

> —Robert Samuelson, "Economic Focus,"
> *Pittsburgh Post-Gazette*

i. When the elaborate methods of preparation of some of the plants used to break down the monotony of life are studied, it becomes quite evident that primitive man must have possessed something other than chance to reveal to

---

*Passing is the phenomenon in which a person who in some sense knows himself or herself to be black "passes" as white because he or she looks white.

him the properties of food and drug plants. He must have been a keen observer of accidents to discover fermentation, the effects and localization of alkaloids and toxic resins, and the arts of roasting and burning a product to gain from it the desired narcotization or pleasing aromas (coffee).

—Oakes Aimes, quoted in Lewis Mumford's
Technics and Human Development

j. It is clear that our *Iliad, Odyssey, Erga,* and *Theogony* are not the first [embodiments of the saga]. These ostensibly primitive poems show a length and complexity of composition which can only be the result of many generations of artistic effort. They speak a language out of all relation to common speech, full of forgotten meanings and echoes of past states of society; a poet's language, demonstrably built up and conditioned at every turn by the needs of the hexameter metre. There must therefore have been hexameter poems before our *Iliad.*

—Gilbert Murray, *The Literature of Ancient Greece*

k. Every state is a community of some kind, and every community is established with a view to some good; . . . . But, if all communities aim at some good, the state or political community, which is the highest of all, and which embraces all the rest, aims at good in a greater degree than any other, and at the highest good.

—Aristotle, *Politics*

l. *Note:* The long-lost bowerbird was found in the Foja Mountains of west New Guinea, and its bower and display were discovered. The bower is a stick tower on a rimmed moss platform, adorned with separate piles of fruit of three different colors. The displaying male extends toward the female a blue fruit set against his golden crest.

In many other kinds of birds, males court females and stimulate them to ovulate by constructing real or mock nests and by ritualized offering of food (courtship feeding). If bower building developed as an exaggerated form of such courtship behavior the bower may represent a gigantic courtship nest. The decoration of bowers by colored objects has been viewed as derived from courtship feeding, since males of all species for which the display is known pick up a decoration and hold it in the bill toward the female, and since these objects are sometimes edible (fruit).

—J. M. Diamond, "Rediscovery of the Yellow-Fronted
Gardener Bowerbird," *Science,* 1982, 216: 431–33

m. The economy will soon be in good shape. A pair of government reports pointed yesterday to an improving economy. The Commerce Department reported that construction spending rose 1.4 percent in December, the second straight monthly gain, and orders to U.S. factories for new manufactured goods rose a strong 4.8 percent.

—Newspaper report

n. [The Assistant Secretary for Health of the Department of Health and Human Services] released the results of the National Household Survey on Drug Abuse, which examined a national sample of Americans over age 12, and the High School Senior Survey.

The surveys showed that one out of three Americans over age 12 has tried some kind of illicit substance.

—Newspaper report

IV. FALLACIES

Fallacies are counterfeit or pseudo-arguments that appear to provide evidence but do not. Fallacies can deceive us in several ways. Sometimes a claim is so attractive that we are ready to accept almost anything that is offered as evidence to support it. Swindlers and "confidence men" present preposterous "evidence" for the reliability of their money-making schemes, but they count on the desire for money to cloud the judgment of their victims. Similarly, a claim may be so repugnant that we will accept almost any statement as evidence against it. Critical thinking requires us to separate the psychological desire to believe or deny a claim from considerations of how well supported that claim is.

In other cases, we may be moved by a strong like or dislike, or respect or disapproval, for the *person* making a claim, which may blind us to such a degree that we fail to consider the nature of the evidence. Fond parents are notorious for their willingness to accept a child's word as sufficient evidence for fantastic claims. Critical thinking requires that we be on guard in this respect as well.

There is a difference between committing a *logical fallacy* and simply making a *factual error*. In ordinary language, the term "fallacy" is sometimes used to refer to false beliefs (particularly ones that are believable because they are attractive to us) but, as used in this textbook, will apply only to logical fallacies. False beliefs are not fallacies in and of themselves in this sense, and merely being in error about something should not be regarded as committing a fallacy. To believe, for example, that Thomas Jefferson did not own slaves is erroneous but not fallacious. The person who doesn't believe that Jefferson owned slaves is ignorant of certain facts, but that person's logical ability is not thereby impugned. To commit a fallacy, we must offer or accept nonevidence as evidence for a claim. A fallacy somehow appears to offer evidence to support the conclusion of an argument without actually doing so.

Aside from being presented in the context of a threat or an enticement, which may distract us from the fact that no evidence is being offered, a fallacy may deceive us by mimicking some aspect of a correct form of argument. We will be better able to understand this property of fallacies after we have studied correct forms of argument in some detail, but a few examples here will make this point somewhat clearer.

Things that are causally connected occur together with some regularity, and the premisses of causal arguments cite such regular connections. But to argue that there is a causal connection *merely* on the basis of the fact that things have occurred together occasionally in the past is to argue fallaciously, because this fact alone is insufficient evidence to show that the joint occurrence is not a mere coincidence. All sorts of things can happen together without any causal connection existing between them. Suppose that you have received good news on Mondays on several occasions in the past. It would be fallacious, solely on this basis, to argue that the day of the week was the cause of the good news.

The following example of a fallacy that mimics a correct argument occurs in Woody Allen's "Love and Death," a film that pokes more than a little fun at philosophy. The hero offers this argument to demonstrate his skill in logic:

All men are mortal. Socrates is mortal. Therefore, all men are Socrates.

The way in which this fallacious argument parodies the classic example of this deductive form of argument is transparent enough to make it amusing rather than deceptive. Life would be simpler if all fallacies were so easy to detect.

Fallacies are frequently committed as a result of thinking in terms of *stereotypes*—fixed, rigid, or conventional mental patterns that leave little room for noting individual variations in information received or for classifying new information appropriately. A blatant example of this kind of fallacy would be to argue that a person was intelligent on the basis of the fact that he or she was a member of some racial or ethnic group. Prejudicial judgments of this type are a particularly invidious form of thinking in terms of stereotypes.

Stereotypic thinking is not always this obvious (or obnoxious). Psychologists have demonstrated the pervasiveness of fallacious reasoning due to stereotypic thinking in the absence of any racial or ethnic prejudice. Two psychologists presented the following problem to several student groups and professional colleagues (Amos Tversky and Daniel Kahneman, "Judgments Under Uncertainty," *Science,* 1974, 185:1124–31). Persons to whom the problem was presented were told that a description had been drawn at random from a sample containing descriptions of 30 lawyers and 70 engineers. This is the description:

> John is a 39-year-old man. He is married and has two children. He is active
> in local politics. His favorite hobby is the collecting of rare books. He is
> competitive, argumentative, and articulate.

The problem is to tell whether John is an engineer or a lawyer.

A large majority of these people answered "lawyer," even though the number of descriptions of engineers outnumbered the number of descriptions of lawyers by more than two to one! (It is much more likely that a description drawn at random from such a collection would be a description of an engineer.) On the basis of the results of this test and similar tests, these psychologists concluded that people are the captives of certain stereotypes pertaining to lawyers and engineers. Presumably, the general stereotype of a lawyer is formed by media (primarily newspaper and television) exposure to high-powered trial lawyers, who are competitive, argumentative, and articulate. Collecting rare books can be an expensive hobby, and many lawyers earn large incomes. In addition, many high-level political offices are held by men and women trained in the law. None of the information presented in the description is incompatible with the engineering profession, however, and a large number of lawyers lead less glamorous lives than many of the people who exemplify the stereotype. If the information that the engineers in the sample far outnumbered the lawyers is ignored, then the judgment that a lawyer (not an engineer) is being described is based on a stereotype rather than on solid information.

V. REVIEW

In Chapter 2, we learned to distinguish deductive arguments from inductive arguments and to understand the general nature of fallacies. In Chapter 3, we will examine some specific types of arguments so that we can develop standards for evaluating them. But before we can do this, we must make certain preliminary distinctions. Once it becomes apparent that an argument is being presented, the pertinent questions to ask and to answer are:

1. What is the conclusion?
2. What evidence is offered in support of the conclusion?
3. Is the evidence conclusive or partial, or is it some sort of counterfeit evidence?
4. If the answer to the third question is unclear, look at the context in which the argument is offered.

Is it a mathematical argument, or some other argument in which the conclusion simply combines or restates information already stated in the premisses? Arguments of this type are probably deductive.

Is it an argument that tries to establish something about the future or the past on the basis of present evidence? Is it an argument designed to show that something is the cause of something else (a causal argument)? Is the argument based on a sample study, or on what happens most of the time, or on similarities? These arguments are probably inductive. Remember, too, to look for words such as "probably" and "necessarily," because they often indicate which type of argument is being presented.

The most important new terms introduced in this chapter are defined below.

Deductive Argument: An argument in which the premisses provide conclusive support for the conclusion.

Factual Information: Information about what the real world is like, in contrast to what is true merely by definition of the terms involved or what is mathematically true.

Fallacy *(Fallacious Argument)*: An argument in which the premisses provide only the illusion of support, not any real support, for the conclusion.

Indirect Proof: An argument in which the denial of the desired conclusion is taken as one of the premisses and used to show that this leads to a contradiction or some obviously false statement. If the premisses in a deductive argument are all true, the conclusion must be true as well; thus, any deductive argument with an obviously false conclusion must contain a false premiss.

Inductive Argument: An argument in which the premisses provide some support, but less than conclusive support, for the conclusion.

Standard Form: A way of writing arguments in which the premisses are listed on separate lines and separated from the conclusion by a solid line.

Truth-preserving: The property of deductive arguments that guarantees that if their premisses are all true, their conclusions will also be true.

VI. EXERCISES

Reconstruct all of the arguments in the following passages. Write them in standard form, and then categorize them as inductive or deductive. Try to identify and supply any missing premisses. If you use any clues from the context of the argument to identify the type of argument and/or any missing premisses, describe them.

1. Fluorescent light is good for houseplants. In an experiment in a commercial nursery, a group of houseplants was exposed to four hours of fluorescent light in addition to normal daylight. These plants grew much more quickly than others that were not exposed to the additional lighting. They were also generally greener and healthier looking.

—*Arizona Daily Star*

2. Of course, the human brain [which weighs about 1,500 grams] is not the largest in the animal kingdom. The elephant's brain weighs 2,500 grams (some five and a half pounds), and the brains of the biggest whales are twice that size.

—Isaac Asimov, *The Intelligent Man's Guide to the Biological Sciences*

3. If we ask precisely wherein consists the greatest good of all, which ought to be the aim of every system of legislation, we shall find that it is summed up in two principal objects, *liberty* and *equality*. Liberty, because any individual dependence is so much force denied to the body of the State; equality because liberty cannot subsist without it.

—Jean-Jacques Rousseau, *The Social Contract*

4. We are bound in duty to pay due respect, not only to what is truly the right of another, but to what, through ignorance or mistake, we believe to be his right. Thus, if my neighbor is possessed of a horse which he stole and to which he has no right, while I believe the horse to be really his and am ignorant of the theft, it is my duty to pay the same respect to this conceived right as if it were real.

—Thomas Reid, *Essays on the Active Power of Man*

5. From an account of Joseph Lister's search for an antiseptic chemical to prevent deaths that followed surgery.

> At the end of 18 months, Lister had used the carbolic acid treatment on 13 cases of compound fracture, with results that could be tabulated as follows:
>
> Deaths 2
> Hospital gangrene 2
> (amputation and recovery . . . . 1)
> (recovery without amputation . . . . 1)
> Recovery without complications 9
>
> These were not enough cases to prove conclusively that carbolic acid was the weapon which Lister sought to fight hospital diseases, but they represented a mortality of only 15 percent as against the usual record of more than twice that figure.

—Agatha Young, *The Men Who Made Surgery*

6. The vandals mutilated five sacred statues, destroyed a sacred book, smeared black paint around, and scribbled obscenities and racial remarks on walls.

Temple leaders said the attack seemed to be planned. They note that the vandals had to bring the paint with them.

—Report about the desecration of a Hindu temple
in suburban Pennsylvania, *Pittsburgh Post-Gazette*

7. An *association* between two or more elements within a geological deposit in no way implies a systematic, behavioral, or dynamic relationship between the components. All that is implied is a roughly coincidental contextual relationship for the events of which the elements were derivatives. For instance, the finding of a whale bone and a tuna vertebrate in a geological deposit in no way implies that whales ate tuna or for that matter that tuna ate whales! Nevertheless, the depositional context of an aquatic environment may be indicated.

—Lewis Binford, *Bones*

8. I recommend that you close the sales tax loopholes which currently exempt cigarettes, alcoholic beverages sold in bars and restaurants, arcade games, cable television, confection products, paper and cleaning products, and non-prescription drugs—most of which are taxed, in fact, in a majority of our states today.

Surely we must question a system that taxes furniture while exempting cigarettes, or taxes the radio while exempting the arcade game, or taxes the prime rib in a restaurant while exempting the martini from the bar of that same restaurant.

—Pennsylvania Governor Richard Thornburgh's
Budget Address, *Pittsburgh Post-Gazette*

9. From a report of an excavation of a Mesolithic site in Ireland, inhabited approximately 9,000 years ago.

At what times of year were the Mount Sandel huts occupied? Could the site have served as a year-round settlement? Our excavations have uncovered much evidence with seasonal connotations. For example, the salmon bones are evidence of summer occupation. Today the main salmon run up the Bann is in mid-summer: June, July, and August. In Mesolithic times there may also have been an earlier run, say in April or May. Although the lower water temperatures [at that time] make it unlikely that the salmon run would continue beyond the fall, eels do run downstream in the fall: September, October and November are the best months of the eel run. Hence the eel bones at the site are evidence of fall residence. So is the presence of hazelnuts, which are ready for picking by mid-fall, and of water-lily seeds, which are best collected in September.

—P. C. Woodman, "A Mesolithic Camp in Ireland,"
Scientific American, 1981, 245, 2:126–27

10. The maximum tax on the first $50,000 of capital gain is 20 percent. Therefore, the tax on the first $50,000 would not exceed $10,000.

—R. J. Cole, *Personal Finance*

11. "Is it possible that he was conscious all that time?" asked Peter Ivanovich.

"Yes," she whispered. "To the last moment. He took leave of us a quarter of an hour before he died, and asked us to take Voloyda away."

The thought of the sufferings of this man he had known so intimately, first as a merry little boy, then as a school-mate, and later as a grown-up colleague, suddenly struck Peter Ivanovich with horror, despite an unpleasant consciousness of his own and this woman's dissimulation. He again saw that brow and that nose pressing down on the lip, and felt afraid for himself.

"Three days of frightful suffering and then death! Why that might suddenly, at any time, happen to me," he thought, and for a moment felt terrified.

—Leo Tolstoy, *The Death of Ivan Ilych*

12. Doctors in Texas have reported finding a virus in patients with multiple sclerosis, a discovery that could help explain the origin of the disease and possibly lead to a way to prevent it.

"What's exciting is that the virus has been found at the time people have the disease," Dr. Melnick said.

Melnick and his colleague, Edward Seidel, analyzed spinal fluid taken from 12 patients with nerve diseases and 27 others without such illnesses.

The virus was found in four of the 12 patients with the diseases; it was not found in any of the patients without nerve ailments.

The scientists bolstered their case by also finding antibodies to the virus in the blood serum of the four patients with the virus. That provides additional evidence that the virus was not a contaminant picked up accidentally in the laboratory.

—*Associated Press* newspaper story

13. Everything would seem to be heading up for the beer business. Per capita consumption of the golden brew in the United States last year reached an all-time high, currently equaling about a six-pack a week for every American 18 and over. Beer sales for the past several years have been going up 4 percent to 5 percent annually; so far the rise this year is running around 2 percent—not bad for a recession year.

—*Time Magazine*

14. A lawyer offers the following argument in a burglary case to prove the defendant's innocence:

Assume that the defendant was burglarizing the store at 7:30 PM, on Friday the 13th of October. This is the time that the burglar alarm sounded. No fewer than six of his co-workers can testify that he was at his job from 4 PM until midnight on that day. In order to break into the store, he would have had to have been in two places at the same time.

15. The question of nutrition is closely related to that of locality and climate. None of us can live anywhere; and he who has great tasks to perform, which demand all his energy, has, in this respect, a very limited choice. The influence of climate upon the bodily functions, affecting their retardation or acceleration, is so great, that a blunder in the choice of locality or climate may not merely alienate a man from his duty, but may withhold it from him altogether, so that he never comes face to face with it. . . . Enumerate the places in which men of great intellect have been and are still found; where wit, subtlety, and malice are a part of happiness; where genius is almost necessarily at home: all of them have an unusually dry atmosphere. Paris, Provence, Florence, Jerusalem, Athens—these names prove this: that genius is dependent on dry air, on clear skies—in other words, on rapid organic functions, on the possibility of continuously securing for one's self great and even enormous quantities of energy.

—Friedrich Nietzsche, *Ecce Homo*

16. A layman seldom sets out the premises from which he is arguing, so it is generally impossible to tell whether some false conclusion is the result of thinking illogically about true premises, or the result of thinking logically about false premises. Or both!

—G. A. Miller, citing John Stuart Mill, "Is Scientific
Thinking Different?," *Bulletin of The American
Academy of Arts and Sciences,* February 1983

17.　An important element in the analyses used to justify the counterforce [nuclear weapons designed to destroy the nuclear weapons of the adversary] race is the idea that it might be possible to fight a nuclear counterforce war in a carefully controlled manner. However, because the means of command and control are inevitably vulnerable to nuclear destruction, it is extremely doubtful that a nuclear war could be limited and prevented from escalating into an all-out civilization-shattering exchange. Moreover, even if a nuclear exchange could be strictly limited to military targets, a strategically significant counterforce attack would probably cause tens of millions of civilian deaths.

> —H. Feiveson and F. von Hippel, "The Nuclear
> Freeze—Pro and Con," *Physics Today,* 1983, 36,1:40

18.　Paleolithic inhabitants who decorated the [Lascaux] cave were predominantly right-handed. Not only do the majority of the animals face right (an orientation generally preferred by right-handed draftsmen), but also the "fossilized" rope depicted . . . was obviously the work of a right-handed individual. Since the natural twisting motion involves the overhand rotation of the thumb away from the body, the twist in this case must have been imparted by the right hand.

> —Letter from T.A. Reisner, *Scientific American,* 1982, 247,4:7

19.　Although incest taboos do possess social functions, these cannot account for their origins, because it is impossible to believe that early men who instituted these rules could have known their possible social advantages.

> —Annemarie deW. Maalfjit, *Images of Man*

20.　Yes, and if oxen and horses and lions had hands, and could paint with their hand, and provide works of art, as men do, horses would paint the forms of gods like horses, and oxen like oxen, and make their bodies in the image of their several kinds.

　　The Ethiopians make their gods black and mule-nosed; the Thracians say theirs have blue eyes and red hair.

> —Xenophanes, *Fragments*

A CLOSER LOOK AT INDUCTIVE ARGUMENTS

I. INTRODUCTION

In this chapter, we will take a closer look at some specific types of inductive arguments. The aim of any inductive argument is to establish that the conclusion is true. This cannot be done with absolute certainty, because, by definition, inductive arguments present less than conclusive evidence to support the truth of a conclusion. But an inductive argument should provide *some* assurance that the conclusion will be true if the premises are all true. The very least we can expect is that an inductive argument will give us some measure of how likely we are to be correct if we draw a conclusion on the basis of the evidence presented.

Our task of studying inductive arguments will be made somewhat simpler if we classify them according to *form*. The concept of form is very important in logic. The term *form of an argument* refers to the structure of the argument, without regard to its subject matter or content. Although you may not have thought about forms of argument before, the term "form" in the sense used here is not unfamiliar to you. You probably have been concerned with structures in many real-life situations.

For example, most high-school students are required to take a civics course in which various forms of government are discussed. In the United States, we have a democratic constitutional form of federal government composed of three main branches—executive, judicial, and legislative. The powers and responsibilities of each of these branches are outlined in our Constitution.

The British form of government, in contrast, is a constitutional monarchy composed of a legislative branch (Parliament), a judicial branch, and a crowned King or Queen, who—except in cases of abdication—holds his or her office for life. The head of government is the Prime Minister, but unlike our President, the Prime Minister is not the head of state. The powers and responsibilities of the various branches of the British government are, like our own, outlined in a constitution.

There are, of course, many other forms of government in addition to constitutional democracies and constitutional monarchies. The Soviet Union has an entirely different form of government. The point is that it is possible to study these various forms of government in a rather *abstract* way, without taking particular notice of the individuals who fill the positions determined by the form of government at any given time. When we study forms of government in this way, we learn something about their parts and how these parts are related to one another. Similarly, when we study forms of arguments, we will learn something about their parts and how they relate to one another.

In the sections that follow, we will identify several forms of inductive argument and establish standards for determining how well the premises in the various argument forms support the conclusions. The correctness of an inductive argument is not determined merely by its form. Other considerations are important as well, and these too will be discussed.

II. ARGUMENTS BASED ON SAMPLES

Arguments based on samples share a common form that is termed, alternatively, simple induction, induction by enumeration, statistical generalization, and inductive generalization. In this text, we will refer to this argument form as *inductive generalization*.

You may have seen or heard inductive arguments defined, somewhat inaccurately, as "arguments from the particular to the general." This can be misleading, because not all inductive arguments have this characteristic. However, inductive generalizations are arguments from the particular to the general. Their premises state what happens in particular cases (for example, what happens in the sample), and their conclusions state what happens in general. Moreover, inductive generalization is such a common form of inductive argument that those who define induction as arguing from the particular to the general perhaps may be excused for focusing on this one important type. However, not all common forms of inductive argument employ particular premises to support a general conclusion.

Inductive generalization is the form of inductive argument political pollsters use to forecast election results. In a national election year, polltakers interview a sample of the population (registered voters who plan to vote in the election) and, on the basis of what members of the sample say about their voting preferences, predict the outcome of the election. The information contained in the premises (called "the statistics") is extended in the conclusion to apply to the entire population. Such an argument might look like this:

1,200 (60 percent) of the 2,000 voters polled plan to vote for the incumbent.

---

60 percent of all voters plan to vote for the incumbent.

Inductive generalization is also the form of inductive argument used in quality-control studies. Suppose that a manufacturer wants to know how many of the products that come off his assembly line are defective. In such a case, an inspector will usually examine a certain percentage of the items as they come off the line. If, over a one-year period, the plant produces approximately 5,000 stereo receivers and 100 are inspected, the argument might look like this:

98 out of 100 receivers that were examined were without defects.

---

98 percent of the receivers produced at the plant are without defects.

Inductive generalizations are used in many types of scientific studies. New drugs are administered to selected individuals to test their effects, and if these individuals suffer no ill effects, the drugs are deemed safe for the general public. The functions of various features of animals, such as their distinctive patterns of coloration, are studied by interfering with one of these features in a sample group and noting how the behavior of the animals is affected. The findings are then generalized to apply to all animals of that type. Investigators recently used this form of reasoning when they applied a harmless black paint to high-contrast wing stripes on tropical butterflies and noted that masking the stripes did not affect survival or wing damage in the sample group.

The generalizations that are the conclusions of inductive arguments of this form may be universal or statistical. *Universal generalizations* state that *all* (100 percent) or *none* (0 percent) of the members of a class have a certain property. *Statistical generalizations* state that some percentage of less than 100 percent, but more than 0 percent, of members of a class have the property. Alternatively, statistical generalizations may be stated in a non-numerical way, using such terms as "most," "almost all," and "very few." The conclusions in the two examples just presented were statistical generalizations, stated numerically. Whether the conclusion of an inductive generalization should be statistical or universal depends on the information contained in the premises. If *all* members of the sample exhibit the property in question, then the conclusion that all members of the population exhibit that property *may*—provided certain other conditions are satisfied—be appropriate.

1. Preliminary Account of the Form of Arguments Based on Samples

We are now ready to consider a preliminary presentation of the abstract form of inductive generalizations:

> *X* percent of observed *F*s are *G*s.
> _____
> *X* percent of all *F*s are *G*s.

The letters *F* and *G* in this form represent such terms as "voters," "voters for the incumbent," "receivers," and "items without any defects," which refer to classes of individuals or to properties possessed by all members of a class. The claim made by the conclusion of such arguments is that the percentage in the population of *F*s that are *G*s is the same as the percentage in the observed sample. (Remember that the percentage need not be expressed numerically.)

2. Standards for Making Correct Inductive Generalizations

When are arguments in this form that have true premises likely to lead to true conclusions? The crucial feature that determines the strength of such arguments is the representativeness of the sample. When samples are representative, the conclusions based on them are strongly supported, for to say that a sample is representative is to say that the features of the population that concern us in an argument (for example, voter preferences) are reflected in features of the sample. When this is the case, what is true of the sample will probably be true of the population as well. It is, of course, not always easy to tell whether or not a sample is representative, but two criteria are important to note:

1. Is the sample large enough?
2. Is the sample varied enough?

To determine whether a sample is large enough, we must have certain background information about the subject matter of the argument. In some cases, a very small sample can support a strong generalization; in others, a very large sample is required. It is quite obvious that a sample of only five voters, all of whom said they would vote for the incumbent, would be too small to use as a basis for predicting a landslide vote for the incumbent in a national election. Such a sample is so small that it is almost worthless. However, if an argument is concerned with the election of the Chairman of the Board of Directors in a small company, the opinions of five voters might constitute a sufficiently large sample for an accurate forecast. The population of voters in such an election may be so small that a sample of five is significant.

A very small sample may be sufficient even when it must represent a very large population *provided* there is a great deal of uniformity in the population. If a cook in a kitchen on top of a mountain is testing samples to determine the boiling point of water at that altitude, one sample—or perhaps two (to check the reading)—would be sufficient, because the population of pans of water is quite uniform with respect to the property of boiling point.

The real question is whether the sample is large enough to capture, or represent, the variety present in the population. This brings us to the second criterion for satisfactory, or *representative,* samples: Is the sample varied enough? The questions of size and variety are not the same, for a very large sample might not represent the variety present in the population. A sample consisting of 10,000 voters in a national election would not be varied properly if all members of the sample were wealthy business executives. It does seem clear that the question of the size of a sample is somewhat less crucial than the question of the variety of a sample. Sufficient size may be viewed as an aid to achieving appropriate variety in samples. A sample that is too small automatically fails to provide the required variety.

A sample that is taken haphazardly from a population may, through luck, be a representative sample. However, arguments based on samples that are gathered without attention to sufficient size and variety do not form a basis for strong arguments. Several techniques are used to obtain representative samples. The use of these techniques does not guarantee that a sample will be representative but does increase the probability that it will be so.

One technique is *matching the sample to the population.* Achieving requisite variety in a sample is easier when we know something about how various segments of the population would be apt to differ with respect to the property (such as voter preferences) that concerns us in the argument. We know, for example, that voting preferences are often shared by persons of similar social class, occupation, and religious or ethnic background. If we also know the proportion of each of these groups in the population of voters, we can construct a sample that "matches" those proportions and be somewhat confident that our sample represents the population. This is the regular practice of such operations as the Gallup Poll and the Harris Poll, which are taken seriously even though their samples usually consist of fewer than 2,000 persons and the population they represent consists of millions of American voters. The predictions of these polls are not always correct, but the arguments on which the predictions are based are strong inductive generalizations.

In the study of logic, it is important to keep separate the *truth* of a conclusion from the *strength* of an argument. Bad or weak arguments may turn out to have true conclusions, and good or strong arguments may turn out to have false conclusions. In inductive logic, the standards for strong arguments are designed to make it *probable* that if the premisses of the argument are true, the conclusion will be true as well. If we adhere to these standards, conclusions that are based on true premisses will usually, but not always, be true.

When a population is known to be highly varied but there is little information about just how it varies, a sampling method called *random sampling,* in which each member of the population has an equal chance of being selected for the sample, is often used. In such a situation, large samples are more likely to capture whatever variety is present in the population.

From what we have said thus far, it is clear that background knowledge plays a large role when we try to assess the strength of an inductive generalization. We not only have to examine the premisses of the argument; we also have to consider whether the sample is representative, and this requires information that is not contained in the premisses. When we cannot tell whether a sample is large or varied enough, we cannot tell whether or not an inductive generalization is strong. This dependence on background knowledge—on information that is not a part of the premisses—is a feature of all inductive arguments. These arguments are often difficult to evaluate for this reason. Success at critical thinking does not demand that we acquire the background knowledge to judge every case. It demands instead that we are aware that certain questions must be raised and that, if these questions cannot be answered, the strength of an argument is in doubt.

3. Fallacies Associated with Inductive Generalizations

We are now ready to consider some fallacies that are associated with this form of inductive argument. One fallacy arises from failing to meet the requirement of obtaining a large enough sample. This fallacy has been called the *fallacy of insufficient statistics, hasty generalization,* or *leaping to a conclusion.* If a friend snaps at you when you ask a question, you would be committing the fallacy of hasty generalization if you argued that this one instance of unfriendly behavior showed that he was no longer your friend. If you conclude that no one likes turnips because none of your friends do, this too would be a hasty generalization. The psychological reasons for leaping to a conclusion are fairly obvious in these cases. In the first, hurt feelings may color your judgment; in the second, personal knowledge of opinions of friends may obscure the fact that they are only a small part of the population. To avoid this fallacy, we must dispassionately take account of the size of the sample before we draw any conclusion from it. If feelings are not the issue, and, instead, there is an inadequate amount of appropriate background information on which to judge whether a sample is large enough, we should try to acquire the information. If this is not possible, it would be advisable to suspend judgment on the conclusion.

The second fallacy associated with this form of inductive reasoning is the *fallacy of biased statistics.* To say that statistics are biased means that the sample lacks proper variety. Biased samples are not representative; they fail to capture, or represent, the variety present in the population from which the sample is taken. Again, background information is required to judge whether a sample is sufficiently varied. Knowing, as we do, that business executives are apt to think alike on political matters, the set of statistics generated by a sample of voters (no matter how large the sample is) that is comprised only of business executives, would be considered biased if these statistics were being used to infer the outcome of a national election.

An example of biased statistics, taken from a newspaper, reported a study in which the investigator tried to show that, in general, when a person is falling in love with someone, the other person is likely to reciprocate the affection. But the investigator's sample was biased, for the group he questioned consisted entirely of couples who had recently become engaged! In another case, again from the daily newspaper, a survey was taken to see whether residents of a large eastern city objected to having a streetcar line out of service for several months while a new subway was being built. Every person questioned objected to the plan, but all the surveying was done on that streetcar line during rush hours when riders were going to and returning from work. The workers who depended on the streetcar for transportation did not constitute a representative sample of city residents.

One way researchers avoid bias is by constructing controlled experiments. Not every statistical study lends itself to this treatment, but it is very useful when it can be done. In a controlled experiment, two samples—the experimental group and the control group—are used. Scientists recently used this technique when they investigated the effects of narcotics on fetuses. The experimental group consisted of 28 newborn infants who had been chronically exposed in the womb to low doses of methadone. (The mothers were former heroin addicts on a methadone maintenance program.) The control group consisted of 30 newborns whose mothers had not been on drugs. The drug-exposed babies all showed more rapid eye movement (REM) sleep and less quiet sleep than the control infants.

The benefit of a controlled experiment, such as this one, is that it helps rule out accidental features in a testing situation. In the study just mentioned, the control group and the experimental group were similar with respect to nutrition, prenatal care, and other factors believed to affect the welfare of newborn babies. The fact that one group of mothers was on drugs and one was not was the only difference known to be important or relevant to the health of the newborns between the two groups.

Here is an example of a study, reported in *Parade Magazine,* that could have been improved by the use of a control group. A Chinese worker developed a toothpaste that was mixed with the Chinese herbs traditionally prescribed for colds. The toothpaste was tested clinically on 3,600 persons who had colds. The Chinese said that 63 percent of the subjects tested reported marked improvement. This statistic is not very impressive, however, when we consider the fact that most colds improve with or without treatment. What we need to know is whether an experimental group with colds improved more quickly than the control group who did not use the new toothpaste. We will return to the discussion of controlled experiments in the chapter on causal arguments, because these experiments are especially useful when inductive generalizations have causal claims as their conclusions.

Still another fallacy associated with inductive generalization has no standard name, but it consists of *rejecting a generalization that is strongly supported* by premises citing sufficient and unbiased statistics when some fact that does not really alter those statisics becomes known. The following case provides an example.

Someone is planning to buy a new car, and carefully collects all the appropriate statistical information. The statistics include comparisons of thousands of automobiles, in terms of performance, safety, repair bills, and other important features. On the basis of these statistics, the person concludes that a certain brand of automobile is the best buy. Before the purchase is made, however, the person announces the decision to a friend at a party and is informed that the friend's brother bought the same car, which turned out to be a real lemon. The friend describes all the things that went wrong with the car in vivid detail. If the person then rejects the conclusion that the chosen brand is the best buy, a fallacy is committed. Can you see why?

It is not that new information should be ignored; additional information—either in the premises themselves or in the form of new background information—can strengthen or weaken inductive arguments. But this new information concerns only one case, and one new case cannot outweigh all the statistical information that has been carefully collected. It is not true that the statistics fail to take account of defective automobiles. The information that some cars of the chosen brand are lemons is already known, but presumably fewer cars of this brand, in general, are lemons. This is what the statistics say, and no reason has been given to doubt their reliability.

Psychologists who discussed a similar example (Richard Nisbett and Lee Ross, *Human Inference*) have carefully studied instances of this fallacy, which David Hume commented on in the eighteenth century, and have agreed with Hume's explanation of why it occurs. The problem, they say, is that new information received about a car from a friend at a party is more *vivid* than an impersonal collection of statistics. When you actually know someone (or someone who knows someone) to whom the lemon belongs, the information seems more startling and impressive than a "mere statistic." The vividness of the new information about a single car psychologically cancels out the far more complete, but less vivid, information about thousands of cars. The expense and inconvenience of owning a lemon is brought home to the prospective buyer in a rather alarming way that can override the better information. It is a fallacy to allow a single vivid case to outweigh strong statistical data. This mistake in reasoning could be called the "fallacy of misleading vividness."

4. The Revised Form of Inductive Generalization

Thus far, we have discussed two criteria for evaluating inductive generalizations (size of sample and variety in the sample), the fallacies resulting from the failure to meet these criteria, and the fallacy of rejecting a strongly supported conclusion when faced with a small amount of vivid information. A further criterion for evaluating the strength of inductive generalizations applies to all other forms of inductive reasoning as well. This criterion is concerned with the strength of the conclusion relative to the strength of the premises in the argument. Remember that an argument is a whole that is composed of parts (the premises and the conclusion). The strength of the whole is determined by considering how much support the premises provide for the conclusion. Thus, an argument can be strengthened by providing better premises (a larger or less biased sample) to support the original conclusion, but an argument can also be strengthened by *weakening the conclusion,* and leaving the premises unchanged. A statement is weakened when it is qualified or guarded in such a way that it presents less information, or less specific information, than the original statement.

Some examples will help to clarify this point. Suppose a poll is taken to determine the outcome of a student-body election. An attempt is made to interview students from various classes, and members of fraternities and sororities, as well as unaffiliated students and students in other organizations who might have different preferences. Approximately 2,000 students are expected to vote in the election, and the size of the sample is 200. Of those interviewed, 80 (40 percent) say they will vote for the Student Conservative Party, and 120 (60 percent) say they will vote for the Student Liberals. The following argument could be constructed:

60 percent of those interviewed said they would vote for the Liberals.

---

60 percent of the students plan to vote for the Liberals.

Even though there is some assurance that the sample is representative, it would be surprising if the popular vote *exactly* matched the preferences expressed in the sample. To express this reservation, it is common to build into the conclusion a departure—a little less or a little more—from the percentage in the sample. This is an example of "weakening" the conclusion relative to the premisses. The altered argument might look like this:

60 percent of those interviewed plan to vote for the Liberals.

Between 55 percent and 65 percent of the students will vote Liberal.

The conclusion might be weakened further by saying that between 50 percent and 70 percent will vote Liberal or that a majority of the students will vote Liberal. There are other standard ways of weakening the conclusion, relative to the premisses, in an argument. For example, if all members of the sample have some property, the conclusion might be that *almost* all the members of the population will have this property.

Because samples, no matter how carefully they are taken, infrequently present an *exact* picture of the population, the conclusion must almost always be guarded in some way. In light of this ever-present possibility of *sampling error,* we will represent the form of inductive generalization in the following way:

$$\frac{X \text{ percent of observed } F\text{s are } G\text{s}.}{X \pm z \text{ percent of all } F\text{s are } G\text{s}.}$$

In this form, z represents the degree of departure in either direction from the observed percentage in the sample. (It is possible to measure the degree of sampling error in some carefully conducted statistical studies, but in general, you should remember that these quantities need not be expressed numerically in every inductive generalization.)

Exercises

Decide whether each of the following arguments is an acceptable inductive generalization or a fallacy. Identify the premisses and the conclusion of each argument. In the case of a fallacy, explain what is wrong. Discuss what sort of additional background information is required, if any further data is needed.

1. A chemistry student is told to determine the boiling point of copper. The student tests two very pure samples of copper and finds that each sample has a boiling point of 2,567° Celsius. The student concludes that this is the boiling point for copper.
2. A nationwide poll of a random sample of thousands of homeowners revealed that 70 percent of them are opposed to increases in welfare payments. Therefore, roughly 70 percent of the adult population opposes such increases.
3. An investigator studied several thousand heroin users and learned that 70 percent of them had used marijuana before they tried heroin. He concludes that 70 percent of all marijuana users will go on to try heroin.
4. It has rained during the last two home football games at our school. Therefore, it will probably rain at all the home games this year.
5. Pueblo sites (prehistoric Indian "apartment villages") are located in many places in Arizona, New Mexico, and Colorado. To determine the number of rooms in pueblo sites that were located by surface surveys but were not excavated, archaeologists examined the relationship between the size of the surface rubble mound prior to excavation and the number of rooms that were ultimately

uncovered in each of six sites excavated in the Upper Little Colorado River region. The number of rooms in each excavated site was equal to (0.10 × Area of rubble mound in square meters) + 4.

6. In 1977 at the University of Pennsylvania, psychiatrists conducted a study to determine the social factors that affect the well-being of coronary patients. There were 93 patients in the study; slightly more than 50 percent of them had pets of some kind (dogs, cats, fish, and one iguana). At the end of a year, one-third of the patients who did not own pets had died but only three animal owners had succumbed. The psychiatrists concluded that pet ownership may have a positive effect on the health of humans.

7. There is no overestimating the importance of pets to people it seems. Katcher [the psychiatrist in charge of the study mentioned in Exercise 6] reported that in one questionnaire, on which people were given the opportunity to indicate whether they thought their pet was an animal or a human member of the family, 48 percent responded that the animal was a human family member.

—"Human-Animal Relationship Under Scrutiny,"
Science, 1981, 214:418

8. Jonathan has to travel to a distant city. He wants to take the safest mode of transport, so he compares statistics over the past ten years on accidents involving buses, trains, automobiles, and planes that occurred between his city and the one he will visit. Jonathan determines that the safety record of buses is far better in terms of lives lost than any of the other forms of travel. As he is about to purchase his ticket, however, he sees a newspaper story about a bus accident in which six people died. Jonathan decides not to buy the bus ticket and to drive instead.

9. Find an example in a newspaper or magazine of an inductive generalization. Discuss the strength of the argument, using the criteria of sample size, lack of bias, and strength of the conclusion relative to the premisses.

III. ARGUMENTS FROM ANALOGY

When we draw an *analogy* between two things or two types of things, we are pointing out an observed similarity between them. We often notice and comment about similarities in everyday life. Analogies—particularly unusual and surprising ones—are, of course, the stuff of which literature, especially poetry, is made. Thus, Boswell (*In Search of a Wife*) draws an analogy between his character and a kind of fabric: "I am a weaker man than can well be imagined. My brilliant qualities are like embroidery·on gauze." Lawrence Durrell (*Reflections on a Marine Venus*) compares the close of days in Rhodes to falling fruit: "In Rhodes the days drop softly as fruit from trees." Open almost any page of Shakespeare and you will find beautiful analogies, which in literature are called "similes" and "metaphors":

> How far that little candle throws his beams!
> So shines a good deed in a naughty world.
>
> —*Merchant of Venice*

When, on the basis of analogies, we conclude that items that are similar in observed ways are also similar in some further, as yet unobserved, respect, we are constructing an *argument from analogy*. In Chapter 2, the argument that concluded that the use of birth-control pills may affect human brain development, on the basis of observed effects of the birth-control hormone on rats (which are physiologically similar to humans) was an argument from analogy.

Not every use of analogy is an *argument* from analogy. For an argument to be present, a conclusion must be drawn on the basis of the noted analogy. The examples from Boswell, Durrell, and Shakespeare are not arguments from analogy, for the analogies that are stated there are not used to support some further unobserved similarity; instead these analogies are used to encourage us to see the world a bit differently by calling our attention to an interesting similarity.

1. Form of Arguments from Analogy

Although arguments from analogy are stated in a variety of ways, they can be reconstructed to exhibit the following basic form:

Objects of type X have properties F, G, H, etc.
Objects of type Y have properties F, G, H, etc., and also an additional property Z.

Objects of type X have property Z as well.

The premisses of these arguments mention the respects (F, G, H, etc.) in which the two types of objects have been observed to be similar. The second premiss also mentions a property (Z) that has been observed in one type of object. The conclusion states that the other type of object has that property as well.

In the argument that concludes that birth-control pills may affect human brain development, the properties F, G, H, etc.—although unspecified in the premisses—are the physiological properties that humans (objects of type X) and rats (objects of type Y) have been observed to share. It is because rats possess these properties that they are used in such experiments. The further property Z of brain development being affected by the birth-control hormone has been observed for rats and is inferred to hold for humans as well.

The practice of giving drugs and other potentially harmful substances to experimental animals and—in the absence of sufficient information about the effects of these substances on humans—concluding that humans will be similarly affected is a familiar practice not only to scientists but also to the general public. In view of this widespread understanding of the role of experimental animals, the similarities between these animals and humans are rarely stated explicitly in the premisses of the analogical arguments that depend on such similarities.

When we reconstruct analogical arguments to judge their strength, we should try to state explicitly any *implicit* points of analogy contained in the premisses. Sometimes it requires a great deal of technical expertise to state the implicit similarities. For example, it probably requires more knowledge of physiology than most of us possess to state precisely the important similarities between experimental animals and humans. When this is the case, it is appropriate to rely on experts' claims that the similarities are present, but we should be aware that the nature of these similarities is crucial to the argument.

2. Standards for the Strength of Analogical Arguments

The primary consideration in determining the strength of an argument from analogy, or an *analogical argument,* is the *relevance* of the similarities mentioned in the premisses to the similarity stated in the conclusion. In the argument we have been discussing, the conclusion states that a certain substance will produce a physiological effect in humans similar to the physiological effect it produces in rats. The truth of the implicit premiss depends on the existence of physiological similarities between rats and humans. The similarities employed in the premisses are relevant to the similarity drawn in the conclusion, because similar physiological features are relevant to whether or not the same substance will produce a similar physiological effect. Of course, rats are not exactly similar to humans in terms of physiological features. Rats are much smaller, their brains are less complex, and there are undoubtedly other important (relevant) differences between rats and humans. Such dissimilarities between rats and humans account in part for the tentative nature of the conclusion of this argument, which is indicated by the use of the term "may."

We will now examine two other criteria for judging the strength of analogical arguments: the number of relevant similarities in the premisses and the number of relevant dissimilarities between the two types of objects. Obviously, if the two types of objects are more alike in relevant ways, the argument will be stronger. If the two types of objects are more unlike, or dissimilar, in relevant ways, the argument will be weaker. The more unlike, or dissimilar, in relevant ways the two types of objects, the weaker the argument is.

One feature is relevant to another if the presence of the first increases (is positively relevant to) or decreases (is negatively relevant to) the probability that the second feature will also be present. Determining which features are relevant in any given situation requires some background knowledge, often a considerable amount of such knowledge. Analogies, like inductive generalizations, may be difficult to evaluate for this reason.

Arguments from analogy are frequently employed in making consumer decisions. You may decide to buy another American car made by the manufacturer of the old car you now own on the basis of its reliable performance. You may be criticized for being guilty of hasty generalization if someone assumes that you are arguing that all cars made by that manufacturer are reliable on the basis of your experience with one car. However, if your conclusion that the new car will be reliable is based on a number of relevant analogies between the old car and the new one, your argument may be a good one. Many features that we believe to be relevant to reliability are incorporated in the type of engine, the braking system, the transmission, and the suspension systems. If these features in the new car are similar to these features in the old one, the conclusion that the new car will be reliable may be strongly supported. However, if the new car has many innovations (perhaps a new fuel-injection system and several new computer-controlled features) or if your old car is a family sedan and the new car is a sports model with radically new design features, your argument from analogy will be considerably weakened. Of course, not every feature of a car is relevant to reliable performance. The color of the car and the style of upholstery, for example, may make no difference at all.

You are already familiar with two other criteria for determining the strength of analogical arguments—the number and the variety of instances in the premisses—from our examination of inductive generalizations. The special value of a larger and more varied sample here is that it facilitates recognition of just which similarities *are* relevant. If the similar properties mentioned in the premisses and the similarity stated in the conclusion are found together in a variety of otherwise dissimilar circumstances, we have reason to believe that their connection with one another is not accidental—that a causal connection or some other real connection exists between the properties.

Suppose, for instance, that you had owned not just one reliable car made by the same manufacturer but had owned and driven six of this manufacturer's cars, in various models and styles. Your argument that another car made by this manufacturer will be reliable will be strengthened, because the additional evidence would tend to show that the manufacturer produces reliable cars and that you were not just exceptionally lucky when you purchased your last car.

Similarly, if experiments had shown that birth-control hormones had an adverse effect on brain development not only in rats but also in monkeys and other experimental animals, then the conclusion that birth-control hormones have an adverse effect on humans would have been strengthened. The additional evidence would tend to show that there is not something special about the reaction of rats that makes them relevantly dissimilar to other mammals (and possibly to humans) in their response to the hormone.

The principle that a variety of cases strengthens an analogical argument may seem to conflict with the principle that says relevant dissimilarities between instances in the premisses and the instance in the conclusion weaken an analogical argument. There is no real conflict between these two principles, however. The instances in the premisses can contain properties that differ in *nonrelevant* ways but must contain similar properties that are relevant to the property inferred in the conclusion.

This discussion of the importance of variety in the premisses of analogical arguments brings out a certain similarity between these arguments and inductive generalizations. Indeed, strong inductive generalizations may be viewed as arguments that are strong by virtue of the high degree of relevant analogy between the sample and the population it represents. Although we can distinguish between the *forms* of the two types of arguments (in inductive generalizations, a general claim is based on what happens in a sample; in analogical arguments, a conclusion about an unobserved similarity is based on similarities that have been observed), ordinary language arguments are often incompletely stated and may not be easily classified as one form of argument or the other. Sometimes there is room for reasonable people to disagree about how an argument can best be reconstructed.

3. Fallacies Associated with Analogical Arguments

As is true of inductive generalizations, arguments that fail to meet the standards for strong analogical arguments but that somehow resemble correct arguments from analogy are fallacious. Arguments that attempt to establish a similarity on the basis of irrelevant analogies are defective in this way. In *A System of Logic* (first published 1843), John Stuart Mill named this fallacy the "fallacy of false analogy." To argue that Joan is probably lazy because her brother John is lazy is an example of this fallacy, for the similarities between Joan and John that are implicit in the premiss (whatever similarities siblings typically share) are not particularly relevant to the property of laziness. Many families have both lazy and industrious children.

One of Mill's own examples of this fallacy is the argument that a paternalistic form of government is superior to other forms of government, on the basis of the success of paternalism in families and a comparison between families and states. Mill points out that the relevant qualities for the successful paternalistic governance of a family—affection of the parents for the children and parental superiority in wisdom and experience—are conspicuously absent in most paternalistic forms of state government. States and families are therefore relevantly dissimilar to one another with respect to how they should best be governed.

Many examples of false analogy are found in early anthropological studies of primitive cultures. Due to the false assumption that certain aspects of these cultures were similar to our own, much of the behavior of individuals in primitive societies was considered perverse or bizarre. For example, knowing that the kinship terms "Mother" and "Father" are applied in our own culture only to a person's biological or adoptive parents, early observers of some tribal cultures noted that those terms are applied in these societies to several persons—not only to the biological parent, but also to the parent's sisters and/or brothers. Since these anthropologists believed that in our own society this could only occur when a child was confused about the identity of the biological parents, they concluded that these societies had—or had formerly had—a system of group marriage in which the terms meaning "Mother" and "Father" were applied to a variety of persons because the child could not know which members of the group were actually the biological parents. Later, and more detailed, anthropological studies—notably those of A. R. Radcliffe-Brown—showed that the kinship terminologies used in our society and in tribal societies are relevantly dissimilar but equally systematic ("logical") and useful in their own contexts. It is no more mysterious for a child in a tribal society with a different kinship terminology to call his or her mother's sister "Mother" than it is for a child in our own society to call his or her mother's friend "Aunt," even though she is not a biological relative and the child knows this to be the case.

4. Analogy in Archaeology and in Legal and Moral Reasoning

We have already discussed the use of analogy in medical research. Archaeology is another science that depends heavily on arguments from analogy. Archaeologists study prehistoric peoples by examining their material remains and often use analogy to infer the functions of implements, artifacts, and buildings. Since the people who made or built these objects are no longer alive, archaeologists cannot directly observe how these things were used by their makers.

However, archaeologists note that other people—who are living now or who are historically documented—use or once used items similar in form to those found in archaeological excavations. On the basis of these observations, archaeologists infer that the prehistoric items were used for similar purposes. Thus, when archaeologists working in caves in Oaxaca, Mexico found awl-like objects made from sharpened deer bones that were analogous in virtually every relevant respect (including patterns of wear) to bone tools used by contemporary Oaxacan farmers to scrape kernels from corn, these archaeologists—who found remains of corn in the caves as well—unhesitatingly attributed the same function to the prehistoric objects.

Judges rule on the legality of actions and cases brought before them in trials. In a civil court, for example, a trial might be held to determine whether a proposed merger between two companies involves a violation of the anti-trust laws. To rule on such actions, judges must be aware of any laws that are applicable to the particular case being tried before them. However, in addition to being guided by laws—which are usually stated rather broadly and are sometimes difficult to apply to complex cases—judges are guided in their rulings by *precedent.* Legal precedents are previous judicial rulings (interpretations of the law for particular cases). Analogical reasoning plays an important role in the legal process, particularly with regard to the use of precedents.

For example, lawyers who are arguing that a merger should be declared illegal will examine previous rulings on mergers. Frequently, they will find an especially important decision, called a "controlling case." If the controlling case is unfavorable to a merger, they will try to present relevant similarities between the case they are arguing and the controlling case in which the merger was denied. Lawyers who are arguing in favor of a merger will try to point out the absence of analogy (relevant dissimilarities) between the controlling case and the case in question.

If there is no controlling case, lawyers on both sides will search through reports of court decisions on mergers and argue relevant similarities between their case and those decisions that are favorable to their position as well as point out relevant dissimilarities between their case and those decisions that are unfavorable to their position. Of course, the judge, after hearing the arguments, decides whether the case in question should be regarded as relevantly similar to the mergers that were denied or permitted in the past.

When we make moral judgments about whether or not a given act deserves blame, we frequently use analogical arguments to show that the act is relevantly similar to other actions that are classified as blameworthy or not. It might be argued, for example, that a case of promise-breaking is excusable, because it occurred under conditions of ignorance similar to the conditions under which other cases of promise-breaking have been excused.

Analogical reasoning is also used to attribute various characteristics, motives, desires, and feelings to other people. This is another way in which analogy is often involved in our moral judgments of others. For example, we might judge a politician to be too weak to be able to handle the stresses of high office because he behaved irresponsibly in situations of similar, but less severe, stress on other occasions. We often make the following sort of judgment:

> Mary should be excused for being short-tempered today, for she had all four wisdom teeth pulled yesterday, and I know how I felt the day after mine were pulled. I couldn't help being cross.

We infer that other persons, who are similar to us in many observable respects, share similar hopes, fears, and feelings when confronted with situations that would inspire those hopes, fears, or feelings in ourselves.

Exercises

Reconstruct the analogical arguments in each of the following passages. Identify the points of analogy in the premises—including any unstated premises—and the analogies argued for in the conclusions. Assess the strength of the arguments on the basis of the criteria presented in this section. Discuss any cases in which further background knowledge is required to determine relevance.

1. Tar (extracted from cigarette smoke) when smeared on the skin of mice in laboratories causes skin cancers. Therefore, cigarette smoking causes lung cancer in humans.
2. My last pair of Brand X running shoes were comfortable, gave excellent support to my feet and ankles, and lasted a long time. I expect my new pair of Brand X running shoes, which have the same design, to give the same kind of service as my old pair.
3. A perfect thought can only come from someone who is perfect. After all, you can't get heat from something cold.

4. Wives, be subject to your husbands as to the Lord, for the husband is head of the wife as Christ also is the head of the church; as the church is subject to Christ, so wives are to be subject to their husbands in every respect.
—St. Paul, Ephesians, 5,22

5. *Note:* This was British physicist Ernest Rutherford's argument in favor of an arrangement of parts of the atom offered in opposition to a "plum pudding" model that held that the electrons were arranged randomly throughout the atom like raisins in a pudding.

> The force that binds planets to the sun (gravity) obeys the same general form of law as the electrical force that binds electrons to the nucleus of an atom. (Both gravity and electricity decrease in strength with the square of the distance between the bodies or particles.) Therefore the electron particles, which have negative charges, when attracted by the positive electricity of the nucleus, should move around it in the same way that the planets move around the sun.

6. From an editorial written in response to a rejection by voters of a measure that would have provided money for additional officers of the court:

> Anyone who has bought a cheap used car knows that paying less for repairs now may prove to be more expensive later. This basic truth is often forgotten by people who call for reduced federal spending. The tendency to let tomorrow take care of itself is exemplified in America's approach to the administration and enhancement of justice. . . .
>
> The path to justice is never easy. Those truly committed to the promotion of justice must be willing to pay the price—a price that must take into account future costs of present inaction. We must not forget principles of preventive medicine when undertaking to remedy social ills. If the public truly desires to ensure the nation's long-term health, it must be willing to pay the doctor's bill for the cures.
>
> —Judge Irving Kaufman, *The New York Times*

7. *Background information:* In the case of *Langridge v. Levy* (1837), the court allowed recovery to the plaintiff, who said that the defendent sold his father a defective gun. The gun had blown up in the plaintiff's hand, and the court ruled that the seller had falsely declared the gun safe when he knew it was defective.

> In *George v. Skivington* (1869), a chemist who compounded a secret hair wash was liable to the wife of the purchaser for injuries caused by the wash. . . . [The court] thought that the imperfect hair wash was like the imperfect gun in the *Langridge* case. It chose to ignore the emphasis in the *Langridge* case on the purported fact that the seller knew the gun was defective and lied. It said, "substitute the word 'negligence' for 'fraud,' and the analogy between *Langridge v. Levy* and this case is complete.
>
> —E. H. Levi, *An Introduction to Legal Reasoning*

8. *Note:* Remains of early (pre-Neanderthal) man were found at Choukoutien, China. All the human skulls there had been carefully opened through the base, presumably to extract the brain. This was regarded as evidence for cannibalism.

> We tend to think of cannibalism as a bestial and inhuman practice, but in fact nothing better demonstrates the humanity of the Choukoutien people. Among living peoples, cannibalism is never a matter of nutrition; no animal, human or nonhuman, eats its dead for food. Rather, it is a solemn ritual act,

sometimes to express family piety toward the deceased or magically to impart the deceased's spirit and qualities to the living. We may be confident that the atmosphere of Choukoutien during the cannibal meal was closer to Mass than to McDonalds.

—C. Jolly and F. Plog, *Physical Anthropology and Archaeology*

9. Johnson told me that he went up thither without mentioning it to his servant when he wanted to study, secure from interruption; for he would not allow his servant to say he was not at home when he really was. "A servant's strict regard for the truth (said he) would be weakened by such a practice. A philosopher may know that it is merely a *form* of denial [that is, a "little white lie"], but few servants are such nice distinguishers. If I accustom a servant to tell a lie for *me,* have I not reason to apprehend that he will tell many lies for *himself?*"

—James Boswell, *Life of Johnson*

Reconstruct the argument that Johnson believes his servants would use if he allowed them to lie for him.

10. 'Tis education forms the common mind;
Just as the twig is bent, the tree's inclined.

—Alexander Pope

11. In the following passage, an analogy is drawn between shade trees and knowledge, or the habit of intellectual activity. The analogy is used to argue for the importance of educating persons during their youth. Discuss whether you think the similarities are relevant.

Knowledge is a comfortable and necessary retreat and shelter for us in an advanced age; and if we do not plant it while young, it will give us no shade when we grow old.

—Lord Chesterfield, *Letters*

12. It seems that the Latin races are far more deeply attached to their Catholicism than we Northerners are to Christianity generally, and that consequently unbelief in Catholic countries means something quite different from what it does among Protestants.

—Friedrich Nietzsche, *Beyond Good and Evil*

13. Find an example of an analogical argument in a magazine or newspaper. Assess its strength according to the criteria discussed in this section.

IV. STATISTICAL SYLLOGISMS

The word "syllogism" is derived from the Greek and literally means "a putting together of ideas." The use of the term in logic is related to this meaning. *Syllogisms* are arguments with two premisses, and a conclusion that "puts together" information presented in the premisses. The argument

All men are mortal.
Socrates is a man.

Socrates is mortal.

is an example of a syllogism. This particular syllogism is deductive, but there is an inductive form of syllogism that closely resembles the deductive form. In the inductive form of syllogism, the first premiss is a statistical generalization, rather than a universal generalization, and this form is therefore referred to as a "statistical syllogism." The argument

90 percent of freshmen at the State University are residents of the state.
Elena is a freshman at the State University.

Elena is a resident of the state.

is an example of a statistical syllogism.

The statistical syllogism is the form of argument we use when we argue that what is generally true (or false) is also true (or false) for a particular case. The first premiss, which is a statistical generalization, is not always stated numerically. "Almost all," "most," "very often," "almost never," and similar expressions may be used to form statistical generalizations. Here is an example:

Hardly any freshmen had a philosophy course in high school.
Oscar is a freshman.

Oscar didn't have a philosophy course in high school.

Reasoning in this form pervades many everyday life occurrences. We don't plan outdoor picnics in Chicago in January because the weather usually won't be favorable. If we are fortunate enough to travel in the south of France, we expect to find good food at the country inns there because that's usually the case. A summons for an audit of our tax return is dreaded because most audits of tax returns are costly and unpleasant.

1. Form of Statistical Syllogisms

With the preceding examples in mind, we are ready to look at the abstract form of statistical syllogisms:

X percent of all Fs are Gs.
a is an F.

a is a G.

In this form of argument, as in an inductive generalization, F and G represent classes of individuals or properties that are possessed by members of a class.

The lower-case letter *a* represents an individual person, place, or thing. The class denoted by *F* is called the *reference class* (the class that the individual mentioned in the second premiss is *referred to* or belongs to.) The class denoted by *G* is called the *attribute class*. (Members of the attribute class have the property *attributed to* the individual in the conclusion.)

Notice that this form of inductive argument proceeds from a generalization in the premiss to a claim about a particular individual in the conclusion. Statistical syllogisms are exceptions to the claim that inductive reasoning goes from the particular to the general!

Since arguments of this form are inductive arguments, their conclusions may be false even though their premises are true. However, as is true of other inductive forms of argument, there are both strong and weak statistical syllogisms. We will now examine some criteria for appraising statistical syllogisms.

2. Standards for the Strength of Statistical Syllogisms

The most obvious standard for judging the strength of a statistical syllogism is the closeness to 100 percent (or 0 percent in the negative case) of the statistical premiss. It is readily apparent that if the premiss in the preceding sample argument had stated that 99 percent instead of 90 percent of the freshmen at State University were state residents, a stronger case would have been presented for the conclusion that "Elena is a state resident." Similarly, the argument would have been weaker if only 85 percent rather than 90 percent of all the freshmen were state residents.

Another standard for strong statistical syllogisms is just as important— perhaps even more important—but is less obvious. This standard requires us to use all available relevant evidence when we select the *reference class* to which the individual is assigned. The problem is that any individual belongs to an *indefinite number* of classes. Let us assume that we have the following information about Elena, for example. She belongs not only to the class of freshmen at State University, but also to the class of women, the class of brown-haired persons, the class of supporters of equal rights for women, the class of 18-year-olds, the class of part-time office workers, the class of members of the Foreign Students' Club, and so on. In constructing an argument with the conclusion "Elena is a state resident," we must take into account *any* class Elena belongs to that might affect the probability that she is a state resident. Suppose, for example, we know that only 2 percent of the members of the Foreign Students' Club are state residents. If we assign Elena to this reference class, ignoring all the other information, we have the following argument:

2 percent of all members of the Foreign Students' Club are state residents.
Elena is a member of the Foreign Students' Club.

Elena is *not* a state resident.

Both this argument and the original argument have true premises, and their statistical premises are very close to 100 percent and 0 percent. So, if we were to use only the standard that requires a strong statistical generalization, both arguments would appear to be strong ones. Yet their conclusions contradict one another. The requirement that we use all available relevant evidence when choosing the reference class—called the requirement of *total evidence*—can prevent this unfortunate result. The statistical premiss must contain the percentage (although this need not be expressed numerically) of freshmen who are members of the Foreign Students' Club and who are also members of any other class Elena belongs to that is relevant to state residency.

Let us assume that the only classes for which information relevant to state residency is available are the class of freshmen and the class of Foreign Students' Club members. A check of school records for past years shows us that generally only 3 percent of freshmen who are state residents join the Foreign Students' Club. We are now in a position to construct the proper statistical syllogism that embodies all available relevant evidence:

> 3 percent of all freshmen at State University who are members of the Foreign Students' Club are state residents.
> Elena is a freshman member of the Foreign Students' Club.
> _____
> Elena is *not* a state resident.

In ordinary language, the statistical premiss is often unstated when it is a generalization that forms part of our common background knowledge. The argument

> The student who sits next to me in logic class doesn't have a home telephone, for he isn't listed in the telephone directory.

is an example of a statistical syllogism with the implicit premiss, "Almost all phone-owners are listed in the telephone directory." As always, when we are concerned with evaluating arguments, we should try to state any implicit premisses. Sometimes when implicit premisses are exposed, we find that they are somewhat questionable, or that they fail to represent all available relevant evidence. When the implicit premiss in this argument is exposed, we may realize that the student belongs to a class of persons who usually do not have their home phone numbers listed, and that a statistical premiss with a different reference class is appropriate.

Exercises

1. In each of the following statistical syllogisms, which are not stated in standard form, identify the reference class and the attribute class and assess the strength of the argument, using the criteria discussed in this section.
   a. About 95 percent of all professional hair dyes and a considerable portion of home dyes now contain paraphenylenediamine or related chemicals

(also called peroxide dyes). My hair was dyed at the hairdresser's. Therefore, peroxide dye was used on my hair.

b. Most Pittsburgh winters include at least one heavy snowfall, so Pittsburgh will almost certainly have one heavy snow this winter.

c. Of all the students who registered this term, 75 percent favor the University requiring students to pay an activity fee to be used by the Student Government. Since Ellen is registered this term, she undoubtedly is in favor of the fee.

d. Very few people dislike chocolate, so Jill will be pleased with the chocolate dessert you made.

e. Since most German Shepherds are easy to train, your German Shepherd puppy should do well in dog-training school.

f. Stocks typically outperform bonds in the first recovery year after a recession. Since this is such a year, stocks should outperform bonds.

2. Each of the following passages gives advice that is based on a statistical syllogism. In each case, reconstruct the argument and explicitly state the statistical premiss, the premiss that refers to a particular individual, and the conclusion.

a. Always remember that the odds in this hobby [mushroom collecting] are heavily against the collector. He is gambling the price of a mess of mushrooms against the doctor and hospital bills. With such odds in mind it is up to the collector to be critical of what he collects.
    —A. H. Smith, *The Mushroom Hunter's Field Guide*

b. Dear Dr. Molnar: I am 56 and considering an operation. Would you advise against it? I've had a loss of hearing since about age 12. On a recent checkup, my doctor said two bones have grown together in the middle ear. He thinks there is an 85 percent chance of improvement to "very good"; 10 percent chance of no improvement; 5 percent chance of further damage.
    Answer: Why should I advise against the operation? Only one chance in 20 of being worse off; 17 chances in 20 of being better off. There are few if any operations in which 100 percent success can be guaranteed. If I were the patient in such a case, I'd take the 17 to 1 odds.
    —"Doctor Molnar," syndicated newspaper column

c. At a Democratic committee meeting, the incumbent prosecuting attorney loses his party's endorsement. He considers running as an Independent, but his advisers tell him not to because hardly any Independents could receive enough votes to win an election in that city.

3. The Fallacy of Incomplete Evidence

Arguments in the form of statistical syllogisms that fail to take into account all available relevant evidence when choosing the reference class (the class denoted by F in "X percent of all Fs are Gs") are fallacious. Any evidence that might influence the probability that the individual (a) has the property (G) attributed to it in the conclusion is relevant evidence. Although we can say what "relevant" means in this context, we require background knowledge to determine whether or not any particular evidence is relevant.

It is even more difficult to interpret the meaning of "available" in this context. How much research is required to be sure that we have accounted for all available relevant evidence? Obviously, we are seldom in a position to spend years of our lives—or even hours—acquiring evidence that is "available" in the sense that it is part of the storehouse of human knowledge. Often, we must make judgments and/or take actions (such as agreeing to an operation) in the absence of evidence that may be "available" but that we are unable to obtain because of time or cost constraints. The requirement of total evidence is not intended to place unrealistic restrictions on reasoning. What it demands is that we make a reasonable effort to find appropriate reference classes and that we do not simply ignore—through carelessness, prejudice, or laziness—evidence that is within our reach. Consider the following example of a fallacious statistical syllogism:

> 98 percent of all medical-school faculty are men.
> Dr. Shirley Jones is a medical-school faculty member.
> _____
> Dr. Shirley Jones is a man.

This argument appears to be a strong one only if we ignore the well-known fact that "Shirley" is almost always a female name and is rarely given to a man. If we accept the argument as it stands, we will be more likely to accept a false conclusion than a true one, for the probability that a faculty member named Shirley is male is surely very low. Even though we do not have exact figures to assign a probability to the proper reference class (male medical-school faculty member named Shirley), we can see that this additional evidence is relevant and that it undermines the original argument.

The argument

> The Governor of this state doesn't have a private home telephone, for there
> is no listing for this in the telephone directory.

is fallacious, for it fails to account for the fact that many government officials have private phones with unlisted numbers. Similarly, it would be a violation of the requirement of total evidence to infer that your bus for work, which is normally on time, will be on time when the city streets are covered with ice.

In statistical syllogisms, the requirement of total evidence is designed to ensure that we choose the right reference class. The requirement of total evidence actually applies to all other forms of inductive argument as well. In other forms of argument, no reference class may be involved, but the requirement demands that we account for any available relevant evidence that would affect the truth of the conclusion of the argument. The rules of critical thinking do not permit us to construct arguments in which we selectively choose evidence that supports our conclusions and ignore available evidence that would undermine them.

Exercises

Each of the following arguments commits the fallacy of incomplete evidence. In each case, discuss what relevant evidence is ignored.

1. Most Russians don't speak English, so the newly appointed Russian ambassador to the United Nations probably doesn't speak any English.
2. Most movie actors aren't politicians, so Ronald Reagan, a former movie actor, is not a politician.
3. Most Americans earn less than $100,000 a year, so the President of General Motors earns less than $100,000 a year.

4. An Incorrect Form of Inductive Argument

The following argument is a correct deductive syllogism:

All humans are animals.
All mammals are animals.

<hr>

All humans are animals.

Letting upper-case letters represent class terms, we can exhibit the form of this argument this way:

$$\text{All } F\text{s are } G\text{s.}$$
$$\text{All } G\text{s are } H\text{s.}$$

$$\text{All } F\text{s are } H\text{s.}$$

As is true of statistical syllogisms, when we change "all" to "most" in the syllogistic form just shown, we are changing a deductive form of argument to an inductive form:

$$\text{Most } F\text{s are } G\text{s.}$$
$$\text{Most } G\text{s are } H\text{s.}$$

$$\text{Most } F\text{s are } H\text{s.}$$

However, this is *not* a good inductive form of argument, because even when we are careful about such factors as sample size, lack of bias, relevance, and total evidence, this form of argument is not likely in general to lead us from true premises to true conclusions. Consider the following argument which contains all true premises:

> Most physicists are men.
> Most men are non-physicists.
> _____
> Most physicists are non-physicists.

Exercise

Construct another example of an argument in this inductive form with obviously true premises and an obviously false conclusion. (*Hint*: Choose classes in such a way that *F* is a much smaller class than *G*, so that it is possible for most *F*s to be *G*s and most *G*s to be *H*s, while most or even *no F*s are *H*s, since the *H*s could simply be just all things that are not *F*s.)

5. Special Types of Statistical Syllogism

A number of special uses of statistical syllogism are so common that they have been given standard names.

i. Arguments from Authority

All of us depend to some extent on the counsel and advice of those who know more than we do. Sometimes when we present arguments, we appeal to what experts have said on the matter instead of presenting any direct evidence to support the claim we are making. Such reliance on experts is not in opposition to critical thinking, for—under certain restrictions—it may be justified as a type of strong statistical syllogism. After all, experts or authorities are almost always, or usually, correct when they make statements about the subject in which they are experts. Talent, training, and experience place them in a position to understand and evaluate evidence in areas that are not easily accessible to everyone else. When the following conditions are met:

(i) The authority invoked is an expert in the area of knowledge under consideration;

(ii) There is agreement among experts in the area of knowledge under consideration; and

(iii) The statement made by the authority concerns his or her area of expertise;

then it is reasonable to take the authority's word on the matter. When these conditions are fulfilled, the form of argument from authority can be stated

> Most of what authority *a* has to say on subject matter *S* is correct.
> *a* says *p* about *S*.
> _____
> *p* is correct.

This form of argument is obviously a version of statistical syllogism. The first premiss is a statistical generalization; the second premiss is a statement about a particular claim (a member of the reference class); and the conclusion attributes the property of correctness to that claim.

Actually, arguments from authority are rarely presented in English in this form. Usually the authority is merely cited or quoted in support of the conclusion claim. For example, a point in advanced physics might be settled by quoting Albert Einstein's views on the matter; a claim concerning the best way to bake a successful souffle might be supported by citing the method recommended by Julia Child. Sometimes, not just one authority but a whole group of authorities is cited: "All the leading physicists agree that the earth is older than 16,000 years." Regardless of the way in which these arguments are stated in English, they are acceptable only when they meet criteria (i)–(iii).

It is always *possible* for the conclusion of an argument from authority to be false even when these three criteria are satisfied. In any inductive argument, the truth of the conclusion is not guaranteed by the truth of the premisses and the correctness of the form of argument. The history of science offers many examples of expert authorities who were mistaken in their beliefs and were proved wrong in the light of new evidence. It often takes time for new evidence to be assimilated and for experts in a field to recognize the significance of the evidence and to change their opinions. Nevertheless, arguments from authority do have an important place in both scientific and everyday reasoning.

ii. Fallacious Appeals to Authority

Arguments that mimic correct arguments from authority but that fail to meet one or more of criteria (i)–(iii) are fallacious appeals to authority. Such arguments can deceive us in several ways. First, some persons set themselves up as authorities—or their followers do—when they actually lack the expertise of a genuine authority. Knowledge of advanced areas of modern science, for example, is achieved only after years of training and study. Yet there always seem to be a few persons who claim to have achieved such knowledge through quite different means (self-study of obscure texts, visions, inspirations, hunches, etc.). Their claims include finding cures for diseases that have eluded standard medical research or explaining major cosmic events in ways that defy the truth of well-accepted scientific theories. People who make such claims, called "cranks" by all but their followers, are not reliable authorities in the subject area in which they profess expertise. Thus, appeals to their authority constitute fallacies.

Second, in certain areas of some fields of knowledge (psychiatry and economics are two important examples) there is still widespread disagreement among those who have all the academic and professional credentials possessed by experts in a field. In criminal cases that invoke an insanity defense, for example, it is common to find "expert" psychiatric witnesses for both the defendant and the plaintiff—one willing to testify, in complete sincerity, to the insanity of the defendant; the other, no less sincere, willing to testify to the sanity of the defendant. When this kind of disagreement occurs among experts in a field, an appeal to the authority of one side or the other is fallacious. There can be no legitimate appeal to authority in such a case, although, of course, the *evidence* presented by the experts may be evaluated on its own merits. When such evidence is considered, however, the form of argument is not an argument from authority but some other type of argument related to the nature of the evidence.

Finally, when someone is a genuine expert in a particular field of knowledge or has achieved success in a difficult and highly competitive enterprise, that person is properly entitled to prestige and recognition for his or her accomplishments. Such persons are often asked to express their views on a wide variety of issues, many of which lie completely outside their field of expertise. Famous physicists are asked their opinions on moral questions; a football hero testifies to the virtues of one brand of panty hose. Their statements cannot carry the weight of a legitimate appeal to authority, for they are obviously speaking about subjects not within their area of expertise. We must be careful not to accept arguments that rely on the glamour or prestige of an authority in one field to support truth of claims in another, unrelated area of knowledge.

iii. Arguments Against the Person (*Argumentum Ad Hominem*)

Closely related to arguments from authority are *arguments against the person,* or, in Latin, *argumentum ad hominem.* In these arguments, the conclusion states that a particular claim is *false* because it is made by a certain individual. Such arguments are legitimate only when there is reason to believe that most of the claims made by the individual concerning a particular aspect of that subject matter are false. Arguments against the person are often made in legal cases when lawyers wish to attack the credibility of witnesses on the opposing side. If a lawyer can show that a witness has committed perjury when questioned about the subject at issue and, moreover, that a lie would benefit the witness in the case under consideration, the argument may be strong. Like arguments from authority, correct arguments against the person can be construed as statistical syllogisms:

> Most of what individual a says about a particular subject matter S is false.
> a says p about S.
> _____
> p is false.

Although the two forms of argument are similar, few of us are ever in a position to claim that most of what an individual says about a subject is false. There are many expert authorities in various fields; there are probably many fewer individuals who lie regularly or who are almost always wrong about a subject. Truth-telling, rather than lying, is the normal mode of human communication. Usually—there are exceptions, of course—people do not go around making pronouncements in subject areas in which they are more often wrong than right. For this reason, special care should be exercised when arguments against the person are evaluated.

With this caution in mind, we can mention other situations (in addition to the courtroom situation just mentioned) in which legitimate arguments against the person can occur. One such situation concerns pronouncements of scientific cranks whose views are in opposition to the collected wisdom of scientists; in the area of their weird theories, scientific cranks are more apt to be wrong than right. Similarly, exaggerated claims about products sold by high-pressure sales-people are probably more often false than true, especially when these people work for organizations that have bad records with the local chamber of com-merce. The records of some stockbrokers are so poor that their clients would be advised to hold off when those brokers say "Buy."

iv. Fallacious Arguments Against the Person

Arguments that a claim is false on the grounds that it was made by a particular individual are *fallacious arguments against the person* unless most claims made by the individual on that subject are false. We may commit this fallacy for several reasons. We may dislike the person who is making the claim, or we may disap-prove of the person's looks, clothing, views, habits, religion, ethnic origin, or some other personal characteristic. Obviously, such prejudices should not be allowed to intrude on our critical judgments of the truth or falsity of claims.

A second reason why we sometimes are misled by fallacious arguments against the person is our desire to believe that the claim made in the conclusion is false. When we disagree with a claim someone makes, we may, in the absence of any evidence against that person's claim, try to discredit it by attacking the character or qualifications—however irrelevant they may be to the issue—of the individual who is making the claim. Samuel Johnson actually defends this falla-cious use of the argument against the person!

> "When there is a controversy concerning a passage in a classic, or concerning a question in antiquities, or some such subject, one may treat an antagonist with politeness and respect. But where the controversy is concerning the government or religion of my country, it is of such vast importance to have the better, that the *person* of the opponent is not to be spared. If a man firmly believes that religion is a great treasure, he will consider a writer who endeavors to deprive mankind of it as a robber; he will look on him as *odious* even though the infidel may think himself in the right." . . .
>
> Dr. Johnson said that when a man voluntarily engages in an important controversy, he is to do all he can to lessen his antagonist, because authority from personal respect has much weight and often more than the reasonings. "If," said he, "my antagonist writes bad language, though that may not be essential to the question, I will attack him for his bad language."
>
> —James Boswell, *The Ominous Years*

Johnson is probably correct in saying that often people are more moved by their respect (or lack of respect) for a person than by the strength of arguments. It is an unfortunate fact that people usually pay less attention to reasons than to the person providing them. Nevertheless, we, as critical thinkers, do not want to be deceived by such ploys!

v. Arguments from Consensus

In an *argument from consensus* some claim is held to be correct (or incorrect) on the basis of the fact that most people, or a great number of people, believe (or reject) the claim. An automobile advertisement arguing that one brand of car is the best states that "50 million Americans can't be wrong!" It is not at all unusual—particularly in advertising campaigns—to try to win acceptance for some claim by saying that "everyone" accepts it. Such arguments, when they are correct, can be cast in the following form of statistical syllogism:

> When most people agree on a claim about subject matter *S*, the claim is usually true.
> *p* is a claim most people make about *S*.
> ───
> *p* is true.

When the form of the argument is exposed in this way, we can see that it may be very difficult to construct arguments in which the first premiss is plausible. In arguments from authority, the authority has acquired expert knowledge that entitles us to accept his or her claims in some subject area. The primary question in arguments from consensus is whether or not majority opinion entitles us to judge a claim to be true in any area. In most cases, when the opinion of the majority is correct, better forms of evidence that would constitute support for the claim are available to almost anyone. Thus, we regard arguments from consensus as extremely weak when they are correct and as fallacious in most cases. In any serious context, such arguments, even when correct, would carry only supplementary weight and the conclusion would have to be supported by other evidence as well.

An apparent exception to these remarks about argument from consensus occurs when majority opinion validates the truth of a claim *by definition.* One example is the recent judicial ruling that a movie is pornographic if it violates local standards of decency (if most people in that community would consider it pornographic). Under these circumstances, the following argument would be correct:

> A movie is legally pornographic if most people consider it pornographic.
> Most people consider movie *M* pornographic.
> ───
> Movie *M* is legally pornographic.

However, careful examination of this argument reveals that it is not of the same form as an argument from consensus. The first premiss is *not* a statistical premiss; instead the first premiss states something that is true as a result of a definition (in this case, the legal definition of "pornographic"). The second premiss, although it is a statistical generalization, states that the circumstances for the application of the definition have been fulfilled for the movie in question; the conclusion states that the movie belongs to the class of pornography thus defined. If the premisses of this argument are true, then the conclusion must be true as well. It is not an inductive argument, but a deductive one. It is a correct argument, but it is not an argument from consensus.

6. Missing Premisses in Statistical Syllogisms

Once the form of an argument is identified, the task of providing any missing premisses becomes somewhat easier. We have already seen that the statistical premiss in statistical syllogisms is frequently suppressed, particularly when it represents a claim that is commonly known. When we supply missing premisses we should, as a rule, try to provide premisses that are both plausible and strong enough to make the argument a good one—that is, we should give the proponent of the argument the benefit of the doubt when we reconstruct the argument. In arguments from authority, arguments against the person, and arguments from consensus, the statistical premiss is almost always suppressed. However, it is important to supply this premiss in order to evaluate these arguments, because they are critically dependent on whether or not most of what an authority says is right, most of what a person says about a subject is false, or majority opinion on a subject is reliable. We can often prevent the acceptance of fallacious arguments by making suppressed premisses explicit.

Exercises

Reconstruct each of the following arguments. Identify the form of each argument, and any fallacious arguments. Discuss any cases in which additional background knowledge is required to evaluate the argument.

1. Charles Colson, a former White House Aide and a convicted perjurer, charged that the CIA knew about the Watergate break-in in advance. Referring to Colson's charge, William Colby, former CIA Director, said, "His lack of credibility should cause the charge to fall of its own weight." (Reconstruct Colby's argument.)
2. My favorite fashion model, Cheryl Teigs, says that Cover Girl cosmetics are safest for delicate skins. Therefore, Cover Girl is the safest brand for sensitive skins.
3. Many prisoners have complained that conditions in the county jail are unsanitary. However, these persons are outlaws, so we can safely deny the truth of their charges.
4. Both the American Medical Association and the American Dental Association have formally endorsed fluoridation of drinking water. Therefore, fluoridation promotes dental welfare and is not generally harmful to people's health.
5. Most people believe that smoking marijuana is dangerous to one's health. Therefore, smoking marijuana is dangerous to one's health.
6. During both the Ford and the Carter administrations, economic advisors to the President agreed that the best way to encourage the United States to conserve

oil would be to impose a tariff of $3 a barrel on imported oil. Therefore, such a tariff would be the best conservation measure.

7. The following argument supports the use of folk medicines or natural remedies.

> I know they have been well reported of and many wise persons have tried remedies providentially discovered by those who are not regular physicians, and have found a blessing in the use of them. I may mention the eminent Mr. Wesley [the founder of Methodism], who, though I hold not altogether with his Arminian doctrine, nor with the usages of his institution, was nevertheless a man of God.
>
> —George Eliot, *Felix Holt*

V. REVIEW

In Chapter 3, we have looked closely at three important and commonly used forms of inductive argument:

1. Inductive generalizations (arguments based on samples)
2. Arguments from analogy
3. Statistical syllogisms

In evaluating arguments in these forms, a number of criteria have been suggested. Some of these criteria apply only to particular forms; others apply to all forms of inductive reasoning.

The strength of *inductive generalizations* depends on whether the sample in the premiss is representative of the population. Two factors are important here: the size of the sample, and the degree of variety in the sample. *Random sampling,* in which each member of the population is equally likely to be a member of the sample, and *matched sampling,* in which relevant variety in the population is proportionately matched in the sample, are two methods frequently used to obtain representative samples.

The strength of *arguments from analogy,* or *analogical arguments,* depends crucially on whether the similarities mentioned in the premisses are *positively relevant* to the similarity inferred in the conclusion. A similarity mentioned in the premisses is positively relevant to the similarity in the conclusion if the similarity mentioned in the premiss increases the probability that the similarity in the conclusion will obtain. Whether or not analogies are relevant depends on background information that is not usually contained in the premisses of the argument. The *number* of relevant similarities and relevant dissimilarities, as well as the *variety* in the instances cited in the premisses, are also important determinants of the strength of these arguments.

Statistical syllogisms are judged on the basis of the strength of their statistical premisses and also on whether or not they meet the requirement of *total evidence.* In statistical syllogisms, the requirement of total evidence demands that we choose the appropriate *reference class* in the premisses of the argument.

Three special cases of statistical syllogism—*argument from authority, argument against the person (argumentum ad hominem)*, and *argument from consensus*—have also been discussed. In their correct form, these arguments contain a statistical premiss that states that in most cases dealing with the subject matter under consideration, the person who makes the claim speaks truthfully, or the person who makes the claim speaks falsely, or the majority opinion is correct.

One criterion to be considered in evaluating any inductive argument is the strength of the premisses relative to the strength of the conclusion. In general, an argument can be strengthened by bolstering its premisses with additional evidence. This might involve providing a larger or more varied sample for an inductive generalization, more relevant analogies in the premisses of an argument from analogy, a stronger statistical premiss, or a more appropriate reference class in a statistical syllogism. Arguments can also be strengthened by *weakening their conclusions*. Since the strength of an argument is determined by how well the premisses support the conclusion, stating a more guarded conclusion, without weakening the premisses, constitutes a stronger argument.

In addition, not only statistical syllogisms, but all inductive arguments are subject to the requirement of total evidence. In constructing an inductive generalization, we are not permitted to ignore or disregard any evidence that, for example, would produce bias in our sample. In an argument from analogy, we cannot ignore any relevant dissimilarities that may hold between types of object mentioned in the argument.

A number of fallacies are associated with these correct forms of argument. In each case, a fallacy occurs when some standard is violated. Not every fallacy has a special name, but many do. A list of named fallacies follows:

Fallacy of Hasty Generalization (also called *insufficient statistics,* or *leaping to a conclusion*): Occurs when the sample in an inductive generalization is too small.

Fallacy of Biased Statistics: Occurs when the sample is not sufficiently varied to represent the population.

Fallacy of False Analogy: Occurs when the types of objects in the premisses of an analogical argument are relevantly dissimilar.

Fallacy of Incomplete Evidence: Occurs when the requirement of taking account of all relevant available evidence is violated.

Fallacy of Misleading Vividness: Occurs when a small amount of particularly vivid information is allowed to outweigh a substantial amount of statistical support for a conclusion.

Fallacious Argument from Authority: Occurs when the authority cited is not a genuine expert in the field of concern, or when the authority is speaking outside his or her field of expertise, or when experts in the area of concern disagree among themselves.

Fallacious Argument Against the Person: Occurs when there are not good grounds to believe that a claim is false because a particular individual says that it is false. (The appropriate statistical premiss—most of what the individual says about a particular subject matter *S* is false—cannot be accepted.)

Fallacious Argument from Consensus: Occurs when majority opinion does not constitute a good reason to believe the truth or falsity of a claim.

Quite a lot of new vocabulary has been introduced in this chapter. In addition to the names of the forms of arguments and fallacies discussed, you should be familiar with the meanings of the following terms:

Attribute Class: The class represented by *G* in the statistical premiss of the form "*X* percent of all *F*s are *G*s" in a statistical syllogism. The conclusion claims that the individual mentioned in the argument is (or is not, in negative cases) a member of this class.

Reference Class: The class represented by *F* in the statistical premiss of the form "*X* percent of all *F*s are *G*s" in a statistical syllogism. The other (particular) premiss claims that the individual mentioned is a member of this class.

Syllogism: An argument with two premisses.

In this chapter, we have treated the various forms of argument separately. In real life, they frequently occur in combination with one another. Often several different forms of argument are presented to support the same conclusion. No inductive argument provides conclusive support, and no combination of these inductive argument forms can provide conclusive support either. However, a conclusion is usually more strongly supported when several types of favorable arguments can be provided than when only a single such argument can be provided. Arguments against the person, arguments from authority, and arguments from consensus are often presented in combination with other arguments.

In other real-life situations, one type of inductive argument is provided to support some conclusion, and another type of inductive argument, employing the previously established conclusion as a premiss, is then presented. For example, the statistical premisses of statistical syllogisms are themselves frequently supported by an inductive generalization.

VI. EXERCISES

1. The following report contains a statistical syllogism, in which the statistical premiss is supported by an inductive generalization. Reconstruct both arguments, and try to evaluate them in light of the criteria developed in this chapter. Are any other argument forms used to bolster either conclusion?

> For a dozen years, Dr. Joseph Stolkowski has researched a theory that a potential mother can dictate the sex of her baby by regulating her diet.
> Dr. Stolkowski is no quack. He is the distinguished chairman of the physiology department of the Pierre and Marie Curie University in Paris. His papers on the preconception selection of sex in humans have been published in the respected medical journals.
> He contends that a woman who wants to give birth to a boy should eat foods rich in potassium and sodium—such as meat, fish, vegetables, chocolate, and salt—beginning at least six weeks before she wishes to become

pregnant. A woman who wants to have a girl should eat foods rich in calcium and magnesium, such as milk, cheese, nuts, beans, and cereals. . . .

In a study of 47 French couples from 1970 to 1980, he says, 39 of them produced a child of the sex they wanted after the wives had followed special diets. In Canada, a study of 224 couples on special diets reveals an 80 percent success rate with this method.

Asked recently how his research was going, Stolkowski told us: "Better than ever. We now have five health centers in Paris and five outside the city where couples are taking their special diets and producing the boy or girl babies they want. Our success rate is approximately 90 percent."

—Lloyd Shearer, *Parade Magazine*

2. Consider the following inductive generalization and tell whether or not as well as *why* the argument would be strengthened, weakened, or unaffected in strength if it were modified in each way suggested. Where applicable, discuss the importance of background information.

All of the 5,000 swans observed in North America and Europe have been white, and no non-white swans have been observed.

All swans are white.

a. Suppose 10,000 white (and no non-white) swans had been observed.
b. Suppose only female swans had been observed.
c. Suppose only 500 swans had been observed.
d. Suppose all observations were made during winters.
e. Suppose swans had been observed in Africa and Australia as well as in Europe and North America.
f. Suppose the conclusion was "All European and North American swans are white."
g. Suppose only adult swans had been observed.
h. Suppose all observations were made on weekends.
i. Suppose all observations were made in areas within 300 miles of a city.
j. Suppose reports from world travelers about black swans had been recorded in seventeenth-century journals, but that no living person had seen a black swan.

3. Samuel Johnson presents the following case supporting the right of a schoolmaster to beat his pupils. What kind of arguments does Johnson employ? Does he commit any fallacies?

The government of a schoolmaster is somewhat of the nature of a military government; that is to say that it must be arbitrary according to particular circumstances. A schoolmaster has the right to beat, and an action of assault and battery cannot be admitted against him unless there is some great excess, some barbarity. Pufendorf [an outstanding legal scholar in Johnson's day] maintains the right of a schoolmaster to beat his scholars.

—James Boswell, *Boswell for the Defense*

4. In the following passage, taken from "Joint Custody as a Fundamental Right," what form of argument is the author using? Identify the premises and the conclusion of the argument.

> The fundamental right of parental autonomy [the right of parents to share in the companionship, care, custody, and management of their minor children] arguably is identical both within the traditionally recognized nuclear family unit and outside that traditional family unit so long as the relationships maintained outside the unit are "family-like" in the previously specified sense [both parents have an active interest in making parental decisions, and neither is prevented from doing so by reasons of distance, disability, or any other incapacitating factor]. Since the state's right to interfere with these rights within the family is limited by a principle far more restrictive than "the best interest of the child," it is hard to see why state interference should become any less restricted after divorce. Normally, the state may interfere with parental rights only to prevent harm or abuse to the child.... Why should a comparable limitation on state judicial power not be present after divorce as well?
>
> —Ellen Canacakos, *Arizona Law Review,* 1982

5. The following passage is taken from a newspaper report concerning the efforts of a consumer group to have the government ban Bendectin, a prescription drug used to treat morning sickness associated with pregnancy. The consumer group claims that the drug has been linked to birth defects in humans. On what type of argument supporting the drug's harmful effects does the group base its petition? Discuss any implicit premises.

> The consumer group's petition cited an unpublished study from the Max Von Pettenkofer Institute in Germany, which found that 16 of 861 rats exposed to high doses of Bendectin developed a condition in which intestines protrude into the chest through a hole in the muscle separating the lung from abdominal muscles.
>
> The group also cited another study conducted in California that used monkeys. That research raised the possibility of an association between the drug and heart defects, the group said.
>
> —*Pittsburgh Press*

6. In each of the following examples, identify the form of argument used and evaluate each argument according to standards for that form.
   a. The Pope, the spiritual leader of millions of Roman Catholics, who believe that he speaks infallibly on matters of faith and morals, has—as have previous Popes—proclaimed abortion to be a form of murder. Therefore, abortion is murder.
   b. In dozens of trials conducted by an independent laboratory, generic brands of laundry detergent performed just as effectively as more expensive name-brand detergents. Therefore, generic brands are just as effective as name-brand detergents for all laundry purposes.
   c. In a recent Harris Poll, 47 percent of a sample (carefully matched to the population) of 2,500 American adults said that they approved of the President's economic policies. Therefore, approximately 47 percent of all American adults approve of the President's economic policies.

d. The movie star whose recently divorced young wife receives alimony of $150,000 per year probably won't have to pay it for very long, since most young women who are divorced remarry within a year of the divorce. (Alimony payments cease upon remarriage.)

e. *Background information*: Lead is sometimes added to molten bronze to increase its fluidity. The amounts normally added range from 5 percent to 25 percent of the volume of bronze.

> The analyses of Bronze Age Greek artifacts made by Craddock, supplemented by those of Renfrew and the Stuttgart group for the Early Bronze Age, show that most copper, arsenical bronze, and tin bronze objects contain less than 1 percent lead. Indeed, out of a total of 185 analyses of Early and Late Bronze Age axes, chisels, swords, daggers, knives, spearheads, arrowheads, and figurines, 161 show lead contents of less than 1 percent, and only nine show more than 3 percent. Catling and Jones found that of 141 Late Minoan II copper and bronze objects from the unexplored Mansion, Knossos, Crete, only three objects had as much as 1 percent lead. . . . The evidence that lead was rarely deliberately added to copper or bronze objects in the Greek Bronze Age seems compelling and indicates that the lead in ancient copper or bronze objects below about 1.5 percent (and certainly below 0.5 percent) is present as an accidental impurity from the copper ore.
>
> —N. H. Gale and Z. A. Stos-Gale, "Bronze Age Copper Sources in the Mediterranean," *Science*, 1982, 216:12–13

f. In the outbreaks of human poisoning from methylmercury in Japan and later in Iraq, one of the most consistent signs in adults was deficits in visual function. . . . The visual system of macaque monkeys resembles that of humans and exhibits the same signs and pathological lesions as that of humans when exposed to methylmercury. Macaques are therefore excellent models for testing the effects of methylmercury on the visual system.
>
> —D. C. Rice and S. G. Gilbert, "Early Chronic Low-Level Methylmercury Poisoning in Monkeys Impairs Spatial Vision," *Science*, 1982, 216:759

7. What steps would you take to find an unbiased sample if you wanted to conduct a poll to determine student opinion at your college or university about the legalization of marijuana?

8. What kind of argument in the passage below supports the conclusion "Over wide areas of Australia, the tame dingo was by no means an effective hunting dog and it contributed relatively little to the Aborigine's larder"?

> At Warburton, the Aborigines denied ever having used dingoes in hunting, especially when pursuing large animals, and this view was echoed by Jankuntjara informants [in South Australia, at the southeastern end of the Western Desert] interviewed by Hamilton. Nor were dingoes ever used for hunting by the desert-dwelling Aborigines we observed in the Clutterbuck Hills-Tikatika region in 1966-1967 or at Pulykara, near Mt. Madley, in 1970.
>
> —R. A. Gould, *Living Archaeology*

9. Can you think of any plausible example in which the opinions of most Americans would constitute the basis for a non-fallacious argument from consensus?
10. Recently, the city of Pittsburgh decided to enforce collection of a personal property tax on stocks and bonds held by city residents. Each resident who owns such property is supposed to file a statement listing their property. The city's resources for detecting ownership of these properties are practically non-existent, since the city does not have access to federal income tax returns filed by residents. Despite this, a letter claiming to know that stocks and/or bonds are owned was sent by the city to each head of household whose earned income exceeded $40,000 per year. (A city income tax is deducted from wages, so these persons were identifiable.) On what type of argument do you think the city based its claim to know that persons earning more than $40,000 owned stocks or bonds?

CAUSAL ARGUMENTS

I. INTRODUCTION

Many of the arguments discussed thus far have been causal arguments. The conclusions of such arguments state that a causal relationship holds (or fails to hold) between two types of things or events. For example, a previous argument concluded that birth-control hormones may affect brain development; another concluded that drugs taken by expectant mothers affect the sleep patterns of their newborn infants; another, that colds disappear more quickly when a medicinal toothpaste is used; and another, that obliterating the high-contrast wing stripes on tropical butterflies does not affect wing damage or flight patterns.

Some of these arguments were inductive generalizations; others were arguments from analogy. Arguments from authority, which, when correct, are statistical syllogisms, are also used to support causal claims. It is clear that causal claims occur as the conclusions of many different forms of argument. In this chapter, we will pay special attention to a variety of ways of establishing causal claims. We will call any argument in which the conclusion is a causal claim a *causal argument,* but we should remember that the term "causal argument" does *not* refer to any single *form* of argument.

Concern with causal connections is prevalent in everyday life. When cars or other mechanical appliances break down, when buses are late, when classes are canceled, when we do well—or poorly—in an examination, or when personal relationships improve or take a turn for the worse, we normally seek the cause or causes of what has happened.

Psychologists (R. Nisbett and L. Ross, *Human Inference*) report that studies have revealed that not only will people readily generate causal accounts of events on the basis of very limited evidence when asked to do so, but also that spontaneous causal analysis is remarkably common.

In one experiment, the investigators "bugged" 13 haphazardly selected conversations at singles' bars, at a picnic for economically underprivileged senior citizens, and at student bull sessions. Using a set of categories that included "gives information," "gives evaluation," "gives advice or suggestion," "makes prediction," and "gives causal analysis," they classified each utterance of a speaker. On the average, statements expressing or requesting causal analysis accounted for 15 percent of all utterances recorded. Even though, as the investigators admit, this was not a carefully controlled scientific study, the proportion of ordinary speech devoted to causes was impressive. The search for causes is clearly not confined to scientific investigations in laboratories and offices. Obviously, concern with causes is a primary influence in our everyday lives.

In Chapter 4, we will be looking closely at causal reasoning and at some methods that have been proposed as aids to discovering causes and supporting causal claims. Although the discovery of causes is an important part of our lives, logic is more particularly concerned with the *justification* of causal claims than with how causes can be discovered. Frequently, no evidence is presented in ordinary life to support causal claims. As critical thinkers, we should be concerned with the quality of the evidence supporting causal claims, or, in other words, with how arguments with causal conclusions are to be evaluated. We should also be aware of common mistakes in causal reasoning (causal fallacies) and learn to avoid them.

II. MILL'S METHODS FOR ESTABLISHING CAUSAL CLAIMS

The problem of justifying causal claims is primarily a problem in *inductive* logic. The reasons offered for the existence of a causal connection are usually less than conclusive, although some causal arguments are better than others. Inductive logic is a much newer branch of knowledge than deductive logic. The latter has been studied in schools continuously since it was first developed—almost single-handedly—by the Greek philosopher Aristotle 2,500 years ago. (Of course, people reasoned logically even before Aristotle formulated the principles of logical reasoning.) In the nineteenth century, John Stuart Mill—well-known for his works *Utilitarianism, On Liberty,* and *On the Subjection of Women*—made a serious and significant attempt to systematize inductive logic by spelling out its rules and principles, just as Aristotle had done with deductive logic.

Mill recognized that scientific knowledge is based on inductive reasoning and that causal reasoning is central to acquiring such knowledge. He was distressed with the flimsy and inadequate basis for many causal claims put forward by scientists of his own day, and he tried to formulate standards that would represent sound scientific practice. Mill thought that causal claims should be based on careful observation and experiment; he believed that if he could make these principles explicit, then people could follow the rules and become more skilled at causal reasoning. The methods that Mill outlined, although they did not always measure up to his exaggerated claims for their success, now provide an important basis for contemporary scientific methodology and are also very useful in ordinary causal reasoning. Although Mill outlined and discussed five methods, only the four most commonly used methods will be treated here. Mill intended his methods to be used both as aids to the discovery of causes and as instruments to justify causal claims. They are in fact used in both of these ways by scientists.

1. The Method of Agreement

Just after a recent Japan Air Lines flight from Tokyo to Europe landed in Copenhagen, 144 passengers were hospitalized and another 51 were treated but did not require hospitalization. All of the ill passengers exhibited symptoms of a gastrointestinal disorder. Doctors immediately suspected that food poisoning was the cause of the illness. The passengers had eaten food put aboard during a refueling stop in Anchorage, and all those who became ill had eaten omelets prepared by a single cook, who worked for the airline's catering service in Anchorage. During a two-week investigation, it was learned that the cook had a sore on his finger. Officials concluded that bacteria from this infection had been the source of contamination and the cause of the food poisoning suffered by the passengers.

This causal inference employed *Mill's Method of Agreement,* which states that when we seek the cause of some event or condition, we should look at the *antecedent circumstances* (the events or conditions that occurred earlier than the event or condition for which the cause is sought). If only one common antecedent circumstance can be identified, then it is likely to be the cause— or a part of the cause—of the event or condition under investigation.

In this case, the illness was diagnosed as food poisoning, and it is known that food poisoning is caused by eating food contaminated by certain bacteria. Contamination can arise in a number of ways. Most people know that harmful bacteria can grow when food is not stored at the proper temperature. Food can also become contaminated through contact with unclean utensils or other things that harbor harmful bacteria. Here, the common antecedent circumstance was contact between the food and a cook whose finger was infected, and this circumstance was judged to be the cause of the illnesses. The important point of *agreement* among the antecedent circumstances of the hospitalized passengers was that all of them had eaten contaminated omelets prior to becoming ill. Schematically, the Method of Agreement can be presented in the following form, where E represents the event or condition for which the cause is sought, and S–Z represent antecedent conditions. The left-hand column numbers each separate case in which E occurs.

Case	Antecedent Circumstances	Event for Which Cause Is Sought
1	X, Y, Z	E
2	X, U, V, Y	E
3	X, W, S	E
4	X, T, Z, W	E
etc.	$X, \ldots$	E

In this schematic representation, X is the only antecedent circumstance in which all occurrences of E agree. In such cases, the use of Mill's Method of Agreement affirms that X is the cause—or a part of the cause—of E. In our example, the number of cases is 195, the total number of cases of food poisoning (E). The antecedent circumstance X represents the circumstance of eating an omelet prepared by the cook with an infected finger. The other letters represent various other antecedent circumstances that were possible causes of the disease; in this example, these antecedent circumstances would include foods and drinks, other than the cook's omelets, that were eaten by various passengers who became ill.

The use of the Method of Agreement does not guarantee that a cause will be discovered, nor does the method constitute an absolute guarantee that the *suspected* cause is the *real* cause of the illness. (This is an inductive form of reasoning, not a deductive form.) There is always the possibility that investigators overlooked the true source of contamination and that the cook's finger was only coincidentally connected with the illnesses. However, this investigation was thorough and the evidence was quite strong, so officials felt there was little room for doubt about the true cause of the passengers' illness.

When we draw up a list of antecedent circumstances, we should confine our attention to possible causal agents—not to every antecedent circumstance indiscriminately. In our example, boarding the plane in Tokyo was also a common antecedent circumstance, but it was not considered to be a possible cause of the illness. We are faced with an unlimited number of antecedent circumstances in most cases of causal inquiry. Without some previous notion of the type of cause sought, there would be no manageable way to use the Method of Agreement.

At the same time, through ignorance or error, a possible cause may be overlooked in constructing the list of antecedent circumstances. If the true cause is not on the list, the Method of Agreement will not disclose it. In such cases, the use of this method may support a false conclusion.

The method is most likely to lead to a true conclusion when we possess general information about the types of causes that bring about the condition or event in question and the method is used to narrow the search for a cause within that general framework. Such general information is called a *causal theory*. In our example, the causal theory that guides the search for a cause of the illnesses is the general information about the nature and causes of food poisoning. It is known that symptoms appear several hours after eating and that the disease is generally caused by consuming food that is bacterially contaminated. It is also known that in certain foods cooked at rather low temperatures, such as omelets, custards, and cream sauces, harmful bacteria can multiply very rapidly. Such foods receive special attention during investigations of food poisoning.

Exercises

For each of the following situations, suggest some possible common antecedent circumstances that you might investigate to find the cause of the event described.

1. You have a flat tire on the way to work. When you finally get to work, you find that three of your coworkers also had flat tires on the way to work.
2. When you arrive home in the early evening, you try to turn on some lights and find that none of them work.
3. Although it is early summer, all of the trees in the woods near your home are turning brown.
4. When you go to a concert downtown and try to park in the lot you normally use, you find that it is full. All of the other parking lots in the area are full as well.
5. Your dog refuses to eat the food you give him four nights in a row.

2. The Method of Difference

Although the newspaper report from which the food-poisoning example was taken did not present all the details, the investigation to find the cause of the illnesses undoubtedly used another of Mill's methods, the *Method of Difference*, to eliminate some possible causes of the disease. Once the illness was diagnosed as food poisoning, the search for a cause concentrated on foods eaten by the various passengers. According to the report, everyone in the first-class section of the plane was served an omelet prepared by that cook, but many of the tourist-class passengers were not. The cook prepared between 207 and 215 omelets, so there were more omelets prepared than passengers who became ill (195). However, no one who had not eaten an omelet prepared by the cook with the infected finger became ill. Mill's Method of Difference tells us that to find the cause of an event or condition E, we should look at cases in which E occurs and E fails to occur and examine the antecedent circumstances of both such cases to see how they differ. Schematically, the Method of Difference can be represented:

Cases	Antecedent Circumstances	Event or Condition for Which Cause Is Sought
1	X, S, T, U, V, W	E occurs.
2	S, T, U, V, W	E does not occur.

Suppose, for example, that a husband and wife were on the Japan Air Lines flight together and were served identical meals. Suppose, further, that the wife was allergic to eggs, so she did not eat the omelet, although she ate all the other foods, and—except in that one respect—ate the same food and drink her husband did. If she did not become ill, and her husband did, the omelet would be judged to be the cause of the food poisoning according to Mill's Method of Difference. The only difference between Es occurring and failing to occur is the presence of X (eating an omelet that was prepared by the cook with an infected finger) in the antecedent circumstances of E. Under these conditions—since unless X occurs, E fails to occur—Mill's Method of Difference states that X is the cause, or an indispensable part of the cause, of E.

Use of the Method of Difference is subject to the same limitations as the Method of Agreement. If the real cause is not listed in the antecedent circumstances, the method cannot detect it. Similarly, the choice of antecedent circumstances in our example is guided by a well-established causal theory concerning possible causes of food poisoning. In the presence of such causal theories, uses of Mill's methods constitute strong evidence for causal claims.

Exercises

For each of the following situations, suggest some antecedent circumstances that may account for the presence of the effect on the one hand and its absence on the other.

1. A friend gives you two tomato plants, which you set out in your garden. One plant produces two dozen tomatoes; the other plant fails to yield a single one.
2. You and a friend go on a hike together. The next day she breaks out with a case of poison ivy, but you don't have any signs of it.

3. You bake a birthday cake, and it turns out just right. You make a second cake a week later, but this one fails.

4. You normally fall asleep within ten minutes of going to bed, but last night you lay awake for at least two hours before you fell asleep.

5. Your new cotton shirt fit perfectly the first time you wore it two weeks ago, but it is now too tight around the collar and its sleeves are an inch too short.

3. The Joint Method of Agreement and Difference

In almost every important use of Mill's Methods of Agreement and Difference, the two methods are combined. Obviously, if the use of both methods points to the same cause, a causal claim is better supported than when only one method is used. Furthermore, the Method of Difference strictly permits a comparison of only two cases—one in which the event or condition under investigation occurs, and one in which it does not. However, the use of just two cases would constitute rather weak evidence, particularly when information about many cases is available. We know, for example, that some people have a natural resistance to disease and that they do not become ill even when they are exposed to the known causal agent of a disease. In most investigations, the Method of Agreement is actually applied to all cases in which the condition occurs and to all cases in which the condition does *not* occur; the Method of Difference is then used to compare the two sets of cases.

The two methods are combined so often that a special name—*The Joint Method of Agreement and Difference*—is given to the combination. Schematically, the joint method looks like this:

Cases	Antecedent Circumstances	Event or Condition for Which Cause Is Sought
1–h	X, S, T, U	E occurs.
i–n	S, T, U, V	E does not occur.

In the schematic representation, the cases (1–h) in which E occurs are grouped together. (In our example, these cases would be the 195 cases of food poisoning.) The cases (i–n) in which E does not occur are also grouped together.

The newspaper report from which our example was taken did not specify the number of cases in which passengers did not become ill, but the plane was a jumbo jet and carried many such persons. The letters S–U represent foods eaten by each passenger. The letter V represents an alternative food to X (for example, an omelet prepared by another cook or a different type of main dish). Although V represents a difference between the two groups, it is not judged to be the cause of the illness, because persons who ate V did not become ill.

The Joint Method of Agreement and Difference is extremely important in studying the causes of and cures for diseases and is a far more powerful tool than either method used alone. For example, if just two persons are given a flu vaccination and one escapes the flu but the other is stricken, we know little about

the effectiveness of the flu vaccine. There are exceptional cases in which exposure to a cause does not produce the effect. The person who did not get the flu
may have had a natural immunity. (We know also that vaccination itself can, in
some cases, be a cause of the disease it is designed to prevent.) If everyone in
a rather isolated community receives a flu vaccine and there is little or no incidence of flu, use of the Method of Agreement would tell us the vaccine was
effective. But we cannot be too confident about this result, for the community
may simply not have been exposed to the flu virus. If, however, hundreds of
students are vaccinated for the flu at the student health clinic and only a few of
them get the flu, but a very large proportion of hundreds of unvaccinated students at the same school get the flu, the Joint Method of Agreement and Difference tells us that there is good reason to believe the vaccine is effective in
preventing flu.

Although Mill's methods are most effective when they are applied within the
structure of a specific causal theory to provide evidence for causal claims, they
can also be used to guide and restrict the search for causes when no specific
causal theory is available. In this way, Mill's methods help investigators formulate
causal theories that can be subjected to further testing. Early studies of cholera,
discussed by B. MacMahon and T. Pugh (*Epidemiology*), illustrate this point.
Even before the germ theory of disease was developed, observers noted that
cholera spread when persons came into contact with infected persons and that
the occurrence of cholera was associated with poverty, overcrowding, refuse,
and filth. Use of the Method of Agreement suggested that the common factor
was exposure to the fecal discharges from cholera patients.

In 1854, one perceptive observer, John Snow, noticed that a group of people
in an area of London where cholera was epidemic were attacked by the disease
with much less frequency than their neighbors. Five years earlier, in 1849, all
groups in London had been uniform with respect to frequency of the disease.
Using the Joint Method of Agreement and Difference, Snow looked for antecedent circumstances that would account for the different frequencies of cholera
present in the two groups in 1854. He discovered that the area was served by
two different water companies. The families supplied by one of the companies,
the Southwark and Vauxhall Company, had a much higher incidence of cholera
than those supplied by the Lambeth Company. In the years between 1849 and
1854, the Lambeth Company had changed its sources of supply from a place near
where the Southwark and Vauxhall Company took its water to a place higher up
on the Thames River. As a result of its move, the Lambeth Company no longer
drew its water from an area near where large amounts of sewage poured into
the river. Snow believed this confirmed his suspicion that fecal contamination
was the cause of cholera.

In the wake of Snow's investigations, efforts were made to provide the citizens of London with clean drinking water, and the incidence of cholera declined
significantly, even though the exact cause of the disease (the specific germ) was
not known until much later. This use of Mill's methods by Snow was an important
step in the development of the germ theory of disease, rather than a use that
depended on that theory.

In the history of medicine, the first search for causes and cures often occurs when investigators notice differences in the geographic distribution of a disease. When a disease is prevalent in one area and much less common in another area, it is natural to look for causes in such general features as differences in diet, soil (which affects food grown there), and water supplies.

Not all attempts to use Mill's methods as aids to discover causes have been as successful as Snow's work on cholera. An incident reported in the *Diary* of Samuel Pepys shows the weakness of Mill's methods in the absence of a causal theory.

During a raging epidemic of the bubonic plague in London in the 1660s, it was noted that not a single London tobacco seller died of the plague. On these grounds, reasoning by what is now called the Joint Method of Agreement and Difference, authorities at Eton, outside London, ordered all school boys to smoke tobacco as a preventive measure when the plague reached that area. Eton is one of the few boarding schools in history where boys were flogged for failing to smoke! Unfortunately, smoking did not prevent the occurrence of bubonic plague at Eton; the use of tobacco was totally unrelated to avoidance of the disease. It was a strange coincidence that London tobacconists had been spared during the epidemic.

We now know that the bubonic plague virus is transmitted through the bite of fleas, which are carried on rodents. The great plague episodes in England during the seventeenth century resulted when rats escaped into the cities from ships, which brought them—and the disease—from foreign ports. This causal connection between rats, fleas, and plague was not discovered, however, until a hundred years after the worst plague years—and it was much later before the immediate cause, a specific virus, was isolated.

Cancer is a current disease with a poorly understood set of causes. Mill's methods are frequently applied at various levels of modern cancer research. It has been observed, for example, that cervical cancer is almost nonexistent among nuns, although it is a rather common form of cancer among women in general. Use of the Joint Method of Agreement and Difference leads investigators to suspect that some aspect of sexual activity or the reproductive process is causally related to cancer of the cervix.

4. The Method of Concomitant Variation

The Method of Difference and the Joint Method of Agreement and Difference are applicable only when the suspected causal agent can be observed to be present in some cases and absent in others. In the investigation of the cause of food poisoning, the suspected omelets were eaten by some passengers but not by others. In the study of cholera, some households received water from one company; some, from another company. In these cases, as in all cases for which the Method of Difference and the Joint Method of Agreement and Difference are applicable, there is a clear distinction between exposure and nonexposure to the suspected agent.

The event or condition that results from the causal agent may be an increased or decreased *rate* or relative frequency of occurrence in a group of persons, rather than specific individual occurrences of the condition for each exposure to the causal agent. This is true in the cholera example. The disease was not present in each case in which the suspected cause (contaminated water) was present. Nevertheless, the water supply was judged to be the cause (or part of the cause) of cholera due to a higher *frequency* of cholera in families supplied by the Southwark and Vauxhall Company. The percentage of Southwark and Vauxhall customers who contracted cholera was much higher than the percentage of Lambeth Company customers who contracted the disease. Drinking the water from a contaminated source did not always result in cholera, but it increased the probability of contracting the disease. The term "cause" is widely used in this probabilistic sense. (We will examine this and various other uses of the term "cause" in Section IV.)

Sometimes when we wish to investigate a causal situation, we are faced with circumstances in which the suspected causal agent is present in all cases. Neither the Method of Difference nor the Joint Method of Agreement and Difference is useful in such cases. When there is more than one common antecedent circumstance in the cases under consideration, the Method of Agreement may be used to limit the number of causal possibilities, but it will not be as helpful as it is when there is only one common antecedent. If, however, the condition or event under investigation *varies in degree or strength* from one case to another, the *Method of Concomitant Variation* may be a useful aid to discovering causes and justifying causal claims.

For example, high blood pressure (hypertension)—a widespread condition among people in all parts of America—is regarded as a major contributor to heart attacks. According to a newspaper report in the *Arizona Daily Star,* an estimated 23 million Americans—10 percent of the population—suffer from high blood pressure. Two scientists suggested that the fact that the death rate from hypertension in Tucson, Arizona, was 41 percent below the national average was caused by the relatively high selenium content of the Arizona soil. (Selenium is a metal found in minute quantities in almost all soils.)

The scientists studied 45 cities. They used the selenium levels measured in grazing food or forage crops as a gauge for amounts of selenium present in state soils. Tucson was among nine cities in seven Western states with high selenium levels and relatively low hypertension death rates. The death rates attributed to high blood pressure in selenium-poor states (Connecticut, Illinois, Ohio, New York, Oregon, Massachusetts, Rhode Island, Pennsylvania, Indiana, and Delaware) are three times greater than these rates in selenium-rich areas.

In this example, the association between selenium levels in the soil (the antecedent circumstance) and death rates from high blood pressure (the condition for which a cause is sought) suggests that selenium may be a causal factor in the prevention of high blood pressure. The method used to discover this connection—or to justify the claim that a causal connection exists between selenium levels in the soil and avoidance of high blood pressure—is Mill's Method of Concomitant Variation. Here is a schematic representation of this Method:

Cases or Groups	Antecedent Circumstances	Event or Condition for Which Cause Is Sought
1	$X+, Y, Z, \ldots$	$E+$ (or $E-$)
2	$X-, Y, Z, \ldots$	$E-$ (or $E+$)

The far left-hand column represents individuals, events, or circumstances— or groups of the same—classed according to the severity or degree of strength of the condition under investigation. There may, of course, be more than two such cases. For example, instead of dividing the individuals into two groups according to whether a condition is present in severe or mild degree, we might divide the individuals into three groups— severe, mild, and moderate. The letter X represents the antecedent circumstance that varies in strength—either in the same direction as the condition under investigation or in the opposite direction. In our example, the death rate from hypertension decreased ($E-$) as the selenium level increased ($X+$). The letters $Y, Z, \ldots$ represent any other common antecedent circumstances that might be suspected to be causally connected with the condition under investigation. In the newspaper report from which our example is taken, no other antecedent circumstances—such as minerals other than selenium—were mentioned.

Another study of disease provides a striking example of the use of the Method of Concomitant Variation. In a large city, such as London, it is usual for a number of deaths due to respiratory problems to occur each day. Until rather recently, most people were unaware of how strongly these deaths were influenced by air pollution. In counting the number of deaths that occurred during a time of severe atmospheric pollution (formerly called "London fog") from November 29 to December 16, 1952, it became apparent, based on Mill's Method of Concomitant Variation, that the intense smog had caused approximately 4,000 deaths. Information concerning the antecedent circumstances (pollution measured in parts per million of sulphur dioxide, SO_2) and the event for which cause is sought (increase in number of deaths) is reproduced in Figure 4–1. This graph shows clearly that the increases and decreases in the number of deaths ($E+$) almost exactly match the increases and decreases in parts per million of sulphur dioxide in the atmosphere ($X+$).

Like the other methods, the Method of Concomitant Variation is most useful within the framework of a specific causal theory. Such a causal theory provides guidance as to which antecedent circumstances among an indefinite number of available antecedents are plausible candidates for causes. If little is known about the specific causal nature of a widespread disease, such as cancer or hypertension, and different frequencies appear to be present in different geographic areas, investigators use the Method of Concomitant Variation to select broad environmental features that vary with intensities that match the variation in frequency of the disease. By doing this, they frequently can control the disease to a certain extent, even when the precise causal agents are unknown.

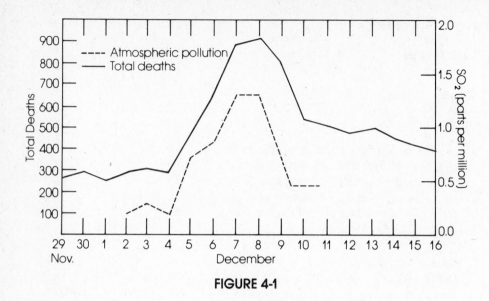

FIGURE 4-1

Atmospheric pollution (in parts per million of sulfur dioxide) and numbers of deaths per day in London, from November 29 to December 16, 1952.

Source: B. MacMahon, T. Pugh, and J. Ipsen, *Epidemiologic Methods* (Boston: Little, Brown, 1960), page 6.

Exercises

In each of the following exercises:

(1) Identify the condition or event for which cause is sought. Be sure to tell whether specific occurrences or rates (relative frequencies of occurrence) are being investigated.
(2) Identify all antecedent circumstances mentioned in the example.
(3) State which of Mill's methods is being used.
(4) Identify the cause, according to the use of Mill's methods.

Note that some of the exercises are taken from newspaper reports and that less than complete information is provided. If more background information is crucial, discuss this point as well. Being aware of what is needed to pass critical judgment on a problem is part of critical thinking! The evidence we receive in newspapers, magazines, and other sources is often incomplete with respect to the conclusions stated there.

1. (From a report in *The New York Times* on the use of a new anti-viral drug, called "ara-A," in the treatment of herpes simplex encephalitis)

Of 28 cases of the disease, 18 received ara-A, and 10 were given an inert substance for 10 days. Five persons in the first group died, and seven in the second group. Thus the mortality rate of the untreated group was 70 percent; the rate of the treated group was 28 percent.

2. Alzheimer's disease is a serious form of senility that afflicts between 5 and 10 percent of all persons over age 65. Recently, researchers discovered that patients who die of Alzheimer's disease have much smaller amounts of a particular enzyme in the cortexes of their brains than persons the same age who do not suffer from the disease. The loss of this enzyme activity has been suspected as a cause of the lesions found on the brains of Alzheimer's patients. In postmortem examinations of five Alzheimer's patients and five people without the disease, it was found that all the diseased patients had lost neurons from the nucleus basalis (a tiny area deep in the brain; its function is not understood by neurologists), while all the people without the disease had the normal number of cells in this area. Scientists who conducted this study believe that the loss of neurons from the nucleus basalis may be responsible for the decreased enzyme activity in the cortex.

3. An anti-smoking campaign aimed at junior high school students has shown significant results. . . . The study involved 750 Houston seventh graders. One group of students was asked about smoking habits—31 percent said they had smoked at least one cigarette in the previous month—and was asked the same question again ten weeks later. No anti-smoking instruction was given to them. [They are members of the control group.] Other groups of students were asked the same question [the report does not tell how they responded], and then participated in various kinds of anti-smoking instruction. By the end of ten weeks, 18.3 percent of the control group—those who were not shown anti-smoking propaganda—had taken up smoking. Among the other groups, fewer students had started smoking—ranging from 8.6 percent to 10.3 percent.

—*Arizona Daily Star*

4. *Background information:* We now know that the disease beriberi is caused by a dietary deficiency in the B complex of vitamins, particularly vitamin B_1. Whole grains provide a common source of this vitamin. The episode described here occurred before anything was known about vitamins. The research was conducted in an asylum for the insane. Cured rice is rice that has been treated to preserve some of the outer hull. Uncured rice (now usually called "polished rice") is rice from which the outer hull—which contains most of the vitamins—is removed.

The lunatics are housed in two exactly similar buildings on opposite sides of a quadrangle surrounded by a high wall. On December 5, 1905, all the lunatics at that time in the hospital were drawn up in the dining shed and numbered off from the left. The odd numbers were subsequently domiciled [housed] in the ward on the east side of the courtyard, and no alteration was made in their diet. They were still supplied with the same uncured rice as in 1905. The even numbers were quartered in the ward on the west of the quadrangle and received the same rations as the occupants of the other ward with the exception that they were supplied with cured rice. . . . On December 5, there were 59 lunatics in the asylum; of these, 29 were put on cured rice and 30 on uncured rice. The next patient admitted to the asylum was admitted to the cured rice ward, and the one admitted after him to the uncured rice ward, the next to cured, and so on alternately to the end of the year.

In the middle of the year, the patients in the east ward were moved to the west ward and those in the west ward to the east, but they continued to receive the same diets. By the end of 1906, among 120 patients eating uncured rice, there had been 34 cases of beriberi and 18 deaths. Among the 123 patients assigned to cured rice, there had been only 2 cases and no deaths, and both cases had been manifested at the time the patients were admitted to the asylum.

—B. MacMahon and T. Pugh, *Epidemiology*

5. In England, which imports most of its sucrose [sugar], records of the last 100 years show a steady increase in per capita consumption of sucrose, from about 20 pounds per year in 1820 to over 100 pounds per year today. Present consumption of sucrose in the United States is about the same. This represents 15 to 20 percent of an individual's caloric requirements. Concomitant with this increased consumption of sucrose has been an almost parallel rise in the prevalence of caries [cavities]. Conversely, surveys in Europe and Japan demonstrated that caries were dramatically reduced during periods of wartime restrictions of sugar, syrup, and all sugar products.

—E. Newburn, "Sugar and Dental Caries: A Review of Human Studies," *Science,* 1982, 217: 418–23.

6. In the newspapers several years ago, there was a story about a doctor in New Jersey who was suspected of—and later tried and acquitted for—murdering a number of patients in a private hospital. Empty vials that had contained curare ("arrow poison") were found in the doctor's locker. The doctor claimed that the curare was used for experiments on dogs, but the man who was supposed to have supplied the dogs denied that he had given or sold any dogs to the doctor. The bodies of the patients, all of whom had been in the hospital for minor operations and who had been in good health otherwise, were exhumed. Sophisticated tests found traces of curare in each of the bodies. On the basis of this evidence, other doctors at the hospital and the authorities insisted that a warrant be issued for the arrest of the suspect.

7. An alarming number of malignant skin cancer cases have been discovered among members of the District of Columbia Police Dept. who were repeatedly exposed to tear gas during the riots and demonstrations of 1968–1971 here.

Dr. Robert F. Dyer, director of the D.C. Police and Firemen's Clinic, said Thursday that one chemical component of tear gas apparently causes cancer.

"Over the past five years I personally have collected a series of 12 patrolmen with malignant melanoma [a form of skin cancer], which in a group of 4,800 men is higher than I would expect," Dyer said.

All 12 officers reported being present at one or more of the many riots and demonstrations quelled with tear gas between 1968 and 1971, he said.

—*Washington Star*

8. Aspirin, taken in large doses by sufferers of arthritis, is being looked at for its effect on the liver.

Gall [the physician conducting the research] said his interest in aspirin and the liver began when a 20-year arthritis sufferer, who had taken aspirin for many years, was found to have high levels of an enzyme in her blood, usually one indicator of hepatitis, a disease of the liver.

When doctors took the woman off aspirin, the high enzyme levels dropped back to normal, Gall said. The test was conducted several times, and each time, the high enzyme levels corresponded to the times when aspirin was taken.

—*Arizona Daily Star*

9. A federal study of 46 cities has concluded that fluoridating water to prevent tooth decay has no adverse effect on public health.

The study by the Center for Disease Control in Atlanta was undertaken to investigate claims that fluoridation is linked to higher cancer rates.

"There is no evidence to suggest that fluoridation does any harm," Dr. J. David Erickson, who conducted the study, said in an interview.

Erickson studied the causes of death of 922,000 people over three years in 46 American cities—24 of them with fluoridated water and 22 without.

After taking into account differences in race, age, sex, education, and population density between the people in the two groups of cities, Erickson found that there was virtually no difference in the death rates. There were 1,124 deaths per 100,000 persons per year in the cities with fluoridated water and 1,137 in those without.

The death rate from cancer was 195 in cities with fluoride and 197 in the cities without.

—Associated Press

10. In a study at Vipeholm, a mental institution in southern Sweden, 436 adult patients on a nutritionally adequate diet were observed for several years. They were found to develop caries [cavities] at a slow rate. Subsequently, the patients were divided into nine groups to compare the effect of various changes in their carbohydrate intake. Sucrose was included in the diet as toffee, chocolate, or caramel, in bread, or in liquid form. Caries increased significantly when food containing sucrose was ingested between meals. Not only the frequency but the form in which sucrose was ingested was important: sticky or adhesive forms were more cariogenic [cavity-producing] than forms which were rapidly cleared from the mouth. After two years on the test diets, the patients were again placed on the control diet, and the caries activity reverted to the pretest pattern.

—E. Newburn, *Science,* 1982, 217:419

III. CONTROLLED EXPERIMENTS

Careful readers will have noticed that *controlled experiments,* which were mentioned in Chapter 3 in connection with preventing bias, were involved in several of the examples and exercises pertaining to Mill's methods. The use of controlled experiments is closely related to Mill's Joint Method of Agreement and Difference. In a controlled experiment, the investigator selects two groups that are similar to one another, except with respect to the antecedent circumstance believed to be causally related to the condition under investigation.

For example, in a controlled experiment to study the effects of a birth-control hormone on brain development in rats, two groups of 100 laboratory rats might be selected from the quite uniform population of laboratory rats. The two groups would be given the same treatment in all respects, except that the experimental group would be given doses of the birth-control hormone with their food and the control group would not be given that hormone. If retarded brain development (or a higher rate of retarded brain development) occurs after this treatment in the experimental group but fails to occur in the control group, then this evidence would provide support for the claim that the birth-control hormone is the cause of the retardation in the experimental group.

In addition, since the experimental group of rats presumably is a representative sample of laboratory rats, what happens to them in the experiment provides a basis for generalizing to what would happen to any laboratory rats that were given the hormone. Similarly, the control group is a representative sample of rats that are not given the hormone, and the results obtained from the controlled experiment can be generalized to the population of laboratory rats. (Drawing an analogy between what happens in rats and what happens in humans depends on a further inference.) Mill's methods are therefore closely related to inductive generalizations.

There are obvious limits to the uses of controlled experiments. Many of you probably felt uneasy about the treatment of "lunatics" in the beriberi experiment. It seems quite cruel to compel a group of helpless people to eat a diet suspected of being connected with a serious disease like beriberi. This diet, however, was common for many people outside institutions at that time as well. Today, government regulations have established strict guidelines for any experiments involving human subjects, and experiments in which humans are forced to participate are less likely to occur.

In addition to moral and legal restraints on controlled experiments involving human subjects, other limitations prevent their use in many cases. To construct a controlled experiment, the investigator must be able to select two groups— the control group and the experimental group. The groups should be as similar as possible in all ways, except that members of the experimental group are exposed to the suspected causal agent whereas members of the control group are not. Furthermore, the control group should be a representative sample of the population that is not exposed to the suspected causal agent, and the experimental group should be a representative sample of the population that might be exposed to the suspected causal agent. Only when these conditions are fulfilled is there strong reason to believe that the results of the study will yield reliable information about what would happen if the population in general were exposed to the suspected causal agent.

Studies performed on experimental animals often meet these ideal conditions. The animals are bred for certain uniform characteristics, so that almost any group of animals is a representative sample of the population. Such animals are not, of course, a representative sample of the human population—only the population of laboratory rats, guinea pigs, or whatever experimental animal is used.

In the physical sciences, it is also possible to perform controlled experiments to study various properties of physical substances. Any bit of pure sodium is a representative sample of that metal, so that it is not difficult for investigators to perform controlled experiments to discover the causal properties of sodium. (Sometimes, however, scientists find it difficult to isolate the item on which they wish to perform a controlled experiment. Nobel Prize winner Marie Curie had to handle tons of pitchblende to isolate enough radium to perform her controlled experiments.)

In the study of causes of human disease, as in many other causal studies of great practical importance, it is extremely difficult to find experimental and control groups that exhibit the required properties. For example, many studies of potential curative treatments are based on controlled experiments in which the control and experimental groups are composed of hospital patients. There is, however, good reason to believe that hospital patients are not a representative sample of the human population. Some hospitals attract patients from one economic group of the population; others, from different economic classes. People who enter a hospital for the treatment of one disease may be more susceptible than the general public to other diseases. In evaluating the effects of curative or preventive treatments, it is important to know about the medical history of a patient's family, but this information is often difficult to obtain. For these reasons, medical scientists are very cautious about projecting the results of controlled experiments on hospital patients onto the general population.

Another problem associated with performing controlled experiments on humans is obtaining large enough samples. In Chapter 3, one causal claim based on a controlled experiment was that the sleep of newborn infants was affected by drugs taken by their mothers when the infants were in the womb. That study of the effects of drugs taken by pregnant women on the sleep patterns of their newborns made an effort to select two groups of mothers who were as alike as possible except for their drug-taking habits, but both the experimental group and the control group were rather small. It is often difficult to obtain samples that are large enough to be representative of even a special subgroup of the human population, such as the subgroup of pregnant women.

Conducting controlled experiments on laboratory animals poses far fewer problems, but if we are interested in effects on humans, then the animal studies are of limited value. We must make a further analogical argument to apply the results of animal studies to humans, and important dissimilarities always exist between the animal and the human populations. Despite these limitations, however, controlled experiments on humans and animals play an extremely important role in causal investigations.

One further problem that should be mentioned in connection with controlled experiments on humans is the elimination of psychological influences that might affect the purity of the results. It is well-known that human illnesses often improve when the patient *believes* in the treatment that is being administered, regardless of any specific physical causal influence of the drug or whatever physical means are employed to effect a cure.

The technique of a *double-blind experiment* is adopted to try to eliminate such psychological influences in judging the effectiveness of possible cures. In an experiment to test a new drug, members of the control group are given some inert substance (called a *placebo*) such as a sugar pill, and members of the experimental group are given the drug being tested. The people receiving these substances do not know whether they are members of the control group or the experimental group; they are "blind" to the type of substance they receive. In addition, the investigators are administering the drugs and placebos "blindly"; the substances are identified by codes, and they cannot be distinguished at the time of the experiment. In this way, the experimenters are able to make judgments about success of treatment in each case and learn who received the drug and who received a placebo only after the experiment is completed.

Double-blind experiments are employed in situations other than drug testing. Recently, the U.S. government completed a three-year study of the effectiveness of cloud seeding in enhancing rainfall. The technique of seeding clouds involves flying over them and sprinkling them with fine particles of silver iodide.

None of the experimenters in the study "knew at the time on which days they were actually seeding clouds with fine silver iodide particles, and on which they were merely sprinkling them with an inert sand 'placebo'" (R.A. Kerr, "Test Fails to Confirm Cloud Seeding Effect," *Science*, 1982, 217:234). Neither those who decided which clouds to seed nor those who judged the amounts of rain that fell from seeded clouds knew whether the clouds had been seeded with silver iodide or sand. After three years, a locked vault that held the secret record of the silver iodide seedings was opened. The experimenters were disappointed to find that this particular double-blind experiment failed to confirm the effectiveness of cloud seeding, but they planned further, more refined experiments and were convinced that weather-modification researchers must continue to use such controlled experiments to test the effectiveness of various weather-modification procedures.

Exercises

1. Review the set of ten exercises at the end of the previous section on Mill's methods, and identify any features that typify controlled experiments.
2. Find a description of a controlled experiment in an outside reading source. (Some good sources are the magazines *Science* and *Scientific American* and the "Science" sections of weekly newsmagazines. Other possible sources are newspaper stories and Sunday supplements, such as *Parade*.) Characterize the important features of the experiment (whether it was double-blind, how the control group was matched to the experimental group, and so on).
3. Design a controlled experiment to test a causal claim that interests you.

IV. DIFFERENT USES OF "CAUSE"

> For want of a nail, the shoe was lost,
> For want of a shoe, the horse was lost,
> For want of a horse, the battle was lost,
> And all for the want of a horseshoe nail.
>
> —Nursery rhyme

Our references to "the cause" of some event or condition tend to conceal the complexity of most causal situations. The term "cause" is used in many different ways, depending on such factors as the state of our knowledge and our practical or theoretical interest in a causal relationship. Consider a murder trial in which the defendant is accused of shooting the victim. The prosecuting attorney, who is interested in showing that the defendant is responsible for the gunshot wound that led to the victim's death, would say that the defendant's action was the cause of death. If in fact the victim did not die immediately, but was taken to surgery and suffocated after an allergic reaction to an anesthetic, the medical examiner's report would cite suffocation as the cause of death. There is no real conflict here; although suffocation was the *proximate* cause (the causal event nearest the occurrence under investigation) of death, the action of the defendant was an earlier part of the causal chain that led to the suffocation. The law is interested in one part of that chain, and the medical specialist is interested in another.

The causal chain leading to the victim's death undoubtedly contains more links. The ambulance that took the victim to the hospital may have been delayed. The anesthetist may have failed to check the victim for allergies. The shooting may have been provoked (caused) by a quarrel resulting from the victim's attentions to the defendant's spouse; the victim's attentions might have been encouraged by the spouse; and so on. All of these events and conditions were a part of the complex causal process leading to the death of the victim. Only a special interest in some part of the complex set of events and processes (such as who is legally responsible or what should be put on the death certificate) leads us to refer to one part of this complex process as "the cause."

This *chain* of causal events that results in the death of the victim is actually oversimplified, for it neglects to take into account various other chains of events that might be interwoven with and that could reinforce or counteract these events. For this reason, it seems more appropriate to use the analogy of a "causal network" rather than that of a "causal chain." Sometimes one aspect of a complex causal process is identified as "the cause" because that aspect is more susceptible to control than other aspects of the causal process. Yellow fever, for example, occurs when the yellow-fever virus enters the bloodstream of a person who is not immune to the disease. The virus, however, is transmitted by the bite of a mosquito, and programs to control yellow fever are usually aimed at eliminating the mosquitoes rather than controlling the specific virus. The mosquito is usually called "the cause" of yellow-fever epidemics.

Many humans have a natural immunity to certain diseases. We do not, however, try to control these diseases through selective breeding, and a lack of natural immunity is almost never cited as "the cause" of disease. Nevertheless, unlike human diseases, plant diseases are often controlled by breeding resistant strains instead of attacking the specific organism responsible for the disease, and we do sometimes say that a plant succumbed to disease because it lacked the immune characteristic.

Sometimes the term "cause" is used in the sense of "necessary causal condition." A condition is called "necessary" if the effect cannot occur without that condition. The presence of oxygen or another gas that will support combustion, for example, is a necessary causal condition for the existence of fires. Our attention often focuses on causally necessary conditions when we are interested in *eliminating* some undesirable effect. When medical scientists are looking for ways to eliminate a disease, they often focus on some necessary causal condition, such as the mosquito carrier of yellow fever. No one, however, would think of trying to prevent forest fires by reducing the oxygen in the atmosphere near forests, even though this would be an effective measure.

Sometimes the term "cause" is used in the sense of "causally sufficient condition." This means that whenever the condition is present the effect is present as well. Decapitation of a person is a causally sufficient condition for that person's death. Atmospheric testing of nuclear bombs is a sufficient causal condition for producing levels of radiation that are hazardous to humans and other animals in the areas near the test sites. Often when we are interested in producing some desired effect, we look for a causally sufficient condition, such as a wonder drug that will bring about a "sure cure" for some disease. It is unusual, however, to be able to isolate a single causally sufficient condition. Usually, the term "sufficent condition" is used to refer to some important causal factor that, against a background of a complex of necessary conditions, is especially proximate, or interesting, or easy to control.

For example, it is reasonable to claim that bringing water up to a temperature of 100° Celsius is sufficient to make that water boil. This is true, however, only when certain necessary background conditions, such as relative freedom of the water from impurities and normal atmospheric pressure, are operative. When the background conditions are fairly normal, or are not subject to great fluctuation, or are not usually under our direct control, we often ignore them and use the term "sufficient causal condition" to refer somewhat loosely to an event or process that we can control directly and that, under normal background conditions, will produce the desired effect.

Sometimes we refer to a set of causal conditions as being "individually necessary and jointly sufficient" for some event to occur. The conditions necessary to cause germination in viable grass seed are (1) adequate water, (2) suitable temperature, (3) oxygen, and (4) light. When all of these conditions are present jointly in the appropriate degree (proportions vary for different types of grasses), the combination is sufficient to cause germination in viable seeds.

However, even when the causes of some type of event are fairly well understood, it is rather unusual to be able to specify complete sets of conditions that are individually necessary and jointly sufficient for the occurrence of the event. An example follows.

Dental caries, the localized destruction of tooth tissue by microorganisms, is a process familiar to most of you, and this process is well understood by medical scientists. There are three main causal factors: (1) the hosts (saliva and teeth), (2) the microorganisms (particularly one called *Streptococcus mutans,* which is found in dental plaque), and (3) the diet.

Experiments have shown that rats fed through stomach tubes do not get cavities even when the caries-producing *S. mutans* is present. Similarly, rats do not get cavities when they are fed orally if their mouths are kept sterile. It would seem then that the presence of teeth, microorganisms, and food are individually necessary and jointly sufficient for cavities in rats. However, rats do not *always* develop cavities under these circumstances—although they do develop cavities at "the normal rate." Some rats, like some humans, apparently are able to resist cavities better than others. For this reason, we would say that the presence of teeth, microorganisms, and a food supply jointly form a *probabilistic* cause of tooth decay, but not a sufficient causal condition for the disease.

Some further necessary conditions may be specifiable in this case (for example, lack of fluoride protection and genetic susceptibility to the disease), but frequently the causal situations are simply too complex to permit us to identify a complete set of conditions. The effort expended by medical scientists in search of additional necessary conditions for a particular type of event depends largely on practical concerns, such as how much knowledge is necessary to *control* the causal process, rather than on theoretical concerns, such as achieving knowledge of a set of jointly sufficient conditions. Although diet has received emphasis recently in the study of dental caries, research formerly focused primarily on host factors (fluoride treatment of teeth and drinking water) and on microorganisms (the possibility of immunization).

We have been looking at some of the different ways in which the term "cause" is used. The point of this discussion is that there are a number of correct uses of the term. Different uses of "cause" are suitable in different circumstances. However, it is important for us to understand the variation in usage of the term, so that we do not fail to identify important causal relationships.

Not all causal claims refer to necessary and/or sufficient causal conditions. It would be foolish, for example, given all the evidence now available, to deny that heavy smoking is a cause of lung cancer, even though not every heavy smoker contracts the disease and not every person who gets lung cancer is or was a smoker. Smoking is a *probabilistic* cause of the disease; it is neither a necessary nor a sufficient causal condition for the occurrence of the disease. We call a causally antecedent condition a *probabilistic cause* when the presence of that condition makes the occurrence of the condition under investigation more probable than it would be in the absence of the antecedent condition. There is very good evidence that heavy smoking is an antecedent condition that is related to lung cancer in this way.

Here is an example, taken from a syndicated newspaper medical advice column, of confusing probabilistic causes and sufficient causal conditions:

> Dear Dr. Steincrohn: Thinking about premature death has caused a serious depression in my husband. Although only 38 and, according to our doctor, physically sound, he lives in fear of dying early.
>
> He blames it on his poor heredity. His father died of a coronary attack at the age of 59 and his mother had a stroke at about the same age. One uncle suffers from extremely high blood pressure.
>
> With that kind of family history, he asks, "What chance have I got?" As a result he smokes too much. Drinks a lot. Has let himself get fat.
>
> He figures how he lives won't make any difference. Have you run into similar problems?
>
> —Dr. P. J. Steincrohn

In answering this letter, the doctor correctly notes that "there may be a hereditary disposition to stroke and heart attacks," but he points out that the man is not inevitably doomed to an early death. He cites records of patients who had good family histories and poor living habits who died earlier than their counterparts who had poor hereditary traits. The husband, at least if his wife's description of the situation is accurate, seems to regard his poor hereditary traits as causally sufficient for an early death rather than as factors that increase the probability of early death. As a result of this misunderstanding, he ignores other factors, such as not smoking, which could counteract a possible predisposition to cancer.

Exercises

For each of the following causal claims, discuss whether "cause" is used in the sense of:

> (1) A proximate or nearest cause in a chain or network of causes.
> (2) An agent causally responsible for some action or event.
> (3) A necessary causal condition.
> (4) A sufficient causal condition.
> (5) A sufficient causal condition against a background of accepted, stable, necessary conditions.
> (6) A probabilistic cause.

1. Martha failed the exam because there wasn't enough time to finish it.
2. Jason will graduate in June because he passed every course he took this year.
3. William went to the party because Jean asked him to go.
4. An arsonist caused the fire at the museum.
5. The house burned down because oily rags were stored in a closet.
6. The criminal confessed because he was promised a light sentence.
7. Nathan caught the measles because he played with the boy next door who had the measles.
8. The crops are poor this summer because there hasn't been enough rain.
9. Rice takes much longer to cook at the observatory because it is on top of an 8,000-foot-high mountain. At that altitude, the boiling point of water is considerably less than it is at sea level.
10. The ice on the sidewalk is melting because salt was thrown on it.
11. Terence caught a cold because he wasn't dressed for the storm.
12. Rats who were injected with massive doses of saccharine developed tumors at a much greater rate than rats who did not receive saccharine, thereby demonstrating that saccharine causes tumors in rats.

V. HUME'S ANALYSIS OF CAUSATION

Thus far in our discussion, we have not attempted to offer a definition of "cause" that would cover the various uses of the term. It is very difficult to define "cause" in a satisfactory way, even though we all seem to grasp the meaning of the term in an intuitive way. In the eighteenth century, David Hume offered an analysis of the meaning of statements of the general form *"A causes B."* Hume was trying to solve the problem of how to justify causal inferences. For the purposes of simplicity, he analyzed the type of causal relationship that held between two rather uncomplicated events, or types of events (the striking of two billiard balls and their movement after the collision). Hume could find nothing in the *ideas* of striking and subsequent motion to connect the two events. That is to say, the concepts of striking and of motion are not related in the way that the concept of bachelor and the concept of unmarried male are related. When Hume turned to experience for a possible justification of causal claims, he said the features we could observe in such relationships were:

1. *A* and *B* are joined with one another in space and time. ("No action at a distance.")
2. *B* follows *A*. (The "effect" does not precede the "cause.")
3. Whenever *A* occurs, *B* occurs; and vice-versa. ("Constant conjunction.")

Hume realized that all three of these relationships might be observed in two events that were only coincidentally connected with one another. (Remember the tobacconists' avoidance of the London plague.) Hume therefore felt that his analysis failed to uncover any "real"—as opposed to coincidental—connection between the two events. His analysis pushed the matter still further, for he showed that there is no logical reason—no correct deductive or inductive argument—to support the view that constant conjunctions that have been observed in the past will continue to hold in the future.

Hume was not entirely satisfied with his results, and he challenged others to find a "real connection," but his own conclusion was skeptical: The inference from cause to effect is based on a psychological habit of expectation, formed as a result of observance of connections in the past. The inference, Hume said, is apparently not grounded in *reasoned* knowledge of real connections but in habit or custom. Since we tend to think that our knowledge of causes, especially what we have learned from scientific investigations, is based on more than mere habit, Hume's well argued and startling conclusion has troubled all who have thought seriously about this problem.

In this text, we cannot discuss Hume's arguments in detail, nor can we consider various attempts to solve the problems he raised. Many serious thinkers reluctantly accept Hume's skeptical conclusion that there is no logical reason to support the view that constant conjunctions that have been observed in the past will continue to hold in the future. Despite this fact, most people also believe that genuine causal connections can be understood as something more than constant conjunction and the habit of expecting repetitions of these conjunctions.

It is important to point out that Hume was *not* recommending that we cease making causal investigations and causal claims or that we give up causal reasoning altogether. He thought that this would not only be foolish, but that it was psychologically impossible. Many philosophers and scientists have adopted the following pragmatic stand in view of Hume's analysis:

> Although we have no logical reason for believing that the future will resemble that past, *if* it does, then our causal judgments that are based on observations of continued regularities (using reasoning of the sort recommended by Mill) will be the ones that provide useful and important information about the world. If the world changes in such a way that the present regularities no longer hold, no other method now available can give us any better information about what regularities—if any—we can expect in the future.

You may have noticed that in Hume's analysis of what it means to say that "*A* is the cause of *B*," he was using the notion of "causally sufficient condition."

This is expressed in the third statement of his analysis: "Whenever *A* occurs, *B* occurs." Another term that is used to distinguish this type of cause from a cause that is probabilistically related to its effect, is "deterministic" cause. A *deterministic cause* inevitably results in its effect.

Determinism is the philosophical principle that everything that happens is a result of causally sufficient conditions. Determinism does not claim that we know, or even that we will someday know, what these conditions are in each case. Determinism is a view about what the world is like, not a view about the knowledge we can obtain about that world. According to the principle of determinism, the fundamental causal structure of the world is deterministic, and references to probabilistic causes are due to ignorance of some part of the causal complex—some "hidden factors" that, if understood, would complete the causal story.

Whether or not all fundamental causes are deterministic is another difficult—and, as yet, unanswered—philosophical question. If the causal structure of the universe is fundamentally deterministic, then our talk about probabilistic causes may simply reflect our ignorance of hidden, deterministic causal factors. In Hume's time, the most advanced science of the day was Newtonian physics. Newton's genius had unearthed an impressive set of deterministic causes, expressed in his Law of Universal Gravitation and in his three Laws of Motion. In view of Newton's successes, it was widely believed that future scientific advances would uncover more and more deterministic causes in cases where previous knowledge had been probabilistic.

Consider our view that smoking is a probabilistic cause of lung cancer. It is certainly possible that further scientific investigation may uncover a genetic property, present in some but absent in others, that predisposes humans to lung cancer when they smoke heavily. Medical scientists might someday be able to specify a set of individually necessary and jointly sufficient causal conditions for the disease.

Nevertheless, there are some areas of modern science, particularly quantum physics, in which—unlike the situation in Hume's time—the best theories available not only have probabilistic causes at the most fundamental level but also cannot even accommodate the discovery of "hidden factors." This point is rather difficult to understand without an appropriate background knowledge of quantum physics. Nevertheless, it is so important that some scientists have considered it the most revolutionary feature of modern science—comparable to Newton's great discoveries in the seventeenth century. Many scientists hope that eventually a different—and, to their minds, a more satisfactory—deterministic theory of quantum physics may be discovered. But they recognize that the present theory cannot be expanded or modified to become a deterministic theory without giving up even more firmly held principles about causality, such as *an effect cannot occur earlier than its cause*. The finest experimental results currently available cannot be accounted for by deterministic causes.

Thus, quantum physics differs from medical science. Medical scientists have discovered that specific microorganisms are causally responsible for such diseases as cholera, plague, tuberculosis, and Legionnaires' Disease, and that deficiencies in specific substances are causally responsible for such diseases as beriberi, rickets, and scurvy. Medical theory is heavily committed to the discovery of such specific causal agents, which, when present or absent against a standard background of necessary causal conditions, are sufficient for the occurrence of specific diseases. In other words, the history of medical science can be viewed in terms of searches for deterministic causes and success in finding such causes. Seventeenth-century physics, which reached its peak in Newton's work, enjoyed similar success in identifying deterministic causes. Until quite recently, Newton's (deterministic) physics represented the most advanced science. The most advanced theory of physics in the twentieth century, however, depends on probabilistic causes.

Probabilistic causation would remain important even if all fundamental causes were deterministic, for at any given time in a subject area, probabilistic knowledge may be the most accurate knowledge available. Furthermore, the search for deterministic causes is frequently guided and motivated by the observance of probabilistic (statistical) regularities. As a practical matter, in science as well as in everyday life, we will continue to be concerned with probabilistic causes.

One final remark: Hume's worries about causation are not solved by replacing a deterministic notion of causality with a probabilistic one. Hume's arguments apply to conjunctions that hold only with probability as well as they apply to constant conjunctions.

VI. CAUSAL FALLACIES

Mistakes in causal reasoning, or *causal fallacies,* can arise through inattention to some important aspect of the nature of causal relationships. Causes are *repeatedly* connected with their effects (although the connections may be probabilistic rather than deterministic). This feature of the causal relationship holds whether we are talking about causally necessary conditions, causally sufficient conditions, proximate causes, or any other special type of cause. We expect causes and their effects to occur together with some degree of regularity. Another standard feature of any causal relationship is that a cause does not occur later in time than its effect.

1. Confusing Coincidental Relationships with Causes (*Post Hoc*)

Sometimes people focus on the second standard feature just mentioned and infer that *A* is the cause of *B* simply because event *B* occurs later than event *A.* To reason this way is to commit a causal fallacy. The fallacy is common enough to be given the special name *post hoc,* which is derived from the first two words of the Latin expression that describes the fallacious pattern of reasoning: *"Post hoc, ergo propter hoc"* ("After this, therefore because of this").

When we think carefully about the matter, we are not likely to claim that a causal connection exists between two events merely on the basis of the fact that one event occurred later than the other. In our critical moments, we realize that it may have been coincidental that one event followed the other in time. But sometimes when the events are striking, unusual, or important to us, we mistake a coincidence for a true causal connection, particularly if such a connection fits more or less within some accepted causal framework. If, for example, an air-conditioning unit breaks down the day after it is is cleaned, its motor is oiled, and its filter is changed by a serviceman on a routine maintenance call, we might suspect a causal connection and blame the serviceman. On inspection, however, the unit may turn out to have broken down due to an entirely unrelated incident (say, the failure of a timing switch that showed no signs of any problem when the unit was serviced).

Post hoc reasoning underlies many superstitious beliefs. If, for example, I receive bad news on three successive Wednesdays and conclude that Wednesday is my unlucky day (that this day of the week somehow causes me to receive bad news), I am committing a *post hoc* fallacy. If I eat a special breakfast (say, bacon and eggs) when I usually have cereal and then do brilliantly on a math examination that afternoon, it would be a *post hoc* fallacy to conclude that the special breakfast was the cause of my unusual performance on the examination.

In addition to constructing unwarranted causal connections between two events that are unusual, or important, and that occur in close succession, the belief that an effect must somehow *resemble* its cause—or that the cause must somehow *contain* whatever is in its effect—is a possible source of *post hoc* fallacies. Mill was especially scornful of this mistake, which he considered to be an undesirable holdover from medieval attempts at scientific reasoning. Mill maintained that proponents of this view might as well argue that pepper had to be in the cook, since there was pepper in the soup! Belief in the efficacy of many folk medicines is based on this kind of reasoning. A causal relationship is considered plausible on the basis of some resemblance, usually between the form of plant and the part of the body that is afflicted. The leaves of the wildflower Hepatica are shaped something like the human liver, so the plant was used as a cure for liver ailments. The blossoms of Plumbago (Lungwort) resemble tiny lungs, and were therefore considered to be an effective lung medicine. Undoubtedly, the supposed "cure" seemed to work in some cases. Many human illnesses clear up regardless of treatment—or lack of treatment— however, and it cannot be assumed that a causally efficacious cure has been found simply because improvement follows treatment in a few cases.

The best way to distinguish coincidental relationships from causal ones is to continue to observe and experiment, when possible, to determine if observed regularities actually persist. After the plague at Eton in the seventeenth century, observers realized that the connection between using tobacco and avoiding the plague was not a genuine causal connection but merely a coincidence, and sustained observation proved this to be true. Mill understood that it was important to use his methods to test suspected causal connections *repeatedly*. This belief is reflected in the modern use of controlled experiments and observations. In this way, irrelevant factors can be eliminated, and the essential components of a causal process—that is to say, a causal theory—can be understood. If opportunities for checking the persistence of regularities are not available, it is wise to suspend judgment about whether a connection is coincidental or causal.

2. Ignoring a Common Cause

Even when observation and experiment assure us that a suspected cause and effect are connected with some degree of regularity, we must be careful to distinguish among various direct and indirect causal connections. For example, when archaeologists excavate sites in Central and North America, they find that sites that contain bits of pottery regularly contain grinding-stone (used for grinding corn) fragments as well. But they do not conclude that the presence of pottery causes the presence of grinding-stone fragments or that the presence of grinding stones causes the presence of pottery. To do so would be to commit the fallacy of *ignoring a common cause*. Pottery fragments and grinding-stone fragments are not directly causally related to one another. Their joint occurrence is a result of an underlying common cause, namely human habitation of those sites.

Examples of regular associations that depend on a common cause are frequently encountered. The measles virus causes both red spots and fever in those people who are afflicted; although the spots and fever are regularly connected, neither directly causes the other. The regular association between storms and falling barometers is due to a common cause—a sharp drop in atmospheric pressure. The tips of many pine trees in my city turned brown recently. This was not the result of the effect of the pine trees on one another; it was the result of a common cause—an atmospheric inversion that allowed atmospheric fluorides to concentrate in the foliage of the pines.

3. Confusing Cause and Effect

A third causal fallacy, the *fallacy of confusing cause and effect,* arises when a direct causal relationship exists between two types of events, but a mistake is made in judging the *direction* of the relationship. An example of this fallacy occurs in one of Graham Greene's spy novels, *The Human Factor.* In one part of the book, a pair of secret agents are discussing a method to "eliminate" a colleague suspected of leaking secrets. One of the agents suggests using peanuts, and offers the following account to his baffled coworker:

> "Peanuts when they go bad produce a mold. Caused by *aspergillus flavus*—but you can forget the name. It's not that important, and I know you were never any good at Latin."
> "Go on, for heaven's sake."
> "To make it easy for you I'll concentrate on the mold. The mold produces a group of highly toxic substances known collectively as aflatoxin. And aflatoxin is the answer to our little problem."

The spy who is so condescending to his colleague has no reason to be smug, since he is guilty of confusing cause and effect. The peanuts do not *produce* a mold when they go bad. The mold attacks the peanuts and is the *cause* of their going bad. The mold, in other words, is a cause—not an effect—of spoiled peanuts.

Effects cannot precede their causes, so the way to avoid the fallacy of confusing cause and effect is to pay special attention to the *temporal order* of two events that have a direct causal relationship to one another. For example, it is well known that the rise in the incidence of lung cancer and the increase in cigarette smoking have been regularly connected over the past 50 years. Most people believe that there is a direct causal relationship between these two events—that the increase in tobacco use is the cause and the increase in cancer is the effect. However, some people have argued that the rise in the incidence of lung cancer may have caused the increase in smoking, because having cancer may create a craving for tobacco. This seems to be a case of the fallacy of confusing cause and effect, for we know that most smokers who develop lung cancer have smoked heavily for years. Their smoking habits were fixed long before they contracted the disease. There is no evidence that people who contracted lung cancer increased their smoking thereafter.

Although the question of which came first—smoking or lung cancer—seems to be a fairly easy one to answer, it is difficult in many causal situations to determine which part of the causal complex occurs earlier in time. For example, there is archaeological evidence that certain areas of the southwestern United States were occupied for a prolonged period of time by one group of people, who disappeared rather abruptly and were succeeded by an ethnically different group of people. The temporal order of this series of events is subject to interpretation. The invasion of the newcomers might have caused the former residents to abandon these areas, or the influx of the newcomers might have been caused, or partially caused, by the decision of the former residents to leave these areas.

Another example of the difficulty of sorting out cause and effect occurs in studies of schizophrenia. There is a well-supported, regular association between schizophrenia in young adults and unstable or disturbed relationships in the families of those who suffer from schizophrenia. But it is not known whether the unhappy family situation is a cause, or part of the cause, of schizophrenia or whether the hardship of living with a schizophrenic tends to cause disturbance in the family. Both schizophrenia (or at least the most obvious symptoms of the disease) and unhappy family situations usually develop over an extended period of time. In such situations, it is almost impossible to determine which event occurred first.

In some cases, further observation and/or controlled experimentation that attempts to interfere with some part of the causal process can enable us to determine the direction of a causal relationship. It is on the basis of many studies of the development of lung cancer and the smoking history of victims of this disease that the claim that cancer causes an increase in smoking can be rejected. In their studies of the abandonment of pueblos in the Southwest, archaeologists look for evidence of warfare and evidence of unfavorable conditions for agriculture, as well as for other evidence—such as the exact dates of leaving and arrival of the different groups—that would help them to decide whether invasion by new people was the cause of pueblo abandonment or an effect of the abandonment.

In some cases, such as cases of schizophrenia, it is very difficult to use experiments to determine causal direction. One experiment that could be performed would be to remove the schizophrenic from the family situation and then to use Mill's Method of Difference to observe whether or not family relationships improved. The results of such an experiment might not be entirely convincing, however. The family situation may have deteriorated during the time spent with the schizophrenic to the point that family patterns of uncooperative behavior may have become too fixed to be changed simply by the removal of the original source of the difficulty.

Although no effect can precede its cause, we must recognize that many causal relationships are complex. Multiple, interacting causes can reinforce and counteract one another to such a degree that isolating the various parts in order to observe or control them separately may not be feasible. In such situations, awareness of the possibility of an underlying common cause, or of the possibility that cause and effect may be confused with one another, can prevent us from accepting unsupported or inadequately supported causal claims.

4. Genetic Fallacy: Reasons and Causes

The term "genesis" can be equated with "origin." The *genetic fallacy* is a mistake in reasoning that occurs when some factor concerning the origin or causal source of a claim is confused with evidence for the truth of that claim. Unlike the three causal fallacies just considered, the genetic fallacy does *not* involve some misunderstanding of the form of evidence required to support a causal claim. It is treated in this section because, after our discussion of the nature of causes, we are in a better position to understand the difference between the *cause* of holding a belief and the *evidence* for the truth of that belief.

When evidence is presented in a logically correct argument, the evidence consists of statements that, if true, provide *reasons* for accepting the conclusion as true. Sometimes, however, beliefs are not held on the basis of reasons but are held because of psychological factors that cause the belief. Among these factors are devotion to the person from whom the belief was acquired, social pressures to conform, and the implantation of a belief at an early age. Any of these factors can be a causal source of a belief, but none of them is a reason for the truth of the belief.

An adult who is afraid of the dark may believe harm will come to him or her from being in a dark room. This belief may be the result of being locked in the closet as a child. The frightening childhood experience is part of a causal explanation of that person's fear of the dark and—as a causal explanation—is probably correct. We have good evidence that such treatment causes fears that persist into adulthood. However, this is not evidence that being in the dark will harm that person. To suppose that the causal explanation of the fear is a reason (in the sense of evidence) why a person ought to be afraid of the dark would be an example of the genetic fallacy. Fallacious appeals to authority, appeals to consensus, and *ad hominem* arguments are also forms of the genetic fallacy, for they involve mistaking some feature of the genesis of a claim (the person who is the source of the claim) as a reason for regarding the claim as true or false.

VII. REVIEW

The aims of Chapter 4 have been to increase understanding of the complexity of causal reasoning, to provide some standards for assessing causal arguments, and to point out some common types of fallacious causal reasoning. The new terminology introduced included the names of four of Mill's methods for discovering causes and justifying causal claims: the *Method of Agreement*, the *Method of Difference*, the *Joint Method of Agreement and Difference*, and the *Method of Concomitant Variation*. Look again at Section II, in which these methods are discussed, and be sure that you are able to recognize examples of the use of these methods.

In our discussion of the term "cause," several types of causes were distinguished:

Necessary Causal Condition: *A* is causally necessary for *B* means that without *A*, *B* will not occur.

Sufficient Causal Condition: *A* is causally sufficient for *B* means that whenever *A* occurs, *B* will also occur.

Deterministic Cause: sufficient causal condition.

Probabilistic Cause: *A* is a probabilistic cause for *B* if the presence of *A* increases the probability that *B* will occur.

Proximate Cause: the causal condition in a causal complex that is nearest in time or space to the event caused.

Another important concept discussed in this chapter is the *controlled experiment*. In a controlled experiment, an experimental group is subjected to a suspected causal agent and a control group is not. The controlled experiment provides a context for the application of Mill's Joint Method of Agreement and Difference. The technique is especially valuable because every effort is made in a controlled experiment to see that the control group and the experimental group differ only with respect to the suspected causal agent; in all other respects, the two groups should be similar. Furthermore, the control group and the experimental group are selected in such a way that they form representative samples of the population. Thus, it is reasonable to infer by inductive generalization that what happens to these groups in the presence or absence of the suspected cause would also happen to the population they represent.

Causal fallacies discussed in this chapter include:

1. *Post Hoc:* The fallacy of arguing that *A* is the cause of *B* just because *B* comes later than *A*. A relationship that is coincidental is judged—on the basis of insufficient evidence of a regular connection—to be causal. Many superstitious beliefs involve this fallacy.

2. **The Fallacy of Ignoring a Common Cause:** When evidence supports the view that there is a regular connection between two events or types of events, the nature of the connection must be investigated before making a causal judgment. *A* and *B* might be regularly connected through some common underlying cause *C*. In such cases, neither *A* nor *B* directly causes the other. Both *A* and *B* are effects of a common cause.

3. **The Fallacy of Confusing Cause and Effect:** When two events or types of events are regularly connected and do not result from a common cause, care must be taken to define which is cause and which is effect. Effects cannot occur earlier than their causes. In complex causal relationships, however, the temporal order of the various parts of the complex may be difficult to investigate.

4. **Genetic Fallacy:** This fallacy occurs whenever something inappropriate about the genesis (source or cause) of a claim or a belief is taken as evidence for its truth or falsity.

VIII. EXERCISES

1. Some people have argued that both smoking and lung cancer are due to some unknown factor, perhaps an obscure hereditary condition. Which fallacy would these people say that those who claim smoking is the cause of lung cancer are committing?

2. Identify any fallacies involved in the following arguments:

   a. Mrs. Jones, who is 89 years old, died two days after receiving a flu shot. Therefore, the flu shot caused her death.

   b. Psychologists who have tested thousands of people working in American businesses have discovered that top executives generally have much larger vocabularies than lower-level employees do. Therefore, if you want to rise to the top in business, you can make this happen by developing a very large vocabulary.

   c. Every time little Johnny approaches the supermarket door, he says "Abracadabra" and then the door swings open. Johnny concludes that saying this magic word causes the door to open.

   d. The results of surveys conducted by a typewriter company indicate that college students who own typewriters are, on the average, better students than college students who do not own typewriters. So if you want to succeed in your college studies, you should get a typewriter.

   e. It has been widely observed that when young children who are usually well-behaved become irritable and difficult, they exhibit the symptoms of a cold or viral infection the next day. It is clear that their misbehavior causes these illnesses.

   f. During the looting and rioting in Detroit in the summer of 1967, the items most commonly stolen were color television sets. Some people argued that one way to prevent such riots would be to distribute free color television sets to those who want them.

g. Tom is being quite reasonable when he regards all his coworkers with suspicion and fear because he feels that they are trying to take over his responsibilities. After all, he grew up in a tough situation and had to fight for everything he has achieved. He became impressed at an early age that others were out to get him.

h. Some people argue that emotional distress is the cause of cancer. Their evidence is the well-known fact that many patients with terminal cancer are severely depressed and unusually irritable.

i. Two students in a large class turn in identical term papers. The teacher accuses them of copying from one another, even though the students can prove that they did not know one another and had no access to one another's work. The teacher maintains that copying could be the only cause of the identical papers. (What fallacy does the teacher commit?)

j. A number of legislators are opposed to legalized abortion on the grounds that women undergoing abortions may be damaged psychologically. We can dismiss the truth of their claims, however, for these legislators are Catholic, and everyone knows the Catholic Church is opposed to abortion.

k. A football coach who is trying to bring his team out of a slump studies the statistics of past games. His research on several teams over a number of years shows that many more passes and attempted passes are almost always made by the losing team than by the winning team. From this information, the coach infers that he can make his team win by restricting the number of passes they throw.

3. The following examples are taken from Friedrich Nietzsche's *Twilight of the Idols*, in which he discusses errors in causal reasoning. Identify the fallacy in each example.

a. Everybody knows the book of the famous Cornaro in which he recommends his slender diet as a recipe for a long and happy life—a virtuous one too. . . . The worthy Italian thought his diet was the *cause* of his long life, whereas the precondition for a long life, the extraordinary slowness of his metabolism, the consumption of so little, was the cause of his slender diet.

b. The church and morality say: "A generation, a people, are destroyed by license and luxury." [I] say: when a people approaches destruction, when it degenerates physiologically, then license and luxury *follow* from this (namely, the craving for ever stronger and more frequent stimulation, as every exhausted nature knows it).

c. This young man turns pale early and wilts; his friends say: that is due to this or that disease. I say: that he became diseased, that he did not resist the disease, was already the effect of an impoverished life or hereditary exhaustion.

d. The newspaper reader says: this [political] party destroys itself by making such a mistake. [I] say: a party which makes such mistakes has reached its end; it has lost its sureness of instinct.

PROBABILITIES AND INDUCTIVE LOGIC

I. PROBABILITY AND INDUCTIVE LOGIC

We know that in a correct inductive argument, the conclusion is *probably* true if its premises are true. We also know that inductive arguments vary in strength. The conclusions of some inductive arguments are highly *probable*; the conclusions of other inductive arguments are only slightly more *probable* than not. Thus far, we have depended on a common-sense understanding of the term "probable," without stating exactly what this term means. In this chapter, we will take a closer look at the concept of *probability* and its relationship to inductive logic.

In the statistical syllogism, a form of inductive argument discussed in Chapter 3, we noted that the statistical premiss may state numerically that a certain percentage of members of the reference class are also members of the attribute class (90 percent of all freshmen are state residents). When such quantitative information is available in the premisses, we can state the degree to which some conclusion is probable.

Sometimes we have a practical interest in knowing exactly *how* probable some conclusion is, particularly when we wish to take some action (such as betting or investing money) on the basis of an argument with a conclusion that is probably true. For example, using a correct statistical syllogism, we can argue that a blind draw from a standard deck of cards will result in a non-heart (that is, a spade, a diamond, or a club being drawn):

> Most cards in a standard deck are non-heart cards.
> *a* is a card drawn "blind" from a standard deck.
> _____
> *a* is a non-heart card.

If we are going to bet that a non-heart will be drawn, we want to know the exact probability of the outcome "*a* is a non-heart," in order to set the proper betting odds. Given our background information about the composition of standard decks of cards, we know that a deck contains 39 non-hearts and 13 hearts. Therefore, the first premiss could be stated quantitatively:

> 39/52 (or 75 percent) of the cards are non-hearts

Knowing this information—which encompasses all relevant available information, given that the draw of the card is made blindly—we can say that the probability of drawing a non-heart is 75 percent, or 3/4.

In an even-money bet, the amount won or lost is equal to the "stake" (the amount that is put at risk). An even-money bet is proper when, as in the toss of a fair coin, there are two possible outcomes and each outcome has a probability of 1/2. When the probabilities of various outcomes are not equal, the betting odds must be altered in an appropriate way to preserve the standard of fairness. For example, betting odds of "3 to 1," in which the return for a winning bet is three times the stake, are fair for an outcome with a probability of 1/4, or 0.25. The "odds" refer to the difference in favor of one side and against the other. On an outcome with a probability of 1/4, such as blindly drawing a heart from a standard deck that contains 39 non-hearts and 13 hearts, there are three times as many ways of losing as there are of winning. A payoff of 3 to 1 balances this disadvantage and makes the bet fair.

The branch of mathematics called *the probability calculus* provides us with a way of calculating, or figuring out, unknown probabilities on the basis of known probabilities. If we know, for example, that the probability of obtaining a head on a single toss of a fair coin is 1/2, then we can use the mathematical theory of probability to figure out the probability of obtaining all heads on three tosses of a fair coin. Since the method of calculating unknown probabilities on the basis of known probabilities is a part of mathematics, it belongs properly to deductive logic rather than to inductive logic. However, the probability calculus has such important applications for inductive reasoning that serious studies of inductive logic always include some treatment of probabilities.

The mathematical theory of probability was developed during the seventeenth century to solve two different types of problems. On the continent, where gambling with cards and dice was a major form of amusement for rich young noblemen, there was a great deal of interest in setting fair betting odds for complicated gambling situations. One such situation involved tossing a pair of dice. Each die has six sides; whatever side is up is called the "face," and 36 different combinations of two faces are possible when a pair of dice is tossed. Only one of these possibilites shows six dots on the face of each die. Thus, the probability that one toss of a pair of fair dice will result in double sixes is 1/36. Obviously, an even-money bet on showing double sixes in one toss would be unfair. Professional gamblers were offering even money bets that at least one pair of double sixes would show in 24 tosses. The Chevalier de Méré, wondering whether these betting odds were fair, put the following question to a friend who was a mathematician:

> How many tosses are required in order for the probability to be at least 1/2 of getting a double six?

The concept of "probability" that is used to assign initial probabilities in situations like this is the *ratio of favorable to possible outcomes*. Remember that the mathematical calculus of probability is used to calculate probabilities on the basis of some initially known probabilities. In coin tossing, if the coin is fair, there are two possible outcomes: heads or tails. Whichever one of these two outcomes is chosen is favorable. The ratio of favorable to possible outcomes in a fair coin toss is therefore 1/2. In dice, each die has six sides. Assuming the die is balanced, the outcome of a particular face showing in a roll of a single die is 1/6. In card games, a standard deck contains 52 cards, divided into 4 suits, with 13 cards in each suit. The probability of blindly drawing a particular single card is 1/52; of drawing any card of a particular suit, 13/52 (1/4); of drawing a particular number, such as an ace, 4/52 (1/13).

It requires considerable mathematical skill to use the known probability of obtaining a double six on a single toss of a pair of fair dice to determine how many times a pair of dice must be tossed to yield a probability equal to 1/2 of obtaining at least one double six. In working out answers to complicated problems such as this, French mathematicians constructed the foundations of the mathematical theory of probability.

Meanwhile, in seventeenth century England, a different sort of interest motivated studies in mathematical probability. There, the problem was not how to figure fair betting odds for games of chance but rather to determine the fair cost of insurance policies. This was the beginning of *actuarial science*—the calculation of risks and premiums for insurance purposes.

The Great Plague had struck England by this time, and people had begun to form associations to share the burden of funeral and burial expenses. To determine fair costs of membership in such associations, it was necessary to know, for example, the probability that a prospective member would survive another 5, 10, 15, or 20 years. Obviously, the understanding of "probability" as a ratio of favorable to possible types of outcomes was not appropriate in these circumstances. Years of life are not parceled out like cards from a deck, with any year being viewed as an equally possible year for death to occur. A different concept of probability from the one used in connection with games of chance was required.

"Probability" in this context is connected with the observed *frequency with which events of a certain type occur*. Information about the ages at which death had occurred for persons living in various areas and following assorted trades and occupations was gathered, mostly from church records, by the burial associations. The information was compiled in "mortality tables," which were used to determine the *relative frequency* with which persons in given situations survived to reach various ages. On the basis of the information in a mortality table, for example, it could be observed that 90 percent of the 25-year-old carpenters living in London survived their thirtieth birthdays. A burial association might then use this information to assign a probability of 0.9 (or 90 percent) that Hawkins, a 25-year-old carpenter from London would be able to pay dues in the association for at least five years and to charge accordingly for his five-year membership.

Mortality tables are still used by insurance companies to determine the cost of life-insurance premiums. Of course, the information contained in modern tables is far more extensive than the data contained in seventeenth-century tables. Similar types of tables, based on records of automobile ownership and accidents, are used as a basis for determining automobile-insurance premiums. Health-insurance costs also are based on actuarial tables.

Both these meanings of "probability"—the ratio of favorable to possible outcomes and the relative frequency of events of a particular type in some reference class of events (See Chapter 3 for the meaning of "reference class")—lend themselves quite naturally to *quantitative* (numerical) expressions of the probability values. When probabilities are expressed quantitatively, the probability that the sentence describing an event is true is stated as a single real number (integer, fraction, or irrational number) between 0 (the lowest value) and 1 (the highest value). A probability may be expressed as a ratio between two numbers (1/4), as a decimal (0.25), or as a percentage (25 percent).

Yet another concept of "probability" is commonly employed when, for example, I say there is an extremely low probability that my mother will attend a Rolling Stones concert during the rock group's next U.S. tour. Here, "probability" does not mean "ratio of favorable to possible outcomes"; nor is my probability assignment based on a notion of relative frequencies. Here, I am using probability as a measure of the *degree to which it is rational to believe certain statements.* My evidence for the belief that my mother won't go to hear the Stones is comprised of a set of beliefs about her taste in music, her lack of interest in pop culture, her dislike of crowded places, and numerous other beliefs about how she prefers to spend her leisure time. The "degree of rational belief" concept of probability can be expressed numerically, but it does not lend itself as naturally to numerical quantification as the other meanings of "probability." If numerical values are assigned to these probabilities, however, the mathematical rules for calculating unknown probabilities on the basis of known probabilities are applicable to degrees of rational belief, just as they are to other probabilities.

II. THE RULES OF PROBABILITY

Before we introduce the mathematical rules, we should note that any assignment of a probability value is conditionally based on specific evidence or on general background information. Probability assignments are always made relevant to the assumed truth of some such information. Thus, the probability of "a single toss of a die shows six dots on the face" being equal to 1/6 is conditional on the die being balanced or fair. Statements of probability values are often standardized as

$$Pr(h|e) = n$$

which can be read "The probability of a statement h, on evidence e, is equal to n." Sometimes, however, when it is clearly understood that a probability value is conditional on general background information and not on any special evidence, we write

$$Pr(h) = n$$

omitting any reference to evidence.

Rule 1. The value n in a sentence of the form

$$Pr(h|e) = n$$

must be a single real number between 0 and 1, inclusive.

In view of Rule 1, the following assignments of probabilities are improper:

Pr(Jones will win the Sweepstakes | Jones bought a Sweepstakes ticket) $= -1$

(No probability values can be negative numbers.)

Pr(The Democrats will win the next presidential election) = 1.25

(No probability value can be greater than 1.)

Rule 2.   If h follows deductively from e, then

$$Pr(h|e) = 1$$

To say that h follows deductively from e means that if e is true, then h must be true also. If this is so, then the probability of h, on evidence e, is 1.

Examples

(a) Pr (Mrs. Jones is married Mrs. Jones has a spouse) = 1
(b) Pr (A black or a red card is drawn | A card is drawn from
      a standard deck) = 1

In this probability sentence, e is "A card is drawn from a standard deck" and h is "A black card or a red card is drawn." If a card is drawn from a standard deck, that card will be either black or red; no other possibilities exist. Thus, $n = 1$.

The probability value of 1 is not reserved exclusively for sentences that follow deductively from the available evidence. Sentences that are certainly true ("sure things") are assigned a probability equal to 1. The type of certainty that is involved here may be practical certainty, rather than certainty based on strict relationships of deductive logic.

Example

Pr (A six-year-old child, using materials found in an ordinary home
    workshop, cannot build a spaceship that will reach Mars) = 1

Notice that no statement of evidence (e) is given in this example; here, the probability is conditional on general background information. This sentence is so likely to be true on the basis of everything we know (it has "practical certainty") that the assignment of 1 to n is appropriate.

Similarly, the lowest probability value (0) is assigned to sentences that are inconsistent with the evidence sentence or that are false as a matter of "practical certainty."

Examples

(a) Pr (5 aces are drawn | 5 cards are drawn, without replacement,
      from a standard deck) = 0

Here, the sentence "5 aces are drawn" is *inconsistent* with the evidence that the deck is standard. (Standard decks contain only 4 aces, and the cards are drawn without replacement.)

(b) Pr (A human being, without any artificial aids, can leap tall buildings in a single bound) = 0

Given our background knowledge of human physiology, this sentence has the "practical certainty" of being false.

Rule 3. If two sentences h_1 and h_2 are *mutually exclusive* (if they cannot both be true), then, on the same evidence in both cases, the probability that their *disjunction* (h_1 or h_2) is true to the *sum* of their individual probabilities.

A disjunction occurs when the components of a compound sentence are connected by "or," as in "The coin came up heads or the coin came up tails." Symbolically, Rule 3 can be expressed

$$Pr(h_1 \text{ or } h_2|e) = Pr(h_1|e) + Pr(h_2|e)$$

Although this rule is stated for any *two* mutually exclusive sentences, it can be generalized to any number of mutually exclusive sentences. This rule allows us to calculate the unknown probability of a disjunction when the probabilities of all the individual disjuncts are known.

Examples

(a) Using as evidence the claim that a fair die is tossed a single time, we know that the probability of throwing a six is equal to 1/6 and that the probability of throwing a two is 1/6. Since the sentences "A six is thrown" and "A two is thrown" are mutually exclusive for a single throw, Rule 3 tells us that the probability of "A six is thrown *or* a two is thrown " is 1/6 + 1/6, or after performing the addition (2/6) and reducing the fraction, 1/3.

(b) Using the evidence in (a), the probability of "A six *or* a two *or* a three is thrown " is equal to (1/6 + 1/6 + 1/6), or 1/2.

Rule 4. The probability of the *conjunction* of two sentences is equal to the probability of the first sentence *multiplied* by the probability of the second sentence, on the condition that the first sentence is true.

A conjunction occurs when the components of a compound sentence are connected by "and," or some other expression such as "moreover," or a semicolon, which indicates that the sentence as a whole is true just in case all of its components are true. "A six showed on one face of a pair of dice *and* a five showed on the other face" is an example of a conjunction. Rule 4 allows us to calculate the probability of a conjunction when the probabilities of the individual conjuncts are known. Symbolically, Rule 4 can be expressed

$$Pr(h_1 \text{ and } h_2|e) = Pr(h_1|e) \times Pr(h_2|e \text{ and } h_1)$$

Like Rule 3, Rule 4 can be generalized to any number of cases, but for simplicity here, it is stated to cover only two conjuncts. When more than two conjuncts are involved, the probability of each successive conjunct is conditional on the truth of all the preceding conjuncts.

Examples

(a) Suppose that a fair coin is tossed twice (the evidence sentence). What is the probability that both tosses yield a head?

Rule 4 tells us to multiply the probability that the first toss will yield a head (1/2) by the probability that the second toss will be a head, on the condition that the first toss yields a head. This probability is also 1/2, since what happens on the first toss has no effect on the second toss (the probability on the second toss is 1/2 regardless of whether the first toss is a head or a tail). Multiplying 1/2 by 1/2 gives us 1/4, which is the probability of "two heads appear on two tosses of a fair coin."

(b) Suppose that two cards are drawn blindly from a standard deck and placed in a drawer together (the evidence). What is the probability that both cards are aces?

We want to know the probability of the conjunction "The first card is an ace *and* the second card is an ace." The probability that the first card is an ace is 4/52. (There are four aces in a standard deck of 52 cards.) The probability that the second card drawn is also an ace, if the first card drawn is an ace, is 3/51. (At the time of the second draw, the deck contains 51 cards; if the first card drawn is an ace, only three aces remain in the deck.) Multiplying 4/52 by 3/51 gives us 12/2,652. This fraction can be reduced to 1/221, which is the probability of drawing two aces from a standard deck in two draws (without replacing the first card drawn).

In example (b), unlike example (a), the probabilities are not the same for the two conjuncts. In coin tossing, what happens on a second or a third toss is *independent* of what happens on any previous toss. When cards are drawn from a deck without replacement after each draw, the probabilities of drawing a particular card are not the same for successive draws. The deck is different after any draw. What happens on the second draw is *not independent* of what happens on the first draw. Of course, if the cards are replaced and the deck is shuffled after every draw, the outcome of each draw is independent of previous draws from the deck.

Example

What is the probability of drawing three aces in three draws from a standard deck without replacement?

Here, we want to apply Rule 4 to more than two conjuncts. The probability that the first draw is an ace is 4/52. The probability that the second draw is an ace, given that the first card drawn is an ace, is 3/51. The probability that the third card is also an ace, given that the first and second cards drawn are aces, is 2/50. Multiplying these three probabilities (a calculator is helpful for such problems), we find that the probability of three aces being drawn from a standard deck in three draws without replacement is equal to 24/132,600. This fraction can be reduced to 1/5,525.

In these examples of the application of Rule 4, it is not difficult to tell whether the events being considered are independent or not. Tosses of coins and rolls of dice are independent events. Draws from a deck, when cards previously drawn are replaced and the deck is reshuffled, are also independent. When cards drawn from a deck are *not* replaced or, as in games such as 21 (Blackjack), when cards that are exposed are then placed on the bottom of the deck and the deck is *not* reshuffled, successive draws are not independent. In applying Rule 4 to many real-life situations, we must pay particular attention to the independence of events. For example, suppose that the probability of getting a busy signal when you call any one of your close friends is 0.05. The probability of getting a busy signal when you call one friend and then getting another busy signal when you call a second friend is *not* equal to 0.05 × 0.05 if those two friends are also friends of one another, because the busy signals are then not independent events. If your first friend is on the phone, this raises the probability that you will also get a busy signal when you try to call the second friend. When we are not dealing with such simple matters as dice and card games, it is often difficult to assign probabilities for nonindependent events, but we should at least be aware of the possibility that nonindependence can affect the calculation of probabilities.

Rules 1–4 (sometimes called *axioms*) form the entire basis of probability theory, just as the axioms of geometry form the basis for that area of mathematics. We will not derive any theorems here, but we will take notice of one useful theorem that makes calculations simpler than they would otherwise be:

Theorem   If $\Pr(h|e) = n$, then $\Pr(\text{not } h|e) = 1 - n$.

Here, "not h" is the negation, or denial, of the sentence h.

Examples

(a) What is the probability of not drawing an ace from a standard deck when a card is drawn blindly?

Since the probability of drawing an ace is 4/52, the probability of not drawing an ace is $1 - 4/52 = 48/52 = 12/13$.

(b) What is the probability of obtaining at least one head in two tosses of a fair coin?

Rule 3 is not applicable in this problem, because "A head occurs on the first toss" and "A head occurs on the second toss" are not mutually exclusive sentences. Heads could occur on both tosses. If we were (mistakenly) to add the probabilities of obtaining a head on the first toss and of obtaining a head on the second toss, the probability would be equal to 1. Obviously, this is incorrect, because it is by no means certain that a head will occur in two tosses. However, the sentence "At least one head occurs in two tosses of a fair coin" is equivalent to the sentence "It is not the case both that a tail occurs in the first toss and that a tail occurs in the second toss." We can use Rule 4 to calculate the probability of obtaining a tail on both tosses ($1/2 \times 1/2 = 1/4$). Then, we can use the theorem to calculate the probability of *not* obtaining a tail on both tosses ($1 - 1/4 = 3/4$).

The *Rasmussen Report,* the most complete study by the U.S. government on the safety of nuclear power, issued in 1975, offers an interesting and important application of this theorem. This report has been called into question by critics of nuclear power. One criticism is that the report presents the probability of a serious accident at a nuclear-power plant (a core-melt accident) in a misleading way (K. S. Shrader-Frechette, *Nuclear Power and Public Policy*).

According to federal government figures, the probability of a serious accident is 1/17,000 per year, per reactor. "Serious accident" in this context refers to a core melt, which, again, according to government estimates, would be equivalent to 1,000 Hiroshimas. The probability of 1/17,000 may sound like a very low probability. However, critics point out that reactors presently operating at 65 nuclear-power plants each have an estimated lifetime of 30 years. The critics feel we should be concerned with the probability that a serious accident will occur at any one plant during its 30-year lifetime.

We can apply the preceding theorem twice to calculate the probability that a serious accident (a core melt) will occur in at least one of these 65 nuclear-power plants over their 30-year lifetimes. This probability is equal to 1 minus the probability that there will be *no* serious accidents in any of these plants during their 30-year lifetimes. The probability that there will be *no* core melts—using the government probability of 1/17,000 per year, per reactor that there will be a serious accident *and* assuming that the events (core melts per year, per reactor) are independent—is equal to

$$[1 - (1/17,000)]^{65 \times 30}$$

or

$$(16,999/17,000)^{1950}$$

which is equal to 0.8916.

We can then apply the theorem a second time to determine the probability that there will be at least one serious accident. "There will be no serious accidents (core melts)" is the denial of "There will be at least one serious accident." To calculate the probability that there will be at least one serious accident, we subtract the probability that there will be no serious accidents (0.8916) from 1:

$$1 - 0.8916 = 0.108$$

Thus, the probability that the United States will be faced with a nuclear-power disaster equivalent to 1,000 Hiroshimas is, according to the government's own figures, slightly more than 10 percent.

The assumption of *independence* for per-year, per-reactor core melts seems somewhat questionable. Nuclear reactors are built along similar designs and have almost identical safety devices. It would seem that if the serious accident were connected with the design of the reactors or the failure of the protective devices, these events could not be considered independent. Of course, there are other possible sources of serious accidents. Another difficult question is whether or not the lack of independence would raise or lower the probability that an accident will occur in at least one plant during its 30-year lifetime. In addition, we could ask whether it is reasonable to assume that the probability of a serious accident in a nuclear-power plant is the same throughout each of its 30 years of use. Some critics of nuclear power have also objected that the figure of 1/17,000 is an unrealistically low estimate of the probability of a serious accident per year, per reactor.

Such questions cannot be answered by simply applying the rules to calculate probabilities. The assignment of initial probabilities and the determination of whether events are dependent or independent require the assemblage and evaluation of evidence, using means far beyond the probability calculus. With suitable evidence in hand, many of the argument forms we considered in earlier chapters—inductive generalizations, statistical syllogisms, and analogies—may be useful in assigning appropriate initial probabilities.

Exercises

1. What is the probability of obtaining either an ace or a king in a single, blind draw from a standard deck of cards?
2. What is the probability of *not* obtaining either an ace or a king in a single, blind draw from a standard deck of cards?
3. What is the probability of obtaining three heads in three tosses of a fair coin?
4. What is the probability of obtaining at least one tail in 3 tosses of a fair coin?
5. What is the probability of obtaining either a head or a tail in a single toss of a fair coin?
6. What is the probability of drawing an ace and a king in two blind draws from a standard deck without replacement?
7. Suppose the probability that a 22-year-old male will survive his forty-seventh birthday is 0.840 and the probability that a 22-year-old female will survive her forty-seventh birthday is 0.910. A man and a woman, who have been close friends at college, are both graduating at the age of 22. They promise to meet each other at their twenty-fifth reunion.
   a. What is the probability that both friends will be alive to keep that promise?
   b. If these good friends fall in love and marry one another after college, would this affect the independence of each friend living another 25 years?
8. Assuming that you know what your birthday is but do not know what mine is, what is the probability that we share the same birthday (day only—not year!)?
9. Suppose that you hold three aces and two different small cards in a game of

draw poker. If you discard the two small cards, what are your chances of improving your hand on the draw? The hand will be improved either by drawing another ace and some other card or by drawing a pair. (*Hint:* Since this is a fair game and you do not know what cards are in the other players' hands, treat their cards as if they were part of the deck.)

10. If my chances of being apprehended for committing some crime are 0.7, my chances of being convicted if I am apprehended are 0.6, and my chances of serving time if I am apprehended and convicted are 0.5, what is the probability that I will serve time if I rob the local grocery store?

III. USING PROBABILITIES TO PLAN A COURSE OF ACTION— DECISION THEORY

"Probability," as Bishop Butler remarked in the eighteenth century, "is the very guide of life." None of us can see what the future holds. We make most choices, decisions, and plans as best we can in the face of less than complete knowledge about what the world will be like and what others will do. Probabilities play an important role in many of these decisions, because we are often in a position to *judge* the probabilities of various outcomes before we make a decision. If we care about seeing a movie from the beginning, we try to arrive at the theater before the show is scheduled to begin because it will probably start on time. We pursue college educations because we believe that what we learn in college will probably enhance the quality of our lives in various ways.

However, the probability that some event or condition will occur is not the *only* consideration on which we base our decision to take a particular course of action. We are concerned with costs and benefits as well. In Exercise 10 in Section II, the probabilities given for apprehension, conviction, and incarceration were not unrealistic, based on government crime statistics. If anything, they were slightly higher than the norm. The probability that someone would actually serve time for robbing a store was quite small (0.21), but even in the absence of any moral or social considerations, a person contemplating such a robbery should surely reflect not only on the probability of serving time but also on the severe unattractiveness of that prospect. It is prudent to avoid even a fairly small risk of falling into such an unhappy situation. Conversely, we think it is reasonable to try to achieve some goals, even though the probabilities of attaining them are small, if the potential benefits are very attractive.

The term *utility* is often used to refer to the desirability (*positive* utility) or undesirability (*negative* utility) of a situation. The term *value* (which can also be positive or negative) is sometimes used as well. We will adopt the somewhat more neutral term *utility*. Thus, we could say that serving time in prison has great negative utility and that this utility should be considered along with the probability of serving time when contemplating an action that could result in a prison sentence.

Decision theory is the area of study that focuses on decision analysis in contexts that vary with respect to the degree of knowledge available. (Here, a "decision" is a decision to take some action.) The goal of decision theory is to develop criteria for rational (reasonable) decision making. In our necessarily brief look at decision theory, we will consider three types of general contexts in which decisions occur:

1. *Decisions under risk:* Contexts in which we can assign various proba- bilities to the outcomes of our actions.
2. *Decisions under certainty:* Contexts in which we know the exact out- comes of our actions.
3. *Decisions under uncertainty:* Contexts in which various outcomes of our actions are possible and we are unable to assign any probabilities to those outcomes.

1. Decisions Under Risk

In one example in the discussion of statistical syllogisms in Chapter 3, a patient whose doctor had suggested an ear operation was trying to make a decision under risk. The operation had three possible outcomes, and each outcome had an assigned probability (improvement to "very good": 0.85; no improvement: 0.10; further damage to ear: 0.05). Although the probabilities in this case are clearly stated, no utilities for the various outcomes are mentioned. Obviously, the first outcome has the greatest utility as well as the highest probability; the second outcome has a lower utility (the hearing problem is unimproved and the patient must endure the pain and expense of an operation); and the third outcome has the lowest utility. If the patient decides against the operation, there is only one outcome to consider (no change in the ear condition). The utility of this outcome ranks higher than utilities of having an unsuccessful operation (no improvement or no improvement and further damage) but ranks lower than the outcome of an operation that results in hearing improvement. Should the patient have the operation or not?

The patient could act as if the most probable outcome of the operation will be the one to occur. However, "Always act as if the most probable outcome of an action will occur" is a poor decision-making rule, since it ignores the utilities of various outcomes and it will lead to apparently irrational decisions in some cases. Following this rule, for example, would lead an immoral robber to hold up the local grocery store on the grounds that no prison sentence was the most probable outcome of that action. Following this rule would also lead a home- owner to refuse to purchase fire insurance, even a very inexpensive policy, because the probability (based on statistics) that a given house will catch fire is very low.

Another possible decision rule for our patient is "Always choose the action with a possible outcome that has a higher utility than any other possible out- come." If the patient follows this rule, the operation will be chosen, for a com- plete restoration of hearing is clearly the outcome with the highest utility, and this outcome is possible only if the patient has the operation, not if any other action is taken. But this rule ignores the known probabilities involved in making a decision under risk, and like the rule "Always act as if the most probable outcome of an action is the one that will occur," it can lead to decisions that most of us would regard as foolish.

To illustrate that this rule is not effective, consider the following case. Suppose that someone has $10,000 to cover college costs. This person places a high utility on having money but also wants a college education very much, and college would be out of the question if this $10,000 were lost. Someone offers this person a chance to invest that $10,000. There is a 10 percent probability that the $10,000 investment will return a profit of $100,000 and a 90 percent probability that the original $10,000 will be lost. Given the high value placed on a college education, most people would consider it unreasonable to invest the $10,000 under these circumstances, even though one possible outcome of this action (money for education and a lot left over for other things) has the greatest utility.

To evaluate decisions under risk correctly, a rule that accounts for both utilities and probabilities is required. "Choose the action that maximizes *expected* utility" is such a rule. To understand this rule, we need to know how to calculate *expected* utilities. Before this can be done, however, we must be able to quantify, or measure, utilities; only then can a calculation be performed.

The problem of measuring utilities is by no means simple. How can we place a numerical value on hearing properly, or on undergoing an unsuccessful operation, or on losing one's hearing? Objectivity is not the issue here. The measurements of utilities need not be objective in the sense that the assigned quantities must be acceptable to any reasonable person. All that is required is that the person confronted with the decision measure his or her utilities, but even that is very difficult in many cases.

Studies of decision theory often begin with examples of decisions that involve money, such as decisions concerning bets or investments. There is a certain sense in which an investment that will return $30,000 is—all other things being equal—three times as desirable as (has three times the utility of) an investment that will return $10,000. If units of money are correlated in this manner with units of utility, it is not difficult to assign a measure of the utility of various amounts of money lost or won, for money already comes in measurable units. We will consider a problem that involves only money to illustrate how expected utilities work; then we will return to the problem of the operation, in which units of utility cannot be identified with dollar amounts.

I am committed to go to a school fair and spend at least $2 there playing a game of chance. I have to decide whether to risk $2 on a punch board or on a dice game. A $2 punch buys the following possible outcomes with associated probabilities: 0.05 for $10, 0.10 for $5, 0.20 for $2, 0.65 for $0. In the dice game, if I roll any matched pair, I win $10; otherwise, I win nothing. To make the problem of measuring utilities correspond to measuring the amounts of money won or lost, I assume that the dice game is no more or no less amusing to me than the punch board and that my sole desire is to gain as much money as possible from my $2 play.

The *expected utility* of a $2 punch is calculated by multiplying each payoff with its associated probability, summing the results, and subtracting the $2 cost:

$$[(10 \times 0.05) + (5 \times 0.10) + (2 \times 0.20) + (0 \times 0.65)] - 2$$
$$= (0.50 + 0.50 + 0.40) - 2 = -0.60$$

In the dice game, the expected utility is also calculated by multiplying payoffs with their associated probabilities, summing the results, and subtracting the $2 cost. In general, the rule for calculating the expected utility of some decision is to multiply the probability of each possible outcome by the number of units (the total amount) of utility associated with that outcome. The sum of these products, minus the initial cost (also measured in units of utility), if any, is the expected utility of that decision.

In the dice game, the probability of rolling a pair of ones, twos, threes, fours, fives, or sixes is 1/6. This probability can be calculated in several ways. The probability of rolling any one pair is 1/36. You can win by rolling any of six mutually exclusive pairs, and (1/36 + 1/36 + 1/36 + 1/36 + 1/36 + 1/36) = 1/6. Or the problem can be viewed another way. The first die shows some number on its face. The probability that the second die will show the same number is 1/6, and this is also the probability that you will roll a pair.

The utility associated with rolling a pair (the payoff) is $10. The probability of *not* rolling a pair is 5/6 (1 minus the probability of obtaining a pair). The payoff for not rolling a pair is $0. Since $10 × 1/6 = $1.67 and 0 × 5/6 = 0, we sum these amounts and subtract the $2 cost (1.67 + 0 − 2 = −0.33). Thus, the expected utility (measured in money) of a play on the punch board is − $0.60 and the expected utility of the dice game is − $0.33. If I followed the rule of maximizing expected utilities, I would choose the dice game and thereby cut my losses.

Now we will return to the problem of measuring the utilities associated with the ear operation. Remember that the measures I assign would be my own in such a situation. You might react differently, and could not be criticized for doing so. The units I assign are just "units of utility." The arithmetic operations of addition, subtraction, multiplication, and division can be performed on these units of utility, but they need not—and perhaps cannot—be translated into monetary amounts.

(i) Units of utility associated with possible outcomes of operation (probabilities are enclosed in parentheses):

Hearing improvement to "very good":   10 (0.85)
No improvement: −2 (0.10)
Further damage: −10 (0.05)

(ii) Units of utility associated with possible outcome of no operation:

No change: 0 (1)

Using these figures and the associated probabilities, the expected utility of the operation is [(10 × 0.85) + (−2 × 0.10) + (−10 × 0.05)] = 7.8. The expected utility of not having the operation is (0 × 1) = 0. The "cost" of the operation was not calculated separately here; it was "figured in" when the utilities were assigned to various outcomes. Following the rule of maximizing expected utility, if I were the patient, I would choose the operation.

In considering candidates for the best rule to follow when making decisions under risk, we saw that different rules may lead to the same decision in some cases. By far the most probable outcome of the operation was also the outcome that clearly had the greatest utility. But the rule "Choose the action that maximizes expected utility" is adequate when other proposed rules appear to offer unreasonable advice. This is frequently the case when an outcome with a low probability has a very high utility or when an outcome with a high probability has a very low utility. That is why the rule for maximizing *expected* utility is generally accepted as a good rule for rational decision making when the probabilities of the possible outcomes of an action are known. This rule is applicable not only when another rule would lead to the correct decision but also when other rules would lead to decisions that seem unreasonable.

2. Decisions Under Certainty

In some situations, we must choose among various actions and each action has only one possible outcome. These decisions are called *decisions under certainty,* but this is something of a misnomer, because the future is never absolutely certain. The world around us might change in a dramatic and unpredictable way between the time of the decision and the outcome of the action. For example, your decision might be between studying for a test in your room and studying for a test in the library. Ordinarily, there is only one possible outcome to each choice—you study in your room if that is your decision, or study in the library if that is your choice. It is, however, *possible* that you decide to study in the library, but find that it is closed due to an unusual and totally unexpected electrical power failure. This is, of course, an unlikely occurrence. In general, when we talk about decisions under certainty, we simply ignore such unusual possibilities.

Decisions under certainty do not require the calculation of any probabilities. The probability associated with the single possible outcome of each action under these circumstances is 1. The rule to apply when making decisions under certainty is simple: "Choose the action that has the highest utility." If no single action has the highest utility, it is reasonable to choose any of the actions that have the highest utility.

Although we do not have to calculate probabilities for decisions under certainty, we may have to give careful thought to how to compare utilities. For example, some products (such as automobile tires and batteries) are sold at various prices with guarantees for various periods of time. If I buy tires with a two-year guarantee at a specified price, I can calculate the cost per year and compare it to the cost per year of tires with a three-year guarantee. But other factors may enter into the decision. How long will I keep my car? How much of a nuisance is it to replace worn tires? Are both sets of new tires equally safe throughout their guarantee period? Comparing utilities almost always involves more than purely monetary considerations, and these additional factors should not be ignored just because they may make the decision more difficult. In many cases (as in the tire-buying decision), the consideration of additional factors involves probabilities (for example, whether or not my car will last for two or three more years is uncertain and may be assigned a probability of less than 1) that can change a decision under certainty into a decision under risk.

In one way, it is simpler to compare utilities for decisions under certainty than it is to compare utilities for decisions under risk. To make the kind of comparison that is required to evaluate decisions under certainty, the utilities need only be ordered by rank (highest, second highest, and so on). Since you do not multiply the amounts of utility by probabilities, there is no need for *units* of utility. In other words, in a decision under certainty, we do not need to be concerned with whether the highest utility is 10 times higher than the next highest utility, or 6 times higher, or exactly how much higher. Units of utility are required, however, when we must perform arithmetic operations such as multiplication, for these operations make no sense unless they are performed on such units.

3. Decisions Under Uncertainty

When we face decisions under conditions of uncertainty, we are aware that various outcomes of our actions are possible, but we have no way of assessing the probabilities associated with these outcomes. Such situations may be rather unusual; in most cases, we are in a position to make at least very rough assignments of probabilities on the basis of past experience or information gathered from other sources. If we can make even rough probability judgments, we should follow the rule for making decisions under risk (choose the action that maximizes expected utility). For the sake of completeness, however, most accounts of decision theory consider the categories of decisions under certainty and decisions under uncertainty as well as decisions under risk.

When we make decisions under uncertainty, since we have no information about probabilities, we base our choices entirely on our consideration of the utilities that are assigned to various outcomes. As usual, the problem of assigning utilities may be difficult. As is true when we make decisions under certainty, in many cases of decision under uncertainty, the various utilities must only be ordered by rank (highest, second highest, and so on) rather than be measured in units that can be multiplied, divided, added, and subtracted—as utilities must be when we apply the rule for decisions under risk. One decision rule for decisions under uncertainty does require units of utility, but this rule does not need to be used in every case.

In a decision under uncertainty, sometimes one action has a possible outcome that is better than the outcomes of any other action and also has no possible outcome that is worse than any other outcome. For a simple decision between two actions, each of which has two possible outcomes, this situation can be represented:

Actions	Outcomes Ordered by Rank (1 is highest)	
	I	II
I	4	3
II	2	1

In this table, Action I has two outcomes, ranked lowest and second lowest in utility. Action II also has two outcomes, ranked highest and second highest in utility. Clearly, Action II is the "best action" and should be chosen; either possible outcome of Action II would be better than either possible outcome of Action I.

In the following case of a decision under uncertainty, a "best action" is available. A football player is offered two nonathletic scholarships—one at State University and one at Out of State University. He doesn't know what his chances are of making the team at either university. He'd like to play ball, but he wants the best education he can get, regardless of whether or not he plays ball, and he believes the academic program at State is better. His utilities are ranked (1) play ball at State, (2) be a non-player at State, (3) play ball at OSU, (4) be a non-player at OSU. Thus, he will be better off at State, whether or not he plays ball. Since a best action is available to him, he should choose it and go to State.

Suppose, however, that another football player assigns his first priority to playing ball. Faced with the same scholarship offers, his ranking of utilities would be (1) play ball at State, (2) play ball at OSU, (3) be a non-player at OSU, (4) be a non-player at State. In this decision under uncertainty, there is no "best action." Going to State not only has outcome with the highest value but also has the outcome with the lowest value. Since no best action is available, the next question is whether there is just one *satisfactory* action—an action that has all acceptable outcomes and no unacceptable ones. If the second player would be satisfied with a utility ranked 3 or higher but would not be satisfied with a utility ranked lower than 3, then choosing State would not be a satisfactory action for him to take. He should follow the rule "Choose the action that is satisfactory" and go to OSU.

Suppose, however, that no utility is completely unacceptable to the football player. He could be happy even as a non-player at State, although for him that outcome has the lowest utility. The rule for choosing *the* satisfactory action does not apply if there is *more than one* satisfactory action. At this point, several strategies (rules for decision) are open to the player.

In cases in which there is no "best action" and no single "satisfactory action," there is no one best decision-making rule to follow. Which strategy our football player follows will depend in part on what sort of person he is. Decision theorists categorize three different types:

1. *The Gambler:* In situations in which only one action has an outcome with the highest utility, one decision strategy is to *take that action.* The gambler is willing to take a chance to get the best. If our player is a gambler, he'll go to State.
2. *The Cautious Player:* The cautious player determines the lowest, rather than the highest, utility for each outcome. The choice is based on which action has the *highest of the low utilities.* The cautious player wants to protect against losses, to "maximize the minimum". Using this strategy, our football player will choose OSU, for the lowest utility associated with that action is 3, whereas the lowest utility associated with State is 4.

3. *The Calculator:* The calculator has to take the trouble to assign units of utility in order to calculate the *average* utilities of the various actions. An average utility cannot be determined merely on the basis of a rank ordering. The strategy is to choose the action with the *highest average utility.*

If our football player is a calculating type, he might assign the following units of utility: play at State (10); be a non-player at State (2); play at OSU (8); be a non-player at OSU (6). The average utility of an action is calculated by adding the utilities of each possible outcome for that action and dividing the total by the number of possible outcomes. The average utility of the decision to go to State is then $(10 + 2)/2 = 6$, and the average utility of the decision to go to OSU is $(8 + 6)/2 = 7$. Following the rule of choosing the action with the highest average utility, our player will go to OSU.

If we examine the calculator's decision-making rule, we can see that when average utilities are assigned, the decision under uncertainty is similar to a decision under risk in which each possible outcome is considered to be just as probable as any other outcome. This method would not be appropriate if available information indicated that one outcome was much less or much more likely to occur than another outcome. In these situations, the problem should be treated as a decision under risk, and probabilities should be assigned in a suitable way.

4. "The Prisoner's Dilemma"

An interesting puzzle about decisions under uncertainty, entitled "The Prisoner's Dilemma," has been widely discussed by decision theorists. Here is one statement of the problem:

A man and a woman are arrested on suspicion of operating a ring of thieves who burglarize homes. The police have sufficient evidence to make the arrests, but the District Attorney doubts that there is enough evidence to convict the pair. In an effort to obtain further evidence, the prisoners are prevented from consulting with one another, and each is offered the following proposition by the District Attorney:

Confess to the crime. If your partner does not confess, you will receive a light sentence of one year in prison, but your partner will receive the maximum sentence of five years.

Each prisoner wants to know what will happen if he or she does confess and the other partner also confesses. The District Attorney tells each prisoner that if both partners confess, each will receive a three-year sentence. The District Attorney also reveals that if neither partner confesses, the case will collapse, but that there is sufficient evidence to convict both partners of a lesser crime, for which they will each receive the maximum sentence of two years.

In making such a bargain, the District Attorney feels confident that both partners will confess, even though they would be better off if neither partner confessed! Can you see why this is so?

The assumption is that each partner is unable to assign any probability to whether or not the other partner will confess. Thus, each partner is faced with a decision under uncertainty. If units of (negative) utility are correlated with the length in years of the possible prison terms, each prisoner is faced with the following choice of actions and the utilities associated with the possible outcomes of those actions (utility rankings are enclosed in parentheses):

	Partner Confesses	Partner Does Not Confess
Confess	−3 (3)	−1 (1)
Do Not Confess	−5 (4)	−2 (2)

In this situation, there is no "best action," for one outcome of confessing carries a lower utility than a possible outcome of not confessing, and vice versa. If there is a satisfactory action, it is to confess, for the lowest utility of all is associated with one outcome of not confessing. If either partner follows the rule of choosing the satisfactory action, that partner will confess. However, if there is no satisfactory action and either partner follows *any* other rule for making decisions under uncertainty, the prisoner will also confess.

The gambler's strategy would be to take the action that has the outcome associated with the highest utility; one of the possible outcomes of confessing has the highest utility. The cautious strategy would be to maximize the minimum utility—in this case, also, to confess. (The worst outcome would then be to spend three years in prison, versus a possible five-year prison term for not confessing.) The calculator would determine that the average utility of confessing is

$$\frac{-3 + -1}{2} = -2$$

whereas the average utility of not confessing is

$$\frac{-5 + -2}{2} = -3.5$$

and would also confess.

The District Attorney feels that both partners will make a *reasonable* decision. Whatever reasonable rule they follow, both partners will confess.

"The Prisoner's Dilemma" raises many interesting problems in decision theory. It is crucial to note that separating the partners, thereby preventing their communication and cooperation, affects their decisions. It is a condition of the problem as a decision under uncertainty that the partners are not able to work out a solution between themselves that would be to their mutual benefit. Nevertheless, if they were able to communicate with one another, each partner would be faced with the problem of whether or not the other partner could be trusted to carry out the mutually agreed on plan. If each partner's decision as to whether or not to trust the other partner is a decision under uncertainty, the dilemma arises again.

"The Prisoner's Dilemma" is an artificial problem, but the same sort of situation often arises in real life. Consider, for example, the problem facing a group of prosperous manufacturers located along a river in which they dispose of manufacturing wastes. The river is in danger of becoming polluted due to their dumping practices, and if pollution levels rise significantly, the manufacturers will be charged stiff penalties. The profits of all manufacturers would increase if their plants could be expanded and no penalties had to be paid. If all manufacturers expand, however, the pollution levels will be high enough to result in penalties, which will reduce profits below their present levels.

The Board of Directors of Plant X is considering expansion. The members of the board figure that if they expand but no other plant expands, the pollution levels will not rise too noticeably and Plant X can count on a 10 percent increase in profit. If Plant X does not expand, but the other plants do, then Plant X not only will have to pay a share of the penalty but, unlike the other plants, will not accrue any additional revenue from an expanded facility to help offset this loss. In such a case, the profits of Plant X would sink to 10 percent below the present level, but the profits of the other plants would sink to only 5 percent below the present level. In the absence of any information about the other manufacturers' plans, the board members of Plant X are in a situation similar to "The Prisoner's Dilemma"; moreover, each manufacturer considering expansion is in the same state as Plant X:

	Others Expand	Others Do Not Expand
X Expands	$P - 0.05P$	$P + 0.10P$
X Does Not Expand	$P - 0.10P$	P

5. "The Petersburg Paradox"

Another famous problem in the history of probability and expected utilities, "The Petersburg Paradox," raises questions about equating units of utility with units of money within the context of a game of chance. The problem and a solution to it were formulated in the seventeenth century by the great Swiss mathematician Daniel Bernoulli, one of the many famous scholarly guests of the Russian Empress Catherine the Great at her court at St. Petersburg.

The game is played this way. A person begins by tossing a fair coin and continues to toss the coin as long as the tosses result in heads. As soon as a tail shows, the game is over. If the first toss is a tail, the game is over and there is no payoff. If only one head shows before a tail appears, the payoff is $4. If two heads show, the payoff is $8. If three heads show, the payoff is $16, and the payoff doubles for each successive head that occurs before a tail appears.

The paradoxical aspect of the game arises when we attempt to determine a fair price to charge for a play of the game. Normally, in games of chance, a price is considered fair if it is equal to, or reasonably close to, the expected value of a play of the game. If units of utility are equated with dollars, the expected utility of a play can be calculated in the usual way—by multiplying the probability of each possible outcome of the game by the associated payoff for that outcome and summing the results. A play of the Petersburg game can be considered to be a set of mutually exclusive outcomes, since a game ends after one toss, or after two tosses, or after three tosses, or after an indefinite number of tosses (n). The probability that a game will end after one toss (that a tail will appear on the first toss) is 1/2, and the associated payoff is $0; the probability that a game will end after two tosses (H, T) is 1/4, and the payoff is $4; the probability that a game will end after three tosses (H, H, T) is 1/8, and the payoff is $8; and so on. In other words, the expected utility in dollars is

$$(1/2 \times 0) + (1/4 \times 4) + (1/8 \times 8) + (1/16 \times 16) + \cdots + (1/n \times n) + \cdots$$

Each of the terms after the first term in this series is equal to 1, and since there is no mathematical limit to the number of tosses, the mathematical sum of the series is an infinite number of dollars! It would seem that the game is worth playing no matter how much a play costs, for any finite cost would be less than the infinite expected utility of the game.

It is highly unrealistic to view a coin tossing game as if it had no end to the number of possible tosses. But the situation is hardly less puzzling if some reasonably large limit is placed on the length of a game. For example, let us say that the maximum number of tosses in a play is 1,001 tosses. The expected utility of that game is $1,000; however, only the most reckless gambler would pay $1,000 to play such a game.

Many different solutions to "The Petersburg Paradox" have been proposed. You may be able to think of a few yourself. Bernoulli's solution is particularly interesting because in it he introduced a significant concept in economic theory—the diminishing marginal utility of money.

Bernoulli distinguished the "physical" value of money from its "moral" (or "practical") value to explain why the addition of a certain fixed amount of money to a large fortune has less value (except to a miser) than the addition of the same amount of money to a small fortune. The principle of the diminishing marginal utility of money can be stated:

> If a certain gain is added to an initial fortune f_0, the utility of this gain decreases as f_0 increases.

According to this principle, a person whose initial fortune is $100 will place a greater value on receiving an additional $100 than a person whose initial fortune is $100,000 will place on receiving another $100. The "physical" value of the $100 is the same in both cases, but the "moral" value is much greater in the first case than in the second. In deciding what price to pay for a play of the Petersburg game, a reasonable person who is aware of the decreasing marginal utility of money will consider the moral value, as well as the physical value, of the expected winnings and will also consider the moral value of the money that must be risked to play the game. In terms of moral value, the loss of even a small amount of his fortune could be very hard on a poor man; the win of a large amount might not mean much to a rich man. (See John Maynard Keynes, "The Application of Probability to Conduct," in J. R. Newman's *The World of Mathematics,* for a further discussion of solutions to "The Petersburg Paradox.")

IV. REVIEW

In Chapter 5, we have considered applications of the mathematical calculus of probability to inductive logic. The term *probability* may be used to refer to the ratio of favorable to possible outcomes of some action or event, to the *relative frequency* with which events of a certain type occur in some series of events, or to the degree to which it is rational to believe certain statements. The mathematical *rules of probability* apply to each of these interpretations of the term "probability." These rules allow us to calculate unknown probabilities when certain other probabilities are known.

Probabilities play an important role in everyday decision making. *Decision theory* is a rather new area of study that focuses on the criteria for making rational decisions. Several rules or strategies for making decisions under various conditions of available knowledge were proposed as guidelines for making rational decisions. The rule "Choose the action that maximizes expected utility" is the most acceptable rule for choosing among actions when the probabilities of the various outcomes of these actions are known. The rule "Choose the action that has the highest utility" is a reasonable rule to use when choosing among several actions, each of which has only one known outcome. When deciding among actions that have more than one outcome with unknown probabilities, the rule "Choose the best action" should be followed if there is a best action. If there is no best action but one satisfactory action is available, the satisfactory action should be chosen. If there is no best action and no satisfactory action, or if there is no best action and more than one satisfactory action, it is reasonable to make decisions using either the *gambler's strategy,* the *cautious strategy,* or the *calculating strategy.*

Decision theory can be used to establish the criteria for making reasonable decisions, depending on the type of information available, but it cannot be relied on to provide the information required for making sound decisions. Obviously, our everyday decisions would be inappropriate and even dangerous if we did not attempt to obtain the most accurate information possible before we made them. The following letter from the president of the Travelers Aid Association, published in a syndicated newspaper column by Ann Landers, makes this point quite strongly:

> Since January, vast numbers of job-seekers have gone to the Deep South in search of employment. Recently, it came to our attention that many of these people are victims of a heartless scam. Ads in newspapers and flyers are offering thousands of fabulous jobs in the offshore oil industry. Information for these jobs costs $10 to $12. For this, the advertiser sends a list of offshore oil companies in Texas and Louisiana.

Travelers Aid Societies in Houston, New Orleans, and elsewhere are seeing an enormous increase in clients who have spent the last of their money on a bus ticket, only to be bitterly disappointed after weeks of fruitless searching for a job.

The unemployed who were desperate enough to risk their last savings on the search for a job thought they were making a reasonable decision, for it appeared, on the basis of deceptive advertising, that the probabilities of finding work were very high. In terms of following the rule of maximizing expected utilities, they did not act unreasonably. However, when the stakes are so high (as they were in this case), it is imprudent—and a violation of the principles of critical thinking—to make judgments about the probabilities of various outcomes on the basis of such poor sources of information. Newspaper advertisements, paid for by profit-seeking organizations, cannot be considered authoritative sources of information. People who base a probability judgment on such a source are apt to be making a fallacious appeal to authority (see Chapter 3). The appropriate way to establish probabilities in such cases is to use strong inductive generalizations, statistical syllogisms (including legitimate appeals to authority), or arguments from analogy. When no reliable probabilities can be established and utilities are so high, decisions can be perilous.

A list of some important terms introduced in Chapter 5 follows:

Best Action: When choosing among several actions, if the outcome of one of the actions has a higher utility than the outcome of any other action in the set and also has no outcome with a lower utility than the outcome of any other action in the set, then that action is a best action.

Conjunction: A compound sentence that is true just in case all of its component sentences are true. "And," "but," and "moreover" are commonly used to join sentences to form conjunctions.

Decision Under Certainty: A choice in which the only possible outcome of each action is known.

Decision Under Risk: A choice in which the probabilities of the various outcomes of the actions are known.

Decision Under Uncertainty: A choice in which the probabilities of the various outcomes of the actions are not known.

Disjunction: A compound sentence that is true if any of its component sentences is true but that is false if all of its component sentences are false. "Or" is commonly used to join sentences to form a disjunction.

Expected Utility: The *utility* of some event is its *value,* which may be positive or negative. For purposes of comparison and calculation, we assign units of utility to various events. The expected utility of an action is calculated by multiplying the probability of each possible outcome of the action by the utility associated with that outcome and summing the results.

Independent Events: Events are independent of one another when the occurrence of one event does not affect the probability of the occurrence of the other event. Tosses of a fair coin are independent of one another; draws from a deck of cards without replacement and reshuffling are not independent of one another.

Mutually Exclusive Events: Events are mutually exclusive if the occurrence of one event rules out the possibility of the occurrence of the other event. On a single roll of a pair of fair dice, rolling a total of six points mutually excludes rolling a total of five points. Sentences are mutually exclusive when the truth of one sentence rules out the truth of the other sentence. If the sentences that form a disjunction are mutually exclusive, only one of them can be true.

Satisfactory Action: When choosing among several actions, if there is no best action but there is an action that has no outcomes with less than an acceptable level of utility, that action is a satisfactory action.

V. EXERCISES

1. The state in which you live operates a lottery. The proceeds of the lottery are used to supplement the state's unemployment insurance fund. You can play the lottery for $1. To play, you choose a three-digit number from 000 to 999, inclusive, and receive an official ticket with that number printed on it. Each evening, a ball is drawn blindly from a container that holds 1,000 balls, each with a different three-digit number on it. If your number is selected in the daily drawing on the date you play, you receive $500 for your ticket. Otherwise, you receive nothing.
   a. What is the expected utility (in dollars) of a single play?
   b. Suppose that you decide to play three times in one day and that you choose the same number each time. (You hold three tickets at a cost of $3.) What is the expected utility (in dollars) of your triple play?
   c. Suppose that you decide to play three times in one day and that you choose a different number each time. What is the expected utility (in dollars) of this triple play?
2. An investor has $1,000 to invest for a period of one year. She must decide whether to invest the money in a recommended stock or in a money-market fund. If she invests in the fund, she will collect $1,200 (her original $1,000 + a profit of $200). If she invests in the stock and there is a merger, she will realize $1,800 (her original $1,000 + a profit of $800). If she invests in the stock and there is no merger, she will receive only $900 (a loss of $100). The probability that there will be a merger is 0.40. Assume that units of utility can be correlated with dollars. (No other utilities are involved in this decision.)
   a. What is the probability that no merger will occur?
   b. What is the expected utility of investing in the money-market fund?
   c. What is the expected utility of investing in the stock?
   d. What decision rule should the investor use?
   e. What is the rational decision in this case?
3. You are in charge of organizing a dinner party that is being held for the sole purpose of raising money for a worthy cause. You must decide whether to schedule an outdoor picnic or an indoor buffet supper. This event must be planned so far in advance that you have no way of assigning a probability to rain

on the day of the party. On the basis of past events of this type, you have the
following information:

> If it does not rain, the outdoor picnic will yield a profit of $500, and
> the indoor buffet supper will yield a profit of $170.

> If it does rain, the outdoor picnic will yield a profit of $80, and the
> indoor buffet supper will yield a profit of $440.

   a. Is this a decision under risk, a decision under certainty, or a decision
      under uncertainty?
   b. Is it reasonable in this case to correlate units of utility with dollars gained
      for the worthy cause?
   c. What decision rule would you follow in this case?
   d. Apply the decision rule, and state what decision you would make. (Show
      your work.)

4. The same conditions stated in Exercise 3 exist, *except* that on the basis of
weather records for the date of the party, you can reasonably assign a probability
of 1/3 to rain on that date.

   a. What type of decision are you faced with now?
   b. What decision rule should you follow?
   c. On the basis of that rule, what is the proper decision? (Show your work.)

5. You are a restaurant manager who is responsible for planning the "daily
specials." You are considering whether or not to introduce a new Thursday
special. If the special is successful, the restaurant will show a profit of $250 for
the night; if the special is not successful, the restaurant will lose $50. If you serve
the usual Thursday special, the restaurant will show a profit of $100. You deter-
mine that the probability that the new dish will be a success is about 1/2. You've
been doing a good job at the restaurant, so you are not afraid that you'll be fired
if you make the wrong decision this time. However, you share in the profits, so
the decision does affect your pay.

   a. What decision rule would you use in this situation?
   b. What would your decision be? (Show your work.)

6. A famous problem in decision theory, called "Pascal's Wager," was formulated
by the French mathematician and philosopher Blaise Pascal in the seventeenth
century. Pascal, who was a devout Christian, offered several formulations of the
problem. Here is one way of looking at "Pascal's Wager":

> There are two possible states of the world: either God exists, or He does
> not. You are faced with two choices: Believe in God, or refuse to believe. If
> God does exist and you are a believer, you will be rewarded with infinite
> happiness in Heaven. If God does not exist and you believe He does, your
> life will be as usual, without any supernatural benefits or penalties. If, on the
> other hand, you refuse to believe and God exists, you can expect everlasting
> punishment in Hell. If you do not believe and there is no God, your life will
> be the usual rewards of life with no Heaven or Hell to face.

   a. Is this version of "Pascal's Wager" a decision under certainty, uncertainty,
      or risk?

    b. If you accept this formulation, is there a "best action"?

    c. Do you think that this way of presenting the problem is reasonable? For example, are there just two choices and two outcomes for each action? Is "life as usual" the same for the believer and the non-believer? Does Pascal make any assumptions about what God is like?

7. Flu shots can offer valuable protection against the flu, particularly in an epidemic year. The shots, however, are not entirely unproblematic. In some people, flu shots can cause an allergic reaction—a kind of mini-flu. This reaction is less severe than a real case of flu and lasts a much shorter time. Another problem is that in order to be effective, the flu shot must be administered before it is known whether or not an epidemic is on the way.

    Suppose that you are trying to decide whether or not to get a flu shot. Based on statistical data, there is a probability of 0.6 that this year will be an epidemic year in your city. You have never had flu in a non-epidemic year and believe the probability that you will get flu is 0 if there is no epidemic. If an epidemic strikes your city and you are not vaccinated, your chances of getting the flu are 0.4 and you will be ill with the flu for nine days. If you are vaccinated, there is a probability of 0.1 that you will have a reaction and be ill for two days.

    Flu vaccination is free at the student health clinic, and you do not particularly mind getting shots. Thus, it is reasonable to equate units of (negative) utility for this decision with days of illness.

    a. What is the probability that you will get the flu if you are not vaccinated?

    b. What is the expected utility of not being vaccinated?

    c. What is the expected utility of being vaccinated?

    d. If you follow the rule of maximizing expected utilities, will you get the flu shot or not?

8. Suppose that a person who needs $1,000 to stay in business (the business is the person's only means of support) is offered the choice between a $1,000 gift or a gamble on a prize of $100,000 if any number but a six is rolled on a single throw of a fair die (but nothing if the six shows). Also suppose that the person has no other way of obtaining the money needed to stay in business.

    a. Is it rational for the person to choose the gamble rather than the gift?

    b. Why or why not?

    c. What does this problem suggest about the practice of equating units of utility with units of money?

    d. What does this problem suggest to you about considering risks as well as possible gains when contemplating an action?

DEDUCTIVE REASONING: CONDITIONAL ARGUMENTS

I. PROPERTIES OF DEDUCTIVE ARGUMENTS: VALIDITY AND THE IMPORTANCE OF LOGICAL FORM

Deductive arguments, as defined in Chapter 2, are truth-preserving. If the premisses of a deductive argument are all true, then the conclusion must be true as well. When an argument is truth-preserving, it is said to be a *valid* argument. Strictly speaking, if we define deductive arguments as truth-preserving, then all deductive arguments are valid arguments. However, terminology varies somewhat, and some logicians distinguish two types of deductive argument: arguments that are truth-preserving, or valid, and arguments that merely purport to be valid. The latter type is called an *invalid deductive argument* or a *deductive fallacy.*

The term "valid" has many uses in ordinary English. We hear people speak of valid beliefs, valid reasons, and valid claims. In the study of logic, however, "valid" and "validity" have special meanings; these terms refer to the truth-preserving property of deductive arguments. One of the chief concerns of deductive logic is to understand the nature of validity. Logicians try to determine how this property relates to other properties of arguments, and they develop methods for testing the validity of various types of arguments.

Although "validity" refers to the truth-preserving character of deductive arguments, arguments can be valid even if their premisses or their conclusions are *not* true. An argument may be truth-preserving even though it contains no truth (its premisses and conclusion are all false) to be preserved. To say that an argument is valid is to claim that regardless of whether the premisses are actually true or not, *if* all of its premisses were true, then its conclusion would be true also.

Thus, it is impossible to construct a valid argument in which all of the premisses are true and the conclusion is false, but valid arguments can contain a false premiss (or premisses) and a true conclusion. Here, for example, is one such argument:

(1)

No mammals can fly.	(false premiss)
All dogs are mammals.	(true premiss)
No dogs can fly.	(true conclusion)

There are also valid arguments with false premisses and false conclusions. Here is one:

(2)

No mammals can fly.
All birds are mammals.

No birds can fly.

In the presentation of arguments (1) and (2), nothing has been done to *prove* that they are valid. At this point, we are relying on intuitive ability to see that if the premisses of these arguments were true, then their conclusions would be true also. Later on, we will prove that these arguments are valid.

Of course, when we present a deductive argument for the purpose of convincing someone of the truth of our conclusion, we want the argument not only to be valid but to have true premisses as well. Nevertheless, the property of validity is so interesting and important that it—rather than the truth of premisses—is the chief focus of deductive logic.

In ordinary life, too, we are sometimes interested in the validity of arguments apart from the truth of their premisses. Occasionally, we may want to trace the consequences (the conclusions that follow deductively) of a variety of premisses, not all of which can be true. We might ask ourselves what would follow if A and B were true and, alternatively, what would follow if A were true and B were not true. Sometimes we want to identify the consequences of sentences but simply have no way of determining their truth or falsity at the time the argument is constructed. If a set of premisses of unknown truth status leads deductively to some obviously false conclusion, then we can say that at least one of those premisses must be false.

The validity of deductive arguments is closely connected with *logical form*. Many logicians believe that any argument that is deductively valid has this property simply by virtue of being an instance of some valid form of argument. You are already familiar with forms of argument from our study of various inductive forms, including analogy, inductive generalization, and statistical syllogism. The form, or structure, of an argument refers to certain logical features that pertain to the argument regardless of its particular subject matter or content. Statistical syllogisms, for example, have two premisses—a statistical generalization that relates an attribute class to a reference class, and a particular sentence that says a given individual is a member of that reference class. The conclusion of a statistical syllogism is another particular sentence that places the individual mentioned in the premiss in the attribute class. (Or, symbolically, "X percent of Fs are Gs. a is an F. Therefore, a is a G.") The form of earlier arguments (1) and (2) can be represented, using our familiar symbols for class terms in generalizations, as

> No Fs are Gs.
> All Hs are Fs.
> _____
> No Hs are Gs.

In a fundamental sense, the strict dependence of validity on the *form* of argument makes it simpler to evaluate deductive arguments than to evaluate inductive arguments. When we tried to evaluate inductive arguments, we had to consider the forms of those arguments, but we also had to take into account all sorts of background information that could affect the strength of the argument. We had to be concerned, for example, with the size of samples, the lack of bias, the relevance of analogies, and other matters. We then had to make judgments about whether the premisses strongly supported the conclusion or supported it to some lesser degree.

In evaluating deductive arguments, we do not need to consider any background information beyond the information required to state implicit premises. Moreover, validity is an all-or-nothing affair. An argument is either valid or not valid. There are no degrees of validity. In addition, if an argument is an instance of a *valid argument form,* then that argument is valid.

In the following sections, we will discuss conditional sentences, introduce some common forms of valid conditional arguments, explain what it means for an argument to be an instance of a valid form, and discuss some fallacies associated with deductive forms of argument.

II. CONDITIONAL SENTENCES

Conditional arguments are arguments that contain conditional sentences as premises, as conclusions, or both. Before we discuss these arguments, we will take a closer look at conditional sentences. *Conditional sentences* are used when we want to say that the truth of one claim depends on (is conditional on) the truth of another claim. Here are some examples:

1. If I study, then I will pass my math exam.
2. Maisie will recover from mono, provided that she takes care of herself.
3. John wouldn't have done that if he had not been forced.
4. You will break your leg climbing that way unless you are careful.

1. The Structure of Conditionals

Each of these conditional sentences (or, briefly, *conditionals*) is a *complex* English sentence—a sentence that contains another sentence as one of its parts. A sentence that is not complex is called *simple.* Conditionals are made up of (at least) two sentences—one that states the condition, and one that depends on the stated condition. In the vocabulary of logicians, the sentence that states the condition is called the *antecedent* and the dependent sentence is called the *consequent.* The antecedent and the consequent may themselves be complex sentences, but first we will consider conditionals with simple antecedents and simple consequents.

In example (1), the antecedent is "I study" and the consequent is "I will pass my math exam." In (2), the antecedent is "she takes care of herself" and the consequent is "Maisie will recover from mono." In (3), the antecedent is "he had not been forced" and the consequent is "John wouldn't have done that." In (4), the antecedent is "you are (not) careful" and the consequent is "you will break your leg climbing that way."

Even this small sample reveals some of the variety of ways in which conditionals are expressed in English. Different verb tenses (past, present, and future) and moods (indicative and subjunctive) are used. Various terms indicate the presence of a conditional: "if . . . then," "provided that," "unless." Sometimes the word that signals the presence of the conditional also functions in another way in the sentence. "Unless," for example, connotes negation; it means the same as "if not." Different word orderings are also used in conditionals. Sometimes, as in (1), the antecedent comes before the consequent; sometimes the antecedent follows the consequent, as in (2), (3), and (4). Subjunctive conditionals are most often used in English to express what would have occurred if something else had occurred, when, in fact, that something else did not occur. These subjunctive conditionals, like example (3), are called *counterfactual conditionals*.

Since the validity of an argument depends on its form, and the form of an argument in turn depends to some extent on the form, or structure, of the sentences that are its premises and conclusion, logicians are concerned with representing the form of conditional sentences in a standard way. To do this, they must ignore all sorts of rhetorical subtleties that are present in the different ways of stating conditionals in English. For the sake of clarity and precision in the study of arguments, logicians forego such refinements.

From the logician's point of view, it is important to know which sentence is the antecedent and which sentence is the consequent in a conditional. A relationship between antecedent and consequent is the crucial logical relationship in these sentences, just as relationships between classes are the crucial relationships in universal generalizations (see Chapter 3). When conditionals that occur in arguments are written in the standard way—"If (antecedent), then (consequent)"—their form is readily apparent. This practice makes it easier to recognize the structure of the argument. We can rewrite examples (2), (3), and (4) in this way [example (1) is already in standard form]:

2. If Maisie takes care of herself, then she will recover from mono.
3. If he had not been forced, then John wouldn't have done that.
4. If you are not careful, then you will break your leg climbing that way.

In addition to the words in these examples, other English expressions are used to indicate conditionals. Here are some of them:

1. Whenever I see a kangaroo, I run. (If I see a kangaroo, then I run.)
2. I run only if I see a kangaroo. (If I do not see a kangaroo, then I do not run.) Note that this is *not* the same as (1) but that it is the same as "If I run, then I see a kangaroo."
3. Given that I see a kangaroo, I run. [Same as (1).]
4. A sufficient condition of my running is my seeing a kangaroo. [Same as (1).]
5. A necessary condition of my running is my seeing a kangaroo. [Same as (2).]
6. I don't run unless I see a kangaroo. [Same as (2).]

2. The Truth of Conditionals

In English, conditionals are used to express various kinds of relationships between the antecedent and the consequent. The conditional "If Maisie takes care of herself, then she will recover from mono" is used, for example, to express a *causal* connection between Maisie's caring for herself and her recovery. Conditionals are also used to express *logical,* or *definitional,* connections between sentences, as in "If two and two are added, then they equal four" or "If porpoises are aquatic, then they live in water." For a causal conditional to be true, there must be a real causal connection between the situation described in the antecedent and the situation described in the consequent. Similarly, if a conditional is intended to express a logical or definitional relationship, it will not be regarded as true unless that connection holds between the antecedent and the consequent.

Another type of connection expressed in English conditionals is called the *material conditional.* An example of a material conditional is "If there is human life on Jupiter, then my great-grandmother was an astronaut." Obviously, there is no causal, definitional, or logical connection between the antecedent and the consequent in this conditional. The point of this sentence, and others like it in English, is to emphasize the falsity of the antecedent. It is a way of expressing, forcefully or humorously, that there is no human life on Jupiter.

Occasionally, we encounter conditional sentences in which the truth of the consequent does not really depend at all on the truth of the antecedent, since the consequent is true whether or not the antecedent is true. An example is

> If Jake continues to smoke, he will eventually die.

Jake will *eventually* die whether or not he continues to smoke—although "eventually" may come a bit sooner if Jake smokes than if he doesn't smoke.

Although material conditionals are used rather infrequently in English, we can learn something logically important about the role of conditionals in valid arguments by examining the circumstances under which material conditionals are true or false.

In a material conditional, the "if . . . then . . . " that connects the component sentences is called a *truth-functional connective,* meaning that the truth of the sentence as a whole is completely determined by (is a function of) the truth of the component sentences. The only circumstance under which we can say a material conditional is false is when it has a true antecedent and a false consequent. That is why the complex sentence "If there is human life on Jupiter, then my great-grandmother was an astronaut" can be used to state the falsity of "there is human life on Jupiter." The consequent of the conditional ("my great-grandmother was an astronaut") is obviously false. Yet the sentence as a whole is taken as true. But if the antecedent were true, then the conditional would be false, for it would have a true antecedent and a false consequent.

When we look at the *form* of a sentence, we ignore its *content* (the *meanings* of the words in the sentence). We are interested merely in the logical relationships between the various terms in the sentence, or between the various sentences that make up a complex sentence. For example, when we express the form of generalizations such as "All *F*s are *G*s," we ignore the meanings of the terms that *F* and *G* represent. Similarly, when we express the form of a conditional—"If (antecedent), then (consequent)"—we ignore the content of its component sentences. However, if we do not pay attention to the content, we have no way of knowing whether a conditional is a causal conditional, a logical conditional, or a material conditional. This matters for some purposes, but is not a disadvantage if our chief concern is the validity of conditional arguments.

All conditionals are like material conditionals in the sense that if their antecedents are true and their consequents are false, then they are false conditionals. (For example, the causal conditional "If the match is struck, then it will light " is shown to be false if the match is struck and the match does not light.) Moreover, for the purposes of determining the validity of conditional arguments, it is reasonable to treat all conditionals as if they were material conditionals. This is so, because any conditional argument that is valid when its conditional components are regarded as material conditionals remains valid if the conditionals happen to be causal conditionals or logical conditionals. Thus, to determine the validity of conditional arguments on the basis of their forms, logicians need to consider only the truth-functional relationship between the antecedent and the consequent in conditional sentences. As we will see, this greatly simplifies the study of the validity of conditional arguments.

In summary, remembering that our primary purpose is the study of the validity of arguments, we can state the general circumstances under which a conditional statement is regarded as true or false by considering only the truth or falsity of its component parts. The only four possibilities are listed in the following table:

Antecedent	Consequent	Conditional Sentence
True	True	True
True	False	False
False	True	True
False	False	True

Exercises

1. Rewrite each of the following sentences in standard conditional form: *If* (antecedent), *then* (consequent).
   a. You can do well in math and logic classes only if you keep up with the assignments.
   b. Unless you want a ticket, you won't park in the faculty parking lot next to the classroom building.
   c. Whenever you want something very much, you work hard to achieve it.
   d. You will get the job provided that you complete your degree this term.
   e. Without complications, life is uninteresting.
   f. In case the teacher asks about her, Jane missed the test because she was ill.
   g. You can pass this class if you really want to pass it.
   h. Having a grade-point average of C or better is a necessary condition for a student being graduated.

    i. Passing one course in logic is a sufficient condition for a student fulfilling the logic requirement.

    j. Only if you care little for your safety will you ride a bicycle on Main Street during rush-hour traffic.

2. In the following exercises, the letters p and q represent component sentences in conditionals. Suppose that p is a true sentence and q is a false sentence. Rewrite each conditional in standard form, and state whether the conditional is true or false. (You may wish to refer to the preceding table.)

    a. p if q.
    b. q if p.
    c. q if q.
    d. If p, q.
    e. p provided that q.
    f. q whenever p.
    g. p is necessary for q.
    h. q is sufficient for p.

III. CONDITIONAL ARGUMENTS

In this section, we will examine two common forms of conditional arguments. Each of these forms has two premises, one of which is a conditional sentence. The conclusions are not conditional sentences.

1. Affirming the Antecedent

The argument

> If we drive nonstop to the coast, we will need two days to recover.
> We are driving nonstop to the coast.
> _____
> We will need two days to recover.

is an example of *affirming the antecedent*. Like many common argument forms, it has a Latin name, *modus ponens*, which can be roughly translated "the way of affirming." One premiss of the argument is a conditional. Using the letters p and q to represent the component sentences of the conditional, and the same letters to represent the same sentences when they occur elsewhere in the argument, we can exhibit the form of the argument in the following way:

$$\text{If } p, \text{ then } q.$$
$$\underline{p}$$
$$q$$

Stated in English, this argument is so simple that its validity is readily apparent. If the premisses of the argument are true, it is easy to see that the conclusion must be true as well. However, now that we understand material conditionals, we are in a position to prove that any argument that has this structure (form) must be valid. We need to show only that there are no circumstances under which the sentences represented by "If p, then q" and "p" are both true and "q" is false.

If the second premiss (p) is true, then the antecedent of the conditional premiss is true. But a conditional with a true antecedent is true only if its consequent (q) is true as well. However, q is not only the consequent of the conditional; it is also the conclusion of the argument. So, if "If p, then q" and "p" (the premisses) are true, then "q" (the conclusion) must be true as well.

In showing that this argument form is valid, we did not take into account any meanings of the sentences that the letters p and q represent. The validity of the form does not depend on the content of the argument. All that is required to show that the form is valid is an understanding of the circumstances under which material conditionals are true or false and the recognition that one of the premisses is a conditional; the other premiss "affirms the antecedent" (claims the antecedent is true), and the conclusion affirms the consequent of the same conditional.

By showing that this argument form is valid, we have also shown that any argument in English that "fits" this form, or is an instance of this form, is also valid. This means that any argument with two such premisses (one, a conditional; the other, a sentence that affirms the antecedent) and a conclusion that is the consequent of the conditional is valid. It is impossible for an argument with this structure to have all true premisses and a false conclusion.

Here are some examples of English-language arguments that are instances of *affirming the antecedent.* These arguments can be rewritten to fit the form without drastically changing the meaning of what is said in English:

1. Sally will go to the dance if Charlie will. But Charlie will certainly go, so Sally will be there.
2. Here comes Rover. Whenever Rover appears, Kitty-cat is not far behind. Therefore, Kitty-cat will be along soon.
3. With persistence, you'll be elected. So you will be elected, for persistence is your strong point.
4. A dead man cannot be robbed unless he can own, spend, claim, or want money. It is impossible for dead men to own, spend, claim, or want money. Therefore, dead men cannot be robbed. (This is a reconstruction of Gaffer's argument in *Our Mutual Friend* in Chapter 1.)

2. Denying the Consequent

The second type of conditional argument, *denying the consequent,* is also very common and only slightly more complicated than *affirming the antecedent.* The Latin name of this argument form is *modus tollens* ("the way of denying"). Here is an example:

If Japanese beetles are present in the garden, then leaves take on a lacy, or skeletonized, appearance.
The leaves in the garden are not lacy, or skeletonized.

Japanese beetles are not present in the garden.

In this argument, as in *affirming the antecedent,* there is a conditional premiss. The other premiss *denies the consequent,* or says that the consequent of the conditional premiss is false. The conclusion of the argument says that the antecedent of the conditional is also false. Using the letters p and q as we did in the previous argument form, we can represent the form of this argument in the following way:

$$\text{If } p, \text{ then } q.$$
$$\text{Not } q.$$

$$\text{Not } p.$$

Again, we appeal to the circumstances under which material conditionals are true or false to show that this argument form is valid. In addition, though, we must consider the meaning of "not." The logical force of "not" is to turn true sentences into false ones, and vice versa. In English, this logical function of *negation* can be accomplished in a number of ways. Sometimes, the term "not" is inserted in a sentence. Other times, sentences are negated by replacing the main verb of the sentence with the negation of that verb: "You can do this."—"You can't do this." The expression "it is not the case that" may precede the sentence to be negated: "You can do this."—"It is not the case that you can do this." A verb that means the same as the denial of the verb in the original sentence may be used: "You passed the test."—"You failed the test." All of this is familiar to competent speakers of English, but here are a few more examples to remind us of the variety of ways in which negation can be accomplished:

1. Harry is happy. Harry is unhappy.
2. She will do it. She won't do it.
3. Jack loves Jill. It is not true that Jack loves Jill.
4. Skeletonized leaves are present. Skeletonized leaves are absent.

As in their treatment of conditionals, logicians ignore various subtleties of English usage and concentrate on the logically important feature of negation—changing a true sentence into a false one, or changing a false sentence into a true one. This is the feature that is important to the validity of arguments. Thus, we adopt a standard way of writing the negation of a sentence in argument forms: write "not" in front of the letter that stands for the sentence that is negated ("Not p").

Now we are ready to consider the validity of the form of *denying the consequent.* One premiss of the argument says that the consequent of the conditional premiss is false. Thus, if the conditional premiss is true, it must have a false antecedent. But the conclusion of the argument simply states that the antecedent of the conditional premiss is false. So, if both premisses are true, the conclusion must be true as well.

As is true of *affirming the antecedent,* any English-language argument that fits the form (is an instance of) *denying the consequent* is a valid argument. Here are some examples of arguments in English that are instances of *denying the consequent:*

1. "Without complications, life is uninteresting. But life is interesting, so there are complications." Here, we have to be concerned with *double negation.* This argument could be stated

   > If there are no complications, then life is uninteresting.
   > It is not the case that life is uninteresting.
   > _____
   > It is not the case that there are no complications.

2. "If you really wanted that car, you would get a job to pay for it. So you must not really want the car, since you won't get a job."

3. "Stupid savages could not devise complex languages without God's help. The languages of these people are complex. Therefore, God helped to construct the languages." This is a reconstruction of Dobrizhoffer's argument in Exercise 11 at the end of Chapter 1. Like example (1), it involves double negation when the conditional is written in standard form:

If God did not help to construct the languages of savages, then these languages could not be complex.
It is not the case that these languages are not complex.
_____
It is not the case that God did not help to construct the languages of savages.

3. Unstated Premisses in Conditional Arguments

It is quite common in written works and ordinary speech to find incompletely stated conditional arguments of the forms *affirming the antecedent* and *denying the consequent.* Frequently, either the nonconditional premiss or the conclusion is omitted. Occasionally, both the conclusion and one of the premisses are missing, and we must depend on the context to tell us that an argument, rather than just a statement of facts, is intended. This is acceptable in many situations because the forms of conditional argument are so well understood. For example, in the *Bible,* St. Paul is obviously arguing for the truth of Christ's resurrection from the dead when he says "If Christ has not risen, vain then is our preaching, vain too is your faith (I. Cor. 15)." Paul intends the argument to be interpreted in the form of *denying the consequent.* Can you supply the missing premiss?

Of course, when premisses are not actually stated, there is always some danger that what is intended as a *modus tollens* may be interpreted as a *modus ponens.* For example, John Wesley (the founder of the Methodist Church), counting on his listeners' faith, is supposed to have said "If you give up belief in witches, then you give up belief in the *Bible.*" Complete Wesley's argument—first as a *modus ponens* (*affirming the antecedent*), and then as a *modus tollens* (*denying the consequent*). Which form do you think Wesley intended? With respect to Wesley's conditional, Bertrand Russell once said "I agree." How did Russell interpret Wesley's argument? (Russell was not a Methodist!)

IV. FALLACIES ASSOCIATED WITH DEDUCTIVE ARGUMENTS

Arguments may somehow purport to be deductive but fail to meet the standards for deductive validity. Such arguments are not truth-preserving and are called *deductive fallacies* or *invalid deductive arguments.* Whether an argument *purports* to be deductive is sometimes difficult to determine but is an important consideration; although inductive arguments are not truth-preserving, it would be inappropriate to regard all inductive arguments as fallacious. Inductive arguments do not purport to be deductive, and the standards for assessing the strength of inductive arguments differ from the standards for evaluating deductive arguments.

1. Fallacious (Invalid) Forms of Arguments

Before we address the question of fallacious arguments in English, we will consider what it means when we say that an *argument form* is "invalid." An argument form is *invalid* (not valid) if it is possible to find an instance of that form with all true premises and a false conclusion. The following form, which resembles *affirming the antecedent,* is an invalid form of argument:

$$\text{If } p, \text{ then } q.$$
$$q$$
$$\overline{\qquad\qquad}$$
$$p$$

To show that this form is invalid, we need to note only that if q were true and p were false, the conclusion would be false but both premises would be true. This is because a material conditional with a false antecedent is true whether its consequent is true or false. This fallacious form is called (not surprisingly) *affirming the consequent.*

It is not difficult to supply an argument in English with two true premises and a false conclusion that is an instance of this form:

If Cincinnati is the capital of Ohio, then Cincinnati is in Ohio.
Cincinnati is in Ohio.
_____
Cincinnati is the capital of Ohio.

The second fallacious form of argument, which is somewhat similar to *denying the consequent,* is called *denying the antecedent:*

> If *p*, then *q*.
> Not *p*.
> ―――――――――
> Not *q*.

The invalidity of this form is evident if we consider that the second premiss denies the antecedent of the conditional premiss (says it is false). But conditionals are true when their antecedents are false, whether they have false consequents (as the conclusion states) or true ones. Since the truth of the premisses cannot guarantee the truth of the conclusion, the argument form is not valid. Again, it is easy to supply an argument in English with true premisses and a false conclusion that is an instance of this form:

> If bats are birds, then bats have wings.
> Bats are not birds.
> ――――――――――――――――――――――――――――
> Bats do not have wings.

To show that an *argument form* is invalid (fallacious), all that is required is to show that it is logically possible for an argument with all true premisses and a false conclusion to fit (or be an instance of) that form. This can be done abstractly, for example, by discussing the circumstances under which sentences of a certain form are true or false. It can also be done concretely by exhibiting an English-language argument that fits the form but that has obviously true premisses and an obviously false conclusion.

2. Fallacious Arguments

It is usually more difficult to show that a given *argument* is fallacious than it is to show that an *argument form* is fallacious. An argument that purports to be deductive is fallacious only if it is not an instance of *any* valid argument form. (Of course, no inductive argument, no matter how strong, is an instance of a valid form. In this discussion of fallacies, we are only considering arguments that somehow resemble deductive arguments.) There are an infinite number of valid argument forms. Thus far, we have considered only two valid argument forms— *affirming the antecedent* and *denying the consequent.* Obviously, we cannot prove an argument is fallacious by showing that it fails to fit either of these forms. For example, the following valid argument does not fit either form:

> All men are mortal.
> Socrates is a man.
> ―――――――――――――――
> Socrates is mortal.

One problem logicians encounter is that a single English-language argument may fit several different argument forms. Forms of argument reflect certain structural features of the components of the argument. Sometimes we are interested in structural relationships *among* various simple sentences in an argument. This is the case in the analysis of conditional arguments. In other arguments, validity depends on structural relationships *within* the simple sentences that make up the argument, such as the relationships between the subject and the predicate in a sentence. This is the case in the syllogism about Socrates. If the validity of a given argument depends on *intra*-sentence structures, we will not prove that it is valid by representing its form in terms of *inter*-sentence structure.

If an English-language argument has obviously true premises and an obviously false conclusion, we know that it is fallacious, for it could not be an instance of any valid argument form. For this reason, it is safe to call the earlier examples of English-language arguments that were instances of *affirming the consequent* and *denying the antecedent* fallacious. In addition, since deductive validity is a matter of form, when we are more familiar with the various types of argument structure and when we can be reasonably certain we have not overlooked any hidden structure by virtue of which some arguments could be valid, we may say that it is highly probable that these *arguments* are fallacious, even though they may not have true premises and false conclusions. For the time being, however, we are on safer ground when we speak of fallacious *argument forms*. When we are presented with an English-language argument that is an instance of one of the known fallacious forms, we should *suspect* it of being fallacious, and it is reasonable to challenge whoever is presenting the argument to prove that it is not.

V. REVIEW

Since the most important material in Chapter 6 can be described in the new vocabulary that was introduced here, the chapter can be reviewed by listing those new terms and their meanings:

Complex Sentence: A sentence that contains another sentence as one of its parts.

Conditional Argument: An argument that contains at least one conditional sentence as a premiss. Some conditional arguments (not the ones studied in this chapter) also have conditionals as conclusions. In this chapter, we studied two valid forms of conditional argument: *affirming the antecedent* (or *modus ponens*), and *denying the consequent* (or *modus tollens*):

Modus ponens	Modus tollens
If p, then q.	If p, then q.
p	Not q.
q	Not p.

We also studied two invalid or fallacious forms of conditional arguments:

Affirming the consequent	Denying the antecedent
If *p*, then *q*.	If *p*, then *q*.
q	Not *p*.
——————	——————
p	Not *q*.

Conditional Sentence (*Conditional*): A complex sentence consisting of an *antecedent* (the sentence that states the condition) and a *consequent* (the sentence that depends on the stated condition). The standard form of a conditional is: "If (antecedent), then (consequent)."

Deductive Fallacy (*Invalid Deductive Argument*): An argument that purports to be deductive but fails to meet the standards of deductive validity.

Invalid Argument: An argument is invalid if it is not an instance of any valid form of argument. An argument that purports to be deductive, but is invalid, is fallacious.

Invalid Argument Form: An argument form is invalid if it is possible for an argument in that form to have all true premisses and a false conclusion. Invalid argument forms are *fallacious* forms.

Material Conditional: A conditional sentence in which the connection between the antecedent and the consequent is merely truth-functional, rather than some "real" causal, definitional, or logical connection. A material conditional is false only when its antecedent is true and its consequent is false.

Truth-Functional Connective: In a complex sentence that is connected by a truth-functional connective, the truth or falsity of the complex sentence depends entirely on the truth or falsity of its component parts. "If . . . then," when interpreted in the sense of a material conditional, is a truth-functional connective. "Not" is also a truth-functional connective. If a sentence "*p*" is true, then "Not *p* " is false. If a sentence "*p*" is false, then "Not *p* " is true.

Valid Argument: An argument is valid if it is impossible for all of its premisses to be true and its conclusion to be false. Strictly speaking, all deductive arguments, as defined in this text, are valid, because the defining characteristic of these arguments is that they are *truth-preserving*. Any instance of a valid argument form is a valid argument.

Valid Argument Form: An argument form is valid if it is impossible for an argument in that form to have all true premisses and a false conclusion.

VI. EXERCISES

Each of the following exercises contains a conditional argument. Assume that all the arguments purport to be deductive, and rewrite each argument (in English) so that its premisses and conclusion are on separate lines. If the conditional premiss is not in standard form, rewrite it. Supply missing premisses or conclusions, if necessary. When doing so, adopt a principle of "charity" and give the proponent of the argument the benefit of the doubt. Then tell whether the rewritten argument is in the form of *affirming the antecedent, denying the consequent, affirming the consequent,* or *denying the antecedent.*

1. Headlines on the *Pittsburgh Press* sports pages on two successive days:

> IF STEELERS BEAT OILERS, THEY GO TO PLAYOFFS
>
> STEELERS BEAT OILERS; GO TO PLAYOFFS

2. You can do well in math and logic classes only if you keep up with the assignments. You keep up with the assignments, so you do well in math and logic classes.

3. The picnic will be held on Thursday, provided that it doesn't rain. But according to the weather reports, there will be no rain on Thursday, so we'll have the picnic.

4. If primitive peoples did not cross the Pacific Ocean, there would not be a strong resemblance between Polynesian artifacts and South American artifacts. But there is a strong resemblance between these artifacts, so primitive peoples did cross the Pacific Ocean.

5. Since there are holes in the carpet, there must be moths in the house; for if there are moths in the house, then they make holes in the carpet.

6. Coyotes howl only when there's a moon, but there's a moon tonight, so they'll be howling.

7. All forms of pantheism [which involves the belief that man is a part of God] must be rejected, because if man is actually a part of God, the evil in man is also in God. But there is no evil in God.

> —Bishop of Birmingham,
> quoted in Bertrand Russell's *Religion and Science*

8. If 2 is not a prime number, then there is a positive integer smaller than 2 and greater than 1 which evenly divides 2. But there are no positive integers smaller than 2 and greater than 1. Therefore, 2 is a prime number.

9. If morals could be taught simply on the basis that they are necessary to society, there would be no social need for religion. But morality cannot be taught in that way.

> —Patrick Lord Devlin, *The Enforcement of Morals*

10. We would not be at the trouble to learn a language when we can have all that is written in it just as well in translation. But as we cannot have the beauties of poetry but in its original language, we learn it.

> —Samuel Johnson

11. The earth is spherical in shape. For the night sky looks different in the northern and southern parts of the earth, and this would be so if the earth were spherical in shape.

> —Aristotle, *Physics*

12. A judgment of acquittal by reason of insanity is appropriate only when a jury verdict of guilty would violate the law or the facts. We cannot say that this was the

situation in Washington's case. Therefore, the district court did not err in its refusal to enter a judgment of acquittal by reason of insanity.

—Bazelon, *Washington v. United States*

13. All history shows that the progress of humanity is accomplished not otherwise than under the guidance of religion. But if the race cannot progress without the guidance of religion—and progress is always going on, and also in our own times—then there must be a religion of our times.

—Leo Tolstoy, *What Is Art?*

14. One could argue that given raw materials of more-or-less equally ideal qualities for axemaking, a simple utilitarian model would predict a wide but more-or-less even pattern of dispersal of axes in all directions from the quarry source. However, such uniformity of dispersal of greenstone [for making axes] from Mt. Williams is emphatically what one does not find in southeastern Australia.

—R.A. Gould, *Living Archaeology*

CONFIRMATION OF HYPOTHESES

I. HYPOTHESES

The first time I baked muffins, they tasted fine but looked peculiar. They were cracked, crooked, wobbly, and peaked. When I told an experienced cook about my muffins, she said they had been baked in an oven that was too hot. This surprised me, for I had followed cookbook directions carefully, but I decided to test her claim. If she is right, I thought, and if I make the muffins the same way but bake them at a lower temperature, they should turn out all right. I baked another batch, lowering the oven temperature 50°. This time, the muffins looked the way they were supposed to, and I believed the cook had been correct in saying that my first muffins had been baked in an oven that was too hot.

This experience illustrates the type of reasoning we will be examining in this chapter. Frequently, we are interested in "testing" certain claims, called *hypotheses,* to learn whether or not they are true. The testing procedure involves *deducing* predictions from the hypotheses and then making observations to see whether the predictions are correct or incorrect. Such tests usually cannot establish hypotheses conclusively as true or false. They can, however, inductively support (*confirm*) the claims or they can inductively undermine (*disconfirm*) them.

Conditional arguments, introduced in Chapter 6, play an important part in the logic of confirmation. Examination of this aspect of inductive logic, which depends partly on deductive reasoning, was postponed until after our study of conditional arguments so that we could better understand the logic of hypothesis testing.

"Hypothesis" has several different uses in ordinary language. Sometimes, it means a guess or suspicion that something is the case: "Our hypothesis is that it will rain on graduation day." Other times, "hypothesis" is used to refer to a belief that is not well established: "The existence of life on any other planet in our solar system is only a hypothesis." Scientists also use "hypothesis" to refer to a sentence that is tested by deducing some prediction from it and checking the truth of that prediction. This last meaning is the one we will adopt in this chapter.

Hypotheses may be formulated about any subject matter. Many hypotheses are causal claims. (We have already said something about using Mill's methods to test causal claims. There are close relationships between the use of these methods and the form of reasoning we will discuss here.) Hypotheses may take different logical forms. Some are universal generalizations: "All human languages have terms for kinship relations." There are also statistical hypotheses: "49 percent of all Americans would say they approve of the way the President is handling foreign affairs." Hypotheses that are not generalizations can also be tested: "A mouse is in the kitchen."

II. THE HYPOTHETICO-DEDUCTIVE METHOD

Most introductory science classes in both high school and college discuss hypothesis testing to some degree. Many texts used in these classes refer to the *hypothetico-deductive method* of testing scientific claims. It will be convenient to introduce this method with a famous example—Galileo's use of the telescope to test the hypothesis that the earth and other planets revolve around the sun.

The prevailing sixteenth-century view of the arrangement of the sun, the earth, and other planets had been proposed 1,400 years earlier by Ptolemy, a Greek astronomer who worked in Alexandria. The Ptolemaic system was *geocentric,* placing our immobile earth at the center of the universe with the other planets and the sun revolving around it. Although the orbits of celestial bodies were very complicated to compute, this system permitted astronomers to make quite accurate predictions of the positions of these bodies over the centuries.

In 1543, Copernicus, a Polish astronomer, proposed a new planetary system that avoided many of the complexities of the Ptolemaic system. The Copernican system was not based on any new observations. By placing the sun at the center with the planets, including the earth, revolving around the sun, the *heliocentric* Copernican system postulated more regular (nearly circular) orbits and accounted for the same observations as the Ptolemaic system, but employed less complicated mathematical calculations of the paths of celestial bodies.

About 50 years after the work of Copernicus was published, a Danish astronomer, Tycho Brahe, introduced still another planetary system in which the earth was motionless, the sun orbited the earth, and the other planets orbited the sun. The Tychonic system had the same mathematical advantages as the Copernican system—postulating simpler orbits with easier calculations than the Ptolemaic system—and it was in accord with all observational evidence. Moreover, in a time when Scripture was considered by many to be a source of information about such things, the Tychonic system agreed with Biblical remarks about the immobility of our earth, found in such passages as Psalm 104: "O Lord my God . . . who laid the foundations of the earth, that it should not be removed for ever." (See O. Gingerich, "The Galileo Affair," *Scientific American,* 247:2, 133.)

All three of these planetary systems were proposed before 1609, the year the telescope was invented. Galileo did not invent the telescope, but he built one that same year and was the first to use the telescope for astronomical observations. Soon after Galileo built his instrument, one of his students suggested to him that if the Copernican system was correct, then Venus, which is between the sun and the earth, should show a full range of phases—from almost dark to crescent to nearly full—similar to the phases of the moon. Galileo turned his telescope on Venus, and, over a period of several months, he was able to observe the full set of phases, as shown in Figure 7-1. (You can observe this yourself with a good pair of binoculars.) Galileo interpreted these data as evidence that the Copernican (heliocentric) system was correct—that the apparently immobile earth actually revolved around the sun.

As a first approach to understanding the hypothetico-deductive method, we can reconstruct Galileo's argument in the following way. His hypothesis is "The Copernican system is correct." On the basis of this hypothesis, a prediction, the truth or falsity of which can be checked by observation (called an *observable prediction*), can be deduced. That is to say, there is an observable prediction that must be true if the hypothesis is true. The prediction in this case is "Venus will show phases."

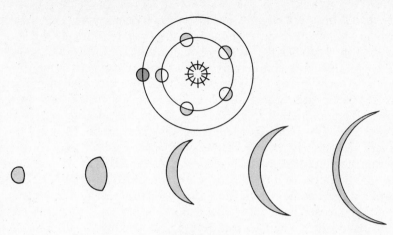

FIGURE 7-1

Phases of Venus

In the Copernican system, Venus can appear nearly full as it passes behind the sun, and its size varies greatly.

Source: Richard S. Westfall, *The Construction of Modern Science: Mechanisms and Mechanics* (Cambridge, UK: Cambridge University Press, 1971). Used by permission of the publisher.

Galileo's argument can be stated

If the Copernican system is correct, then Venus will show phases.
Venus shows phases.

The Copernican system is correct.

Here, the first premiss is a conditional sentence; its antecedent is the hypothesis, and its consequent is the observable prediction. The second premiss says that the prediction was observed to be true. The conclusion asserts the truth of the hypothesis.

The argument, thus formulated, fits one of the patterns of conditional arguments discussed in Chapter 6. It can be stated generally

If the hypothesis is true, then the prediction is true.
The prediction is true.

The hypothesis is true.

This argument is an instance of *affirming the consequent:*

If p, then q.
q

p

This argument form is, as we know, fallacious. A purported deductive argument of this form is a fallacy, unless the argument fits some other valid form.

However, we should remember that arguments provided in support of hypotheses are intended to be inductive arguments, not deductive arguments. The truth of their premisses only makes it probable that their conclusions are true. These arguments are said to *confirm* hypotheses. *Confirmation* refers to positive inductive support, rather than to a guarantee of truth.

Nevertheless, it would be awkward to have to admit that a fallacious deductive form was a satisfactory form of inductive argument. Fortunately, this is not necessary, for the form of reasoning we use to confirm hypotheses requires additional premisses and is actually more complicated than *affirming the consequent.*

III. COMPLEXITIES IN THE HYPOTHETICO-DEDUCTIVE METHOD

The *deductive* part of the hypothetico-deductive method refers not to the overall structure of the arguments, but rather to the *connection* between the hypothesis and an observable prediction that is deduced from it. This means that the connection between the antecedent and the consequent in the conditional premiss of these arguments should be such that if the antecedent is true, then the consequent must be true as well.

1. Auxiliary Hypotheses

Even in the fairly simple example of hypothesis testing just discussed, we must make several additional assumptions to connect the hypothesis deductively with the observable prediction. The truth of these assumptions, called *auxiliary hypotheses,* is not in question at the time of the test, but these assumptions must be made if the observable prediction is to follow deductively from the hypothesis. One of Galileo's assumptions (auxiliary hypotheses) was "Venus lies between the earth and the sun." Another was "The telescope is a reliable instrument for observing celestial bodies." The conditional premiss in Galileo's argument, if these auxiliary hypotheses were stated rather than assumed, would read

> If the Copernican system is correct, and if the telescope is a reliable instrument of observation, and if Venus lies between the earth and the sun, then Venus will show a complete set of phases.

There are two important types of auxiliary hypotheses. One type has to do with *proper testing conditions.* In general, these auxiliary hypotheses are concerned with whether or not all of the equipment and materials to be used in a test are in proper working order and the observers of the outcome of the test are capable of correctly assessing the outcome.

The second type of auxiliary hypothesis has to do with *theoretical background knowledge.* Most hypothesis testing is carried out against a background of some other claims that are assumed to be true. Tests of hypotheses concerning the curative powers of many drugs assume that certain theories of human physiology and microbiology are true. The physical theory of optics plays a background role in any tests that use microscopes or telescopes. When theoretical knowledge is not itself being tested but its truth is assumed in a test of some other hypothesis, it belongs to the set of auxiliary hypotheses.

When we remember that Galileo was the first person to use a telescope to observe the heavens, we can see that hypotheses about the reliability of telescopes could easily be questioned. In the tremendous controversy that followed Galileo's discovery (he was censored, then silenced, and finally tried by the Inquisition and placed under house arrest by the Catholic Church), he suggested that his critics look through the telescope to observe what he had seen. With his remarkable new instrument he had observed not only the phases of Venus, but also the moons of Jupiter and the mountains on our own moon. Many critics refused to look, on the grounds that what was seen through a telescope did not constitute observation because telescopes could not be relied on to show what was really there.

In Galileo's time, the questions raised about his telescope were chiefly theoretical. That is to say, not just the accuracy of Galileo's own instrument, but the principles of optics on which the construction of telescopes were based, were doubted by some influential thinkers. It seemed too implausible that putting together two curved lenses—each of which would distort the appearance of objects—could enable an observer to see far-away objects more clearly. Prior to the invention of the telescope, people had used curved lenses and mirrors for the explicit purpose of distorting images, in a way similar to that employed by "fun houses" in amusement parks today.

It is usually in a context like this, when a widely held belief is apparently overturned by a new test, that auxiliary hypotheses are brought into question. When things occur pretty much the way we expect them to and when our beliefs are confirmed by tests, we don't take the trouble to ask what assumptions are involved. But those assumptions—auxiliary hypotheses—nevertheless play an important part in hypothesis testing.

In the dispute between those who believed the Copernican system was correct and those who denied it, the reliability of some auxiliary hypotheses was unquestioned by both parties. No one, for example, doubted that Venus was positioned between the earth and the sun.

Recognizing that auxiliary hypotheses are important in the logic of confirmation leads us to revise the simple form of the conditional arguments used to confirm hypotheses. In representing the form of these arguments, H denotes the hypothesis that is being tested, $A_1, \ldots, A_n$, represent auxiliary hypotheses (there may be any number of these), and P stands for the observable prediction:

If H and $A_1, \ldots, A_n$, then P.
P is true.

H and $A_1, \ldots, A_n$ are true.

This form of argument is not deductively valid. It does, however, by including the auxiliary hypotheses in the premisses, make the role of these hypotheses in the argument explicit.

2. Alternative Hypotheses

The form of argument to support the truth of hypotheses we have just examined is more complicated than the simplest forms of conditional arguments, but it still does not represent the full complexity of the logic of hypothesis testing because it fails to account for the importance of *alternative hypotheses*. An *alternative hypothesis* is one that, along with the same auxiliary hypotheses, would yield exactly the same observational prediction as the hypothesis that is being tested.

In Galileo's time, three competing planetary systems were proposed by leading astronomers. Tycho's system, which was geocentric even though it was not the same as Ptolemy's system, predicted the same phases of Venus that Galileo observed. Tycho's system agreed with the Copernican system in all points of observation that could be obtained using the telescopes of that day. Our previous account of confirmation, even with the added complexity of auxiliary hypotheses, does not say anything about how to choose among incompatible alternative hypotheses with the same observable predictions. To see that problem more clearly, let us look at another example in which an alternative hypothesis plays an important role.

The question of when humans first came to America is perplexing. It is widely believed that the first American immigrants came from Asia across the Bering Strait, probably over an "ice bridge." From there, they (or their descendants) spread out all over the North and South American continents. The big question— When did this happen?—is especially puzzling because there is a lot of good evidence indicating that humans were all over both continents 10,000–12,000 years ago. Presumably, only rather small numbers of humans crossed from Asia, so it must have taken a long time for this widespread settlement to occur. However, there is almost no evidence that humans were anywhere in North America much before 12,000 years ago, and what little evidence there is has been highly disputed.

Several years ago, two archaeologists (W. Irving and C. Harrington, "Upper Pleistocene Radiocarbon-Dated Artifacts from the Northern Yukon," *Science,* 1973, 179:335-40) made an important discovery that they took as confirmation of the hypothesis "Humans were in Beringia [Alaska] 27,000 years ago." They found mammoth bones that showed traces of having been shaped by humans. Bones can be "worked" (shaped into tools) only when they are in a fresh state. After a relatively short time, they become so brittle that they splinter. Mammoths did coexist with humans for a time in the New World, but they have long been extinct. The worked bones, when subjected to radiocarbon dating, showed that this mammoth had died approximately 27,000 years ago. (The correctness of radiocarbon dating is an important auxiliary hypothesis.)

Nevertheless, many archaeologists did not accept these dated bones as confirmation of the hypothesis that humans were in America 27,000 years ago. They pointed out that an alternative hypothesis could accommodate the dates of the worked bones just as well. This hypothesis is that the bones were from an animal that died 27,000 years ago but was frozen in the tundra for approximately 15,000 years. Then, during a thawing period around 12,000 years ago, the mammoth remains were found by newly arrived humans, who worked the bones. The long freeze had preserved the bones from brittleness, so that when they thawed, they could be worked just like fresh bones.

This alternative hypothesis may seem a bit far-fetched, but actually it is not. In recent times, long-frozen mammoths have been heaved from the earth in Siberia during thawing and freezing cycles. Their meat was eaten; their ivory tusks were sold on the market; their stomachs were examined to see what food they had eaten before they died; and people made tools from their bones. Since archaeologists knew about these occurrences and since, at the time of the discovery of the worked bones, there was no solid evidence to support the presence of humans in that region before 12,000 years ago, they believed the hypothesis that the bones had been frozen for 15,000 years before being worked was initially more plausible than the hypothesis of early occupation of the area by humans.*

We are now in a position to learn how to choose among alternative hypotheses that have the same observable predictions. One hypothesis is considered to be *better* confirmed than an alternative hypothesis by an observable prediction that follows from either of them when that hypothesis was more plausible (or had a higher *prior probability*) before the test occurred.

Prior probabilities—the probability that a hypothesis is true prior to (before) taking account of a particular test of that hypothesis—play an important role in the logic of confirmation. Not only do these probabilities help us to decide which hypothesis among several alternatives is confirmed by a particular test; they also help us to decide which hypotheses are worth taking the trouble to test. If a hypothesis is wildly implausible (if its truth is almost impossible to imagine), scientists are reluctant to spend any time, effort, or money on testing it. Furthermore, if a hypothesis has a very high prior probability—such as the geocentric hypothesis in Galileo's time—then, even when tests apparently disconfirm it, efforts are made to "save the hypothesis" by questioning auxiliary hypotheses. The debate between supporters of the heliocentric system and the geocentric system went on for nearly 100 years after the Copernican system was first published. The Law of Universal Gravitation and the Laws of Motion, formulated by Newton, who was born the year Galileo died, were accepted by almost all scientists, and these laws showed that geocentric systems required motions that were impossible. It took that work—and some further important observations (such as stellar parallax) with better instruments—to finally overturn geocentric hypotheses.

*This situation may change. Archaeologists are diligently searching for remains of early man, and new and better evidence may be found at any time. Recent discoveries, for example, show that humans were in Australia—long thought to be the most recently populated continent—some 40,000 years ago.

The prior probabilities of hypotheses can depend on a number of factors. Previous studies or tests may have contributed to the probability of a hypothesis. The prior probability of a hypothesis that is compatible with well-established scientific theories is greater than the prior probability of a hypothesis that conflicts with accepted views. A hypothesis proposed by a legitimate "authority" has a greater prior probability than a hypothesis proposed by a crank. In some cases, only rough estimates of prior probabilities can be made. In others, precise quantitative values can be assigned, as we will see in Section VI on Bayesian confirmation.

3. Form of Inductive Arguments of Confirmation

We can now present the structure of reasoning that is used to confirm hypotheses. It is considerably more complex than the first simple formulation of the hypothetico-deductive schema, which treated arguments of confirmation as simple conditional arguments. This new formulation shows how conditional arguments play a part in reasoning about hypotheses, but it also exhibits the overall inductive structure of these arguments. The conclusion "The hypothesis is true" is probably true if the premises are true. The truth of the premises does not guarantee that the hypothesis is true. As in any inductive form of argument, there are strong cases and weak cases. The strength of confirmation depends partly on the quality of the tests (a topic to be discussed later) and partly on whether any alternative hypothesis has a prior probability as high as that of the hypothesis being tested.

The structure of arguments to confirm hypotheses can be summarized as follows:

1. The hypothesis is initially plausible. (It has some degree of prior probability.)
2. If the hypothesis and the auxiliary hypotheses are true, then the observable prediction is true.
3. The observable prediction is true.
4. No alternative hypothesis has as high a prior probability as the hypothesis that is being tested.
5. Therefore, the hypothesis is true.

In these arguments of confirmation, there are four premisses. The first premiss states the plausibility of the hypothesis to be tested. The second and third premisses are the same premisses as those in the simple conditional argument form. The conditional premiss states the deductive connection between hypothesis and prediction, and the third premiss states the truth of the prediction. The fourth premiss again appeals to prior probabilities. If a test confirms a number of alternative hypotheses, the hypothesis that is best confirmed *after* the test is the one that *started out* with the greatest degree of plausibility. A positive prediction that follows deductively from several hypotheses confirms each of them; after the test, however, the hypothesis that was most probable before the test remains most probable. The only way to change this relative ranking is by negative (disconfirming) evidence, as we will see in Section V.

4. Confirming a Causal Hypothesis

Edward Jenner's confirmation of the hypothesis that an attack of cowpox confers immunity to smallpox is classic in the history of medicine.

Smallpox is a very serious disease that has long been the source of widespread death and disfigurement. Recently, the World Health Organization announced that smallpox has at last been completely eliminated; there is not a single case of the disease in the entire world. Since smallpox spreads only by contact among humans (no other carriers of the disease are known), this is a significant step toward the achievement of worldwide health.

Smallpox is highly contagious. When a few of Columbus's sailors first brought it to America, whole tribes of Indians, who had never been exposed to the disease, were destroyed by it. Smallpox epidemics were common in Europe and the Middle East before the twentieth century, and the disease was a serious problem in some parts of the world until just a few years ago. Within the last 20 years, New York City was thrown into near panic when it became known that a foreign traveler with an active case of smallpox had spent several hours in Grand Central Station.

For centuries, doctors have tried to discover a way to prevent smallpox. It was long known that people who survived an attack of the disease were immune to further infection. It was also well known that some persons contracted a relatively mild form of the disease. Thus, one method of trying to protect against a severe case of smallpox was to be scratched with the infectious material from a sore from someone with a mild case of the disease. This method, called "inoculation," was extremely hazardous and frequently resulted in the very condition it was designed to prevent. Nevertheless, it was widely practiced in the Middle East as early as the seventeenth century.

In England, persons who lived and worked near dairy farms were susceptible to a somewhat similar but much milder disease, "cowpox," that attacked both cows and humans. The disease was never fatal, and left only a few faint scars. Jenner—a doctor who lived and worked in the dairy country of Gloucestershire—was aware of the belief, commonly held in that area, that an attack of cowpox conferred immunity not only to further attacks of that disease, but to smallpox as well.

Jenner decided to test the hypothesis "An attack of cowpox confers immunity to smallpox." A report of his test is given by Isaac Asimov in *The Intelligent Man's Guide to the Biological Sciences:*

> In 1796, he [Jenner] decided to chance the supreme test. First, he inoculated an eight-year-old boy named James Phipps with cowpox, using fluid from a cowpox blister on a milkmaid's hand. Two months later came the crucial and desperate part of the test. Jenner deliberately inoculated young James with smallpox itself.
>
> The boy did not catch the disease. He was immune.

We can reconstruct Jenner's argument, using the model for confirmation listed in the preceding section.

1. *The hypothesis "An attack of cowpox confers immunity to smallpox" is initially plausible.*

    It was widely believed in Gloucestershire that an attack of cowpox produced this benefit. Dairymaids and others who worked around cows, although very susceptible to cowpox, never seemed to get smallpox, even during raging epidemics. Another factor influencing the plausibility of the hypothesis was that mild attacks of smallpox conferred immunity to further attacks, and cowpox produced symptoms similar to those of *extremely* mild cases of smallpox. All of this made the hypothesis worth testing.

2. *If an attack of cowpox confers immunity to smallpox, then Phipps, who has had cowpox and is inoculated, is immune.*

    The consequent follows deductively from the antecedent, with three auxiliary hypotheses:

 (i) The smallpox matter with which Phipps was inoculated had not lost its potency.
 (ii) Jenner knew how to inoculate, and he was qualified to observe whether or not Phipps actually had cowpox and whether or not he contracted smallpox.
 (iii) Persons who are inoculated and who do not contract even a mild case of smallpox are immune.

    The first two auxiliary hypotheses refer to the conditions of the test; the third is a theoretical background assumption, based on past experience with the disease.

3. *The observable prediction is true.*

    Phipps was immune.

4. *No alternative hypothesis has as high a prior probability as the hypothesis that is tested.*

    Jenner's hypothesis is a *causal hypothesis* (having cowpox *causes* immunity to smallpox). Causal hypotheses are especially difficult to test because there are usually a number of alternative possible causes for what is observed. For example, some persons have natural immunities to some diseases. Phipps may have been one of those fortunate few who are naturally immune to smallpox. The alternative causal hypothesis "Phipps has natural immunity to smallpox," along with the same auxiliary hypotheses, has exactly the same observable prediction: Phipps is immune (even though he is inoculated).

    The hypothesis of natural immunity, however, has a lower prior probability than the cowpox hypothesis. Although exact statistics were unavailable, it was known that natural immunity to this highly contagious disease was relatively rare.

5. *Therefore, an attack of cowpox causes immunity to smallpox.*

    The hypothesis is confirmed.

Exercises

In each of the following:

(1) Identify the hypothesis.

(2) Try to state some observable predictions that follow from the hypothesis. Identify any auxiliary hypotheses that are required for your predictions.

(3) Try to formulate an alternative hypothesis to account for what has been observed.

(4) Compare (in a rough, non-numerical way) the prior probabilities of the original hypothesis and the alternatives you suggest. Indicate the sources on which your probability assignments are made. (For example, you might assign a very high prior probability to H because it fits well with established scientific theories; or you might assign a very low prior probability to H on the basis of your past experience with similar types of hypotheses.)

1. Medical scientists have noticed recently that the incidence of severe heart attacks in young and middle-aged men is far greater in a particular small area of Finland than in any other region of the world. Most of these men work as lumberjacks. Their diets consist of large amounts of meat, eggs, cream, and rich pastries—foods that are high in cholesterol. The medical scientists believe that the diet is the cause of the high incidence of heart attacks.

2. A plastic surgeon who specializes in face-lifts recently commented that his youngest patients are frequently actresses. He believes that actresses seek face-lifts at an earlier age than other women because actresses' faces "fall" as a result of extensive massaging when they put on and take off their make-up.

3. In the chapter from S.J. Gould's *The Mismeasure of Man,* entitled "The Real Error of Cyril Burt," Gould discusses the views of one of the leading developers of "intelligence testing." Answer questions about Burt's hypothesis.

> [Burt] wonders about the intellectual achievements of Jews, and attributes it, in part, to the inherited myopia [near-sightedness] that keeps them off the playing fields and adapts them for poring over account books.

4. On the basis of annual data, Mr. Ehrenhalt [Regional Commissioner for the Bureau of Labor Statistics] said, fewer teen-agers (16 to 19 years old) in proportion to the youth population are working in New York City than in other central cities. While New York is at the bottom in the proportion of its young people actually holding jobs, he said, the city's rate of unemployment for that group has run below that in the major middle western cities hard hit by the recession.

The seeming contradiction, he explained, stems from the fact that a large element of youths here in the 16- to 19-year-old bracket have not been looking for jobs and, in many cases, have probably not even been thinking about working because jobs for young people are so hard to get here. Consequently, they are not counted as unemployed in population surveys, he said.

—Damon Stetson, *The New York Times*

5. Counseling and home placement programs can substantially reduce the number of juveniles locked up for minor status offenses . . . according to a federally funded study.

The study, done by University of Southern California researchers, evaluates a program undertaken at eight sites where efforts were specifically made to help juveniles stay out of detention facilities.

The Southern California researchers reported there was a reduction of 43 percent from preprogram levels in the total number of juvenile status offenders placed in detention at the eight sites.

Their evaluation added "Although this does not constitute proof that the program caused the reduction, since such reductions were part of the larger national trend in any case, knowledge of particular program activities makes us confident that a substantial portion of the reductions can be attributed to the program."

—Howard Benedict, Associated Press

6. [John Ferguson McLennan (1827–1881)] was interested in the early history of society, and charged that no one before him had attempted to reconstruct the social conditions of primitive peoples. . . .

His major item of reconstruction was bride capture, which is still carried out in mock battles in some contemporary societies. Thus, among the Kalmucks, a prospective groom would go to the village of his bride, pay the bride price, and then carry the girl away on his horse, while the people of her village pursued them or made mock resistance. Or again, among the Welsh, the groom and his friends engaged in a mock battle with the friends of the bride, until the latter inevitably lost. Postulating that these customs were survivals from former actual situations of bride capture, McLennan set out to explain why women should have been taken in this manner. He arrived at the logical conclusion that there must have been a shortage of women [due to the practice of female infanticide].

—A. deW. Maalfjit, *Images of Man*

7. A rare Amazon "sea cow," one of only two manatees of its kind in the nation, died yesterday at the Pittsburgh Zoo.

The 200-pound, $5\frac{1}{2}$-foot creature was found dead in its tank at 8 A.M. It had been in apparent good health.

An autopsy by Robert Wagner, zoo veterinarian, failed to reveal the cause of death, but zoo officials speculated that a drop in water temperature during a heating failure Monday night might have been a contributing factor.

"It wasn't an old animal, as manatees go," Goodlett [Director of the Aquazoo] said. "They're believed to live about 35 years." [The 15-year-old manatee had been in the zoo for 13 years.]

Goodlett said the building's furnace went off at about midnight Monday night. Tuesday morning, the water temperature stood at 64° F, he said. The water is usually kept at 75–78° F.

—H. Pierce, *Pittsburgh Post-Gazette*

8. In the following excerpt from *The Bog People,* P.V. Glob is referring to studies of three Iron Age men found in Danish peat bogs, where they had been buried for nearly 2,000 years. The circumstances of the burials, as well as their location, showed that the men had been deliberately killed, probably in conjunction with some ceremony. Bog water, which is saturated with soil-acids, prevented deterioration of the bodies, and the contents of the stomachs and intestines of the three men were examined and analyzed.

In each of these last meals no trace was found of summer or autumn fruits, such as strawberries, blackberries, raspberries, apples, or hips; nor was there any trace of greenstuffs. There are thus grounds for thinking that all three men met their deaths in winter or early spring, before everything had come into leaf. From this we may conjecture that the deaths took place at the time of the mid-winter celebrations whose purpose was to hasten the coming of spring. It was on just such occasions that bloody human sacrifices reached a peak in the Iron Age.

IV. INCREMENTAL CONFIRMATION AND "ABSOLUTE" CONFIRMATION

When tests such as Jenner's test of the cowpox hypothesis and Galileo's test of the heliocentric hypothesis confirm, they usually do so in a relative or *incremental* sense. This means that the probability of the hypothesis *after* such a test is greater than it was *prior* to the test. A hypothesis is said to be confirmed in the "absolute" sense only when it is so strongly supported by evidence that it is *almost* certainly true. (Its probability is close to 1.) Many tests may have to be performed before a hypothesis is "absolutely" confirmed.

Even when a hypothesis is "absolutely" confirmed, there is always the possibility that new evidence will prove that it is false. Before Europeans learned about platypuses, the hypothesis "All mammals bear live young" was considered absolutely confirmed. When Europeans first heard reports of Australian egg-laying mammals, they assumed that the aboriginal Australians who described these strange animals were either mistaken or dishonest. However, the aboriginals were correct; platypuses are mammals.

Newton's Laws of Motion, long regarded as universally applicable and absolutely confirmed, are now—in light of Einstein's work on relativity— considered restricted in their application to particles that are not moving at speeds close to the speed of light or that are not located in strong gravitational fields. To say hypotheses are "absolutely" confirmed means they are very strongly supported, and there is no evidence available that counts against them. It does not mean that there is no chance that they will be rejected in light of future evidence.

Controlled experiments and Mill's methods are often used to test causal hypotheses. Observable predictions deduced from hypotheses may be predictions about the outcome of a controlled experiment. The Method of Difference and the Joint Method of Agreement and Difference are sometimes useful in eliminating alternative hypotheses. In controlled experiments, special attention is paid to auxiliary hypotheses that might affect the outcome of a test. The use of varied samples and the repeated use of Mill's methods play a role in the confirmation of hypotheses, for no important hypothesis is firmly accepted or rejected on the basis of a single test.

Any observable prediction that can be deduced from a hypothesis may be used to test it, but some predictions are more important than others. Consider, for example, the hypothesis that the very large mammals (megafauna) that once roamed North America and Australia became extinct because man "overhunted" them. One "prediction" that follows from the overhunting hypothesis is that these mammals coexisted with man over a period of time. Archaeological investigation has proved this to be true. But this evidence does not confirm the overhunting hypothesis nearly so strongly as archaeological evidence of massive "kill sites" or "butchering sites" would, and such evidence has not been found. In fact, many archaeologists believe that the long period of coexistence between man and these animals counts *against* the overhunting hypothesis.

In general, we can say that the more unlikely it is for a prediction to be true *unless* the hypothesis is true, the better the truth of that prediction confirms the hypothesis. In some cases, it would be very surprising if a prediction turned out to be true unless the hypothesis which gave rise to it were also true. However, a long period of coexistence for humans and megafauna would not be particularly surprising or unlikely, even if the animals became extinct as a result of some cause other than overhunting by humans. We know that extinctions sometimes occur as a result of destruction of habitat—which may be a result of human activities or of some natural force, such as severe droughts—rather than from human predation. Giant Pandas in China are now threatened with extinction due to loss of habitat, despite human efforts to prevent their extinction. Thus, the evidence of coexistence does not greatly increase the probability of that hypothesis.

Proponents of pseudo-scientific theories often try to find acceptance for their theories by pointing to successful predictions based on these theories. An example of this is found in *dianetics*—a pseudo-psychological theory that predicts the remission of neurotic symptoms for people who undergo the therapy prescribed by dianetic theory (see W. Salmon, 1967, p. 119). Many persons undergoing this treatment did improve. However, the spontaneous remission of neurotic symptoms is very common. Many people recover from their neuroses with no treatment at all, so the true predictions of dianetics do not strongly confirm the theory.

Astrology attracts many believers, who faithfully read their "horoscopes," follow the advice given, and note that many of the predictions contained therein turn out to be true. Consider some typical examples of these astrological forecasts, which are printed in many daily newspapers:

> What appeared to be immovable will now prove to be flexible.
>
> Apparent obstacle actually proves to be a stepping-stone toward goal.
>
> Be ready for significant change which could ultimately result in journey.
>
> Member of opposite sex does care, will plainly show it.
>
> Many people miscalculate when judging your capabilities.

All of these "predictions" are couched in such vague terms that they could be applied to many different types of situations that are not at all unusual or surprising in the lives of most people. The truth of such "predictions" does nothing to confirm the hypothesis that our lives are influenced by the positions of the stars and planets.

Exercise

Give an example of some popular pseudo-scientific theory, and discuss the nature of predictions made by the theory.

V. DISCONFIRMATION

Before we discuss the nature and quality of predictions further, we should examine the other aspect of the hypothetico-deductive method—arguments used to *disconfirm* hypotheses. In this connection, you may have heard it said that scientific hypotheses cannot be *proved;* they can only be *disproved.* An even stronger claim, made by Sir Karl Popper, is that induction plays no role in science at all; the only legitimate scientific reasoning is the deductive rejection of hypotheses, using the argument form of denying the consequent. Let us look at this suggestion in connection with the heliocentric–geocentric controversy.

If we assume—as everyone now does—the truth of auxiliary hypotheses concerning the reliability of telescopes and the location of Venus between the earth and the sun, then according to the Ptolemaic system, Venus will not show a full set of phases; it will always have a crescent appearance, although the crescent will vary somewhat in width (see Figure 7-2).

Galileo could have used the following argument to *disconfirm* the hypothesis "The Ptolemaic (geocentric) system is correct":

If the Ptolemaic (geocentric) system is correct, then Venus will not show a full set of phases.
Venus does show a full set of phases.

The Ptolemaic system is not correct.

The observable prediction that follows deductively from this hypothesis—and the auxiliary hypotheses that we are assuming are true—is "Venus will not show a full set of phases."

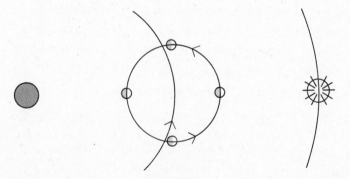

FIGURE 7-2

In the Ptolemaic system, Venus must always appear more or less crescent-shaped.

Source: Richard S. Westfall, *The Construction of Modern Science: Mechanisms and Mechanics* (Cambridge, UK: Cambridge University Press, 1971). Used by permission of the publisher.

In the conditional premiss of this argument, the hypothesis is the antecedent and an observable prediction—which must be true if the hypothesis is true—is the consequent. This time, however, the observable prediction turns out to be false. The argument fits the *valid* conditional form of *denying the consequent*:

> If p, then q.
> Not q.
> _____
> Not p.

Thus, there is an apparent difference between *confirmation* of hypotheses, which is supposed to be inductive, and *disconfirmation* of hypotheses, which can be deductively valid. However, as we have seen in looking at the argument in its historical context, an attempt is often made to save a hypothesis by rejecting one or more auxiliary hypotheses. The Ptolemaic system is now rejected by astronomers; in Galileo's time, however, its prior probability was too great to be outweighed by observations with an instrument that was considered by many to be unreliable. If the disconfirming argument were fully stated, it would read

If the Ptolemaic system is correct, and if the telescope is a reliable instrument of observation, and if Venus lies between the earth and the sun, then Venus will not show a complete set of phases.
Venus does show phases.
_____
Either the Ptolemaic system is incorrect, or the telescope is unreliable, or Venus is not between the earth and the sun.

Faced with this conclusion, most of Galileo's contemporaries were willing to reject the reliability of the telescope rather than the Ptolemaic system. It took repeated and varied tests to settle this issue.

Hypothetico-deductive arguments of disconfirmation have this form:

> If H and $A_1 \ldots A_n$, then P.
> P is false.
> _____
> Either H is false or A_1 or $\ldots$ or A_n is false.

In this argument form, the conclusion follows deductively from the premisses, but it is not a conclusive rejection of the hypothesis. The conclusion says merely that either the hypothesis is false or one of the auxiliary hypotheses is false.

Even in cases in which there is no doubt about auxiliary hypotheses, the method of arriving at the truth by disconfirming false hypotheses has its limitations, because an infinite number of possible false hypotheses may have to be eliminated. A situation in which there are only two competing hypotheses with any plausibility and in which the rejection of one hypothesis "forces" us to accept the other hypothesis is unfortunately rare.

1. Crucial Tests

Occasionally, scientists find themselves in the happy situation of being faced with only two competing hypotheses about a given issue, with agreement about auxiliary hypotheses, and with an observable prediction that confirms one hypothesis at the same time it disconfirms the other. These *crucial tests* delight scientific investigators. Jenner's test of the cowpox hypothesis on young Phipps comes close to the ideal situation. There was a very small chance that Phipps was naturally immune to smallpox, but this was so unlikely that the inoculation seemed to settle the issue between the two real contenders: "Cowpox confers immunity to smallpox," and "Cowpox does not prevent smallpox."

In this case, as in most cases of crucial testing, the test that seems to absolutely confirm one hypothesis and absolutely disconfirm the other becomes possible only after prolonged investigation and many noncrucial tests. It is unrealistic to call even this kind of scientific reasoning "purely deductive," for the deductive rejection of one hypothesis is embedded in a series of complex inductive arguments. These inductive arguments serve to support the truth of auxiliary hypotheses, to establish prior probabilities, and to eliminate some alternative hypotheses. Such work is usually necessary before reaching the stage of performing a crucial test. The following example illustrates what typically happens in attempts to disconfirm well-established hypotheses.

2. Disconfirming a Causal Hypothesis

Different Indian groups, each with distinct languages and cultures, live in the region of the Amazon River. Some of these groups are extremely hostile to neighboring tribes and are constantly engaged in violent warfare. The Yanomamö are known to be among the most warlike of the groups. Many anthropologists have long believed that the cause of their hostile behavior is the scarcity of protein in their diets. The warlike tactics, say those anthropologists, enable the Yanomamö to compete for scarce resources in an environment that is inadequately supplied with enough protein for those who live there.

However, when the hypothesis "Warlike behavior among the Yanomamö is caused by a diet deficient in protein" was recently tested, it was rejected by the two anthropologists who conducted the test (N. Chagnon and R. Hames, "Protein Deficiency and Tribal Warfare in Amazonia: New Data," *Science,* 1979, 203: 910–73).

Chagnon and Hames spent 13 months living with the Yanomamö, carefully recording the foods they ate and calculating the amounts of protein in those foods. They found that the protein intake of the Yanomamö was greater than standard minimum daily requirements—that their diet was not deficient in protein. The argument for disconfirmation can be reconstructed as follows:

1. *The hypothesis has initial plausibility.*
    The truth of this hypothesis was the prevailing view among the anthropologists who had studied these people. This hypothesis is con-

sistent with a widely accepted theoretic approach to the study of human culture, which views the material conditions in which people live as the chief factors in determining their behavior. It is also known that protein deficiencies have various effects not only on human physiology but also on human behavior.

2. *If warlike behavior among the Yanomamö is caused by a diet deficient in protein, then the diet of the Yanomamö will exhibit protein deficiency.*

    This observable prediction follows deductively from the hypothesis and three auxiliary hypotheses:

    (i) The methods used by the investigators to measure amounts of available protein in the diet of the Yanomamö were accurate.
    (ii) The field study that lasted 13 months was long enough to provide a correct picture of the normal eating patterns of the Yanomamö.
    (iii) The "minimum daily requirement of protein" is a good measure of the amount needed to avoid protein deficiency.

    The first two auxiliary hypotheses refer to the conditions of the test. The third auxiliary hypothesis is derived from generally accepted theoretical knowledge of human nutritional requirements—the theory that is the source of information you see printed on boxes of breakfast cereal.

3. *The diet of the Yanomamö is not deficient in protein.*

    The observable prediction is false.

4. *Therefore, warlike behavior among the Yanomamö is not caused by protein deficiency in their diet.*

    However, although the observation that the diet is not deficient in protein disconfirms the hypothesis, it does not conclusively establish that this hypothesis is false. This argument, like the arguments that confirm hypotheses, is inductive—if we regard the falsity of the hypothesis as its conclusion. Deductively, all we can say is that either the hypothesis is false or some auxiliary hypothesis is false.

Some anthropologists have questioned whether the 13-month study was long enough (the second auxiliary hypothesis). Those who study the diets of people who live by hunting and gathering, as do the Yanomamö, have found that there are often sharp variations in the amounts of available protein from one year to another. Epidemic diseases in animals that are hunted or excessive rains or droughts (events that do not occur on a yearly basis) greatly affect the amounts of available protein-rich food. Hunter-gatherers cannot count on steady supplies when environmental conditions are unusually severe. This particular study may have been conducted in an unusually good year for gathering and hunting.

Obviously, the testing conducted during the 13-month study was significant and important. However, this one result is not enough to convince those who believe that the prior probability of the protein-deficiency hypothesis is very high. Additional tests, carried out over a period of years, would (if the results were similar to the results of the 13-month study) eventually overturn the hypothesis. In a situation such as this one, it is difficult to see what sort of crucial test could be devised to help us choose between the hypothesis being tested and some other hypothesis. No other causal hypothesis (except the negative "Warlike behavior is not caused by protein deficiency") was even formulated in this study.

Exercises

For each of the following, identify the hypothesis that is disconfirmed and reconstruct (insofar as possible) the disconfirming argument, with reference to plausibility, disconfirming observations, and alternative hypotheses.

1. A student tells the teacher that a family crisis may require a trip out of town at the time of the next class period, when a test is scheduled. The student fails to appear for the test, and the teacher surmises that the student left town to deal with the crisis. Then, immediately after the test ends, the teacher sees the student with a group having lunch at the Student Union.

2. You oversleep and are concerned about missing an appointment, so you dress hurriedly, skip breakfast, and get out of the house as quickly as you can. When you return in the evening, you find the front door ajar and immediately suspect that a burglar is responsible. When you go inside, however, nothing is disturbed. The house looks exactly the way it did when you left in the morning, so you stop worrying about a burglar.

3. Cauterization was the only known treatment [for gangrene]; sometimes the patient was cured by it and sometimes the gray slough would reappear. Most surgeons regarded hospital gangrene and the other septic diseases as inescapable scourges, without troubling to do more than to speculate about their causes. Young Lister [Joseph Lister, 1827–1912, who revolutionized surgery by the introduction of antiseptics], however, examined the results of the cautery treatment and reasoned that if some patients recovered and some did not, though all had been exposed to the oxygen in the air which most doctors vaguely assumed to be the cause of the trouble, then oxygen could not be responsible.

—A. Young, *The Men Who Made Surgery*

4. Researchers [at the national Centers for Disease Control] say they are convinced that, despite earlier worries, the [new hepatitis B] vaccine is not linked to the deadly acquired immune deficiency syndrome.

The vaccine, which became generally available last July, prevents one common type of hepatitis, a viral infection that causes inflammation of the liver.

Of more than 200,000 people who have been given the vaccine, only 118 became ill. Fifty-six of the illnesses were found to be unrelated to the vaccine. Only six of the people were seriously ill, the centers said.

The centers found no cases of immune deficiency in people who had received the vaccine since July, and just two cases, both in homosexual men, in the initial study and trial of the vaccine.

Acquired immune deficiency, a mysterious and often fatal breakdown of the body's disease-fighting system, has been found in more than 1,200 people in the United States, most of them homosexual men.

Hepatitis B vaccine, first licensed in 1981, is made from the blood plasma of donors who have hepatitis B, most of whom are homosexual men. Because most of the donors are homosexual men, the centers said, there has been concern that the vaccine could be linked to acquired immune deficiency.

—*The New York Times* (March 21, 1983)

5. In an attempt to make ecological sense out of a diversity of practices, including food choices and taboos, much attention has been given to protein as a necessity in potentially short supply. These various studies identify a particular potential for protein scarcity in a given situation and seek to demonstrate that the ecologically most important effect of certain aspects of behavior is the alleviation of this scarcity. Support for these interpretations has been offered in the form of the almost universal preference for meat over plant foods, a preference that, while not instinctual, is "biologically and culturally conditioned" and makes good nutritional sense as well.

Yet this general "Protein Hypothesis" faces a number of problems. Proteins per se are not recognized by most peoples of the world and thus are not considered in their evaluations. Furthermore, all meat is not preferred over all plants, and preference orders among animal foods do not correspond to protein contents. Certainly, high-quality protein is a requirement for survival, but since many peoples can give reasons for their food preferences, and since these reasons do not include the protein content of different foods, it becomes necessary to explore the link between stated preferences and nutritional consequences that include protein intake. One possible link between the two is the suggestion that, for lack of a better name, may be called the "Fat Hypothesis."

There are numerous examples of stated preferences for fat as a major attribute of food desirability. Animal foods are often clearly ranked according to fat content....

—M.A. Jochim, *Strategies for Survival*

6. *Background information*: Some birds, such as Clark's nutcracker, hide seeds and recover them later.

Few people would want to wait several months near a nutcracker's cache, hoping to learn whether it was eventually dug up by the bird that buried it.

Diana Tomback of the University of Colorado at Denver reasoned, however, that much could be learned from the way Clark's nutcrackers search for caches. She took advantage of the fact that birds leave a record of their searches in the form of beak marks in the snow and the earth where they dig. Moreover, successful searches can be identified by the presence of piñon-seed coats next to the holes from which seeds were taken. If nutcrackers search at random, successful probe holes and clusters of unsuccessful holes should be more or less evenly distributed over landscapes where the birds have searched. Tomback found, on the contrary, that unsuccessful probes were clumped around successful ones. The pattern indicated that nutcrackers were not searching for caches by trial and error. Furthermore, in the early spring (before rodents had found many of the caches), about two-thirds of the probes were successful, far more than one would expect of a random search.

Tomback's observations do not prove unequivocally that the birds could remember where their caches were. They might have smelled them (although again it is an unlikely possibility). Alternatively, they could have searched mainly in places of the kind that are likely to contain caches. Recent laboratory studies done by Stephen B. Vander Wall at Utah State University seem to rule out these possibilities.

—S.J. Shettleworth, "Memory in Food-Hoarding Birds," *Scientific American*, 248:3, 106

7. In 1678 the Dutch physicist Christian Huyghens suggested [contrary to the accepted theory that light was made up of tiny particles] that light consisted of tiny waves. If it was made up of waves, there was no difficulty about explaining the different amount of refraction of different kinds of light through a refracting medium, provided it was assumed that light traveled more slowly through the refracting medium than through air. The amount of refraction would vary with the length of the waves: the shorter the wavelength, the greater the refraction. This meant that violet light (the most refracted) had a shorter wavelength than blue light; blue, shorter than green; and so on. It was this difference in wavelength that distinguished colors to the eye. And of course, if light consisted of waves, two beams could cross without trouble. (After all, sound waves and water waves crossed without losing their identity.)

But Huyghens' wave theory was not very satisfactory either. It didn't explain why light rays traveled in straight lines and cast sharp shadows, nor why light waves could not go around obstacles, as water waves and sound waves could. Furthermore, if light consisted of waves, how could it travel through a vacuum, as it certainly did in coming to us through space from the sun and stars? What medium was it moving?

—I. Asimov, *The Intelligent Man's Guide to the Physical Sciences*

8. Most any textbook [on the subject of pre-Neanderthal man] tells us that the men of Choukoutien cooked meat over hearths, predominantly ate venison, but also ate elephants, rhinoceroses, beavers, bison, and wild pigs, and on occasion one another.

Evidence for the use of fire was summarized by Teilhard de Chardin as so extensive as to need no further comment! In this judgment I must agree, but the evidence hardly justifies the picture one gets from textbooks of early man seated around his hearth roasting meat and carrying on a fireside chat.

The thickest layer of ash in the upper-middle part of the cave deposit is up to *six meters* [more than 19 feet] deep. Stone tools and fossilized small vertebrates—rats and bats—were numerous in this layer, *sometimes indeed forming their own layers.* The ash deposit here is not in piles, but spread out in even layers, apparently the result of water movement. In the lower-middle part of the cave deposit, the ash layer is thicker near the south wall. *At its maximum, it is four meters deep.* It was around the fringe of this ash layer that most of the human fossils and stone tools were unearthed.

—Lan-Po, *The Cave Home of Peking Man*

—L. Binford, *Bones*

Note: The emphasis in the quoted passage is Binford's. His alternative hypothesis to the claim that early man was a cave-dwelling hunter of large animals is that early man was more of a scavenger who used caves, but who did not live in them, and who feasted mainly on the marrow in bones left by animal predators.

VI. BAYESIAN CONFIRMATION

When the hypothetico-deductive method is supplemented with considerations of prior probabilities, as suggested in preceding sections of this chapter, and when the requisite probabilities can be expressed quantitatively, *Bayes's Theorem*—a theorem of the mathematical calculus of probability (discussed in Chapter 5)—provides a formal model for arguments of confirmation and disconfirmation. In this section, we will look at Bayes's Theorem first, and then we will see how arguments similar to those we have already examined can be analyzed along Bayesian lines.

1. Bayes's Theorem

The probability calculus is used to calculate unknown probabilities on the basis of some already known probabilities. Thus, we can use the "multiplication rule" (Rule 4, Chapter 5, Section II) to calculate the probability of a conjunction when the probabilities of individual conjuncts are known:

$$\Pr(h_1 \text{ and } h_2|e) = \Pr(h_1|e) \times \Pr(h_2|e \text{ and } h_1)$$

Sometimes, we have information about a "set-up," such as the composition of a deck of cards, and we are interested in the probability of some outcome that has not yet occurred, such as drawing an ace. Such "pre-trial" problems were discussed in Chapter 5. Other times, however, we may have already observed an outcome, such as four successive tosses of a coin resulting in a head, and we may be interested in what kind of set-up gave rise to that outcome (for example, was the coin that was tossed and landed heads four times in a row a fair coin?). Bayes's Theorem, which can be derived from the four rules of probability presented in Chapter 5, enables us to calculate these "inverse" or "post-trial" probabilities when certain other probabilities are known. To illustrate the theorem, we will consider the question just raised about whether a coin that lands heads four times in a row is fair.

Before we can use Bayes's Theorem, some prior probabilities must be known. In our example, we need to know the prior probability that the coin is fair as well as the prior probability that the coin is unfair. (Here, let's say that "unfair" means the coin is weighted to yield a head on every toss.) These prior probabilities are usually not the result of calculations, but are assigned on the basis of certain background knowledge. If the coin is received in change from the grocery store, then there is a very high prior probability that it is a normal, fair coin. But if the coin is in the possession of a person who is known as a prankster or a slick gambler who seems to be winning heavily, we might reasonably assign a very low prior probability to the fairness of the coin. For the sake of our example, we will assume that the slick gambler holds the coin and that the prior probability that it is fair is only 0.1. Then, since the coin is either fair or not fair, the prior probability that it is *not* fair is $1 - 0.1 = 0.9$.

The next probabilities we need to know are the *likelihoods* that the observed outcome (four heads in a row) would have happened if the coin was fair and if the coin was not fair. If the coin is fair, the probability of obtaining four heads in a row is $(1/2)^4$, or 0.0625. If the coin is unfair (weighted to show only heads when it is tossed), the likelihood of getting four heads in a row is 1. If the *evidence statement* follows deductively from a hypothesis, then its likelihood is 1.

In addition, we need to know the probability that the observed evidence would occur whether or not the hypothesis were true. This is called the *total probability* for the evidence statement. It is based on the prior probabilities of each of the hypotheses that could give rise to the observed evidence as well as on the probability that the evidence would occur, given the truth of each of the hypotheses. Suppose, for example, that we want to know the probability that a white ball will be drawn (e) when the ball may be drawn blindly from either of two urns (h_1) or (h_2). Let us say that either of the urns has an equal probability of being chosen (the prior probability for h_1 is equal to the prior probability for h_2, and both are 1/2). But suppose that the first urn contains 50 white balls and 50 black balls, and the second urn contains 75 white balls and 25 black balls. If the ball is selected from the first urn, the probability that it will be white is 1/2; but if it is selected from the second urn, the probability that it will be white is 3/4. The total probability of drawing a white ball, regardless of which urn is selected, is

$$[Pr(h_1) \times Pr(e|h_1)] + [Pr(h_2) \times Pr(e|h_2)]$$

which, in this case, is [1/2 × 1/2] + [1/2 × 3/4]. This is equal to 1/4 + 3/8, or 5/8, which is the total probability of "A white ball will be drawn, given that it is drawn from one of the two urns, each with a probability of 1/2 of being selected, one of which contains 1/2 white balls and the other of which contains 3/4 white balls."

Finally, uses of Bayes's Theorem require that the prior probability of the hypothesis being tested be greater than zero. The reason for this will be clear when we look at the mathematical formulation of the theorem.

We now return to our problem about whether or not the coin held by the slick gambler is fair. In the following representation of Bayes's Theorem, let h represent the hypothesis "The coin is fair," let $\sim h$ (not h) represent the other hypothesis "The coin is unfair," and let e represent the evidence "Four heads appeared in four tosses of the coin." Thus, $Pr(h)$ is the prior probability that h is true, and $Pr(\sim h)$ is the prior probability that $\sim h$ is true. $Pr(e|h)$ is the likelihood that four heads will appear if the coin is fair, and $Pr(e|\sim h)$ is the other likelihood. Finally, $Pr(h|e)$ is the *inverse probability* that we want to calculate—the probability that the coin is fair, given the evidence of four heads appearing in four tosses.

Bayes's Theorem. Assuming that $Pr(h)$ is not equal to 0

$$Pr(h|e) = \frac{Pr(h) \times Pr(e|h)}{[Pr(h) \times Pr(e|h)] + [Pr(\sim h) \times Pr(e|\sim h)]}$$

(The probability in the denominator is the total probability for e. It is the probability that four heads will occur, regardless of which hypothesis is true. Also, we can see that if $Pr(h)$ were zero, then the value on the left would be zero as well.)

Inserting the values for likelihoods and prior probabilities just assigned into this equation gives us

$$\Pr(h|e) = \frac{0.1 \times 0.0625}{[0.1 \times 0.0625] + [0.9 \times 1]} = 0.0068$$

The quantity on the right, called the *posterior probability* of the hypothesis that the coin is fair, is lower than the prior probability of that hypothesis. In other words, the evidence of four tosses turning up heads disconfirmed that hypothesis, reducing its probability from 0.1 to 0.0068.

Exercises

1. Among 300 freshmen attending a certain college, 100 are from out of state and 200 are state residents. Cars are owned by 50 of the out-of-state students and by 50 of the state residents.
   a. If a student is selected *randomly* (if each student has an equal probability of being selected), find:
      (1) The probability of selecting an out-of-state student without a car.
      (2) The probability of selecting a state resident without a car.
      (3) The probability of selecting a student with a car.
   b. If the student who is selected randomly has a car, find:
      (1) The probability that the student is an out-of-state student.
      (2) The probability that the student is a state resident.
2. A total of eight points on a pair of dice can be rolled the "hard way" (4–4), or the "easy way" (3–5, 5–3, 2–6, 6–2). There is a prior probability of 1/36 of rolling an eight the hard way, but a prior probability of 4/36 of rolling an eight the easy way. (Can you see why this is so?)
   Suppose you know that someone has rolled an eight (this is the evidence), but you did not see the way the dice came up. What is the probability that the eight was rolled the hard way?
3. The object of a game of chance is to draw a white ball blindly from one of two jars, each of which contains 100 balls. One of the jars contains 75 white balls and 25 black balls. The other jar contains 25 white balls and 75 black balls. The outcome of a toss of a fair die determines from which jar the ball is to be drawn. If the die shows a six, the ball is drawn from the jar with 75 white balls. If any other face shows, the ball is drawn from the jar that contains only 25 white balls. Suppose you agree to play the game.
   a. What is the prior probability that you will be able to draw from the jar containing 75 white balls?
   b. What is the prior probability that you will have to draw from the jar containing only 25 white balls?
   c. What is the likelihood that you will draw a white ball if you draw from the jar containing 75 white balls?
   d. What is the likelihood that you will draw a white ball if you must draw from the jar containing only 25 white balls?
   e. What is the total probability that you will draw a white ball (the probability of drawing a white ball no matter which jar is selected)?

f.   Suppose that someone ahead of you plays the game and loses by drawing a black ball. What is the probability that your opponent's ball came from the jar containing 75 white balls and 25 black balls?

2. Using Bayes's Theorem to Test Hypotheses

In this section, we will see how Bayes's Theorem can be used to disconfirm a hypothesis concerning prehistoric agriculture in America: "The diet of people in Ecuador during the Valdivian Phase (3000 B.C.) was based on intensive maize agriculture." The prehistoric beginnings of agriculture are of great interest to anthropologists, and the claim that maize agriculture was practiced at this early date in coastal Ecuador has been strongly defended by some investigators. This hypothesis was also initially very plausible because the ecological setting in coastal Ecuador is similar to many other areas in which there is evidence of early agricultural activity. Although in this case—unlike the exercise in which the prior probability of selecting one of the jars depended on the outcome of a toss of a fair coin—we have no precise way of assigning a prior probability, we do know that the prior probability is rather high, so we will assign 0.7 to it. Then, the prior probability that the diet was not agriculturally based is $1 - 0.7 = 0.3$. Bayes's Theorem formally requires that $\Pr(h)$ be greater than zero, and this is reflected in our informal requirement that there is at least some plausibility for the hypothesis to be tested.

Anthropologists learn some things about the diets of prehistoric peoples by examining their skeletal teeth. Dental caries (cavities), for example, are most frequent and severe in people whose diets are agriculturally based, less severe in gathering-collecting-hunting peoples, and least severe among strictly meat-eating hunters. (This is an important auxiliary hypothesis.)

The agricultural hypothesis was tested by a physical anthropologist, Christy Turner ("Dental Caries and Early Ecuadorian Agriculture," *American Antiquity*, 1978, 43:694–96), whose evidence consisted of a sample of 76 teeth recovered from six crania of individuals who had been buried in a Valdivian-period cemetery. These individuals were judged to have lived to an age at which they would be susceptible to caries (another auxiliary hypothesis). Two additional auxiliary hypotheses were stated by Turner:

(i)   Maize, as it is usually prepared for eating, has strong cariogenic potential (clings to the teeth and causes cavities).

(ii) T.D. Stewart's dental pathology review (*American Journal of Anthropology*, 1931) provides a good measure for incidence of dental caries among prehistoric Central American Indians whose diet was agriculturally based. (According to Stewart's review, 15.5 percent of all teeth of these individuals have one or more carious lesions.)

Using the agricultural hypothesis and these auxiliaries, the observable prediction was that in a sample of 76 teeth, approximately 12 (76 × 0.155) should have had at least one cavity. However, when the teeth were examined, there was not a single cavity on any of the teeth. (This is the evidence *e.*)

Using the expected average of 12 bad teeth in a sample of 76 to determine the likelihood of finding no cavities when our hypothesis is true and making certain assumptions about the randomness of the sample and the normal distribution of cavities in the population, there is only about one chance in 100 of finding no cavities in a sample of 76 teeth: $Pr(e|h) = 0.01$.

Because our auxiliary hypotheses assure us that the incidence of cavities is much lower when the diet is not agriculturally based, let us assign the likelihood of 0.1 to discovering no cavities if the diet is not agriculturally based:

$$Pr(e|\sim h) = 0.1$$

Now we are ready to apply Bayes's Theorem to determine the posterior probability of the hypothesis in light of the evidence:

$$Pr(h|e) = \frac{0.7 \times 0.01}{[0.7 \times 0.01] + [0.3 \times 0.1]} = \frac{0.007}{0.037} = 0.19$$

The posterior probability that the diet was agriculturally based during the Valdivian period has been dramatically reduced by this test—from 0.7 to 0.19. The probability that the diet was not agriculturally based (since that is the only alternative) has been correspondingly enhanced—up from 0.3 (its prior probability) to 0.81.

The role of alternative hypotheses, which was not explicit in the hypothetico-deductive method, is apparent in Bayesian confirmation. To know what support some piece of evidence lends to a hypothesis, we need to know how probable the evidence would be if the hypothesis were false—that is, if some alternative hypothesis were true. For simplicity in our example, we considered only two alternatives, but we could have treated each alternate hypothesis about subsistence strategy (hunter-gatherer-collector, hunter, and agriculturalist) separately by assigning each one a prior probability and considering the likelihood that the evidence would occur for each case.

Bayes's Theorem helps us to understand why some tests are more valuable for confirming or disconfirming hypotheses than other tests. The evidence of no cavities is particularly damaging to the hypothesis because this would be so unlikely (only one chance in 100) if the hypothesis were true. Furthermore, there are many cases of hypotheses that we would like to test, but that do not deductively imply any observable predictions even when we consider the auxiliary hypotheses. In these cases, it is reasonable to ask how *likely* (or probable) a certain prediction would be if the hypothesis were true or if some alternative hypothesis were true. Bayes's Theorem helps us to see how these *likelihoods* raise or lower posterior probabilities by various amounts. The posterior probability is not as affected by an outcome that is very likely to occur whether or not the hypothesis is true as it is affected by an outcome that would be very surprising unless the hypothesis were true. Compared to the hypothetico-deductive method, this Bayesian pattern, or model, for arguments of confirmation and disconfirmation seems to capture much better our insights and intuitions about using the outcomes of predictions to judge whether a hypothesis is true or false.

Exercises

1. Breast cancer strikes approximately one out of every ten American women between the ages of 30 and 60. Early detection is important to prevent fatalities. Suppose that doctors develop an early-warning screening test that is inexpensive and "noninvasive" (it does not involve X-rays or any surgical technique). When the test is negative, the patient almost certainly does not have incipient breast cancer. However, in about 40 percent of all cases with a positive test result, no cancer is present. When a test is positive, the patient is advised to undergo further testing with X-rays. Mrs. Griffen, age 40, has no symptoms but is considering having the screening test performed.
   a. What is the prior probability that Mrs. Griffen will contract breast cancer?
   b. Suppose that Mrs. Griffen has the test and that the result is positive. What is the probability that she has breast cancer?
2. Suppose you see an announcement that all cars of your make and model are being recalled due to a suspension problem. These models were produced at two plants: X and Y. You have no way of checking to determine which plant produced your model, but plant X produced about 80 percent of the make and model of your car, whereas plant Y produced only 20 percent. The automobile manufacturer estimates that about 90 percent of the models produced by plant Y have the suspension problem but that only 50 percent of the models produced by plant X have this problem.
   a. What is the probability that the suspension in your car will be defective?
   b. Suppose you take your car in to be tested and find out that the suspension is defective. What is the probability that your car was produced by plant X?
3. Based on recent statistics, the probability that a smoker who lives in a rural area will die of lung cancer is 0.00065 and the probability that a smoker from an urban area will die of lung cancer is 0.00085. The probability that a nonsmoker from an urban area will die of lung cancer is 0.00015; the probability that a rural nonsmoker will die of lung cancer is 0.00001. Approximately 70 percent of the population lives in urban areas, and about 30 percent lives in rural areas. Assume that 20 percent of urban dwellers are smokers and that 10 percent of rural dwellers are smokers.
   a. What is the probability that an urban dweller will die of lung cancer?
   b. What is the probability that a person from a rural area will die of lung cancer?
   c. Given only the information that a person died of lung cancer, what is the probability that this person was an urban dweller?
   d. Given only the information that an urban dweller died of lung cancer, what is the probability that this person was a smoker?

4. A murder has been committed, and the police have brought in two suspects on the basis of circumstantial evidence. The suspects are similar in physical appearance, but one is a redhead and the other has brown hair. The police feel that one of the two suspects almost certainly committed the crime, but they think there is a greater chance (80 percent) that the redhead, who has a previous record, is guilty. A witness who saw someone running from the scene of the crime says that the person had brown hair, so the brunette is brought to trial. The defense attorney insists that the witness be tested for reliability, and a test is set up. In lighting and other circumstances similar to those in which the crime occurred, the witness identifies redheads of similar size and body build as brunettes in 90 percent of the cases.

   a. Taking the performance of the witness into account and accepting the prior probabilities offered by the police, what is the probability that the brunette is guilty?

   b. If the witness had correctly distinguished the redhead from the brunette in 50 percent of the test cases, what would the probability that the brunette is guilty have been?

VII. REVIEW

This chapter provides an introduction to the logic of *confirmation*. This methodology is based on the concept that certain claims that are not accessible to direct observation can be inductively supported or undermined by checking the truth or falsity of *observable predictions* based on those claims. Confirmation is of the utmost importance in scientific reasoning, and is also commonly used in everyday life. Confirmation often employs deductive arguments as well as inductive arguments, but its overall structure is inductive. The conclusions reached by using this form of reasoning may be false even though the premises are all true. This is to be expected, since these arguments make claims about what is unobserved on the basis of observations; future observations can lead us to reject claims that we currently consider to be highly confirmed. Several formulations of the *hypothetico-deductive method of confirmation* were considered, but these were shown to be inadequate and were rejected in favor of a *Bayesian model of confirmation*, developed informally in Section III and formally in Section VI.

Brief definitions of the key concepts examined in this chapter follow.

Alternative Hypotheses: Hypotheses that are distinct from the hypothesis being tested but that could yield the same observable predictions.

Auxiliary Hypotheses: Claims (often unstated) that are assumed to be true in the context of a test of a hypothesis. Auxiliary hypotheses are used in conjunction with the hypothesis being tested to derive observable predictions. There are two chief categories of auxiliary hypotheses: (1) those that claim that the conditions of the experiment or observation are "normal" (that reliable instruments are used by competent observers, etc.), and (2) theoretical auxiliary hypotheses that assume the truth of background theories.

Bayesian Confirmation: A method of confirmation that, like the hypothetico-deductive method, considers the observable predictions derived from the hypothesis and the auxiliary hypotheses. In addition, Bayesian confirmation requires taking into account the prior probabilities not only of the hypothesis being tested but also of the alternative hypotheses. A true prediction confirms the hypothesis if that hypothesis had a higher prior probability than any of the alternative hypotheses. This method of confirmation also accommodates observable predictions that follow inductively rather than deductively from the hypothesis and the auxiliary hypotheses. When numerical values can be assigned to certain probabilities, *Bayes's Theorem* provides a quantitative model for Bayesian confirmation.

Confirmation: Positive inductive support for hypotheses. "Confirmation" can be used in either an *incremental* or an "absolute" sense. Hypotheses are incrementally confirmed by tests that raise their probability. Hypotheses are considered to be "absolutely" confirmed only when there is overwhelmingly strong support for them and when there is no available evidence against them. However, it is always possible for an "absolutely" confirmed hypothesis to turn out to be false.

Crucial Test: A test used when only two incompatible hypotheses are plausible and the outcome of a particular test would confirm one hypothesis and disconfirm the other.

Disconfirmation: When predictions based on hypotheses are observed to be false, the hypotheses are said to be "disconfirmed." "Disconfirmation" can be used in either an incremental or an "absolute" sense.

Hypothesis: Any claim about the unobserved that is tested by considering observable predictions derived from the hypothesis.

Hypothetico-Deductive Method: A method of confirming hypotheses that requires that an observable prediction be deduced from the hypothesis being tested, along with any auxiliary hypotheses. If the prediction is true, the hypothesis is confirmed. If the prediction is false, the hypothesis is disconfirmed.

Likelihood: The probability that the observable prediction (the evidence) would be true if the hypothesis were true and if the alternative hypotheses were true; employed when using Bayes's Theorem as a model of confirmation.

Posterior Probability: The probability that a hypothesis is true after taking into account the results of a particular test; employed when using Bayes's Theorem as a model of confirmation. If the posterior probability is higher than the prior probability, the hypothesis is confirmed. If the posterior probability is lower than the prior probability, the hypothesis is disconfirmed.

Prior Probability: The probability of a hypothesis before taking into account the results of a particular test or observation.

VIII. EXERCISES

The following set of true–false questions is designed to check your understanding of some of the basic concepts introduced in Chapter 7.

1. The facts that some hypothesis is similar to other well-supported scientific hypotheses and that it does not conflict with any well-confirmed hypotheses are relevant to determining its prior probability.

2. Prior probabilities can be based on objective evidence rather than on personal beliefs about how likely a hypothesis is to be true.

3. All we need to know to determine whether a hypothesis is well-confirmed is whether or not it has any true observable predictions.

4. In assessing arguments for the truth of a hypothesis, we must consider whether any alternative hypotheses are strongly confirmed by the observable evidence.

5. Observable evidence can establish any scientific hypothesis as conclusively true or false.

6. In the hypothetico-deductive method, the argument from the truth of the observable prediction to the truth of the hypothesis is inductive.

7. In most cases, an observable prediction may be deduced directly from a scientific hypothesis without any additional assumptions as premises.

8. No matter how carefully a scientific hypothesis is tested, there is always a possibility that it may be rejected later in light of the discovery of new evidence.

9. In most cases, there is only one scientific hypothesis that is compatible with all the available evidence.

10. There are no degrees of confirmation. A hypothesis is either totally confirmed or totally disconfirmed by the evidence.

11. It is always possible to construct and carry out a crucial test to determine once and for all which of two competing hypotheses is correct.

12. A scientific hypothesis is usually nothing more than a summary of the observable evidence on which it rests.

13. When testing a hypothesis, we simply assume that all of the auxiliary hypotheses required to support the observable prediction are true. In other circumstances, however, hypotheses that are used as auxiliaries may be subjected to tests.

14. If the prior probability of a hypothesis is zero, then it is not suitable for testing using the Bayesian method of confirmation, because its posterior probability will be zero as well.

15. A hypothesis may have a very low prior probability initially but may become strongly confirmed as a result of repeated favorable tests.

16. If a hypothesis has a very high prior probability, then one unfavorable test result will not necessarily absolutely disconfirm it.

ARGUMENTS IN WHICH VALIDITY DEPENDS ON CONNECTIONS AMONG SENTENCES

I. INTRODUCTION

In this chapter, we will again take up the analysis of arguments in which validity depends on *truth-functional* connections among sentences. We have already discussed *affirming the antecedent* (*modus ponens*) and *denying the consequent* (*modus tollens*), as well as the fallacious forms that mimic these valid forms of inference. Two sentential connectives—"if . . . then" and "not"—were introduced in Chapter 6, and their truth-functional meanings were presented in truth tables there.

Other connectives (terms used to form complex sentences)—"or," "and," and "if and only if" can be assigned truth-functional definitions also, thereby allowing a large class of English-language arguments to be analyzed in truth-functional terms. We will begin by introducing a few more common forms of truth-functional arguments, and then present a general method for determining the validity or invalidity of *any* argument form in which validity depends on truth-functional connections.

It may be useful to point out that this area of logic, called "truth-functional logic," "sentential logic," or "propositional logic," is based on two important principles:

1. Every sentence is either true or false.
2. No sentence is both true and false.

The first principle is sometimes called *the principle of the excluded middle*; the second principle, *the principle of contradiction.* The first principle assures us that a sentence such as "It is raining" is either true or false; the second principle assures us that the sentence "It is raining" cannot be both true and false. It should be understood that these principles apply to declarative sentences in a *specific context of utterance.* For example, the time and place to which the claim "It is raining" refers is either understood or expressed. If this were spelled out explicitly, the sentence would be something like "It is raining on March 15, 1984, in Washington Square in New York City." Obviously, the sentence "It is raining" is true when it applies to places and times when it is raining, and it is false when it applies to places and times when there is no rain, but when the sentence is understood as referring to a particular time or place, the principles apply. Some sentences (generalizations) are understood as implicitly referring to all times and all places ("All men are mortal"). Properly understood, the principles of the excluded middle and contradiction seem obvious enough, and we will accept them in our study of logic.

1. Hypothetical Syllogisms

Hypothetical syllogisms have two conditional premisses, and a conditional conclusion. The following argument is an example of a hypothetical syllogism:

If inflation can be controlled, then businesses will expand.
If businesses expand, then unemployment will decrease.

If inflation can be controlled, then unemployment will decrease.

As in the conditional arguments discussed in Chapter 6, these conditional sentences are treated as *material conditionals.* The connective "if . . . then" yields a false complex sentence only if the antecedent is true and the consequent is false. We can represent the form of this argument by letting p, q, and r stand for the antecedents and consequents in the premisses and conclusion, using the same letter for the same simple sentence in each case:

If p, then q.
If q, then r.

If p, then r.

For this argument form to be *invalid*, it must be possible for the conclusion to be false while both premisses are true. However, this is impossible, since the only way the conclusion could be false would be for p to be true while r is false. But if p is true, then q must also be true for the first premiss to be true. If the second premiss has a true antecedent (q), then its consequent (r) must also be true, or it will not be a true premiss.

In other words, if p is true, the sentence represented by r would have to be categorized as "false" in the conclusion and as "true" in the second premiss for this argument form to be invalid. But no sentence can be both true and false, so the argument form is valid. The English argument just presented is an instance of this valid form, so it is a valid argument.

2. Dilemmas

In English, the term *dilemma* is often used to refer to a situation in which a choice between two disagreeable alternatives must be faced ("Tom is in a dilemma; he must either give up the big party weekend or fail some of his midterms next week"). The original meaning of the term "dilemma" refers to a form of argument in which one of the premisses states the choice between the two alternatives. The two meanings are connected, for someone like Tom who is in a dilemma often faces the following sort of argument:

If I spend the weekend partying, then I will fail some midterms.
If I spend the weekend studying, then I will miss out on some good times.
I will party this weekend, or I will study.

I will fail some midterms, or I will miss out on some good times.

This argument is valid. (Remember that for an argument to be valid, the premisses do not have to be true. If it is impossible for the argument to have all true premisses and a false conclusion, then the argument is valid.)

You have probably noticed that this argument is similar to, but slightly more complicated than, arguments that take the form of "affirming the antecedent." In this dilemma form of argument, called the *constructive dilemma,* there are two conditional premisses. The third premiss states that one or the other of the antecedents is true, and the conclusion states that one or the other of the consequents is true. Using letters to represent simple sentences, this form of argument can be symbolized:

> If *p*, then *q*.
> If *r*, then *s*.
> *p* or *r*.
> ———————
> *q* or *s*.

Before we show that this argument form is valid, we need to consider the truth-functional meaning of the sentential connective "or." Complex sentences that are connected by "or" are called *disjunctions*. Disjunctions may be *exclusive,* in which case "or" is roughly interpreted "one or the other, but not both." When a menu says "Soup or salad is included in the price of the meal," we understand that the disjunction is exclusive. If you want both soup and salad, you must pay extra.

Disjunctions may also be *inclusive.* In these sentences, "or" means "one or the other, or possibly both." When a road sign says "This bridge is open to automobile or truck traffic," we understand that the disjunction is inclusive. The English "or" is thus ambiguous; it has two distinct meanings. Some languages, such as Latin, have two different words for the two senses of "or."

For the purpose of analyzing forms of arguments, it is desirable to eliminate ambiguity in the important sentential connectives by agreeing on a single meaning. Logicians have selected the inclusive sense of "or," since any arguments that are valid based on this interpretation remain valid when "or" is interpreted exclusively, but not vice-versa. The truth-functional meaning of "or" is given in the following table, where *p* and *q* represent any two sentences:

p	*q*	*p* or *q*
True	True	True
True	False	True
False	True	True
False	False	False

The table can be summarized by noting that a disjunction is true whenever one or both of its components (*disjuncts*) is true, and false only when both disjuncts are false.

Now we can see that this dilemma form of argument is valid, for when the truth-functional meanings of "if . . . then" and "or" are adopted, if all the premisses are true, the conclusion must be true as well. For the disjunctive premiss (p or r) to be true, at least one of its disjuncts must be true. Then, the conditional premiss that has that disjunct as its antecedent must have a true consequent to be true. But this means that either q or s (the conclusion) is true if all of the premisses are true. The English argument representing Tom's dilemma is valid, since it is an instance of a valid argument form.

Another version of the dilemma, called the *destructive dilemma*, is closely related to *denying the consequent* (*modus tollens*). Here is an example of an English-language argument that is an instance of a destructive dilemma:

> If the reporter was doing his job, he was present at the political meeting.
> If the reporter is intelligent, he would have known what was happening there.
> Either the reporter wasn't present at the meeting, or he didn't know what was happening there.
> _____
> Either the reporter wasn't doing his job, or he isn't intelligent.

The form of this argument is represented below:

$$\begin{array}{l} \text{If } p, \text{ then } q. \\ \text{If } r, \text{ then } s. \\ \text{Not } q \text{ or not } s. \\ \hline \text{Not } p \text{ or not } r. \end{array}$$

This argument form is valid. (You can convince yourself that this is so by analyzing the form in a similar way to the analysis of the constructive dilemma just presented.)

There are several other variations of the dilemma form of argument. Frequently, the antecedent of one of the conditionals is the denial of the antecedent of the other conditional, and the disjunctive premiss then takes the form "p or not p." When this is the case, the disjunctive premiss is often unstated in English, since it is obviously true. In many cases, the conclusion is also unstated.

James Boswell, in his *Journal,* describes such an argument, offered by Pasquale de Paoli, the "George Washington of Corsica," when Paoli was trying to decide whether or not to marry:

> If he [the commander of a nation] is married, there is a risk that he may be distracted by private affairs and swayed too much by a concern for his family.
> If he is unmarried, there is a risk that not having the tender attachments of a wife and children, he may sacrifice all to his ambition.

Can you complete Paoli's dilemma with an appropriate premiss of the form "p or not p" and a conclusion?

In another variant of the constructive dilemma, both conditionals have the same consequent:

> If I win a scholarship, I'll have enough money for tuition.
> If I get a part-time job, I'll have enough money for tuition.
> I'll win a scholarship, or I'll get a part-time job.
>
> ---
>
> I'll have enough money for tuition.

This obviously valid argument illustrates another feature of dilemmas. Dilemmas do not necessarily present *unattractive* alternatives in the disjunctive premiss. We can be in a "happy dilemma," facing two pleasant alternatives, as well as an unhappy one.

3. Disjunctive Syllogisms

In *disjunctive syllogisms,* one of the premisses is a disjunction and the other premiss states the denial of one of the disjuncts. The conclusion affirms the truth of the other disjunct.

> Either the home team will win the pennant, or the fans will be unhappy.
> The home team won't win the pennant.
>
> ---
>
> The fans will be unhappy.

This argument is an instance of the following valid form:

$$p \text{ or } q.$$
$$\text{Not } p.$$
$$\overline{}$$
$$q$$

If the first premiss is true, then at least one of the disjuncts (p, q) must be true. The second premiss says that one of those disjuncts is false (p). The conclusion simply says that the other disjunct (q) is true, which must be so if both premisses are true.

A variation on the disjunctive syllogism is

$$p \text{ or } q.$$
$$\text{Not } q.$$
$$\overline{}$$
$$p$$

In this form, the second disjunct, rather than the first, is denied in the second premiss, and the conclusion affirms the truth of the first disjunct.

Because we have agreed to interpret "or" in its inclusive sense, the following argument form, which resembles disjunctive syllogism, is *not* valid:

$$p \text{ or } q.$$
$$p$$

Not q.

Since "p or q" is true not only when one of the disjuncts is true but also when both disjuncts are true, affirming the truth of one of the disjuncts in the second premiss does not rule out the truth of the other disjunct. However, the conclusion in this argument form states that the other disjunct is false.

Nevertheless, the following English-language argument is valid:

Joshua either failed the exam, or he passed it.
Joshua failed the exam.

Joshua did not pass the exam.

In this argument, "or" is clearly intended to be exclusive, because it is impossible for Joshua to both fail and pass the same exam. However, since we have agreed to use "or" only in its inclusive sense, we cannot represent the form that demonstrates the validity of this argument unless we find another way to express the meaning of the exclusive "or." We could do this by introducing a *new* connective (we could call it "eor"), but it is also possible to use the sentential connectives "or," "and," and "not" in the following way to express "or" in its exclusive sense:

$$p \text{ or } q, \text{ and not both } p \text{ and } q$$

The valid form that the English argument is an instance of is

$$p \text{ or } q, \text{ and not both } p \text{ and } q.$$
$$p$$

Not q.

("And" is another important truth-functional connective. Its meaning will be discussed in the next section.)

Exercises

Which of the argument forms discussed in this section most closely fits each of the following English-language arguments?

1. If Roxanne knew that Cyrano spoke to her, she would have fallen in love with him. If she had fallen in love with Cyrano, Christian would have been disappointed. So, Christian would have been disappointed if Roxanne knew that Cyrano was speaking.

2. If stocks go up, bonds go down. If interest rates rise, bonds go down. Therefore, since stocks or interest rates will go up, bonds will go down.

3. Tim has football scholarship offers at State University and at Smalltown College, one of which he'll accept. But he certainly won't take the offer at Smalltown, so he'll go to State University.

4. To pass a logic class, you must work exercises. To get a degree, you must pass a logic class. So if you intend to get a degree, you should do your logic exercises.

5. If the team wins next week, they'll go to the bowl game. If the team ties next week, they'll win the conference championship. But they will either win or tie next week, so they'll go to the bowl game or win the conference championship.

6. Either you buy a lottery ticket for the school library fund, or you care nothing about the library. But surely you care about the library, so you'll buy a lottery ticket.

7. If your lottery ticket wins, you'll receive a good book for a prize; if your lottery ticket loses, you'll be supporting the school library fund. So either way, you'll get something good for your ticket.

8. If I stay up late to cram for the exam, I'll do poorly because I am so tired. If I don't stay up late to cram, I'll do poorly because I haven't read the material. So it looks like I'll do poorly on the exam.

9. If I keep up my studies during the term, I won't have to cram for the final exam. If I don't have to cram for the final, I'll do well on it. So if I keep up my studies during the term, I'll do well on the final.

II. SYMBOLIZING CONNECTIVES

Since we are treating validity as a matter of logical form, our task of formal analysis will be simplified if we introduce symbols to represent truth-functional connectives. This will simplify writing argument forms, and it will also serve to remind us that the truth-functional meanings of such expressions as "if . . . then," "or," and the other connectives are considerably more restricted than the meanings of these terms in ordinary language. The English connective "if . . . then" has various meanings, but we will interpret it as a material conditional connective, since every argument that is valid based on this "weak" interpretation remains valid if "if . . . then" is understood as a connective for a causal conditional or for a logical conditional. Similarly, every argument that is valid when "or" is understood in its "weak" or inclusive sense remains valid in the stronger exclusive sense.

In addition to the following truth-functional connectives:

1. *Arrow* ($\rightarrow$): The connective "if . . . then" will be represented by a "$\rightarrow$" (called an "arrow") between two sentences.
2. *Tilde* ($\sim$): The connective "not" will be represented by a "$\sim$" preceding the sentence that is negated.
3. *Wedge* (v): The connective "or" will be represented by a "v" between two sentences.

we will also employ the truth-functional conjunction "and," represented by a "•" (dot) between two sentences.

In ordinary English, a conjunction with two conjuncts, such as "John went to the movies, and Mary played racquetball," is true just in case both conjuncts are true. Otherwise, it is false. This is the logically important feature of conjunction, and it expresses the whole of the truth-functional meaning of "and," as shown in the following table. (The dot symbol (•) is used instead of "and." "True" is abbreviated "T," and "false" is abbreviated "F.")

p	q	$p \cdot q$
T	T	T
T	F	F
F	T	F
F	F	F

A conjunction can be expressed in a number of different English terms, including "also," "but," "furthermore," "moreover," and "while." Sometimes a semicolon is used to conjoin sentences. These different expressions carry varying connotations. For example, "but" implies a *contrast* between the two sentences that are conjoined ("Jane won the election, but John lost"). "And" is sometimes used to connote *temporal succession* in the sense of "and then" ("Rosie finished the marathon and went to a dance that night"). However, as with the other connectives, logicians ignore these subtleties to concentrate on the logical force of conjunction as it affects the validity of arguments. The preceding table, called a *truth table,* assigns an unambiguous meaning to the dot symbol by stating conditions under which sentence forms containing the dot are true or false.

In addition to the truth table for "and" (the dot), the following three truth tables completely define the other truth-functional connectives introduced thus far:

p	$\sim p$		p	q	$p \rightarrow q$		p	q	$p \vee q$
T	F		T	T	T		T	T	T
F	T		T	F	F		T	F	T
			F	T	T		F	T	T
			F	F	T		F	F	F

It is a little unusual to regard negation ($\sim$) as a *connective,* since it does not connect two sentences, but it is similar to other connectives in most ways. Negation is called a "unary" connective; the others are "binary" connectives. Every negated sentence does contain another sentence (the sentence that is negated), so a negated sentence fits our definition of a "complex sentence."

It will be convenient to define one more truth-functional connective—the *material biconditional.* In English, the expression closest in meaning to this connective is "if and only if." The sentence "The roof leaks if and only if it is raining" obviously means that if the roof leaks, it is raining *and* if it is raining, the roof leaks. Thus, the material biconditional is equivalent to the conjunction of two material conditionals, in which the antecedent of one is the consequent of the other, and vice-versa. Since this is so, we could simply use the arrow and the dot to express this relationship: $(p \rightarrow q) \cdot (q \rightarrow p)$. The left conjunct represents "p only if q," and the right conjunct represents "p if q." However, the relationship represented by the material biconditional is common enough in argumentation to use a special symbol $\leftrightarrow$ (double arrow) to denote it. The truth table for the material biconditional is

p	q	$p \leftrightarrow q$
T	T	T
T	F	F
F	T	F
F	F	T

A material biconditional is true when both components are true or when both components are false; otherwise, a material biconditional is false.

III. SYMBOLIZING ENGLISH SENTENCES

For the purposes of analyzing English arguments in which validity apparently depends on truth-functional connections between sentences, we will symbolize the arguments by using letters (p, q, r, s, and so on) to denote simple sentences and the connective symbols ($\rightarrow$, $\cdot$, v, $\leftrightarrow$, and $\sim$) to denote truth-functional connectives. When arguments are symbolized, the resulting expressions are argument forms.

Sentence forms are symbolic expressions that consist of letters for sentences and symbols for connectives. The relationship between sentence forms and English sentences is analogous to the relationship between argument forms and English-language arguments.

Before we can symbolize English sentences that contain more than two simple sentences, one last feature of our symbolism must be introduced. Some form of punctuation is necessary to avoid ambiguity in these sentences. In English, various punctuation marks (commas, dashes, semicolons) serve to eliminate ambiguity. Certain terms in English, such as "either," "neither," and "both," also perform this function. Our logical symbolism has just one form of punctuation— parentheses—which are used here just as they are in arithmetic and algebra.

For example, the expression

$$7 + 5 \times 3$$

is ambiguous, because one value is obtained when 7 is added to 5 and then multiplied by 3, and another value is obtained when 7 is added to the product of 5 and 3. When the expression is written

(1) $$7 + (5 \times 3)$$

the value is clearly 22. When the expression is written

(2) $(7 + 5) \times 3$

the value is 36. Parentheses tell us which expressions belong together and which arithmetic operations we should perform first. To determine a numerical value for an expression, we perform the operation *within* parentheses first and the operation that is indicated by the *main connective* last. Parentheses are used to indicate that the sign for addition in expression (1) and the sign for multiplication in expression (2) are the *main connectives*. In a similar way, parentheses indicate the main connective in sentence form, telling us whether the sentence form in question is a conditional, a disjunction, a conjunction, a biconditional, or a negation.

The following examples illustrate how parentheses are used in translating English sentences into formal symbolism.

1. Either Andretti won the race and the prize money is large, or his backers will not be happy.

    p: Andretti won the race.
    q: The prize money is large.
    r: His backers will be happy.

    (1) $(p \cdot q) \, v \sim r$

    In this sentence, "either" serves to group together all the components that precede "or." Both the occurrence of "either" and the comma prevent us from understanding the sentence in the following way:

    (2) $p \cdot (q \, v \sim r)$ (incorrect translation)

    Just as in numerical cases, a difference in the placement of parentheses can make a difference in the *truth value* assigned to the complex sentence. Suppose that p is false, q is true, and r is false. Then $\sim r$ is true. Since (1) is a disjunction (its main connective is "v") that contains one true disjunct, (1) is true. However, (2) is a conjunction (its main connective is "•"), and the first conjunct (p) is false; based on the same assignment of truth values to sentence letters, (2) is therefore false.

2. Neither rain nor sleet can keep the postman away, but only Superman could deliver mail in this snowstorm.

    p: Rain can keep the postman away.
    q: Sleet can keep the postman away.
    r: Only Superman could deliver mail in this snowstorm.

    $$\sim (p \, v \, q) \cdot r$$

In this sentence, "neither" and the comma indicate that the main connective is the conjunction (in English, "but"). "Neither rain nor sleet can keep the postman away" has the same meaning as

(1)   "It is not the case that either rain can keep the postman away or sleet can keep the postman away," or symbolically, $\sim(p \vee q)$.

Alternatively, the "neither . . . nor" could be rendered

(2)   "Rain cannot keep the postman away and sleet cannot keep the postman away," or symbolically, $\sim p \cdot \sim q$.

We see that expressions (1) and (2) are equivalent by examining the following truth table:

			(1)			(2)
p	q	$p \vee q$	$\sim(p \vee q)$	$\sim p$	$\sim q$	$\sim p \cdot \sim q$
T	T	T	F	F	F	F
T	F	T	F	F	T	F
F	T	T	F	T	F	F
F	F	F	T	T	T	T

In this truth table, as in all standard truth tables, the initial columns display all possible truth values of the relevant sentence letters. There are just two sentence letters in this case (p and q). The third column displays the truth value of $p \vee q$ for each combination of truth values of the sentence letters. The fourth column displays the values of $\sim(p \vee q)$. The values in this column are opposite to the values in the preceding column ($\sim$ converts true sentences into false ones, and vice-versa). The fifth and sixth columns display values of the negation of p (opposite to values in the first column) and the negation of q (opposite to values in the second column), respectively. The final column, which is identical to the $\sim(p \vee q)$ column, gives the values of the conjunction of $\sim p$ and $\sim q$. Thus, the table shows that whatever values are assigned to the sentence letters p and q, expressions (1) and (2) always have the same truth value. When this relationship holds between two sentence forms, the forms are said to be *logically equivalent*.

The logical equivalence of expressions (1) and (2) is an example of *De Morgan's Laws*. The logician Augustus De Morgan (1806–1871) pointed out important similarities between some aspects of logic and ordinary algebra. The laws that bear his name can be stated in English:

1. The negation of a conjunction is logically equivalent to the disjunction of the negations of the conjuncts.
2. The negation of a disjunction is logically equivalent to the conjunction of the negations of the disjuncts.

3. The conjunction of two sentences is logically equivalent to the negation of the disjunction of their negations.
4. The disjunction of two sentences is logically equivalent to the negation of the conjunction of their negations.

In symbols, the laws can be expressed more simply:

1. $\sim(p \cdot q) \leftrightarrow (\sim p \cdot \sim q)$
2. $\sim(p \vee q) \leftrightarrow (\sim p \vee \sim q)$
3. $(p \cdot q) \leftrightarrow \sim(\sim p \vee \sim q)$
4. $(p \vee q) \leftrightarrow \sim(\sim p \cdot \sim q)$

Exercises

1. Translate each of the following English sentences into the sentence form that most nearly captures the meaning of the English sentence, using the suggested sentence letters and their assigned interpretations. Be sure to use parentheses when necessary to prevent ambiguity.

> p: Logic is easy.
> q: Logic is fun.
> r: Symbols can be used.

a. Logic is fun, but logic is not easy.
b. Logic is not easy unless symbols can be used.
c. Logic is fun only if symbols can be used.
d. Logic is easy, and logic is fun if symbols can be used.
e. Logic is not fun if symbols can't be used.
f. Symbols can be used, or it is not the case that logic is easy.
g. Logic is fun if and only if it is easy.
h. Logic is neither easy nor fun.
i. It isn't true that symbols cannot be used.
j. Logic isn't easy if and only if symbols can't be used.
k. Logic is fun, but it isn't easy.
l. Logic is easy; moreover, it is fun.

2. Using the preceding interpretations for p, q, and r, translate the following sentence forms into English sentences:

a. $p \cdot \sim r$
b. $\sim(p \cdot r)$
c. $\sim(q \vee r)$
d. $q \leftrightarrow \sim r$
e. $p \cdot (\sim r \rightarrow q)$
f. $(p \vee q) \cdot \sim(p \cdot q)$
g. $r \rightarrow (p \rightarrow q)$
h. $(r \cdot p) \rightarrow q$

    i. $q \cdot (p \leftrightarrow q)$
    j. $(q \rightarrow r) \cdot (r \rightarrow q)$

3. Construct a truth table to show that the expressions $p \leftrightarrow q$ and $(p \rightarrow q) \cdot (q \rightarrow p)$ are logically equivalent. This will be a four-row truth table, like the one that showed the logical equivalence of $\sim(p \lor q)$ and $\sim p \cdot \sim q$. Be sure to include separate columns for $p \rightarrow q$ and $q \rightarrow p$.

4. Construct a truth table to show whether each of the following pairs of sentences is logically equivalent. Be sure to indicate whether or not your truth table shows they are equivalent.

    a. $p \rightarrow q \, ; q \rightarrow p$
    b. $p \rightarrow \sim q \, ; \sim(p \rightarrow q)$
    c. $p \rightarrow q \, ; \sim(p \cdot \sim q)$
    d. $p \rightarrow q \, ; \sim p \lor q$

IV. DETERMINING THE TRUTH VALUES OF COMPLEX SENTENCES

When complex sentences are formed from simple sentences and truth-functional connectives and when the truth values of simple sentences are known, the truth values of the complex sentences can be determined. Consider the following examples of sentence forms, when it is known that p is true, q is true, r is false, and s is false.

1. $r \rightarrow (p \cdot q)$ is true.

    This sentence form is a conditional with a simple sentence as the antecedent and a conjunction as the consequent. Since its antecedent is false, it is a true conditional. We do not need to consider the truth value of the consequent in this case, because any conditional with a false antecedent is true.

2. $(p \lor r) \rightarrow (q \lor s)$ is true.

    This sentence form is a conditional with a disjunction as its antecedent and another disjunction as its consequent. The antecedent has a true disjunct (p), so it is true. The consequent also has a true disjunct (q), so it is true. A conditional with a true antecedent and a true consequent is true.

3. $p \cdot (r \lor q)$ is true.

    This sentence form is a conjunction. Its first conjunct is a simple sentence (p) with a true value. Its other conjunct is a disjunction with one true disjunct (q), so this conjunct is also true. The conjunction of two true sentences is true.

4. $(p \cdot r) \lor s$ is false.

    This sentence form is a disjunction. Its second disjunct is a simple sentence with a false value. Its first disjunct is a conjunction with one false conjunct (r), so the conjunction is false. Thus, the disjunction has two false disjuncts and is false.

5. $p \leftrightarrow \sim q$ is false.

This sentence form is a material biconditional. One of its components is a simple sentence (p) that is true. Its other component is the negation of a true sentence, so that component is false. Thus, the two components of the biconditional have different truth values, and the biconditional is false.

The general method for determining the truth values of complex sentence forms is to work from the innermost parentheses out, considering the sentences connected by the main connective last of all.

Exercises

Suppose that p is true, q is false, r is true, and s is false. What is the truth value (T or F) of each of the following complex sentence forms?

1. $p \vee q$
2. $q \vee s$
3. $p \cdot (q \vee \sim q)$
4. $(p \cdot q) \vee (r \cdot s)$
5. $(p \cdot r) \vee (q \cdot s)$
6. $p \rightarrow s$
7. $p \rightarrow (s \rightarrow r)$
8. $p \rightarrow (r \rightarrow s)$
9. $(p \cdot s) \rightarrow r$
10. $\sim (r \cdot s)$
11. $r \rightarrow (p \rightarrow (q \vee s))$
12. $r \cdot (q \rightarrow p)$
13. $\sim (r \vee s)$
14. $q \leftrightarrow s$
15. $(q \leftrightarrow r) \rightarrow p$

V. DETERMINING THE VALIDITY OR INVALIDITY OF ARGUMENT FORMS

Truth tables similar to those used to define truth-functional connectives may be used to prove the validity or invalidity of argument forms. Since every valid argument in which validity depends essentially on truth-functional connectives is an instance of a valid truth-functional *argument form*, the truth-table method provides an indirect test of validity for truth-functional *arguments* in English. Consider the following argument:

> If primitive peoples did not cross the Pacific Ocean, there would not be a strong resemblance between Polynesian artifacts and South American artifacts. But there is a strong resemblance, so primitive peoples did cross the Pacific.

Assume that sentence letters p and q are interpreted in the following way:

p: Primitive peoples crossed the Pacific Ocean.
q: There is a strong resemblance between Polynesian artifacts and South American artifacts.

Then the English argument is an instance of the following argument form:

$$\sim p \rightarrow \sim q$$
$$q$$
$$\overline{}$$
$$p$$

To prove the validity of this form (and thus the English argument), we need to construct a truth table with four rows to display all possible combinations of the truth values of the component sentence letters (p, q):

(1)	(2)	(3)	(4)	(5)
p	q	$\sim p$	$\sim q$	$\sim p \rightarrow \sim q$
T	T	F	F	T
T	F	F	T	T
F	T	T	F	F
F	F	T	T	T

In addition to the two initial columns for the sentence letters p and q, there will be a column for each sentence form that is a premiss and a column for the sentence form that is the conclusion of the argument. There may also be additional columns for complex sentence forms that are components of the premisses or the conclusion. (In this case, we will have columns for $\sim p$ and $\sim q$. This will simplify reading the table, because to determine the truth value of $\sim p \rightarrow \sim q$, we need only look at the columns for $\sim p$ and $\sim q$.)

To check the validity or invalidity of the argument form, look at the premiss *columns* (5) and (2) and the conclusion *column* (1). Note any *rows* in which the premisses are *all* true. (The first row is the only row in which both premisses are true). Now check that row (or rows) to see whether the conclusion is true as well. If the conclusion is true in each case in which *all* the premisses are true, as in the truth table here, then the argument form is valid. If in some row the premisses are all true but the conclusion is false, then the argument form is invalid. The argument form above is valid. In the first row, the only row in which all the premisses are true, the conclusion is true as well.

Since a truth table displays all *possible* combinations of truth values of the premisses and conclusion, an examination of truth tables settles the question of whether or not it is *possible* for an argument in that form to have all true premisses and a false conclusion. By definition, an argument (also, an argument form) is valid if it is not possible for it to have all true premisses and a false conclusion.

Here is another example of an argument in English that can be tested by the truth-table method:

If we drive nonstop to New York, we'll need at least two days to recover, for if we drive nonstop we'll be on the road for 24 hours, and if that happens we'll need at least two days to recover from the trip.

The conclusion is stated at the beginning of the argument, which is an instance of *hypothetical syllogism*. If we assume that sentence letters *p*, *q*, and *r* are interpreted

> *p*: We drive nonstop to New York.
> *q*: We'll be on the road for 24 hours.
> *r*: We'll need at least two days to recover from the trip.

then the argument is an instance of the following form:

$$p \to q$$
$$q \to r$$
$$\overline{}$$
$$p \to r$$

This argument form contains three distinct sentence letters. An eight-row truth table is required to display all possible combinations of the truth values of these three letters. (In general, a table of 2^n rows is required when there are n distinct sentence letters.) In addition to the three initial columns for the sentence letters *p*, *q*, and *r*, the truth table contains a column for each premiss and a column for the conclusion:

(1)	(2)	(3)	(4)	(5)	(6)
p	*q*	*r*	$p \to q$	$q \to r$	$p \to r$
T	T	T	T	T	T
T	T	F	T	F	F
T	F	T	F	T	T
T	F	F	F	T	F
F	T	T	T	T	T
F	T	F	T	F	T
F	F	T	T	T	T
F	F	F	T	T	T

Here, columns (4) and (5) display truth values of the premisses and column (6) displays the corresponding truth value of the conclusion. Both premisses are true in only the first, fifth, seventh, and eighth rows. The conclusion is true as well in these rows. Thus, no row contains all true (T) premisses and a false (F) conclusion. This argument form is valid, and any English-language argument that is an instance of this form is valid.

Truth tables can also be used to demonstrate the invalidity of argument forms. *Affirming the consequent* is a fallacious (invalid) argument form:

$$p \rightarrow q$$
$$q$$
$$\overline{}$$
$$p$$

with the following truth table:

(1)	(2)	(3)
p	*q*	$p \rightarrow q$
T	T	T
T	F	F
F	T	T
F	F	T

Here, the premisses are given in columns (2) and (3) and the conclusion is given in column (1). Note that in this truth table, as in many others, the initial columns do "double duty." When a sentence letter is either a premiss or a conclusion, there is no need to repeat it in a separate column. In the third row, both premisses are true but the conclusion is false. The table demonstrates that this argument form is invalid, because it is possible for an argument of this form to have all true premisses and a false conclusion.

Although the truth-table method can prove the invalidity of an argument *form* conclusively, we should remember that such a proof does *not* show that any English-language argument of that form is invalid. Since not all valid arguments are valid truth-functional arguments, the English argument may be an instance of some other valid form. (Some valid forms, for example, depend on connections *within* the sentences in the argument rather than on connections among the sentences.) To prove that an argument is invalid, it must be shown that the argument is not an instance of any valid argument form.

Indirect arguments, also called *proofs by contradiction,* which were discussed in Chapter 2, can be handled by the truth-table method. In an indirect argument, the proponent tries to prove some claim by taking the denial of the claim as a premiss and then showing that this assumption leads to some absurdity—either an obviously false sentence or an outright contradiction. (In Latin, this type of argument is called *reductio ad absurdum*; the assumed premiss is reduced to absurdity.) Since if all the premisses are true in a valid argument, the conclusion must be true as well, a valid argument that leads to an obviously false conclusion must contain at least one false premiss.

As we mentioned in Chapter 2, in ordinary language, the claim used as a premiss in an indirect argument is frequently supported by an opponent but rejected by the person constructing the argument. Indirect argument is a powerful method of proof in mathematics. Students of higher mathematics encounter this method frequently and recognize that assuming the denial of what they are supposed to prove provides a convenient starting point for constructing a proof.

Consider the following example of a proof designed to show that there is no largest prime number:

> Suppose there is a largest prime number (k). Let n be the number obtained by multiplying together all prime numbers less than or equal to k. Consider $n + 1$. This number is clearly larger than k, and it is a prime number, for it leaves a remainder of 1 when divided by any of the prime numbers less than or equal to k. But if $n + 1$ is prime, then k is not the largest prime number. Hence, k is not the largest prime number.

To represent the form of this argument, we will use these sentence letters and interpretations:

> p: There is a largest prime number (k).
> q: There is a prime number ($n + 1$) greater than k.

The conclusion of the argument form is $\sim p$. To use the indirect method of proof, the denial of the conclusion (p) is taken as a premiss, and it is pointed out that if this is so, it has as a consequent another sentence q. In addition, q has as a consequent the denial of p. The form of the argument can be represented

$$p$$
$$p \rightarrow q$$
$$q \rightarrow \sim p$$
$$\overline{}$$
$$\sim p$$

The following truth table shows that this form is valid:

(1)	(2)	(3)	(4)	(5)	(6)
p	q	$\sim p$	$\sim q$	$p \rightarrow q$	$q \rightarrow \sim p$
T	T	F	F	T	F
T	F	F	T	F	T
F	T	T	F	T	T
F	F	T	T	T	T

Columns (1), (5), and (6) are premiss columns and column (3) is the conclusion. In this truth table—unlike the others we have considered so far—there are *no* rows in which all the premisses are true. Although this may seem to invalidate the form, in fact it guarantees its validity. If there are no rows in which all of the premisses are true, then there can be no rows in which all of the premisses are true and the conclusion is false! There are no rows in which all the premisses are true because the premisses contradict one another; at least one of the premisses must be false. Since the purpose of this argument is to show that the first premiss is false (it is the denial of the conclusion), this should not be too surprising. Any argument in which it is *impossible* for all of the premisses to be true is valid, for in such arguments, it is automatically impossible for all of the premisses to be true and the conclusion to be false.

It should be mentioned that when an argument of this form has more than one premiss, the argument may not indicate *which* of the premisses is false—only that at least one of them must be false. The preceding valid argument is said to guarantee the truth of its conclusion ("There is no largest prime number") because the other premisses are not considered questionable.

Exercises

1. Use truth tables to determine the validity or invalidity of each of the following argument forms. Be sure to say whether the form is valid or invalid.

a. $p \cdot q$
    p
    $\sim p \lor \sim q$
    _____
    q

b. $(p \lor q) \rightarrow (p \cdot q)$
    $p \cdot q$
    _____
    $p \lor q$

c. $(p \lor q) \rightarrow (p \cdot q)$
    $\sim(p \lor q)$
    _____
    $p \cdot q$

d. $p \rightarrow q$
    $\sim(q \lor r)$
    _____
    $\sim p$

e. $p \rightarrow q$
    $p \rightarrow \sim q$
    _____
    $\sim p$

f. $p \rightarrow q$
    $\sim p \rightarrow q$
    _____
    q

g. $p \rightarrow (q \rightarrow r)$
$\underline{q \rightarrow (r \rightarrow s)}$

$p \rightarrow s$

2. Using sentence letters and connective symbols, symbolize the following arguments and construct truth tables to help you decide whether the resulting argument forms are valid or invalid.

a. Either the game has been sold out, or it has been canceled. If it's been sold out I won't be able to see it, and if it's been canceled I won't be able to see it. So I won't be able to see the game.

b. Either Jeremy won a scholarship, or he borrowed money for tuition. But he hasn't borrowed money. Therefore, Jeremy won a scholarship.

c. If it doesn't rain for two weeks in June, the garden will fail. If the garden fails, we won't have fresh tomatoes in July. So if it doesn't rain for two weeks in June, we won't have fresh tomatoes in July.

d. If the public is very interested in a sport like baseball, the public will pay plenty to see the games. The public does pay a lot to see baseball, so the public is very interested in baseball.

e. Professional baseball players can command big salaries, and they could do so only if the public supported them strongly. So the public strongly supports professional baseball players.

f. If I buy a new car, I'll be broke (because of the insurance payments). But if I buy an older car, I'll be broke (because of the cost of keeping it in shape). I must buy either a new car or an older car, so I'll be broke.

3. The following passage occurs in Sophocles's play *Antigone*. Antigone has admitted burying her brother, against the tyrant Creon's orders, and has been sentenced to death. Reconstruct her argument as a truth-functional argument, and translate it using appropriate symbols:

> *Antigone*: This punishment will not be any pain.
> Only if I had let my mother's son
> Lie there unburied, then I could not have borne it.
> This I can bear.

4. Reconstruct the following argument from *Les Liasons Dangereuses* (C. de Laclos, translated by P.W.K. Stone) as a truth-functional argument, and translate it using appropriate symbols:

> Either you have a rival or you don't. If you have one you must set out to please, so as to be preferred to him; if you don't have one you must still please so as to obviate the possibility of having one. In either case the same principle is to be followed: so why torment yourself?

5. Reconstruct the following argument, using truth-functional connectives and the suggested interpretations of sentences:

> In England under the blasphemy laws it is illegal to express disbelief in the Christian religion. It is also illegal to teach what Christ taught on the subject

of nonresistance. [Therefore], whoever wishes to avoid being a criminal must profess to agree with Christ's teaching, but must avoid saying what that teaching was.

—Bertrand Russell

p: You express disbelief in the Christian religion.
q: You break the law.
r: You teach what Christ taught on the subject of nonresistance.

6. Consider the following passage from *Middlemarch*:

Poor Mr. Casaubon was distrustful of everybody's feelings toward him, especially as a husband. To let anyone suppose that he was jealous would be to admit their (suspected) view of his disadvantages; to let them know that he did not find marriage particularly blissful would imply his conversion to their (probably) earlier disapproval.... All through his life Mr. Casaubon had been trying not to admit even to himself the inward sores of self-doubt and jealousy.
   Thus Mr. Casaubon remained proudly, bitterly silent.

—George Eliot

Try to cast Mr. Casaubon's reasoning into argument form, stating the premises and the conclusion. Then select sentence letters, with appropriate interpretations, and construct the argument form that this argument fits. Use a truth table to test the validity of the form.

7. Consider the following argument from *Nuclear Power and Public Policy*:

Now either nuclear power is safe and catastrophic accidents are impossible, in which case no limit on liability is needed to protect the nuclear industry from bankruptcy. If the limitation is needed, it can only be so because successful claims can be made against the industry. But successful claims can be made against the industry only when injury can be shown to be the result of a nuclear accident. And if this can be shown, nuclear power is not safe. Hence one cannot argue consistently, both that there is a need for a limit on nuclear liability and that nuclear reactors are safe.

—K.S. Shrader-Frechette

a. Represent the form of this argument, using the following interpretations of sentences:

p: Nuclear power is safe.
q: Catastrophic accidents are possible.
r: A limit on liability is needed to protect the nuclear industry from bankruptcy.
s: Successful claims can be made against the industry.
t: Injury can be shown to be the result of a nuclear accident.

b. How many rows would there be in the truth table for this argument form?

VI. TAUTOLOGIES, SELF-CONTRADICTIONS, AND CONTINGENT SENTENCES

Some sentences have the interesting property of being true simply on the basis of their truth-functional structure. An example of such a sentence is "If it is snowing, then it is snowing." This sentence is an instance of the form $p \rightarrow p$, and it is obviously true regardless of what the weather happens to be. Sentences of this type are called *tautologies*. Truth tables can be used to determine whether or not sentence forms are tautologous. If the column under the sentence form contains only Ts, that sentence form is tautologous. If a sentence is an instance of a tautologous sentence form, then that sentence is a *tautology*.

Some truth tables of tautologous sentence forms follow.

1.

p	$p \rightarrow p$
T	T
F	T

This truth table shows that $p \rightarrow p$ is a tautology. Any English conditional in which the antecedent and the consequent are identical is an instance of this tautologous form.

2.

p	$\sim p$	$p \vee \sim p$
T	F	T
F	T	T

Any English sentence that is a disjunction with two disjuncts, one of which is the denial of the other, is an instance of this tautologous form. Examples are:

a. It is snowing, or it is not snowing.

b. John loves Mary, or he does not.

3.

p	q	$q \rightarrow p$	$p \rightarrow (q \rightarrow p)$
T	T	T	T
T	F	T	T
F	T	F	T
F	F	T	T

An English instance of this tautologous sentence form is "If there's gold in the mine, then if the prospector finds gold, there's gold in the mine."

Tautologies belong to the class of sentences that are *logically true*. Their truth is a matter of their logical form and not a matter of what they say about how things are in the world. A sentence such as "If it is snowing, then it is snowing" tells us nothing at all about the weather, or anything else in the world.

The meaning of "tautology" in the logician's vocabulary is somewhat different from the common usage of the term to refer to any obvious or uninteresting claim. Because of the empty or uninformative nature of logical tautologies, however, the two senses are related. Despite the fact that logical tautologies do not provide information about what the world is like, these sentences, which are true as a result of their form rather than their content, are interesting to logicians. One widely held philosophical view of the nature of mathematical truths is that they are all tautologies, and few people would deny the importance of mathematics.

Just as some sentences are true by virtue of logical structure rather than their connections with the way the world is, other sentences are false by virtue of their truth-functional logical structure. These sentences are called *self-contradictions*. In a truth table, the column under a self-contradiction will contain only Fs. An obvious example of a self-contradictory sentence form is $p \cdot \sim p$, with the following table:

p	$\sim p$	$p \cdot \sim p$
T	F	F
F	T	F

The English sentence "It is snowing, and it is not snowing" is an instance of this self-contradictory form. Obviously, any conjunction that contains one conjunct that is the negation of another conjunct is self-contradictory. However, there are more subtle forms of self-contradictory sentences, such as

$$(p \rightarrow q) \cdot ((q \rightarrow r) \cdot (p \cdot \sim r))$$

It may not be apparent, without constructing a truth table, that this is a contradictory sentence form.

When the truth or falsity of a sentence depends not merely on its logical structure but also on how the world actually is, it is called a *contingent sentence*. Because the truth value of these sentences is contingent on actual states of affairs, they may be either true or false. Any truth-functional sentence form that is not a tautology or a self-contradiction is contingent. The truth-table column under such a sentence form will contain a mixture of Ts and Fs.

The following important relationship holds between the truth-functional validity of arguments and the tautologousness of sentences:

> An argument is valid truth-functionally if and only if its corresponding conditional is a tautology.

The *corresponding conditional* to an argument is a conditional sentence with the following structural properties:

1. The antecedent of the conditional is the conjunction of all of the premisses of the argument.
2. The consequent of the conditional is the conclusion of the argument.

The corresponding conditional to the form *affirming the antecedent* (*modus ponens*) is

$$((p \rightarrow q) \cdot p) \rightarrow q$$

The corresponding conditional to the form *hypothetical syllogism* is

$$((p \rightarrow q) \cdot (q \rightarrow r)) \rightarrow (p \rightarrow r)$$

Exercises

1. Explain why any argument with a tautologous conclusion is valid.
2. Explain why any argument with a self-contradictory premiss is valid.
3. Explain why there can be no valid argument that has all tautologous premisses and a contingent conclusion.
4. Is the following claim true? "If two sentence forms are logically equivalent, then the statement of their material biconditional is a tautology." Explain.
5. Write the corresponding conditionals for each of the following argument forms:

a. $p \vee q$
   p
   _____
   $\sim q$

b. $p \rightarrow q$
   $p \vee r$
   $r \rightarrow \sim s$
   s
   _____
   q

6. Construct truth tables to show whether the following sentence forms are tautologous, self-contradictory, or contingent. Be sure to say what the truth table shows.

a. $(p \rightarrow q) \rightarrow (q \rightarrow p)$
b. $p \rightarrow \sim p$
c. $\sim p \rightarrow p$
d. $q \rightarrow (p \vee \sim p)$
e. $(p \rightarrow q) \rightarrow (p \rightarrow (p \cdot q))$

7. Using sentence letters to represent simple sentences in English, translate each of the following into an appropriate sentence form that most closely captures the truth-functional structure of the sentence. Use a truth table to decide whether

the sentence as translated is a truth-functional tautology, self-contradiction, or contingent sentence.

   a. You can't win if you don't try.
   b. The rain falls on both the rich and the poor.
   c. You win some, and you lose some.
   d. If you really love her, you'll tell her so.
   e. You're either with me, or against me.

VII. LOGIC AND COMPUTERS: APPLICATION OF TRUTH-FUNCTIONAL LOGIC

The ability to perform many calculations at incredible speeds is one important feature of modern computers. The speed of computers depends on their electronic components; the calculating ability of computers depends on their logical design. Although computers work at remarkable speeds, they can accomplish their tasks only when the problems they are to solve can be analyzed in terms of basic logical operations, such as negation, conjunction, and disjunction.

Following a few preliminary remarks, we will briefly discuss the role of truth-functional logic in the logical design of computers, using a rather primitive adding machine as an example.

1. Representation of Numbers

Numerals are symbols that are used to name numbers. You are familiar with *Roman numeral symbols* (I, X, V, L, C, D, M) and with *Arabic numeral symbols* (0, 1, 2, etc.). In addition to the various types of symbols that may be used to name numbers, there are many possible different *systems of numerals*. These numeral systems are distinguished by the number of distinct numeral symbols used to represent numbers.

i. Decimal System

The system familiar to all of you is the *decimal system*. It employs ten distinct symbols (0, 1, 2, 3, 4, 5, 6, 7, 8, 9). The numbers zero through nine can each be represented by a single digit. Numbers greater than nine must be represented by more than one digit, using the familiar *place system*, which employs powers of 10. (Remember 10^0 is equal to 1, 10^1 is equal to 10, 10^2 is equal to 100, and so on.)

In the decimal system, the *rightmost* digit stands for the number of units (10^0). The place left of that stands for the number of tens (10^1); the place left of that stands for the number of hundreds (10^2); and so on.

Some examples are

67 represents 6 tens and 7 units, or

$$(6 \times 10^1) + (7 \times 10^0)$$

342 represents 3 hundreds, 4 tens, and 2 units, or

$$(3 \times 10^2) + (4 \times 10^1) + (2 \times 10^0)$$

1001 represents 1 thousand, no hundreds, no tens, and 1 unit, or

$$(1 \times 10^3) + (0 \times 10^2) + (0 \times 10^1) + (1 \times 10^0)$$

The decimal system is sometimes called a *base-ten numeral system.*

ii. Binary System

In the binary system, sometimes called a *base-two numeral system,* there are only two digits (0 and 1). The numbers zero and one can each be represented by a single digit. Numbers greater than one must be represented by more than one digit, and a *place system,* employing powers of two, is used in which the rightmost digit stands for the number of units (2^0; any number raised to the 0 power is equal to 1). The place left of that stands for the number of twos (2^1); the place left of that stands for the number of fours (2^2); and so on.

Some examples are

1001 represents the number nine, because it signifies

$$(1 \times 2^3) + (0 \times 2^2) + (0 \times 2^1) + (1 \times 2^0)$$

111 represents the number seven, or

$$(1 \times 2^2) + (1 \times 2^1) + (1 \times 2^0)$$

The binary system is not especially convenient for human calculators who use paper and pencil, because it requires many more marks than are needed in the decimal system to represent the same numbers. However, any number can be represented in either system; the fact that there are only two distinct symbols in the binary system is not a limitation in that sense. Furthermore, under some circumstances, it is more convenient to use a binary system than a decimal system. If information about numbers is being transmitted as a series of electrical impulses on a wire, then it is simpler to have to distinguish only two types (using high current and low current) than ten types. Electrical impulses can be transmitted very quickly, so the disadvantage of having to write down long strings of symbols—as a human calculator who uses paper and pencil must do—does not apply.

2. Binary Addition

Binary addition works just like addition in the decimal system. In the following addition table, the numbers above the lines (rows *p* and *q*) are the numbers to be added; below the lines, the left digit (c) is the carry digit and the right digit (s) is the sum digit:

p	1	1	0	0
q	1	0	1	0
cs	10	01	01	00

To summarize the table, the first column shows us that one plus one is equal to two (10 in binary notation); the second and third columns show us that zero and one added yield one (although it is written down here, the carry digit can be omitted when it is zero); and the final column gives the result of adding two zeros. The information about addition may be viewed in a form analogous to that of a truth table:

p	q	c	s
1	1	1	0
1	0	0	1
0	1	0	1
0	0	0	0

3. Constructing an Adder

To analyze addition as a *logical* operation, we can consider which of our familiar truth-functional connectives can be used to capture the functions represented in the c and s columns.

In the c column, there is a high value (1) when both p and q have the high value; otherwise, the value is low (0). If we read 1 as T and 0 as F, the addition table for c is exactly analogous to the truth table for logical conjunction ($\bullet$).

Turning now to the s column, we can see that when p and q have the same value, s takes the low value (0), whereas when p and q have different values, s takes the high value (1). This is exactly the opposite situation from the one represented by the material biconditional connective. So one way of representing this s function is

$$\sim(p \leftrightarrow q)$$

Another way of representing this s function is

$$(p \bullet \sim q) \vee (\sim p \bullet q)$$

Exercise

Construct a truth table to show that these two forms are logically equivalent.

Now suppose that we have electrical switches that can physically realize the logical functions of conjunction, disjunction, and negation. For example

Conjunction (see Figure 8-1): There are two input wires (p, q). When both wires carry high current (1), the single output wire from the switch carries high current. When either or both input wires carry low current (0), so does the output wire.

FIGURE 8-1
Conjunction

Disjunction (see Figure 8-2):   This switch also has two input wires and one output wire. When either or both input wires carry high current, so does the output wire. When both input wires carry low current, so does the output wire.

FIGURE 8-2
Disjunction

Negation (see Figure 8-3):   This switch has one input wire and one output wire. It changes the current on the input wire from high to low and from low to high.

FIGURE 8-3
Negation

Using switches of this type, we can build our simple adding machine. We want to feed numbers, represented by impulses of high and low current, into the machine on the input wires p and q and to have output wires that represent the carry digit c and the sum digit s.

FIGURE 8-4
Adding Machine (external view)

Figure 8-4 is a "black box" representation of such a machine, so-called because although we can observe the inputs and the outputs, we cannot see how the machine works.

The internal workings of the machine are represented in Figure 8-5.

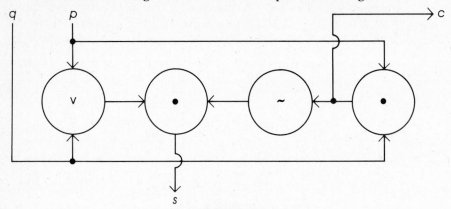

FIGURE 8-5
Adding Machine (internal view)

The simple adding machine, called a *half adder*, is quite primitive. Although it can add any two digits, it cannot add the carry digit from a previous addition. To construct a *full adder*, we need to consider binary addition for three digits (p, q, and a carry-in digit c_{in} from a previous addition). The following table provides the required information about binary addition:

p	q	c_{in}	c_{out}	s
1	1	1	1	1
1	1	0	1	0
1	0	1	1	0
1	0	0	0	1
0	1	1	1	0
0	1	0	0	1
0	0	1	0	1
0	0	0	0	0

Examination of this table reveals that c_{out} takes the high value in rows 1, 2, 3, and 5 (when all three inputs p, q and c_{in} are high, as they are in row 1, or when any two inputs are high and the third input is low). In row 2, p and q are high; in row 3, p and c_{in} are high; in row 5, q and c_{in} are high. Thus, we can express c_{out} as the following function of p, q, and c_{in}:

$$(p \cdot q \cdot c_{in}) \vee (p \cdot q \cdot \sim c_{in}) \vee (p \cdot \sim q \cdot c_{in}) \vee (\sim p \cdot q \cdot c_{in})$$

The same type of reasoning may be used to formulate s as a function of p, q, and c_{in}. The high value is assigned to s in rows 1, 4, 6, and 7. The high value is assigned whenever an odd number of components (either one or three) takes a high value; otherwise, s is low. Thus, we can express s as the following function:

$$(p \cdot q \cdot c_{in}) \vee (p \cdot \sim q \cdot \sim c_{in}) \vee (\sim p \cdot q \cdot \sim c_{in}) \vee (\sim p \cdot \sim q \cdot c_{in})$$

The full adder will have three input wires and two output wires. Using three types of switches to realize the functions of negation, conjunction, and disjunction, the adder might be constructed as shown in Figure 8-6.

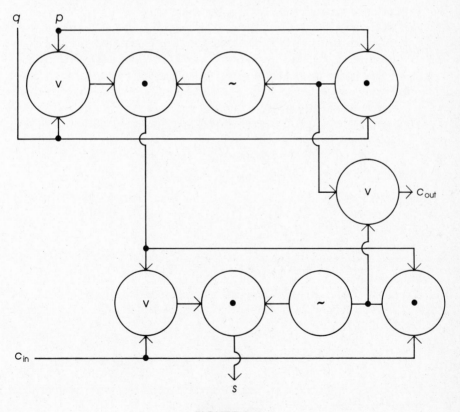

FIGURE 8-6
A Full Adder

Many logical problems of computer design resemble these rather simple problems just presented, although, of course, they can be considerably more complicated.

4. Disjunctive Normal Forms

A *disjunctive normal form* is a disjunction, each disjunct of which is a conjunction. Furthermore, each conjunction contains exactly one occurrence of every sentence letter in that sentence form; the one occurrence may be either negated or unnegated. (The sentence forms for c_{out} and s above are called disjunctive normal forms.) It can be proved that for any truth-functional sentence form, there is a logically equivalent disjunctive normal form. Sometimes it is desirable to design computers using only three kinds of switches (for negation, disjunction, and conjunction). In such cases, it is useful to have a method for translating sentence forms that contain other connectives into sentence forms that contain only tildes, dots, and wedges. One method for constructing the disjunctive normal form that is logically equivalent to any sentence form was first proposed by Lewis Carroll (*Symbolic Logic*):

1. Construct a truth table for the sentence form.
2. Note any rows in which the truth value of the sentence form is T.
3. For each row in which the sentence form is assigned T, form a conjunction in which each sentence letter occurs exactly once and is negated if and only if the sentence letter is assigned F in that row.
4. Form a disjunction using each of the conjunctions (constructed according to step 3) as disjuncts.
5. This disjunction is in disjunctive normal form and is logically equivalent to the original sentence form.

Exercises

1. Construct logically equivalent disjunctive normal forms for each of the following sentence forms:
   a. $p \rightarrow q$
   b. $p \leftrightarrow q$
   c. $\sim(p \rightarrow q)$
   d. $p \rightarrow \sim q$

2. Sometimes computers are designed with just one kind of switch, called a "nand" switch and symbolized by a stroke ($|$). This switch represents the negation of a conjuction:

$$(p \mid q) \text{ is logically equivalent to } \sim(p \bullet q)$$

It is possible to use only the stroke connective to represent *any* truth-functional connection between sentences. Some examples are
   $\sim p$ has the same truth table as $p \mid p$.
   $p \rightarrow q$ has the same truth table as $p \mid (q \mid q)$.
   $p \lor q$ has the same truth table as $(p \mid p) \mid (q \mid q)$.

Using only the stroke connective, construct a sentence form that is equivalent to:

    a. $p \cdot q$
    b. $p \leftrightarrow q$

3. Design a circuit with two input wires p and q and one output wire s, using only the connectives $\sim$, $\cdot$, and v, that functions as an exclusive "or" switch.

4. Many lights are wired in such a way that they can be turned on or off at either end of a room. Use the logical connectives for conjunction, disjunction, and negation to work out a design for the circuit that controls these lights.

VIII. REVIEW

Chapter 8 was devoted to the study of various forms of truth-functional arguments, the translation of English arguments into argument forms, the use of symbols for sentence letters and connectives, and the use of truth-table tests to determine the validity and invalidity of argument forms. The *truth-functional connectives* "if. . . then," "and," "or," "not," and "if and only if" were given truth-table definitions. Sentences that are true by virtue of their truth-functional structure (*tautologies*) and sentences that are false by virtue of their structure (*self-contradictions*) were also examined. The truth-table method for settling questions of validity and tautologousness can be cumbersome if many distinct sentence letters occur in the sentence forms and argument forms that are tested. An alternative method for proving validity or invalidity of argument forms and for determining whether sentence forms are tautologies, contingent sentence forms, or self-contradictions is presented in the Appendix to this text. This method is more convenient to use if more than four distinct sentence letters occur in an argument form or sentence form. In the last section of Chapter 8, an important application of truth-functional logic—the logical design of computers—was discussed, using the construction of a simple adder as an example.

A list of important definitions and argument forms covered in this chapter follows.

Truth-table definitions of logical connectives:

Conjunction:	p	q	$p \cdot q$
	T	T	T
	T	F	F
	F	T	F
	F	F	F

Disjunction:	p	q	$p \lor q$
	T	T	T
	T	F	T
	F	T	T
	F	F	F

Material Biconditional:

p	q	$p \leftrightarrow q$
T	T	T
T	F	F
F	T	F
F	F	T

Material Conditional:

p	q	$p \rightarrow q$
T	T	T
T	F	F
F	T	T
F	F	T

Negation:

p	$\sim p$
T	F
F	T

Some important valid argument forms:

<table>
<tr><td>Constructive Dilemma:</td><td>Destructive Dilemma:</td></tr>
<tr><td>

$p \rightarrow q$
$r \rightarrow s$
$p \vee r$
───────
$q \vee s$

</td><td>

$p \rightarrow q$
$r \rightarrow s$
$\sim q \vee \sim s$
───────
$\sim p \vee \sim r$

</td></tr>
<tr><td>Disjunctive Syllogism:</td><td>Hypothetical Syllogism:</td></tr>
<tr><td>

$p \vee q$
$\sim p$
───────
q

</td><td>

$p \rightarrow q$
$q \rightarrow r$
───────
$p \rightarrow r$

</td></tr>
</table>

Contingent Sentence: The truth or falsity of a contingent sentence depends on its content as well as on its logical structure. A sentence form is contingent if its column in a truth table contains both Ts and Fs.

Corresponding Conditional: Every argument (and every argument form) has a corresponding conditional in which the antecedent is the conjunction of all of the premises and the consequent is the conclusion of the argument.

Logical Equivalence: Two sentences (or sentence forms) are logically equivalent if they always have the same truth value. If two sentences are logically equivalent, then the statement of their material biconditional is a tautology.

Self-Contradiction: A complex English sentence is a self-contradiction if it is false by virtue of its logical structure, regardless of its content. A sentence form is a truth-functional self-contradiction if its column in a truth table contains only Fs.

Tautology: A complex English sentence is a tautology if it is true by virtue of its truth-functional structure, regardless of its content. A sentence form is a tautology if its column in a truth table contains only Ts.

Truth Table Test for Validity or Invalidity of Argument Forms: Construct a truth table with an initial column for each distinct sentence letter in the argument. (If there are n such letters, the truth table will have 2^n rows.) Construct a separate column for each premiss and the conclusion. (There may be additional columns for complex components of these sentence forms as well.)

If there is some row in which all of the premisses are assigned T and the conclusion is assigned F, the argument form is invalid. If there are no such rows, the argument form is valid.

Valid Truth-Functional English Argument: An English argument is valid truth functionally if it is an instance of some valid truth-functional argument form. (Note that a valid argument may also be an instance of some invalid argument form. An English argument is invalid only if there is *no* valid form of which it is an instance.)

CHAPTER 9

CATEGORICAL SYLLOGISMS

I. INTRODUCTION

Discussions of deductive validity in earlier chapters included examples of obviously valid categorical syllogisms, similar to the following:

(a)   No birds are mammals.
                 All bats are mammals.

                 No birds are bats.

(b)   All birds can fly.
                 Some mammals cannot fly.

                 Some mammals are not birds.

(c)   All presidents are politicians.
                 Some presidents are statesmen.

                 Some statesmen are politicians.

In this chapter, the forms of categorical syllogisms will be analyzed and two different methods for determining their validity will be presented.

Categorical syllogisms, like hypothetical syllogisms and disjunctive syllogisms (discussed in Chapter 8), are arguments with two premises. However, categorical syllogisms are *not* truth-functional arguments. Techniques other than truth tables are required to assess the formal validity of categorical syllogisms. All three of the preceding categorical syllogisms are valid. The validity of these arguments, however, does not depend on truth-functional connections among sentences. *Intrasentence structures*—connections between classes named by subject terms of categorical sentences and classes named by predicate terms of categorical sentences—must be considered.

II. CATEGORICAL SENTENCES

In arguments (a), (b), and (c), only four basic types of sentences occur. These are the four types of *categorical sentences.* If we let the letter S represent the subject terms and the letter P represent the predicate terms, we can characterize the forms of the four types of categorical sentences in the following standard way:

1. All S are P.
2. No S are P.
3. Some S are P.
4. Some S are not P.

The form of the first type of categorical sentence, "All S are P," is the already familiar *affirmative universal generalization.* Sentences of this form state that all the members of the *class* denoted by the term S are members of the *class* denoted by the term P. Another way of stating the same thing is to say "the subject class is included in the predicate class." (The logic of categorical syllogisms is some-times called "the logic of classes.") "All Juniors at the University are undergrad-uates" is an example of an affirmative universal sentence.

The second type of categorical sentence, "No *S* are *P*," is a *negative universal generalization*. This type of sentence states that no members of the class *S* are members of the class *P*. Alternatively, this sentence could be interpreted as "the subject and predicate classes do not overlap" or "the subject and predicate classes exclude one another." "No professional football players are ballerinas" is a neg-ative universal sentence.

The third type of categorical sentence, "Some *S* are *P*," is an *affirmative particular generalization,* also called an *affirmative existential generalization*. This type of sentence says that at least one individual is a member of the class *S* and also of the class *P*. (This is a *general* sentence because no member is actually identified; the sentence just says there is *some* such member.) Another way of stating the same thing is to say "the subject and predicate classes overlap to the extent that they share at least one member." "Some dogs are brown" is an example of an affirmative existential generalization.

The fourth type of categorical sentence, "Some *S* are not *P*," is a *negative existential* (or *particular*) *generalization*. Sentences of this form state that some-thing (at least one thing) that is a member of the class *S* is not also a member of the class *P*. That is to say, there is at least one member of *S* such that given any individual member of *P*, that member of *S* is not identical to that individual. This alternate formulation, although quite awkward in English, will be useful in our later discussion of an important feature of the negative existential general-ization. "Some dogs are not brown" or "There is at least one dog such that no brown thing is identical with it" is an example of a negative existential generalization.

1. The Square of Opposition

Syllogistic logic was developed by Aristotle more than 2,300 years ago. Aristotle made the first attempt to formalize principles of valid arguments and was so successful that much of what he developed has continued to be studied in logic classes from antiquity to the present day. Only the geometry developed by Euclid, at roughly the same time Aristotle achieved his results, has secured a comparable position in western intellectual history. In addition to his interest in the validity of syllogisms, Aristotle was concerned with various relationships among the four types of categorical sentences when each had the same subject and predicate. These relationships can be considered by displaying the four types of sentences in a square of opposition, shown in Figure 9-1.

(*A*) All *S* are *P*.   (*E*) No *S* are *P*.

(*I*) Some *S* are *P*.   (*O*) Some *S* are not *P*.

Figure 9-1
Square of Opposition

The letters *A, E, I,* and *O* have been used since medieval times to denote the four types of categorical sentences. *A,* which represents the universal affirmative, is the first vowel of the Latin "Affirmo," or "I affirm." *I,* which denotes the particular affirmative, is the second vowel of the same Latin word. *E,* which identifies the universal negative, is the first vowel of the Latin "Nego," or "I deny," and *O,* which represents the particular negative, is the second vowel of the same Latin word.

Before we discuss the relationships among these categorical sentences, we need to consider an important issue. When we employ sentence forms, such as those presented in the square of opposition, we disregard all *content* in the sense that we do not concern ourselves with the nature of the subject class or the predicate class. All that interests the logician is the relationship between those classes. Does one class include or exclude the other? Do the two classes share a common member? Is there a member of one class that does not belong to the other class? We are already familiar with some advantages of employing sentence forms rather than sentences when we are concerned chiefly with the validity or the invalidity of an argument. However, such abstraction from content requires us to make certain decisions about how terms are to be treated.

i. Existential Assumption

A logically important feature of the *A* and *E* forms of categorical sentences is that we sometimes use universal generalizations in English when we are aware that there are no members of the subject class ("All ghosts are invisible"). We also sometimes use universal generalizations when we *hope* there will be no members of the subject class ("All students who do not meet the deadline for term papers will receive a failing grade"). But if we consider a sentence form such as "All *S* are *P*" rather than an English sentence, we have no way of knowing whether or not there are actually any *S*s. To avoid ambiguity, logic—insofar as it focuses on forms rather than content—requires us to treat the subject terms of categorical sentences in the same way for each occurrence. Thus, an agreement must be reached as to whether or not we will assume that members of the subject class exist.

We have already made similar choices for the purpose of clarity and precision in dealing with truth-functional sentence forms. For example, it was decided to interpret "or" inclusively, as defined in the truth table for "v," and similarly to interpret all conditionals as material conditionals. Aristotle's treatment of class logic assumed that members of the subject class do exist. This decision is called the *existential assumption.* (For reasons that will be discussed later, modern systems of logic do not make this assumption.)

ii. Relationships Among Categorical Sentences

If we adopt the existential assumption (that is, if we assume that there are members of the subject class *S*), then the following relationships hold between pairs of sentences:

1. The *A* sentence and the *O* sentence are *contradictory* to one another, as are the *E* sentence and the *I* sentence.

To say that two sentences are *contradictories* means that when one sentence of the pair is true, the other sentence must be false. Clearly, if "All *S* are *P*" is true, then it must be false that "Some *S* are not *P*." And if it is true that "Some *S* are not *P*," then it cannot be the case that "All *S* are *P*." With regard to the *E* and *I* sentences, if "No *S* are *P*," it must be false that "Some *S* are *P*." Similarly, if it is true that "Some *S* are *P*," then it must be false that "No *S* are *P*." The sentence forms that are *diagonally* opposite one another on the square of opposition are "opposites" in the sense that they are logically contradictory to one another.

2. The *A* sentence and the *E* sentence are *contrary* to one another.

Two sentences are *contraries* when they could not both be true, although they could both be false. The sentences "All dogs are brown" and "No dogs are brown" are contraries, and both sentences are false. The sentences "All football players are athletes" and "No football players are athletes" are contraries, but only the second sentence is false. The sentence forms that are opposite one another at the *top* of the square of opposition are "opposites" in the sense that they are logically contrary to one another.

It is proper to use the terms *contradictory* and *contrary* to apply to pairs of sentences that are not categorical sentences. For example, "My only brother weighs more than my only sister" and "My only sister weighs more than my only brother" are contraries, even though neither sentence is categorical. Both of these sentences could not be true, although they could both be false (if my siblings weigh exactly the same).

Referring to truth-functional sentence forms, any pair of the forms *p* and ∼*p* is a contradictory pair, whether or not *p* is a categorical sentence. (Remember that a sentence letter may represent any sentence whatsoever, although when we were interested in capturing structural relationships among sentences, we used sentence letters to represent *simple* sentences.) The sentences "It is raining" and "It is not raining" are obviously contradictories.

In critical thinking, it is important to be clear about the difference between contradictory and contrary pairs of sentences. It would be a mistake, for example, to conclude "Sally hates me" from the premiss "Sally doesn't love me." Although the sentences "Sally hates me" and "Sally loves me" are contrary to one another, they are not contradictory. Therefore, we cannot conclude that because one of them is false, the other must be true. They could both be false. The English term "incompatible" is ambiguous when it is applied to pairs of sentences that do not "agree" with one another. "Incompatible" sometimes refers to contraries and sometimes refers to contradictories.

3. The *I* and the *O* sentences could not both be false, but they could both be true.

Sentences that stand in relationship to one another in this way are called *sub-contraries*. The English sentences "Some dogs are brown" and "Some dogs are not brown" are sub-contraries; both are true. The pair "Some men are mortal" and "Some men are not mortal" are sub-contraries, but only the first sentence is true. The sentences on opposite sides of the *bottom* of the square of opposition are "opposite" in the sense that they are sub-contraries. Contrary pairs of sentences are frequently mistaken for contradictories, but sub-contraries are not often mistaken for contradictories. When this mistake does arise, it can often be traced to confusion about the placement of "not" in English sentences. For example, the sentences

(i) "Elizabeth II is the Queen of England."
(ii) "Elizabeth II is not the Queen of England."

are contradictories. In sentence (i), inserting "not" after the verb has the same logical force as prefixing sentence (i) with "It is not the case that."

Despite superficial grammatical similarities, however, existential generalizations are logically different from (i) and (ii), and inserting a "not" after the verb has a different logical force than prefixing "It is not the case that." Consider the following pair of sentences:

(iii) Some women are Queens.
(iv) Some women are not Queens.

These sentences are not contradictories. They are both true, and they are sub-contraries.

4. The *I* sentence is a logical consequence of (is implied by) the *A* sentence, and the *O* sentence is a logical consequence of (is implied by) the *E* sentence (see Figure 9-2).

Clearly, if there are *S*s (the existential assumption), then if "All *S* are *P*," it must be the case that "Some *S* are *P*." Similarly (if there are *S*s), if "No *S* are *P*," then it must be the case that "Some *S* are not *P*."

This relationship between the *A* and *I* sentences and between the *E* and *O* sentences is called *sub-implication,* because the sentences at the top of the square of opposition *imply* the sentences below them. If the *A* sentence is true, then the *I* sentence must be true as well; if the *E* sentence is true, then the *O* sentence must be true also.

Figure 9-2

The relationships among categorical sentences in the Aristotelian square of opposition can be represented by arrows, as shown in Figure 9-3.

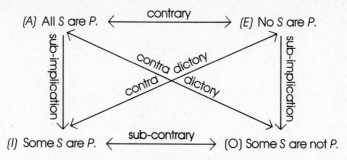

Figure 9-3
Aristotelian Square of Opposition

Exercises

1. Assume that there are members of the subject class in each of the following. Answer each question with a *categorical sentence* in English.
    a. What is the contradictory of "All fiddlers are bass fiddlers"?
    b. What is the contrary of "No politicians are statesmen"?
    c. What is the contradictory of "Some politicians are statesmen"?
    d. What is the sub-contrary of "Some cats are Persians"?
    e. What sentence must be true if "All cats are Persians" is true?
    f. What sentence must be true if "No cats are Persians" is true?
    g. What is the contradictory of "Some cats are not domestic"?
    h. What is the contradictory of "No football players are pre-med students"?
    i. What sentence is contrary to "All doctors are rich"?
    j. What is the sub-implication of "No rich persons are doctors"?
2. Give an English sentence (it need not be categorical) that is contrary to each of the following:
    a. It never rains in southern California.
    b. Mary Ann has two blue eyes.
    c. His only pet is a dog.
    d. Johnny is rich.
    e. Chocolate desserts are delicious.
    f. Chocolate is my favorite flavor.
    g. You always complain about the homework.
    h. When it rains, it pours.
    i. Many a hero has gone unsung.
    j. Parakeets are the easiest pets to keep.
3. Give an English sentence (it need not be categorical) that is contradictory to each of the following:
    a. Peas are not usually eaten with a knife.
    b. Carrots are orange.
    c. Baseball is less interesting than football.
    d. Every rose has its thorn.

e. The grass is always greener on the other side of the fence.
f. This movie glorifies criminals.
g. Mary Stuart was the only reigning Queen of Scotland.

2. The Modern Square of Opposition

If we do not assume that there are some members of the subject class (the existential assumption), the square of opposition is drastically simplified. Many relationships between forms of categorical sentences with the same subject and predicate terms no longer hold. Only the contradictory relationships between the pairs of categorical sentences diagonally opposite one another remain intact. This *modern square of opposition* is shown in Figure 9-4.

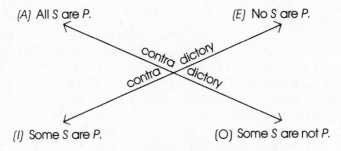

Figure 9-4
Modern Square of Opposition

The logical structure of the *A* and *E* sentences is understood to be that of *conditional sentences*:

(A)   If anything is an *S*, then it is a *P*.
(E)   If anything is an *S*, then it is not a *P*.

As is true of all material conditionals, if the antecedent is false, the conditional is true. In other words, if it is false that anything is an *S*, then the *A* sentence "All *S* are *P*" is true and the *E* sentence "No *S* are *P*" is also true. Since we do not *assume* there are *S*s and since the *A* and *E* sentences themselves do not state that there are *S*s, it is *possible* that the *A* and *E* sentences could both be true. The only circumstances under which we regard a sentence in conditional form as false is when it has a true antecedent and a false consequent. Thus, the relationship of being *contrary* does not hold in general between these two *forms* of sentences, although it is still proper to call many instances of these two forms in English "contraries" when it is known that members of the subject class do in fact exist.

The superficial grammatical similarity between the forms "All *S* are *P*" and "Some *S* are *P*" can be misleading. "All *S* are *P*" has the logical form of a conditional sentence, whereas "Some *S* are *P*" is logically equivalent to a type of conjunction: "There is something that is *S,* and that same thing is also *P.*" Similarly, the *O* sentence "Some *S* are not *P*" is equivalent to the conjunction: "There is something that is an *S,* and it is not a *P.*" No existential *assumption* must be made with respect to the particular affirmative and the particular negative, because these sentences contain as one of their conjuncts the claim that there is at least one thing that is an *S*. The *I* sentence and the *O* sentence each *state* that some *S* exists, and this assertion of existence is reflected in the name *existential generalization.*

Now if in fact there are no *S*s, then both "Some *S* are *P*" and "Some *S* are not *P*" are false, since each of these sentences contains a false conjunct. Thus, the relationship of being sub-contraries (the relationship that says both sentences may be true but cannot both be false) does not hold in general between these sentence forms.

The relationship of sub-implication also fails when the existential assumption is abandoned. If there are no *S*s, then the *A* and *E* sentences are both true. But if there are no *S*s, then the *I* and *O* sentences are both false. So it is possible (when there are no members of the subject class) for the *A* sentence to be true while the *I* sentence is false and for the *E* sentence to be true while the *O* sentence is false.

Consider the following four categorical sentences in which "unicorn" is the subject term and "white things" is the predicate term:

A: All unicorns are white things.
E: No unicorns are white things.
I: Some unicorns are white things.
O: Some unicorns are not white things.

We do not assume that unicorns exist. In fact, we know that unicorns do not exist. Accordingly, the *A* and *E* sentences are both true, and the *I* and *O* sentences are both false. The *A* sentence does not imply the *I* sentence; the *E* sentence does not imply the *O* sentence. *A* and *E* are not contraries; *I* and *O* are not sub-contraries. However, *A* and *O* are contradictories, as are *E* and *I*.

There are two primary reasons why modern logicians have abandoned the existential assumption about members of the subject class. First, the general tendency in modern logic is to make as few assumptions as possible, on the grounds that the fewer assumptions one makes, the less apt one is to be mistaken. Logic, we should remember, is a subject that deals with *possibilities,* not with what the world is actually like. Existential assumptions commit us to the view that the world is made up in a certain way—that certain kinds of things exist in the world. Most modern logicians now make just one very innocuous existential assumption: "There is at least one thing that exists." This assumption is much weaker than the assumption that there are members of any subject class that one cares to mention.

Referring to the weaker modern assumption, one logician has said "We might be wrong about that, but we could never know we were wrong." Moreover, if we make the stronger assumption that there are always members of the subject class, we know that we are going to be wrong sometimes. In addition, giving up this existential assumption deprives us of nothing essential, for when it is appropriate to do so, we can always simply *state* (as an additional premiss) that there are members of the subject class, rather than assuming that this is so.

The second reason for abandoning the existential assumption is a practical one. Modern logic, which is a highly symbolic enterprise, works more smoothly without the complexity introduced by the Aristotelian existential assumption. In Chapter 10, we will develop some of the symbolic techniques that have already been introduced, and then it will be possible to show some of the simplicity that has been gained through modern treatments of the logic of classes. In the rest of this chapter, we will follow the practice of adopting the modern attitude toward the existential assumption, unless otherwise stated.

Even though we will reject the existential assumption in our formal treatment of the syllogism, the relationships among categorical sentences in the traditional Aristotelian square of opposition are important in everyday reasoning in ordinary language. For that reason, it repays our careful attention. Arguments in ordinary reasoning often depend on the fact that one sentence is contrary to another, or is sub-contrary to another, or is a sub-implication of another. We should be able to recognize and assess such arguments.

III. TRANSLATING ENGLISH SENTENCES INTO STANDARD CATEGORICAL FORMS

It should come as no surprise that there are many ways of expressing an English-language sentence that assumes the logical form of one of the four types of categorical sentences. With sufficiently clever linguistic manipulation, many English sentences that do not appear to be categorical sentences can fit one of these categorical forms. For example, a sentence such as "It never rains but it pours" can be "translated" into "All times of raining are times of pouring," which is a standard *A* sentence.

1. *A* Sentences

Consider the following English sentences:

1. All trespassers are persons who will be prosecuted.
2. Trespassers will be prosecuted.
3. Anyone who trespasses will be prosecuted.
4. If anyone trespasses, that person will be prosecuted.
5. No trespasser will fail to be prosecuted.
6. It is false that some trespassers will not be prosecuted.
7. All persons who will not be prosecuted are non-trespassers.

All of these sentences are equivalent to one another in the logically important sense that each sentence states that the class of trespassers is included in the class of persons who will be prosecuted. The following remarks about each of these sentences are designed to make this equivalence apparent:

1. This sentence is already in standard categorical form. "Trespassers" denotes the subject class, and "persons who will be prosecuted" denotes the predicate class.
2. In English, the *quantifier* ("all" or "some") is frequently dropped when context makes clear which quantifier is intended. For example, the sentence "Whales are mammals" is to be understood as "All whales are mammals." But in "Watch your language. Children are present," the second sentence is understood to mean "Some children are present." Also, noun phrases such as "persons who," "things which," and similar expressions are frequently dropped from the predicate term.
3. In this sentence, we can easily see that "Anyone who trespasses" means the same as "all trespassers."
4. This is the standard translation of an *A* sentence into a form that makes its conditional nature apparent: "If anything is an *S,* then it is a *P.*"
5. This sentence is obviously equivalent to the *E* form: "No trespassers are persons who will not be prosecuted." In addition to changing the "all" in the original sentence (1) to "no," the predicate "persons who will be prosecuted" has been replaced by "persons who will not be prosecuted." In general, an *A* sentence may be transformed into an equivalent *E* sentence in the following way:
   a. Replace "all" with "no." Changing an affirmative sentence to a negative sentence, or a negative sentence to an affirmative sentence, is called "changing the *quality* of a categorical sentence."
   b. Replace the predicate term of the sentence with its *complement.* The complement of a class is the class of all things that are not in the original class. For example, the complement of the class of cats is the class of non-cats; the complement of the class of non-men is the class of men. The term that refers to the complement class is called the *complement* of the original term.
      The process of changing the quality of a categorical sentence and replacing the predicate term with its complement is called *obversion.* When any categorical sentence (*A, E, I,* or *O*) is *obverted,* a sentence that is equivalent in meaning to the original sentence results.
6. This sentence is equivalent to the *denial* of an *O* sentence: "*It is not the case that* some trespassers are persons who will not be prosecuted." The *O* sentence that is contradictory to "All trespassers are persons who will be prosecuted" is "Some trespassers are persons who will not be prosecuted." The denial of the contradictory of a sentence is logically equivalent to the original sentence.
7. In this sentence, the subject term is the complement of the predicate term in (1) and the predicate is the complement of the subject term in

(1). This transformation is called *contraposition*. The contraposition of *A* sentences yields *A* sentences that are equivalent in meaning to the original sentence.

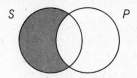

Figure 9-5

The relationship between subject and predicate in the *A* sentence can be represented graphically in the *Venn diagram** of the *A* sentence shown in Figure 9-5. Against a background of all of the types of things in the universe, the overlapping circles represent two classes, or types of things in that universe: *S*s and *P*s. These classes may or may not have members. Shading is used to indicate the emptiness of a region. Thus, for the *A* sentence, the region in the *S* circle that lies outside the *P* circle is shaded, for any *S*s (if there are any) must lie within the part of the *S* circle that is included in the *P* circle.

2. *E* Sentences

Consider the following English sentences:

1. No whales are fish.
2. Whales aren't fish.
3. Nothing that's a whale is a fish.
4. None but non-fishes are whales.
5. If anything is a whale, then it is not a fish.
6. All whales are non-fish.
7. It is false that some whales are fish.

Each of these sentences says that the class of whales and the class of fish is non-overlapping, or in other words, that no members are common to both classes. Comments on each of these sentences follow:

1. This sentence is in standard *E* form.
2. This sentence is equivalent to the categorical *A* sentence "All whales are non-fish." In ordinary English, we might be tempted to say "All whales are not fish," but this sentence is ambiguous; it leaves open the possibility that some whales are fish, and in the original sentence (2), the intent seems to be to deny that any whales are fish. The sentence form "All *S* are not *P*" is not a categorical sentence form, and due to its ambiguity, is not equivalent to the categorical "All *S* are non-*P*," which is a variant of the *A* form.

---

*After John Venn (1834–1923), an English clergyman who made important contributions to mathematics and logic.

3. "Nothing that's a whale" in this context clearly has the same meaning as "no whales," and "is a fish" agrees better grammatically with this version than "are fish."

4. "None but non-fishes are whales" means the same as "Only non-fishes are whales" or "If anything is not a non-fish, then it is not a whale." This in turn can be seen to be equivalent to "If anything is a fish, then it is not a whale." This sentence states that there is no overlap between the classes of fish and whales, which is what the original *E* sentence (1) says.

5. This is the standard translation of the *E* sentence into an equivalent conditional. "No *S* are *P*" becomes "If anything is an *S*, then it is not a *P*."

6. This sentence represents the standard transformation of an *E* sentence into an equivalent *A* sentence by *obversion*. The quality of the sentence is changed from negative to affirmative, and the predicate term is replaced by its complement.

7. This sentence is the denial of the contradictory of the original *E* sentence (1). In general, the categorical sentence "No *S* are *P*" is equivalent to the noncategorical sentence "It is false that some *S* are *P*."

E sentences (including all the English variants of the standard form of *E* sentence) can be represented by the Venn diagram shown in Figure 9-6.

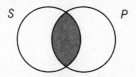

Figure 9-6

As in the Venn diagram of the *A* sentence, the two circles represent the classes *S* and *P*. The shading in the overlapping area indicates that this region is empty (that there are no things belonging to both classes).

Inspection of the Venn diagram should make it clear that the sentence forms "No *S* are *P*" and "No *P* are *S*" are equivalent. This means that the subject term and the predicate term may be interchanged in an *E* sentence without changing the meaning of the sentence. This transformation is called *conversion*. Conversion does not always preserve meaning when it is applied to *A* sentences. For example, "All elephants are mammals" does not mean the same as "All mammals are elephants." Examination of the Venn diagram of the *A* sentence makes its lack of symmetry with respect to subject and predicate terms apparent.

3. *I* Sentences

The following are all English variations of the same *I* sentence:

1. Some logical principles are things difficult to grasp.
2. Some logical principles are difficult to grasp.

3. Some things are both logical principles and difficult to grasp.
4. There are logical principles that are difficult to grasp.
5. Some logical principles are not things that are not difficult to grasp.
6. Some logical principles are not easy to grasp.
7. It is not the case that no logical principles are difficult to grasp.
8. It is not the case that all logical principles are easy to grasp.
9. Some things that are difficult to grasp are logical principles.

Some of these equivalences are discussed below. You should convince yourself of the equivalences of the rest.

1. This sentence is in standard *I* form.
3. This form makes the conjunctive nature of *I* sentences apparent.
5. An *O* form that is equivalent to the *I* form can be constructed by changing the quality from affirmative to negative and replacing the predicate term with its complement (obversion).
7. The *E* sentence that is the contradictory of the *I* sentence is negated. The resulting sentence is equivalent to the original *I* sentence.
9. Since the *I* sentence has the logical form of a conjunction and since the order of the conjuncts is irrelevant to the truth of the conjunction, "Some *S* are *P*" is equivalent to "Some *P* are *S*." As in the *E* sentence, the subject and predicate terms in the *I* sentence may be interchanged without changing the meaning of the sentence. Conversion preserves meaning in *I* sentences.

In constructing the Venn diagram for the *I* sentence, two overlapping circles are again used to represent the classes *S* and *P*. An **x** is used to represent the fact that a class has a member. Since the *I* sentence says that the classes *S* and *P* share at least one member, an **x** is placed in the overlapping region, as shown in Figure 9-7.

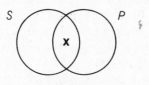

Figure 9-7

4. *O* Sentences

The following are all English variations of the same *O* sentence:

1. Some runners are not vegetarians.
2. Some runners are non-vegetarians.
3. Some non-vegetarians are runners.
4. Not all runners are vegetarians.

5. There are non-vegetarian runners.
6. Some non-vegetarians are not non-runners.

The principles by virtue of which these sentences are equivalent to one another have all been introduced by now. The first sentence (1) is in standard *O* form. The second sentence (2) is the obverse of (1). The quality of sentence (1) is changed from negative to affirmative (that is, from an *O* sentence to an *I* sentence), and the predicate term is replaced by its complement. Sentence (3) is the converse of (2), in which the subject and predicate terms of that *I* sentence are interchanged. Sentence (4) is the denial of the *A* sentence that is contradictory to the original *O* sentence. Sentence (5) exhibits the conjunctive nature of the *O* sentence. Finally, sentence (6) is the *contrapositive* of sentence (1). Contraposition preserves sameness of meaning in *O* sentences as well as in *A* sentences.

Again, using overlapping circles and an **x** to show that a class has some member, the Venn diagram in Figure 9-8 represents all variants of the *O* sentence. In this case, the **x** is drawn outside the *P* circle but within the *S* circle.

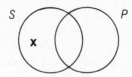

Figure 9-8

Exercises

For each of the following English sentences, construct an English sentence in one of the four standard categorical forms that captures the meaning of the original sentence as nearly as possible. Draw a Venn diagram for each sentence and clearly label the subject class circle and the predicate class circle.

1. Only a mother could love him.
2. If students don't keep up with the assignments, they're lost.
3. The longest mile is the last mile home.
4. Happy is the bride the sun shines on.
5. No one may be admitted except juniors and seniors.
6. Not all apples are red.
7. If it isn't genuine, it isn't worth owning.
8. The home team always wins at football.
9. Valuable lessons are never easily learned.
10. Not every good dancer is a good person.
11. American warships are in the Indian Ocean.
12. The easiest course is not always the most satisfying.
13. It never rains in southern California.
14. She brings sunshine everywhere she goes.
15. Cosmic radiation is all around us.

16. Times like these try persons' souls.
17. It's an antique only if it's more than 100 years old.
18. The last exercise is always the best.

IV. TESTING FOR VALIDITY WITH VENN DIAGRAMS

Categorical syllogisms in standard form are arguments with two premisses and a conclusion that also have the following properties:

1. Both the premisses and the conclusion are categorical sentences in standard form.
2. Only three terms occur in the argument. One of these terms occurs once in each premiss; each of the other two terms occurs once in one of the premisses and once in the conclusion.

When we represent the forms of these arguments, we will use *S* to refer to the subject term of the conclusion, *P* to refer to the predicate term of the conclusion, and *M* to refer to the term that occurs in both premisses.

An argument is deductively valid if its conclusion does not contain any information that is not already present at least implicitly in the premisses. If no new information occurs in the conclusion, then it is impossible for the premisses to be true while the conclusion is false.

We have already seen how the information contained in categorical sentences can be represented in Venn diagrams. A Venn diagram can show whether or not one class is included in another, one class excludes the other, classes share a common member, or one class has a member that lies outside the other class (see Figure 9-9).

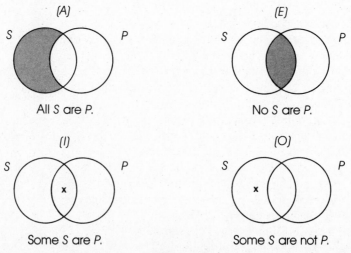

(A)

All S are P.

(E)

No S are P.

(I)

Some S are P.

(O)

Some S are not P.

Figure 9-9

To apply the Venn diagram technique to categorical syllogisms, we need three overlapping circles—one for each of the three terms in the argument. The circles are arranged in the standard way shown in Figure 9-10.

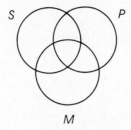

Figure 9-10

To test a syllogism for validity, we use shading or **x**s to mark information contained in the premisses on this standard blank diagram. Then we inspect the diagram to see whether or not the information in the conclusion sentence can be "read off" the diagram. If, after the premisses are diagrammed, the conclusion can be "read off" the diagram, then the argument is a valid syllogism. If the conclusion cannot be "read off" the diagram, then the argument is an invalid syllogism.

Examples

(a)   All sensitive persons are dreamers.   All S are M.
             All dreamers are poets.   All M are P.
             _____
             All sensitive persons are poets.   All S are P.

In this argument, S is the class of sensitive persons, P is the class of poets, and M is the class of dreamers.

To diagram the first premiss, we consider only the two circles labeled S and M. The first premiss is an A sentence, with S as the subject term. Thus, we shade all of the S circle that lies outside the M circle, as shown in Figure 9-11.

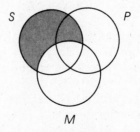

Figure 9-11

To diagram the second premiss, we consider the two circles labeled P and M. The second premiss is also an A sentence with M as the subject term, so we shade all of the M circle that does not lie within the P circle, as shown in Figure 9-12.

S   P

M

Figure 9-12

After diagramming these two premisses, we stop and inspect the Venn diagram to see whether or not we can "read off" the conclusion. The conclusion is an *A* sentence with *S* as the subject term and *P* as the predicate term. On the diagram, all of the *S* circle that lies outside the *P* circle has been shaded. (A part that lies inside the *P* circle has been shaded as well, but this does not conflict with the claim that if anything is an *S* then it is a *P*; it simply provides the additional information that any of the *S*s that are *P*s are *M*s as well.) Thus, we *can* "read off" the sentence "All *S* are *P*" from the Venn diagram, and the argument is shown to be valid.

(b)   All statesmen are honorable persons.   All *S* are *M*.
            Some honorable persons are politicians.   Some *M* are *P*.
            ─────────────────────────────────────   ──────────────
            Some statesmen are politicians.   Some *S* are *P*.

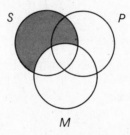

S   P

M

Figure 9-13

In Figure 9-13, the first premiss, "All *S* are *M*," is diagrammed by shading the part of the *S* circle that lies outside the *M* circle.

In Figure 9-14, the information contained in the second premiss, "Some *M* are *P*" is added to the diagram of the first premiss. The overlapping region between the *P* circle and the *M* circle is itself divided into two parts. One of these parts lies within the *S* circle; the other part lies outside the *S* circle. Since the information in the premiss tells us only that there is a member somewhere in this overlap, we cannot locate an **x** definitely in one region or the other. Instead, we use the "floating **x**" (two **x**s connected by a dashed line) to indicate that a member lies somewhere in that region.

However, when we try to "read off" the conclusion "Some *S* are *P*," we see that the diagram tells us only that an **x** *may* lie in the region overlapping *S* and

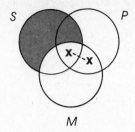

Figure 9-14

P or that it *may* lie in the region overlapping *P* and *M* but outside *S*. Thus, we cannot "read off" the conclusion from the diagrammed premises, and the syllogism is invalid. It is *possible* for both premises to be true and the conclusion to be false.

(c)　　　　No unicorns are black things.　No *S* are *M*.
　　　　　Some black things are dogs.　Some *M* are *P*.
　　　　　_____　_____

　　　　　No unicorns are dogs.　　　　No *S* are *P*.

In the Venn diagram in Figure 9-15, the first premiss requires us to shade the overlapping area between the *S* and the *M* circles. An **x** is then drawn in the overlapping area between the *M* and the *P* circles. In this case, as a result of diagramming the first premiss, we can see that the area of overlap between *M* and *P* that also lies within the *S* circle is empty, so we do not need to use a "floating **x**." The **x** can only be drawn in the area between *M* and *P* that is unshaded.

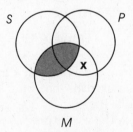

Figure 9-15

In order for us to "read off" the conclusion from this diagram, the area of overlap between the *S* and the *P* circles would have to be shaded. Since this is not the case, the syllogism is invalid.

(d)　　　　No intelligent persons are gluttons.　No *P* are *M*.
　　　　　Some famous persons are gluttons.　Some *S* are *M*.
　　　　　_____　_____

　　　　　Some famous persons are not intelligent.　Some *S* are not *P*.

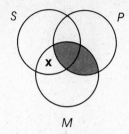

Figure 9-16

The first premiss is diagrammed in Figure 9-16 by shading the overlapping region between the *P* and the *M* circles. The second premiss requires that we place an **x** in the overlap between the *S* and the *M* circles. The **x** is placed in the unshaded portion of this overlap. In order to "read off" the conclusion, there must be an **x** in the portion of the *S* circle that lies outside the *P* circle. This is the case, and so the diagram shows the validity of this syllogism.

(e)   Some animals are furry.   Some *S* are *M*.
         Some furry things are cats.   Some *M* are *P*.

         Some animals are cats.   Some *S* are *P*.

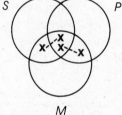

Figure 9-17

To diagram the first premiss, we place an **x** in the overlap between *S* and *M*. There are two parts to this overlap—one within the *P* circle and one outside the *P* circle (see Figure 9-17). The premiss does not tell us where to place the **x**, so we must use a floating **x**. The second premiss tells us that there is a member of both *P* and *M* but does not tell us whether or not this member belongs to *S*. Therefore, we must use another floating **x**. The conclusion requires that an **x** be in the overlapping region between *S* and *P*. But since both **x**s are floating, we cannot tell whether or not either **x** lies in that region. Thus, the conclusion cannot be "read off" the diagram, and the syllogism is invalid.

Exercises

1. For each of the following syllogisms:

     (i) Identify the *S*, *M*, and *P* terms.

(ii) Draw a Venn diagram.

(iii) Tell whether the syllogism is valid or invalid.

Diagramming will be simplified if whenever a syllogism contains both a universal and a particular premiss, the universal premiss is diagrammed first. This will minimize the use of floating **x**s.

a. All animals feel pain. All things that feel pain are able to think. Therefore, all animals are able to think.

b. All patriots are chauvinists. Some chauvinists are fanatics. Therefore, some patriots are fanatics.

c. No good persons are cruel to animals. Some children are cruel to animals. Therefore, some children are not good persons.

d. No elephants are easy to train. Some dogs are not easy to train. Some dogs are not elephants.

e. All messengers who bring bad news are unwelcome. All messengers who bring bad news are punished. Therefore, some unwelcome persons are punished.

f. Some awards are worthless. Some worthless things are fun to have. Therefore, some awards are fun to have.

g. All diets require will power. No things that require will power are simple. Therefore, no diets are simple.

h. Some syllogisms are not valid arguments. All syllogisms have two premisses. Therefore, some arguments with two premisses are not valid.

i. No syllogisms are arguments with four terms. Some arguments with four terms are invalid. Therefore, no syllogisms are invalid.

j. Some arguments are invalid. Some invalid arguments are not syllogisms. Therefore, some arguments are not syllogisms.

2. Consider each of the following pairs of sentences to be premisses. Using an appropriately labeled three-circle Venn diagram, tell what syllogistic conclusion, if any, can be drawn from these premisses.

a. No football players are weaklings.
No ballerinas are weaklings.

b. Some dogs have fleas.
Some things with fleas are good pets.

c. No students are boring.
Some professors are boring.

d. All mariners are sailors.
All mariners love the sea.

e. Some valuable things are inexpensive.
Some inexpensive things are not bargains.

f. No valuable thing is free of charge.
All immunizations at the Health Center are free of charge.

g. All champions are hard workers.
Some hard workers are unsuccessful.

h. All birds are egg-layers.
Some mammals are egg-layers.

i. No birds are cold-blooded.
   All reptiles are cold-blooded.
j. All reptiles are cold-blooded.
   Some dinosaurs are not cold-blooded.

V. DISTRIBUTION OF TERMS

A term is said to be *distributed* in a categorical sentence if and only if that sentence says something about *every* member of the class to which the term refers. In the *A* sentence, for example, the subject term is distributed. When we say that "All logic students are hard-working," we are saying that *every* logic student is a hard-working person. However, the predicate term in the *A* sentence is not distributed, because that sentence does not say something about every hard-working person.

In the *E* sentence, both the subject and predicate terms are distributed. The sentence "No NFL football players are ballerinas" says of every NFL football player that he is not a ballerina and also says of every ballerina that she is not an NFL football player.

In the *I* sentence, neither the subject term nor the predicate term is distributed. This sentence says only that the two classes share at least one member. The *I* sentence says nothing about every member of either the subject class or the predicate class.

In the *O* sentence, the subject term is not distributed; as in the *I* sentence, the subject term in the *O* sentence refers to only some member or members ("some" may mean more than one) of the class, not to every member. Although it is not immediately obvious, however, the predicate term is distributed in the *O* sentence. The awkward alternate formulation of the *O* sentence presented earlier ("There is at least one member of *S* such that, given any individual member of *P,* that member of *S* is not identical to that individual") illustrates that the *O* sentence says something about every member of the *P* class—namely, that at least one member of *S* is not identical with any member of *P*. Thus, the claim that "Some dogs are not brown" has the same meaning as "There is at least one dog that is not identical with any brown thing." It should be clear that the latter sentence says something about every member of the class of "brown things."

These facts about the distribution of terms, which will play an important role in the second method for assessing the validity of categorical syllogisms, can be summarized as follows:

> *Universal sentences:*   Subject term is distributed.
> *Negative sentences:*   Predicate term is distributed.

Fallacies of distribution can occur if the distinction between using a term distributively (to refer to every member of a class) and using a term collectively (to refer to the class as a whole) is not recognized. Consider the following arguments, neither of which is a categorical syllogism:

1. I infer that this stew will be delicious because each ingredient that went into it is delicious.

2. Mary's room at college must be large, for she lives in a very large dormitory.

In the first of these arguments, the conclusion that a *collective whole* (a stew) has a certain property is based on the information that its *parts* (distributively or individually) have that property. But this type of inference is not reliable. We all know that you can put together a collection of individually fine football players or singers and still end up with a poor team or a choir that sings badly. What is true of the parts is not *necessarily*—or even *probably*—true of the whole. The mistake of reasoning that what is true of the parts of a whole is also true of the whole, or that what is true of the individual members is true of the class, is called the *fallacy of composition*.

The second argument depends on the principle that what is true of the whole must be true of its parts. But this is also mistaken reasoning. Very large machines can be constructed from parts that are individually very small. A herd of cattle can be small even though none of its members is small. The fallacy involved in argument (2) is called the *fallacy of division*. Like the fallacy of composition, the fallacy of division involves confusing the distributive use of a term with its collective use.

Exercises

1. The following argument occurs in Book V of Lucretius's (ca. 100–55 B.C.) great philosophical poem *On the Nature of the Universe*. What fallacy does Lucretius commit here?

> In the first place, since the elements of which we see the world composed—solid earth and moisture, the light breaths of air and torrid fire—all consist of bodies that are neither birthless nor deathless, we must believe the same of the world as a whole.

2. Does the following argument commit a fallacy of distribution? Explain.

> Science tells us that physical objects are made up entirely of tiny particles—electrons, positrons, neutrons, etc.—that are invisible, although their motions can be detected by sophisticated instruments. Science also tells us that these particles are in constant motion and that there are spaces between them. Yet we can see physical objects, feel their solidity, and see that they are not always in motion. So science must be wrong; physical objects cannot be composed of atomic and subatomic particles.

3. What fallacy occurs in the following passage?

> What is prudence in the conduct of every private family can hardly be folly in that of a great kingdom.
>
> —Adam Smith, *Wealth of Nations*

VI. RULES FOR TESTING THE VALIDITY OF SYLLOGISMS

The use of Venn diagrams provides a general method of determining which conclusions follow validly from premisses in categorical syllogisms. This technique is simple to apply and provides a practical test for validity.

Various other techniques may be used to determine whether syllogisms are valid or invalid. Deductive logicians are not as concerned with assessing the validity of *particular arguments* as they are concerned with formulating and testing *general principles* related to what conclusions follow from what premisses. The truth tables and the proof method discussed in the Appendix to this text embody such general principles for truth-functional arguments. A number of different systems of principles governing what follows from what in categorical syllogisms have also been investigated by logicians, beginning with Aristotle.

Aristotle's treatment of syllogisms was quite different from the Venn-diagram method. To understand his approach to the problem, the concept of a *figure of a syllogism* must be introduced. In categorical syllogisms, we see that the *S* term may be either the subject or the predicate of the premiss in which it occurs; similarly, the *P* term may be either the subject or the predicate of the premiss in which it occurs. Thus, four possible arrangements, or figures of the syllogism, can be distinguished:

$$
\begin{array}{cccc}
MP & PM & MP & PM \\
SM & SM & MS & MS \\
\hline
SP & SP & SP & SP
\end{array}
$$

Since the order in which the premisses of an argument are stated has no bearing on the validity of the argument, variations in form that depend on this feature do not need to be considered. Both the premisses and the conclusions of these arguments are sentences in *A, E, I,* or *O* form. There are 64 possible combinations of these four types of sentences, taken three at a time (two sentences as the premisses and one sentence as the conclusion), and each of the 64 combinations (called *moods*) can occur in each of the four figures. Thus, there are only a finite number of forms of categorical syllogisms. Although the number is rather large (256), it is possible to use Venn diagrams to test each form. (Only a few of these forms are valid.)

Aristotle's own system of principles for testing validity involved taking as axioms those syllogisms in the first figure that were obviously valid and showing that all valid forms in the other figures could be reduced (by obverting sentences, exchanging subject and predicate terms in *E* and *I* sentences, and other transformations discussed in Section III) directly or indirectly to these obviously valid forms. To show the invalidity of forms, Aristotle used the method of counter-example, providing arguments in those forms with obviously true premisses and obviously false conclusions. Aristotle's treatment of syllogistic logic was therefore similar to Euclid's treatment of geometry as a deductive system and different from the methods for testing validity discussed in this chapter.

1. Three Rules for Valid Syllogisms

In this section, we will consider a system of three rules for testing the validity of categorical syllogisms. This system of rules is an alternative to the Venn-diagram method, and some people find it easier to use than the diagrams.

All of the properties required for a syllogism to be valid can be stated compactly in the three following rules.*

1. *The* middle term *must be distributed exactly once.* (This means that the middle term must be distributed in one of the premisses and must be undistributed in the other premiss.)
2. *No* end term *can be distributed exactly once.* (This means that the S term can be distributed in the conclusion *if and only if* it is distributed in a premiss; the same is true of the P term.)
3. *The number of negative conclusions must equal the number of negative premisses.* (That is to say, there can be a negative conclusion *if and only if* there is exactly one negative premiss.)

Although these requirements are not immediately obvious, they are easy to memorize and provide an extremely simple way of testing for the validity of categorical syllogisms.

If a categorical syllogism violates none of these three rules, then it is valid. If *any* one of these rules is violated, then the syllogism is invalid. Understanding what it means for a term to be distributed is crucial to understanding why these rules work. However, all we need to know to *apply* these rules to syllogisms is *which* terms are distributed—not what "distribution" means.

If a term is distributed in the conclusion, then the conclusion says something about every member of the class to which the term refers. In any valid syllogism, the occurrence of that term in the premiss must be distributed as well; otherwise, the conclusion would "go beyond" the premiss in the sense that the conclusion—but not the premiss—would say something about every member of that class.

For similar reasons, one of the occurrences of the *middle term* (the M term, which occurs in each premiss but not in the conclusion) must be distributed, because it is through the middle term that the S and P terms (*end terms*) are connected. This connecting function of the middle term shows up clearly in Venn diagrams. If one of the premisses did not say something about every member of a class, then there might be no connection between the subject term and the predicate term of the conclusion.

The preceding remarks offer *partial* justification for the rules. A justification has been given for why the middle term must be distributed *at least* once, but nothing has been said about why it must be distributed *at most* once. It has been shown why an end term that is distributed in the conclusion must be distributed in the premiss, but it has not been shown why an end term that is distributed in the premiss must also be distributed in the conclusion. All of the other less

---

* These rules are presented by Wesley Salmon in *Logic,* 3rd ed., and were adapted from a set given by James T. Culbertson, *Mathematics and Logic for Digital Devices.*

obvious features of the rules can be justified, but the proofs are often tedious "proofs by cases," in which one must go through all the possible figures of the syllogism in which the rule is applicable to show why it works.

For example, to show that no valid categorical syllogism can have two negative premisses, we note that each negative premiss either states that the middle term and the end terms completely exclude one another or that some member of one of these classes does not belong to the other class. From this, however, it may not be apparent that nothing at all can be said with certainty in the conclusion about the relationship between the two end terms. In a "proof by cases," we can use Venn diagrams to consider the following possibilities.

(i) Both premisses are *E* sentences.

Since the subject and the predicate terms are interchangeable in *E* sentences, we do not need to consider each figure separately. The Venn diagram for any syllogism with two *E* premisses looks like the one shown in Figure 9-18. An inspection of the Venn diagram shows that no conclusion relating the end terms can be drawn from such premisses.

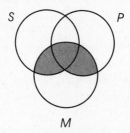

Figure 9-18

(ii) Both premisses are *O* sentences.

If the middle term is not the predicate term in at least one of the *O* sentences, then the middle term is undistributed. Thus, the third figure is invalid:

$$MP \quad (O)$$
$$MS \quad (O)$$
$$\overline{}$$
$$SP$$

For the other three figures, Venn diagrams will show that no syllogistic conclusion can be drawn from two *O* premisses.

(iii) One premiss is an *E* sentence, and the other premiss is an *O* sentence.

There are two possibilities:

(a) The premiss containing the *P* term is the *E* sentence. Two Venn diagrams are relevant here (see Figure 9-19). The left one diagrams

"Some *S* are not *M*"; the right one diagrams "Some *M* are not *S*." Neither shows a syllogistic conclusion.

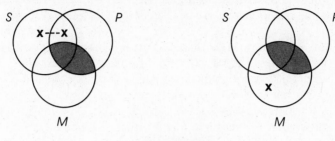

Figure 9-19

(b) The premiss containing the *S* term is the *E* sentence. Two Venn diagrams are relevant here (see Figure 9-20). The left one diagrams "Some *P* are not *M*"; the right one diagrams "Some *M* are not *P*." Neither yields a syllogistic conclusion.

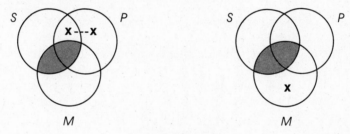

Figure 9-20

A *part* of the third rule has thus been justified in this "proof by cases", for we have shown that any syllogism in which the number of negative premisses is *greater than* the number of negative conclusions is invalid. (Obviously, any syllogism can have only one conclusion.)

Exercise

Show, by a demonstration similar to the preceding "proof by cases," that any syllogism in which the number of negative conclusions is greater than the number of negative premisses is invalid. (Show that any valid syllogism with a negative conclusion must have at least one negative premiss.) Be sure to consider all possibilities.

2. Examples of Using the Rules to Test Validity

Remember that the subject terms are distributed in universal sentences and that the predicate terms are distributed in negative sentences. All distributed terms will be denoted by the subscript $_d$ in the argument forms.

(a)   All soldiers are brave persons.   All M_d are S.
         Some soldiers are not daredevils.   Some M are not P_d.
         _____   _____
         Some brave persons are not daredevils.   Some S are not P_d.

1. The middle term is distributed in the first premiss but not in the second premiss. Thus, the middle term is distributed exactly once.
2. S is not distributed in the first premiss or in the conclusion. P is distributed in both the second premiss and the conclusion. Thus, no end term is distributed exactly once.
3. The second premiss is the only negative premiss. The conclusion is negative. Thus, the number of negative premisses is equal to the number of negative conclusions.

The syllogism is valid.

(b)   All football fans are fanatics.   All P_d are M.
         Some fanatics are silly people.   Some M are S.
         _____   _____
         Some silly people are football fans.   Some S are P.

1. The middle term is not distributed in either of the premisses.

The syllogism is invalid. (Violation of one rule is sufficient to show invalidity. However, notice that the second rule is also violated, since P is distributed exactly once.)

(c)   No difficult subjects are worthless.   No M_d are P_d.
         Some logic classes are not difficult.   Some S are not M_d.
         _____   _____
         Some logic classes are not worthless.   Some S are not P_d.

1. The middle term is distributed in both premisses.

The syllogism is invalid. (Also note that the third rule is violated. There are two negative premisses and one negative conclusion.)

Exercises

1. Identify the premisses and the conclusions of the following categorical syllogisms. Put the premisses and the conclusions into standard categorical form. Use the rules you have learned in this section to determine the validity or invalidity of the arguments. If a syllogism is invalid, say which rule or rules it violates.
    a. Some birds are non-flyers, for ostriches are birds and all ostriches are non-flyers.
    b. No persons who aren't in great shape are runners, so no smokers are runners, for all smokers are persons who aren't in great shape.

   c. Not all generals are war-mongers, but some admirals are war-mongers; so no admirals are generals.

   d. Some bridge games are interesting to observe, but no canasta games are interesting to observe. Hence, some bridge games are not canasta games.

   e. Whales have lungs, but no fish do; so whales aren't fish.

   f. All gem-stones are expensive, but some cubic zirconias are not expensive; so cubic zirconias are not gem-stones.

   g. All feminists supported the ERA, but some women did not support the ERA. Hence, some feminists are not women.

   h. All porpoises are mammals, but no fish are mammals; so no porpoises are fish.

   i. Ostriches never fly, but birds always do; so ostriches aren't birds.

   j. Not all sofas are beds, but some beds are uncomfortable; so some sofas are uncomfortable.

2. Some systems of rules for valid syllogisms include the following rule:

No syllogistic conclusion can be drawn from two particular premisses.

Provide a justification for this rule. (*Hint*: You may provide a "proof by cases," using Venn diagrams to support each case. Or you may appeal to the set of three rules for a valid syllogism and show that this rule follows from that set.)

VII. REDUCING THE NUMBER OF TERMS IN SYLLOGISMS

By definition, a categorical syllogism cannot contain more than three terms. However, many arguments that do contain more than three terms can be transformed to equivalent categorical syllogisms. *Synonyms* are often used in ordinary-language arguments for rhetorical purposes. Language is more interesting if the same term is not repeated several times. Obviously, when we wish to reconstruct these arguments to assess their validity, synonyms can be treated as different occurrences of the same term.

In other cases, arguments contain both pairs of a complementary set of terms. In such cases, it may be possible to reduce the number of terms by performing an *obversion* (changing the quality and replacing a predicate term with its complement) on some categorical sentence. Since obversion can reduce the number of terms only when the extra term occurs in the predicate position, it may be necessary to exchange the subject and predicate terms before obverting. (Remember, this exchange is legitimate only in *I* and *E* sentences!) Consider the following argument, in which both premisses are categorical sentences and the conclusion is a categorical sentence, but there are four terms:

All puzzles are interesting.
All logic exercises are puzzles.
_____
No logic exercises are uninteresting.

First, we note that the terms "interesting" and "uninteresting" are complementary. If the first premiss is obverted, it becomes "No logic puzzles are uninteresting." In this way, we obtain a categorical sentence equivalent to "All puzzles are interesting," but we reduce the number of terms in the syllogism to three. The result is a syllogism in standard form that can be tested by the rules for a valid syllogism or by the Venn-diagram method:

> No *M* are *P*.
> All *S* are *M*.
> ————————
> No *S* are *P*.

Another way of reducing the number of terms in this English argument is to obvert the conclusion instead of the first premiss. Then, the conclusion becomes "All logic exercises are interesting." Again, a categorical syllogism results, but of the following form:

> All *M* are *P*.
> All *S* are *M*.
> ————————
> All *S* are *P*.

(In this form, the *P* term is "interesting," whereas in the preceding form, the *P* term is "uninteresting.") Is this a valid form of syllogism?

The following argument contains five terms:

> Some non-believers are freethinkers, because no believers are atheists and some atheists are non-freethinkers.

Letting *P* represent freethinkers, *S* represent believers, and *M* represent atheists, we can represent this argument as follows:

> No *S* are *M*.
> Some *M* are non-*P*.
> ————————
> Some non-*S* are *P*.

First, we obvert the second premiss. We change the *I* sentence to an *O* sentence, and change non-*P* to *P*:

> Some *M* are not *P*.

Next, we reduce the pair of terms *S* and non-*S*. We begin by exchanging the subject and the predicate terms in the conclusion. This is legitimate, since the conclusion is an *I* sentence:

> Some *P* are non-*S*.

Then, this sentence can be obverted to yield

> Some *P* are not *S*.

The reconstructed argument, which contains only three terms, has this form:

> No *S* are *M*.
> Some *M* are not *P*.
> _____
> Some *P* are not *S*.

Is this a valid form of syllogism?

Exercises

Reconstruct each of the following arguments as a categorical syllogism in standard form. Test each syllogism for validity, using either the rules for a valid syllogism or Venn diagrams.

1. Some men are non-sexists, since all sexists oppose equal rights for women and some men do not oppose equal rights for women.
2. Some strong persons are sensitive, but no poets are insensitive. Hence, some poets are strong persons.
3. All modern-style architecture is stark, but some recently constructed buildings are ornate; so not all new buildings are in the modern style.
4. Some edible things are non-poisonous, for all insects are edible and some insects are poisonous.
5. No man is willing to die; but women aren't men, so some women are not unwilling to die.
6. No one who speaks Latin lives in Latin America; but not all Latin Americans live there, so some Latin Americans are Latin-speakers.
7. Carrot-eaters are health-food freaks, and no one who is crazy about health food eats chocolate; so chocolate-freaks aren't carrot-eaters.

(Exercises 8–10 are taken or adapted from *The Art of Thinking*, also called *Port-Royal Logic*, a seventeenth-century logic text designed by Antoine Arnauld to teach a young nobleman everything there was to know about logic in ten days.)

8. That which has no parts cannot perish by dissolution of its parts.
   The soul has no parts.
   _____
   The soul cannot perish by dissolution of its parts.

9. No virtue is offensive.
   Some zeal is not inoffensive.
   _____
   Some zeal is non-virtuous.

10. All liars are unbelievable.
 Every upright person is believable.

 All liars are persons who are not upright.

VIII. RECONSTRUCTING ORDINARY-LANGUAGE ARGUMENTS AS SYLLOGISMS

Many arguments that are incompletely stated in English or that contain sentences not in categorical form can be reasonably reconstructed as categorical syllogisms.

Examples

(a) Consider the following passage from Simone de Beauvoir's *The Ethics of Ambiguity*:

> In *Plutarch Lied* Pierrefeu rightly says that in war there is no victory which cannot be regarded as unsuccessful, for the objective which one aims at is the total annihilation of the enemy and this result is never attained.

This argument can be stated in syllogistic form:

All successful victories in war achieve total annihilation of the enemy.
No actual victories in war achieve total annihilation of the enemy.

No actual victories in war are successful victories in war.

(b) The following argument from Chapter 12 of Leo Tolstoy's *What Is Art?* can also be recast as a syllogism:

> Accustoming people to something resembling art disaccustoms them to the comprehension of real art. And that is how it comes about that none are more dull to art than those who have passed through the professional schools and have been most successful in them. Professional schools produce an hypocrisy of art.

Syllogistically, this argument can be expressed

All who have successfully passed through professional schools of art have been accustomed to something resembling art.
All who have been accustomed to something resembling art are persons most dull to real art.

All who have successfully passed through professional schools are persons most dull to real art.

(c) The next argument is from St. Augustine's *Confessions*, Book X. When an unstated (but obviously intended) premiss is supplied, it can be viewed as a categorical syllogism:

> [A] happy life is not seen with the eye, because it is not a body.

In syllogistic form, this argument becomes

> No happy lives are bodies.
> All things that can be seen with the eye are bodies.
> _____
> No happy lives are things that can be seen with the eye.

(d) The final example is taken from *The Mismeasure of Man* by Stephen Jay Gould:

> If I had any desire to lead a life of indolent ease, I would wish to be an identical twin, separated from my brother and raised in a different social class. We could hire ourselves out to a host of social scientists and practically name our fee. For we would be exceedingly rare representatives of the only really adequate natural experiment for separating genetic from environmental effects in humans—genetically identical individuals raised in disparate environments.

A syllogistic reconstruction of this argument is

> All genetically identical individuals raised in
> disparate environments are representatives of the only
> adequate natural experiment for separating genetic
> from environmental effects in humans.
> All representatives of the only adequate natural
> experiment for separating genetic from environmental
> effects in humans are persons who can command a
> sufficient fee from social scientists to lead a life of
> indolent ease.
> _____
> All genetically identical individuals raised in disparate
> environments are persons who can command a
> sufficient fee from social scientists to lead a life of
> indolent ease.

IX. QUASI-SYLLOGISM AND SORITES

I. Quasi-Syllogism

A syllogism with a universal premiss, a premiss stating that a given individual is a member of the subject class, and a conclusion stating that the individual is a member of the predicate class, such as

> All men are mortal.
> Socrates is a man.
> _____
> Socrates is mortal.

is called a *quasi-syllogism*. Although this is obviously an instance of a valid form of reasoning, it is not a categorical syllogism as it stands, because the sentences that mention a specific individual (called *singular sentences*) are not categorical. Some treatments of syllogistic logic cover this fundamental form of argument by interpreting singular sentences as disguised universal generalizations:

All members of the class in which the only member is Socrates are men.

If the singular sentences are interpreted in this way, the preceding quasi-syllogism becomes an instance of the valid form:

$$\text{All } M \text{ are } P.$$
$$\text{All } S \text{ are } M.$$
$$\overline{\text{All } S \text{ are } P.}$$

Quasi-syllogisms can also occur with negative universal premisses:

No whales are fishes.
Shamu is a whale.
_____
Shamu is not a fish.

The conclusion in this syllogism is interpreted as

No members of the class in which the only member is Shamu are fishes.

Interpreting the singular premiss as in the other quasi-syllogism, this quasi-syllogism becomes an instance of the valid categorical form:

$$\text{No } M \text{ are } P.$$
$$\text{All } S \text{ are } M.$$
$$\overline{\text{No } S \text{ are } P.}$$

An alternative way of interpreting the quasi-syllogism will be discussed in Chapter 10.

2. Sorites

A *sorites* is an argument with more than two categorical sentences as premisses, from which a final categorical conclusion may be drawn by performing a series of syllogistic inferences. In a sorites with three premisses, the intermediate syllogistic conclusion drawn from a pair of the stated premisses is used as an additional premiss and combined with the third premiss to yield the final conclusion of the argument.

In a sorites with more than three premisses, the process of drawing intermediate conclusions and using them as additional premisses is performed as often as may be required to reach the final conclusion. Lewis Carroll, the brilliant logician who is best known as the author of *Alice in Wonderland,* discusses this type of argument in his *Symbolic Logic.* All of the following examples are taken from this work. Solutions to the first two examples are given. The remaining sets of premisses are intended as exercises.

Examples

(a)

    (i) No ducks waltz.
    (ii) No officers ever decline to waltz.
    (iii) All of my poultry are ducks.

Taking "ducks" as a middle term, the first and third premisses can be combined to yield the intermediate conclusion:

    (iv) No poultry of mine waltz.

"No officers ever decline to waltz" can be obverted to obtain "All officers waltz." This can then be combined with the intermediate conclusion (iv) to yield the final conclusion:

    (v) No officers are poultry of mine.

The conclusion "No poultry of mine are officers," which is equivalent to (v), could also be drawn from these premisses.

(b)

    (i) No potatoes of mine that are new have been boiled.
    (ii) All my potatoes in this dish are fit to eat.
    (iii) No unboiled potatoes of mine are fit to eat.

Taking "things that are fit to eat" as a middle term, premisses (ii) and (iii) can be combined to provide an intermediate conclusion:

    (iv) No unboiled potatoes of mine are my potatoes in this dish.

Before this intermediate conclusion can be combined with (i), the number of terms must be reduced. Since "boiled" and "unboiled" are complementary, we will obvert (i), in which "boiled" occurs in the predicate position. Obverting (i) gives us

    (v) All potatoes of mine that are new are unboiled (potatoes of mine).

Combining (iv) and (v), we have the final conclusion:

No potatoes of mine that are new are my potatoes in this dish. (Or, less awkwardly, "None of my new potatoes are in this dish.")

As an exercise, show that the conclusion "All of my new potatoes are unfit to eat" follows from the three original premisses.

(c)
    (i) No one takes in the *Times* unless he is well-educated.
    (ii) No hedgehogs can read.
    (iii) Those who cannot read are not well-educated.

(d)
    (i) Everyone who is sane can do Logic.
    (ii) No lunatics are fit to serve on a jury.
    (iii) None of your sons can do Logic.

(e)
    (i) All hummingbirds are richly colored.
    (ii) No large birds live on honey.
    (iii) Birds that do not live on honey are dull in color.

(f)
    (i) No birds, except ostriches, are 9 feet high.
    (ii) There are no birds in this aviary that belong to anyone but me.
    (iii) No ostrich lives on mince pies.
    (iv) I have no birds less than 9 feet high.

X. REVIEW

We would expect a rather specialized terminology to have developed in connection with a subject that has been studied in classrooms for more than 2,000 years. Certainly, this has been the case with *syllogistic logic*. Although some of this terminology is used predominately in logic classes, much of it has found its way into the everyday vocabulary of educated people. A list of the important new terms used in this chapter, with brief definitions, follows.

Categorical Sentence: There are four standard forms of categorical sentences. Letting S represent the subject term and P represent the predicate term, these forms are:

1. All S are P. (universal affirmative, or A sentence)
2. No S are P. (universal negative, or E sentence)
3. Some S are P. (particular affirmative, or I sentence)
4. Some S are not P. (particular negative, or O sentence)

Categorical Syllogism: The following features characterize this type of argument:

1. Two premisses and a conclusion, each of which is a categorical sentence.
2. Only three terms occur in the argument. One of the terms occurs once in each premiss; the other two terms occur once in one of the premisses and once in the conclusion.

Complementary Terms: A pair of terms is complementary when one term of the pair refers to a class and the other term of the pair refers to its *complement* (the class in which the members are all things that are not members of the original class).

Contradictory Sentences: When one sentence in a pair is the negation of the other sentence, the pair of sentences is contradictory. In a pair of contradictory sentences, one is true and the other is false. For categorical sentences with the same subjects and predicates, the *A* and *O* sentences are contradictory, as are the *E* and *I* sentences.

Contraposition: The *contrapositive* of an *A* or an *O* sentence is formed by exchanging the positions of the subject and predicate terms and replacing each with its complement. Contraposition preserves meaning for *A* and *O* sentences, but not for *I* and *E* sentences.

Contrary Sentences: When a pair of sentences is related in such a way that they could both be false but could not both be true, the sentences are contrary to one another. If it is assumed in categorical sentences with the same subject and predicate that there are members of the subject class, the *A* and *E* sentences are contraries.

Conversion: A categorical sentence is *converted* when the subject and predicate terms are interchanged. Converting *I* and *E* sentences yields sentences with the same meaning as the original sentences; converting *A* and *O* sentences does not.

Distribution of Terms: When a sentence refers to every member of a class, the term referring to that class is said to be *distributed*. In *universal* categorical sentences, the subject terms are distributed; in *negative* categorical sentences, the predicate terms are distributed.

Existential Assumption: The assumption that there are some members of the subject class referred to in a universal categorical sentence.

Fallacies of Distribution: Mistakes in reasoning that occur when a term that is used collectively in the premises is interpreted distributively in the conclusion (*fallacy of division*) or when a term that is used distributively in the premises is interpreted collectively in the conclusion (*fallacy of composition*).

Figure of a Syllogism: The arrangement of the end terms and the middle term in the premises. There are four figures:

MP	*PM*	*MP*	*PM*
SM	*SM*	*MS*	*MS*
SP	*SP*	*SP*	*SP*

Obversion: A categorical sentence is *obverted* when the quality of the sentence is changed and the predicate term is replaced with its complement. The resulting sentence is a categorical sentence that is logically equivalent to the original sentence.

Quality of a Categorical Sentence: The quality of a categorical sentence refers to whether the sentence is negative or affirmative. The quality of *A* and *I* sentences is affirmative; the quality of *E* and *O* sentences is negative.

Quasi-Syllogism: A three-term syllogism with a universal premiss, a singular premiss, and a singular conclusion.

Sorites: An argument with more than two categorical sentences as premisses and with a categorical conclusion that is reached by drawing an *intermediate* syllogistic conclusion from two of the premisses and then using this conclusion in combination with another premiss to draw a further syllogistic conclusion. This pattern is repeated, using the remaining premisses, until the final conclusion is reached.

Sub-Contrary Sentences: When a pair of sentences is related in such a way that they could both be true but could not both be false, the sentences are sub-contraries. If it is assumed that there are members of the subject class, the *I* and *O* sentences are sub-contraries in categorical sentences that have the same subject and predicate.

Venn Diagrams: Sets of overlapping circles, which may be marked to indicate class membership, class exclusion, and class inclusion. These diagrams are used to diagram categorical sentences and to test for the validity of syllogisms.

XI. EXERCISES

1. For each of the following incomplete arguments, supply a premiss that will make the argument a valid categorical syllogism or quasi-syllogism. (Use the rules for valid syllogisms or Venn diagrams, if helpful.)
   a. Marijuana should not be legalized because it is potentially dangerous.
   b. Marijuana should be legalized because it is no more dangerous than alcohol, which is legal.
   c. Abernathy must be rich, since he never wears an overcoat.
   d. Female office workers work just as hard as male office workers and are just as productive. Therefore, female office workers should receive the same pay as male office workers in comparable positions.
   e. Since John gets sick only when he is nervous, his illness must be psychogenic.
   f. Not all Socialists deserve to be persecuted, for some Socialists are champions of human rights.
   g. Those who do not sin need not fear God, so you don't need to be afraid of God.
   h. Terry is a mathematician, so she must be musically talented.
   i. You had no right to take away his gun, because that gun was private property.
   j. If you failed, it's because you didn't try hard enough.
2. What syllogistic conclusion, if any, can be validly drawn from the following pairs of premisses? (Use of the rules for valid syllogisms or Venn diagrams will prove helpful.)
   a. All beautiful things are expensive. Some beautiful things are made of inexpensive materials.
   b. Some sailors are adventurous. Some adventurous persons like long sea voyages.

   c. Whoever lives by the sword will perish by the sword. Some soldiers perish by the sword.

   d. Whatever goes up must come down. Stock prices are going up.

   e. Anything I say can be misinterpreted. Some misinterpretations are harmless.

   f. All grains are cereals. Some fruits are grains.

   g. No salt is an element. Some salts are soluble.

   h. All metals are fusible. Some conductors are non-metals.

   i. All gondolas are boats. All gondolas have gondoliers.

   j. All children like candy. Some adults like candy.

3. Reconstruct each of the following arguments as a categorical syllogism, supplying plausible premises when necessary. Test each syllogism for validity, using the rules for valid syllogisms or Venn diagrams.

   a. Some valid arguments have false conclusions, but not all syllogisms are valid; so some syllogisms have true conclusions.

   b. None but the rich can afford to be idle. Anyone who can afford to be idle is a threat to the Puritan work ethic, so some rich persons threaten the Puritan work ethic.

   c. Skillfully handcrafted items that are beautiful, enduring, and useful are never inexpensive, so Navajo rugs command a high price.

   d. A clever cook avoids making souffles for dinner parties. No home economics major is not a clever cook. Therefore, no home economics major fails to avoid making souffles for dinner parties.

   e. Some custards are soft, but no ices are soft; so some ices are not custards.

   f. Fallacious arguments are unconvincing. None of your arguments are fallacious. Therefore, all of your arguments are convincing.

   g. Some professors are ignorant. None who are ignorant are fit to teach college students. So some who are unfit to teach college students are professors.

   h. He who hesitates is lost, but the lost shall be found; so hesitators won't stay lost.

   i. All reporters are aggressive. None but reporters have daily deadlines. So no non-aggressive persons have deadlines.

   j. Syllogisms all have two premises. Not all syllogisms are categorical. Some non-categorical syllogisms have two premises.

   k. Decent newspapers cannot attain a wide circulation, for they do not emphasize sensational material. We all know that papers that emphasize sensational material attain a wide circulation.

ARGUMENTS IN WHICH VALIDITY DEPENDS ON RELATIONS

I. INTRODUCTION

In preceding chapters, we analyzed two important types of arguments: truth-functional arguments and categorical syllogisms. For each type of argument, validity was shown to be a matter of *form*. The validity of truth-functional arguments is dependent on logical connections between the sentences that make up the argument, whereas the validity of categorical syllogisms is dependent on logical connections between the subject terms and the predicate terms within sentences. In our analysis of both truth-functional and syllogistic arguments, we ignored the *content* of the arguments. Simple sentences in truth-functional arguments and class terms in categorical syllogisms were represented by letters of the alphabet, allowing us to express the forms of these arguments in a general way. In the case of truth-functional arguments, further formalization was introduced by the use of symbols to represent the truth-functional connectives "and," "not," "or," "if . . . then," and "if and only if."

Most logicians hold the view that *any* deductively valid argument is an instance of some valid *argument form*. Accordingly, the history of logic has been the history of an increasing awareness of the formal properties of arguments that are recognized intuitively as valid. Aristotle's theory of syllogisms was the first formal account of arguments. Shortly after Aristotle, the Stoic logicians developed a comprehensive theory of the forms of truth-functional arguments. Only much later did another important class of arguments receive formal treatment. The validity of these arguments depends on certain formal *properties of relations* mentioned in them. These *relational arguments* will be the subject of this chapter.

II. EXAMPLES OF RELATIONAL ARGUMENTS

The following arguments are obviously valid:

(1)   New Maseratis are more expensive than new Cadillacs.
New Cadillacs are more expensive than new Fords.

New Maseratis are more expensive than new Fords.

(2)   Jack is older than Jill.

Jill is not older than Jack.

(3)   One British pint is equal to 570 milliliters.

570 milliliters is equal to one British pint.

We cannot represent the forms by virtue of which any of these arguments are valid through the application of the techniques of truth-functional logic or of syllogistic logic. In each case, the validity of the argument depends essentially on some property of the relations ("more expensive than," "older than," "equal to") referred to in the arguments.

III. IMPORTANT PROPERTIES OF RELATIONS

Argument (1) is valid because if one thing is more expensive than a second, and the second is more expensive than a third, then the first is more expensive than the third. When a relation such as "more expensive than" exhibits this feature, the relation is said to be *transitive*. Many ordinary relations are transitive. Some other examples are "older than," "younger than," "prettier than," "equal to," "greater than," "ancestor of," "descended from."

Not all relations are transitive. Some are *intransitive*. If the fact that one member is related to a second and the second has the same relation to a third *rules out* the first member standing in that relation to the third, then the relation is intransitive. The following argument is valid because the relation "mother of " is intransitive:

> Ruth is the mother of Betty.
> Betty is the mother of Claudia.
> ———————————————————
> Ruth is *not* the mother of Claudia.

Other examples of intransitive relations are "father of" and "twice as large as."

Some relations are neither transitive nor intransitive. ("Transitive" and "intransitive" are contrary terms, not contradictories.) In these *nontransitive relations,* if the first member stands in that relation to the second and the second has that relation to a third, then the first member *may or may not* be related to the third in that way.

"Cousin of" is a nontransitive relation. If James is a cousin of Alice and Alice is a cousin of Richard, James may or may not be Richard's cousin. No conclusion can be drawn regarding the relation between the first and third members on the basis of a nontransitive relation between the first and second and the second and third. Some other nontransitive relations are "takes a class with," "likes some of the same foods as," "is a friend of," "loves," and "is in a carpool with."

All of the relations mentioned thus far are relations between things or individuals that are considered *two* at a time. These are called *binary relations,* or *two-termed relations.* The two things that are related by a binary relation are called the *terms* of the relation. Not all relations are binary. In "Clarissa bought her books from Edward," a relation connects three terms: Clarissa, her books, and Edward. The following sentence involves a four-term relation: "Tony gave money to Sally for the hospital fund-raiser." Although it becomes awkward to construct English sentences involving relations with more than four or five terms, theoretically any number of terms can be related. To avoid complexities and to focus on some important properties of binary relations, our discussion in this chapter will be confined to binary relations that relate only two terms.

If we limit our consideration to binary relations, then the following claim is true: Any relation whatsoever falls into *exactly one* of the following categories: transitive, intransitive or nontransitive.

The relation mentioned in argument (2) in Section II ("older than") is a transitive relation. However, the validity of this argument does not depend on the transitivity of that relation but on another of its properties. "Older than" is an *asymmetric relation*. In asymmetric relations, if the first member is related to the second, then the second is *not* related to the first in that way. "Greater than," "less than," "weighs more than," and "mother of" are familiar examples of asymmetric relations.

If the fact that the first member has a relation to the second *implies* that the second has that same relation to the first, then the relation is said to be *symmetric*. "Equal to," "weighs the same as," "not identical with," and "sibling of" are all symmetric relations. The validity of argument (3) in Section II depends on the symmetry of "equal to."

There are also *nonsymmetric relations* in which the fact that the first member is related to the second *neither* implies *nor* rules out the second member having that relation to the first. "Brother of" is a nonsymmetric relation. Two individuals can be related in such a way that one is the brother of the other but the second is not the brother of the first (when the second is female). Of course, in the case of two males, if the first is brother to the second, then the second is brother to the first. Since either situation is possible for two arbitrarily selected individuals, "brother of" is a nonsymmetric relation.

Every binary relation falls into *exactly one* of these three categories: symmetric, asymmetric, or nonsymmetric.

If an individual or a thing is related to itself by some relation, then that relation is said to be *reflexive*. Obviously, "identical with" is a reflexive relation; everything is identical with itself. Other examples of reflexive relations are "equal to" and "is the same color as."

When a relation is such that no individual or thing can have that relation to itself, then the relation is said to be *irreflexive*. Examples of irreflexive relations are "unequal to," "different from," "not the same as," and "greater than."

Some relations are *nonreflexive*. Individuals or things *may or may not* bear such relations to themselves. "Loves," for example, is nonreflexive; some persons love themselves, but others do not.

It may seem a bit odd to regard a relation as two-termed when the "two" things being related are one and the same. Nevertheless, it makes perfectly good sense to speak of a thing either having or failing to have some relation to itself. In general, the terms in any binary relation need not refer to distinct individuals.

Exercises

1. State whether each of the following relations is:

   (1) Transitive, intransitive or nontransitive.
   (2) Symmetric, asymmetric, or nonsymmetric.
   (3) Reflexive, irreflexive, or nonreflexive.

a.	Loves	b.	Cousin of
c.	Belongs to	d.	Looks like
e.	Less than	f.	Is preferred to
g.	Plays better than	h.	Is taller than
i.	Is identical with	j.	Is the same age as

2. Name ten different binary relations, and categorize each as transitive, symmetric, reflexive, etc.

IV. USING QUANTIFIERS TO EXPRESS RELATIONS

Aristotle used *variables* (letters of the alphabet) to represent class terms when he formulated principles of reasoning. Using variables in this way simplifies the expression of principles and makes it easier to recognize the formal properties of arguments. The use of letters to represent sentences in truth-functional logic is a twentieth-century innovation. We can grasp some of the simplicity that we gain by applying this technique if we compare our formulation of *affirming the antecedent*:

$$p \to q$$
$$\underline{p }$$
$$q$$

with the formulation of the ancient Stoic logicians:

If the first, then the second.
The first.
_____
Therefore, the second.*

When truth-functional argument forms involve numerous simple sentences, the use of sentence letters becomes even more attractive. (Try to express one of the dilemma forms of argument using expressions such as "the first," "the second," "the third," etc.)

Twentieth-century developments in the symbolization of logic enable us to express the properties of relations in a compact way. The symbolic languages commonly used by modern logicians provide an adequate formulation of categorical syllogisms as well and, by employing symbols common to various types of arguments, serve to make apparent important logical similarities among truth-functional arguments, syllogistic arguments, and relational arguments.

In the following sections, we will speak of *translating* English expressions into artificial symbolic language. These translations are not intended to capture all of the nuances that could be expressed in the English language. Their purpose is to identify the features of arguments that are important for determining their validity. The symbols that you will be introduced to here are designed to capture only those features.

For any translation to be possible, the symbols of the artificial language must be *interpreted*. *Interpretations* specify the meanings of the symbols to the extent that truth conditions (the conditions under which sentences in the artificial

*Benson Mates, *Elementary Logic,* p.214.

language are true or false) are clearly specified. We have already done this (using truth tables) for the symbols used in truth-functional logic. Since the same connectives will be used here, the following summary is provided (remember, p and q are sentence letters):

1. $\sim p$ is true if and only if p is false.
2. $(p \lor q)$ is false only in cases when both p and q are false; otherwise, it is true.
3. $(p \cdot q)$ is true only in cases when both p and q are true; otherwise, it is false.
4. $(p \rightarrow q)$ is false whenever p is true and q is false; otherwise, it is true.
5. $(p \leftrightarrow q)$ is true whenever p and q have the same truth value; otherwise, it is false.

Other features of interpretations will be discussed in context as they arise.

1. Symbolizing the Universal Quantifier

In the universal affirmative form "All S are P," "all" is called a *universal quantifier*. We have already discussed the logical structure of these *universal affirmative sentences*, and we know that they are best understood as *conditional sentences*. Expressed as a conditional, the universal affirmative becomes

If anything is an S, then it is a P.

An alternative conditional formulation is

For any individual (person, place, or thing), if it is an S, then it is a P.

The universal quantifier is commonly symbolized by a lower-case letter from the end of the alphabet enclosed in parentheses. Examples are

(x) Read: "For any x"
(y) Read: "For any y"
(z) Read: "For any z"

In symbolizing the universal affirmative sentence, the same letter that is in the quantifier is used in place of pronouns such as "it" to refer to the same individuals. Thus, to symbolize "For any individual, if it is an S, then it is a P," we write

$$(x)(Sx \rightarrow Px)$$

Parentheses enclose the expression following the quantifier to indicate that the xs in this expression are those referred to by the quantifier that precedes the expression. The letters used in this way are called *individual variables*; the upper-case letters used to represent *classes* of individuals are called *predicate letters.*

Now, suppose that we want to translate the English categorical sentence "All suffragettes are feminists" into a symbolic sentence that represents the meaning of the English sentence as closely as possible. The first step is to specify a *domain of interpretation,* or the *set of all individuals* that we will refer to in the artificial language. This domain may vary from interpretation to interpretation. In one situation, we may be talking only about numbers and can choose the *set of all numbers* as our domain of interpretation. In another situation, we may be referring only to persons and can choose the *set of all persons* as our domain. The domain of interpretation can be any nonempty set of individuals. To simplify matters for all interpretations in this chapter, unless otherwise noted, we will select as our domain of interpretation the set of all individuals. (The members of this domain are all persons, things, numbers, etc.)

Predicate letters will be interpreted as referring to *classes* (sets) of individuals in the domain. To translate our sentence, we need to interpret one predicate letter as referring to the class of suffragettes and a second predicate letter as referring to the class of feminists. We will interpret S as the class of suffragettes and F as the class of feminists. Then "All suffragettes are feminists" can be translated into

$$(x)(Sx \rightarrow Fx)$$

The universal negative sentence ("No S are P"), which also has the structure of a conditional sentence ("For any individual, if it is an S, then it is not a P"), is written

$$(x)(Sx \rightarrow \sim Px)$$

To translate the sentence "No chihuahuas are guide-dogs," we interpret

C: the class of chihuahuas
G: the class of guide-dogs

and write

$$(x)(Cx \rightarrow \sim Gx)$$

2. Symbolizing the Existential Quantifier

The quantifier "some" is called the *existential quantifier. Particular affirmative sentences* and *particular negative sentences* assert both that some individual *exists* and that the individual either *has* or *lacks* some property. These sentences are said to have *existential import.* Universal sentences lack existential import, since they do not assert the existence of members of the subject class.

The *I* and *O* sentences have the structure of conjunctions:

> *I:*   Some *S* are *P.*
> There is some individual that is an *S and* also a *P.*
>
> *O:*   Some *S* are not *P.*
> There is some individual that is an *S and* not a *P.*

The existential quantifier is symbolized by a backward "E" followed by an individual variable and enclosed in parentheses: $(\exists x)$.

To symbolize the existential, or particular, affirmative categorical sentence, we write

$$(\exists x)(Sx \cdot Px)$$

which can be read "There is some *x* such that it is *S* and it is *P.*"

To symbolize the existential (particular) negative categorical sentence, we write

$$(\exists x)(Sx \cdot \sim Px)$$

which can be read "There is some *x* such that it is *S* and it is not *P.*"

Exercises

Provide suitable interpretations for predicate letters and translate the following sentences into the symbolic language:

1. Some dogs have fleas.
2. Some cats are not independent.
3. No dogs are vegetarians.
4. All cats are independent.
5. There are wild cats.
6. Cats are quadrupeds.
7. Not all dogs bark.
8. All dogs bark, and all cats meow.
9. Some dogs bark, but some do not.
10. Dogs and cats are fine pets.

3. Symbolizing Relational Sentences

With a minor modification, the symbols used to represent categorical sentences can be adapted to express relations. The class terms that occur in categorical sentences may be thought of as *one-place predicates.* Using symbols, we indicate that an individual x is a member of a class S by writing a predicate letter followed by a single individual variable: Sx. In a similar manner, we can think of binary relations as *two-place predicates*. Using symbols, we indicate that an individual x stands in a relation R to an individual y by writing that predicate letter followed by the pair of variables, taken in the proper order: Rxy.

Two-place predicate letters are interpreted as referring to sets of *ordered pairs* of individuals who are related by the relation in question. For example, we could interpret the predicate letter L as referring to the set of all pairs of individuals such that the first member of the pair loves the second member of the pair. In specifying such interpretations, we use the following notation:

$$L: \underline{\quad} loves \ldots$$

Using quantifiers, predicate letters, and individual variables, generalizations that involve relations can be expressed in symbols. For example, if we interpret L as above, we can translate "Everything loves everything" into symbols:

$$(x)(y)(Lxy)$$

If we want to translate the sentence "Everybody loves everybody," we need to use a predicate letter to represent the class of persons. If we interpret P in this way, then the sentence is translated

$$(x)(y)((Px \cdot Py) \rightarrow Lxy)$$

which can be read "Given any x and any y, if x is a person and y is a person, then x loves y." Note that if we choose to limit our domain of interpretation to the set of all persons, then "Everybody loves everybody" is translated

$$(x)(y)(Lxy)$$

Given the same interpretation of L, "Something loves something" is translated

$$(\exists x)(\exists y)(Lxy)$$

Again, interpreting P as the class of persons and L as loves, "Somebody loves somebody" is translated

$$(\exists x)(\exists y)(Px \cdot Py \cdot Lxy)$$

In addition to generalizations about relations, sentences such as "Ruth is the mother of Betty" state that some specific individual is related to another specific individual. In our symbolic language, lower-case letters from the earlier part of the alphabet (a–t) are interpreted as referring to individuals. These letters, called *individual constants,* perform the same function in the symbolic language as proper names perform in ordinary language. For example, we could symbolize the sentence "Socrates is mortal" by interpreting s to refer to Socrates and M to refer to the class of mortals and writing

$$Ms$$

Socrates, one of the most important philosophers of all time, was married to Xanthippe. If we interpret H to refer to ___ is husband of . . . , s to refer to Socrates, and a to refer to Xanthippe, then

$$Hsa$$

is true, for it says that Socrates is the husband of Xanthippe. Given the same interpretations

$$Has$$

is false, for it says that Xanthippe is the husband of Socrates. Obviously, "husband of" is an asymmetric relation.

Using quantifiers, individual variables, and two-place predicate letters, we can conveniently and precisely characterize important properties of binary relations. If R is some two-place relation, then we can symbolically express any of the following properties of R:

1. R is reflexive: $(x)Rxx$
   The symbolic formula can be read "Given anything, it stands in relation R to itself."
2. R is irreflexive: $(x)(\sim Rxx)$
   "Given anything, it is not related by R to itself."
3. R is nonreflexive: $\sim(x)(Rxx) \cdot \sim(x)(\sim Rxx)$
   "It is not the case that R is reflexive, and it is not the case that R is irreflexive." (Or, "R is not reflexive, and R is not irreflexive.")
4. R is symmetric: $(x)(y)(Rxy \rightarrow Ryx)$
   "Given any x and any y (not necessarily distinct), if x bears relation R to y, then y bears relation R to x."
5. R is asymmetric: $(x)(y)(Rxy \rightarrow \sim Ryx)$
   "Given any x and any y (not necessarily distinct), if x bears relation R to y, then y does not bear relation R to x."
6. R is nonsymmetric: $\sim(x)(y)(Rxy \rightarrow Ryx) \cdot \sim(x)(y)(Rxy \rightarrow \sim Ryx)$
   "R is not symmetric, and R is not asymmetric."
7. R is transitive: $(x)(y)(z)((Rxy \cdot Ryz) \rightarrow Rxz)$
   "For any three individuals x, y, z (not necessarily distinct), if the first bears relation R to the second and the second bears relation R to the third, then the first bears relation R to the third."
8. R is intransitive: $(x)(y)(z)((Rxy \cdot Ryz) \rightarrow \sim Rxz)$
   "For any three individuals x, y, z (not necessarily distinct), if x bears relation R to y and y bears relation R to z, then x does not bear relation R to z."

Exercises

Express each of the following in symbols, providing interpretations for symbols when necessary. Be sure to specify the domain of interpretation.

1. R is nontransitive.
2. Mary loves someone.
3. John loves himself.
4. John loves himself and Mary.
5. Mary does not love John.
6. Someone loves Mary.
7. Everyone loves John.
8. No one loves John.
9. Mary loves no one.
10. Everyone loves John, or everyone loves Mary.

4. Multiple Quantifiers

To symbolize most generalizations involving relations, we must use more than one quantifier. For example, to state the property of transitivity of a relation, three universal quantifiers are required. When multiple quantifiers are all of the same type (all universal or all existential), the order in which they are placed at the beginning of the symbolized expression is irrelevant. Assuming that R is interpreted the same way in each case, there is no difference in meaning among the following:

$$(x)(y)(z)((Rxy \cdot Ryz) \rightarrow Rxz)$$
$$(y)(x)(z)((Rxy \cdot Ryz) \rightarrow Rxz)$$
$$(z)(y)(x)((Rxy \cdot Ryz) \rightarrow Rxz)$$

Likewise, there is no difference in meaning between

$$(\exists x)(\exists y)(Rxy \cdot Ryx)$$

and

$$(\exists y)(\exists x)(Rxy \cdot Ryx)$$

However, when there are multiple quantifiers of both types in a single expression, care must be taken, for the meaning may not be preserved when quantifiers are reordered. Consider the sentence "Everybody has a mother." Let us limit our domain to the set of persons:

$$M: \underline{\quad} \text{ is the mother of} \dots$$

The symbolic sentence is

$$(x)(\exists y)(Myx)$$

Based on the given interpretation for M, the symbolic sentence can be read

Given any x, there is some y such that y is the mother of x.

In other words, the sentence says that for any person, there is someone who is the mother of that person.

If the order of the quantifiers is reversed, the symbolic sentence becomes

$$(\exists y)(x)(Myx)$$

Based on the given interpretation for M, this sentence can be read

There is some y such that given any x, y is the mother of x.

In other words, someone is the mother of everyone! When "someone" occurs at the beginning of the expression, it means "some one person," and it is clearly false that some one person is the mother of everyone. When "someone" occurs in the position shown in the first translation, it means "someone or other," and it is true that every person has someone or other as a mother. Thus, although these two symbolic expressions differ only in the order in which the quantifiers are placed at the beginning of the expression, they have very different meanings.

Exercise

Using the set of persons as the domain of interpretation and interpreting L as ___ loves . . . , express each of the following in symbolic language.

1. Everyone loves someone (or other).
2. No one loves everyone.
3. No one loves anyone.
4. Someone loves everyone.

5. The Fallacy of Every and All

It was—and is—widely believed that everything that happens does so as a result of some cause. In antiquity, the claim "Everything that happens has a cause" was used as a premiss to infer that there is some "first cause" of everything. If this argument is valid, however, it must be an instance of some form other than

$$\frac{(x)(\exists y)(Cyx)}{(\exists y)(x)(Cyx)}$$

because this form is invalid. Based on the intended interpretation (C: ___ causes . . .), the symbolization provides a reasonable translation of the argument, as just stated. However, it is possible to interpret C in such a way that the premiss is obviously true but the conclusion is obviously false (C: ___ is mother of . . .). Since an instance of the argument form is invalid, that is (when the domain of interpretation is the set of all persons)

$$\frac{\text{Everyone has a mother.}}{\text{Someone is everyone's mother.}}$$

the form itself is invalid. For an argument form to be valid, every interpretation of the nonlogical symbols (predicate letters and individual constants) must result in a valid argument.

This fallacious form of argument is called the *fallacy of every and all*. We must remember, however, that an argument that is an instance of some fallacious *argument form* may not be an invalid *argument*. The argument is invalid only if it is not an instance of any valid argument form. Nevertheless, as is true of truth-functional arguments, we should at least suspect invalidity when an argument is an instance of an invalid form and when no analysis of the argument is provided to show that it is an instance of some valid form.

Aristotle's argument for the existence of a first cause, or "prime mover," actually involved at least one further premiss: an infinite series of causes and effects is impossible. We might symbolize Aristotle's rejection of an infinite regress of causes—the claim that there must be some cause that is not the effect of any other cause—as

$$(\exists y)((\exists x)(Cyx) \cdot \sim(\exists z)(Czy))$$

or "There is a y such that y causes some x and no z causes y." Even the addition of this premiss does not allow us to conclude that there is just one first cause, however, for there may be more than one "uncaused cause." ("Some" means "at least one"; it does not mean "exactly one.")

Although it is difficult to analyze some of Aristotle's arguments due to difficulties in translating the language as well as the loss or alteration of texts, many interpreters impute the fallacy of every and all to Aristotle in more than one context. In commenting on Aristotle's apparent use of the premiss that every action has a final end to support the conclusion that there is one and the same end to all actions, called the "Supreme Good," a contemporary philosopher has said in defense of the founder of logic:

This is a type of reasoning [relational logic] that lies beyond the reach of his own formal logic. He may, for this reason, have been more easily deceived by this fallacy.*

V. SYMBOLIZING ARGUMENTS

One of the advantages of modern symbolic languages is the fact that they expose important similarities in structure between various types of arguments. Consider, for example, the following quasi-syllogism:

> All princesses are beautiful.
> Diana is a princess.
> _____
> Diana is beautiful.

Based on the interpretation

> P: the class of princesses
> B: the class of beautiful persons
> d: Diana

the argument can be translated

$$(x)(Px \rightarrow Bx)$$
$$Pd$$
$$\overline{}$$
$$Bd$$

Ignoring for a moment the presence of the quantifier, this form is obviously quite similar to the form of *affirming the antecedent*:

$$p \rightarrow q$$
$$p$$
$$\overline{}$$
$$q$$

We can also consider the fact that a universal generalization is a sentence that says something about every individual in the domain of interpretation. If what the universal generalization says is true of every individual in the domain, then it is true of any *particular* individual in the domain. For example, based on the given interpretation, if

$$(x)(Px \rightarrow Bx)$$

*D.J. O'Connor, "Aristotle," in *A Critical History of Western Philosophy,* edited by D. J. O'Connor.

is true, then so is

$$Pd \rightarrow Bd$$

If we replace the first premiss with a particular instance of the generalization $(Pd \rightarrow Bd)$, then the argument becomes

$$Pd \rightarrow Bd$$
$$Pd$$
_____
$$Bd$$

This is obviously the same form as *affirming the antecedent* and is therefore a valid argument form. Thus, the original quasi-syllogism is valid. This method of determining the validity of the argument form of quasi-syllogisms seems less arbitrary than the treatment suggested in Chapter 9. There, sentences like "Diana is a princess" were treated as a type of universal generalization: "All members of the class of which Diana is the only member are princesses." This method was somewhat artificial because universal generalizations lack existential import, but the sentence "Diana is a princess" ordinarily would be regarded as false if she did not exist.

A detailed discussion of the systems of logic that employ quantifiers is beyond the scope of this text. It is worth noting, however, that all these systems have a rule of inference that permits a move to be made from universally quantified sentences to their particular instances. Other rules treat removing existential quantifiers and replacing both types of quantifiers after they have been removed. With this in mind, consider the similarity between the following syllogistic form of argument and the truth-functional form of hypothetical syllogism:

$$(x)(Sx \rightarrow Mx) \qquad p \rightarrow q$$
$$(x)(Mx \rightarrow Px) \qquad q \rightarrow r$$
_____
$$(x)(Sx \rightarrow Px) \qquad p \rightarrow r$$

Similarities between syllogistic arguments, truth-functional arguments, and relational arguments also become apparent when we use this symbolic language. For example, the validity of the argument "Marcy ran faster than Sam, and Sam ran faster than Carrie; therefore, Marcy ran faster than Carrie" depends on the true but unstated premiss that "ran faster than" is a transitive relation. The argument can be symbolized, using the following interpretation:

$R:$ ____ ran faster than . . .
$m:$ Marcy $s:$ Sam $c:$ Carrie

$$(x)(y)(z)((Rxy \cdot Ryz) \rightarrow Rxz)$$
$$Rms \cdot Rsc$$
_____
$$Rmc$$

Here, too, the symbolism shows the similarity between this form and *affirming the antecedent.*

The value of symbolic techniques in modern logic should not be underestimated. The use of appropriate symbols has allowed advancements to be made in this field that are comparable to the advancements in mathematics that resulted from the replacement of the system of Roman numerals with the system of Arabic numerals.

VI. REVIEW

In Chapter 10, you have been introduced to arguments in which validity depends on the *properties of binary relations* referred to in the arguments. You have also been introduced to some of the symbolic techniques used in modern logic to express the forms of these arguments and have been shown how some of these forms resemble familiar truth-functional forms.

Every *binary relation* falls into exactly one of each of the following categories:

1. Transitive, intransitive, nontransitive.
2. Symmetric, asymmetric, nonsymmetric.
3. Reflexive, irreflexive, nonreflexive.

You should review the definitions of these properties of relations presented in this chapter and be able to categorize examples of binary relations according to these properties.

In many arguments in which validity depends on some property of a relation referred to in the argument, the premisses do not include a statement of that property. You should be able to recognize such unstated premisses and to supply them when you reconstruct these arguments.

You should be able to translate categorical sentences and sentences involving relations from English into the logical symbolism that reveals their logical structure. To do this, you need to remember that *universal sentences* are to be treated as *conditional sentences* and that *existential (particular) sentences* are to be treated as *conjunctions*.

Finally, you should be able to recognize apparent instances in English of the *fallacy of every and all.* This fallacy occurs when sentences containing both *universal* and *existential quantifiers* are treated as if truth is always preserved when the order in which their quantifiers occur is exchanged. The ability to symbolize such English sentences helps us to avoid this fallacy.

VII. EXERCISES

1. For each of the following arguments, name the property of the relation that makes the argument valid:
   a. Horses can outrun greyhounds, and greyhounds exist. But greyhounds can outrun rabbits, so horses can outrun rabbits.

   b. 7 is greater than the square root of 48, so the square root of 48 is not greater than 7.

   c. John is married to Sarah, so Sarah is married to John.

2. Relations that are transitive, symmetric, and reflexive are called *equivalence relations*. Can you give three examples of equivalence relations?

3. Relations that are transitive, asymmetric, and irreflexive are called *ordering relations*. Can you give an example of an ordering relation?

4. When an individual *a* is related by a relation *R* to individual *b*, then *b* is said to be related to *a* by a relation called the *converse of R*. What is the converse of each of the following relations?

   a. Husband of

   b. Parent of

   c. Greater than

   d. Greater than or equal to

5. When a relation is symmetric, what can we say about its converse?

6. Provide a suitable interpretation and translate the following into the symbolic language developed in this chapter, using relational predicates when appropriate:

   a. Cats make better pets than dogs.

   b. Some cats are smarter than any dog.

   c. Every dog fears some cat.

   d. Some cat is feared by every dog.

   e. Christopher is Virginia's brother.

   f. Not everyone has a cousin.

   g. Cats and dogs are smarter than goldfish.

   h. Snakes eat mice.

   i. Every rich woman owns a piano.

   j. Some poor people own pianos.

7. Provide a suitable interpretation and symbolize all three of the arguments in Exercise 1 of this set. Be sure to symbolize the unstated premises concerning the properties of the relations involved as well as the stated premises.

8. The following argument is an example of fallacious reasoning presented by G.E.M. Anscombe in *An Introduction to Wittgenstein's Tractatus*. What is wrong with it?

> At all times there is a possibility of my abstaining from smoking. There is a possibility of my abstaining from smoking at all times.

9. Construct (or find) an example of an argument in English that apparently commits the fallacy of every and all.

10. Give an example of a relation that is reflexive but not symmetric.

PAYING SPECIAL ATTENTION TO THE LANGUAGE OF ARGUMENTS: DEFINITIONS

I. AMBIGUITY AND VAGUENESS

Assessing the correctness of deductive or inductive arguments requires paying special attention to the language in which the arguments are cast. Before we can decide whether or not the conclusion of an argument follows from its premisses, we must understand what the premiss sentences and the conclusion sentence mean. This task can be complicated by the *vagueness* or the *ambiguity* of many English expressions. We have already adopted certain conventions to eliminate ambiguities in logical connectives, such as "or" and "if . . . then," which have helped us to represent the formal structures of arguments and the application of simple tests for validity. In this section, we will discuss how ambiguity and vagueness in expressions that are not logical connectives affect arguments.

1. Ambiguity

An expression is *ambiguous* if it has more than one distinct meaning. In English, the word "pen" is ambiguous. It can be used to refer to an instrument for writing, an enclosure for animals, or a penitentiary, and its intended meaning within the context of an expression may not be obvious. Frequently, the sentence in which the word occurs does make its meaning clear. Sometimes, a broader context— several sentences, or an account of the circumstances in which the sentence is uttered or written—may be required to eliminate ambiguity. For example, in the sentence "Mark's pen won't write," the meaning of "pen" is clear. However, more information than "Mark couldn't get out of the pen" is needed to know whether Mark was trapped in an animal pen or in a penitentiary.

When we evaluate syllogisms and quasi-syllogisms, we must be sure that expressions are used in the same sense in each occurrence within a single argument. If ambiguous expressions occur, there may be more than three terms in the argument, even though the same English expression is used for two of the terms. Consider the following argument:

Mad men should not be permitted to make important decisions concerning the lives of others.
My father is mad.

My father should not be permitted to make important decisions concerning the lives of others.

Suppose that this argument is offered in the following context: My father, whose mental competence is not in question, is mad (angry) at me because I took a curve at a reckless speed and rolled his car over. He has refused to let me drive his car in the future—a decision that significantly inconveniences me.

The first premiss is plausible only if the term "mad" is understood in the sense of "not mentally competent." But in the second premiss, the meaning of "mad" is different: here, "mad" means the same as "angry." So although the argument resembles a quasi-syllogism, it actually contains more than three terms and is not a valid argument.

When the persuasive force of an argument depends essentially on such shifts of meaning in ambiguous terms, called *equivocations,* the argument is said to commit the *fallacy of equivocation.* In the preceding example, the equivocation involves the single ambiguous word "mad." In other cases, the equivocation may result from the ambiguity of a whole sentence or larger unit of language. Consider the following extract from the *Journal* of John Wesley (the founder of Methodism):

> 1751.   London.   I was carried to the Foundery and preached, kneeling (as I could not stand) on part of the Twenty-third Psalm.

Wesley had sprained his ankle and had preached in a kneeling position. His text was the Twenty-third Psalm. However, the sentence could be understood to mean that he knelt on a copy of the Psalm as he preached.

This type of ambiguity, sometimes called *amphiboly,* is the result of ambiguous sentence structure instead of a single ambiguous term. Such ambiguities can occur when commas are omitted or improperly placed or when grammatical rules for the placement of modifiers are ignored. For example, "He has two grown sons and a daughter in the nunnery" is a puzzling sentence, for it suggests that the sons as well as the daughter are in the nunnery. The ambiguity is resolved when a comma is placed after "sons." Another example is "The guards and prisoners who refused to join in the prison break were tied and left behind," which sounds as if there were guards who refused to break out of prison! There should be a comma following "guards" and a comma following "break." The sentence "They have brown and green eyes" is ambiguous; it could mean that the persons referred to have multi-colored eyes, but it is probably an attempt to express "They have brown eyes and green eyes."

Other ambiguities arise through the use of adjectives and adverbs that are *relative terms.* "Small" and "large" are examples of such terms. A large mouse is not a large animal. A small skyscraper is probably not a small building.

Ambiguity can also arise as a result of shifting the *accent* or emphasis on certain words when a passage is read or spoken. Boswell, in his *Journal,* criticized a fellow lawyer for inferring that it was all right to lie *for* his client on the grounds that the Ninth Commandment, which is usually interpreted as a prohibition of lying, actually says "Thou shalt not bear false witness *against* thy neighbor."

There are no recipes for avoiding and detecting fallacies of equivocation; but the recognition that many words do have more than one meaning, that grammatical constructions may be misleading, and that shifts in emphasis can change the meaning of a passage, provide some defense against the most serious mistakes. In some situations, it may be necessary to ask for or to give a definition of an ambiguous term to prevent misunderstanding. (Techniques for definition will be discussed in Section II.)

When our primary purpose is to present or to evaluate evidence for some claim, it is advisable to resolve ambiguities and to make all claims as explicit and precise as possible. Nevertheless, conveying information to be used in arguments is only one use of language. Ambiguities play an important role in the expressive language of poetry, in which the use of words and expressions to evoke a number of different images and to convey several meanings is crucial. Puns and other forms of humor also depend on ambiguity. Our language would be terribly impoverished without such ambiguities.

Exercises

Discuss the ambiguities on which the following arguments depend:

1. Mary is a person who is a good dancer. Therefore, Mary is a good person.
2. Jumbo is a small elephant. Therefore, Jumbo is a small animal.
3. All women are not feminists. Betty Freidan is a woman. Therefore, she is not a feminist.
4. Camels are the ships of the desert. Ships, in order to move, must be propelled by motors, sails, or oars. Therefore, camels must be propelled by motors, sails, or oars.
5. *Lord Caversham*: Good evening, Lady Chiltern! Has my good-for-nothing young son been here?

   Mabel Chiltern (coming up to Lord Caversham): Why do you call Lord Goring good-for-nothing?

   Lord Caversham: Because he leads such an idle life.

   Mabel Chiltern: How can you say such a thing? Why he rides in the Row at ten o'clock in the morning, goes to the Opera three times a week, changes his clothes at least five times a day, and dines out every night of the season. You don't call that leading an idle life, do you?

   —Oscar Wilde, "An Ideal Husband"

2. Vagueness

An expression is *vague* if "borderline cases" occur in which it is unclear whether or not the expression is applicable. Vagueness differs from ambiguity in that an ambiguous term is one that has at least two distinct, *nonoverlapping* meanings. Some English words, such as "kid," are both ambiguous and vague. "Kid" is ambiguous because it can refer to a young goat or a young child. In the first sense, "kid" is not vague, for goats stop being kids when they are one year old. However, there is no clear cutoff point at which a person is no longer a "kid." In this section, we will ignore possible ambiguities of the terms discussed so that we can concentrate on vagueness.

A standard example of a term that is vague in the sense that it has borderline cases of application is "bald." A person with no hair at all is bald; a person with a full head of hair is not bald. But there are cases in which it is unclear whether the term "bald" is applicable or not. Other examples of terms that are vague in this sense are "old," "happy," "rich," "thin," and most color terms.

Vague terms, like ambiguous terms, can cause difficulties in arguments. For example, the argument that concludes a man is not religious on the grounds that he does not attend church regularly is defective because it fails to recognize that "religious" is a vague term. There are a number of distinct criteria for being religious, including—but not limited to—belief in a supernatural being; membership in an organized religion; adoption of an ethical code or set of altruistic values; performance of acts of devotion or piety; and a sense of reverence toward fellow humans, other living things, or even the entire universe. It is appropriate to call a person "religious" when some, but not all, of these criteria are applicable.

Since "religious" is a vague term, it is unclear just how many of these criteria must be met in order to apply the term "religious" to someone. If all of them are applicable to some person, that person is religious. If none of these criteria apply, the person is not religious. Evidence that someone does not attend church regularly appeals to only one of the criteria and is clearly not enough to support the conclusion that the person is not religious.

Vagueness is a pervasive, important, and useful feature of language, and it would be foolish—if not impossible—to try to eliminate all vague terms. Ordinary social conversation would be severely limited without such comfortable but vague expressions as "See you soon," or "I'll call you sometime," or "How have you been?—Just fine." International diplomacy depends heavily on vague language. Sentiments can be expressed by using such expressions as "The government has warned that it will take strong measures if its territorial waters are violated" without giving away any secrets or risking loss of face.

In some circumstances, however, vague words should be given precise definitions. For example, although the vagueness of the term "religion" poses no problems in most ordinary contexts, some historical situations demand a precise definition of this term. For a long time in the United States, conscientious objectors to military service who were members of some religion were treated differently from conscientious objectors who were not religious. Religious objectors were assigned to alternate nonmilitary service. Nonreligious objectors went to jail.

Leaving aside the question of whether any religious test should be applied to conscientious objectors, obviously when something as serious as a prison sentence is at stake, it is important to state precisely the conditions under which someone will be assigned to prison. What is needed in this particular situation is a definition of "religion" that will reduce its vagueness. In the next section, various techniques for defining terms as well as several types and purposes of definition, including definitions to reduce vagueness, will be discussed.

II. DEFINITIONS

Many books have been written on various aspects of linguistic meaning. In this text, we will touch briefly on only a small part of this fascinating subject. Here, we will be concerned primarily with the meanings of words only insofar as their meanings affect the understanding and evaluation of arguments. A number of different ways of defining words (giving their meanings) are suitable for different purposes.

1. Ostensive Definition

One of the most primitive forms of definition is the technique of indicating individuals, things, or events to which a term applies by pointing to them, displaying them, or using some other nonverbal method of drawing attention to the objects being defined. Parents use this technique to introduce many words to their infants by pointing to baby's eyes, nose, and ears, to dogs, cats, and birds, and to many other objects, while uttering the words that refer to them. This technique is called *ostensive definition*. This type of definition is fundamentally important because it establishes a link between *words* and *objects* in the world that are referred to by using words.

There are limits to the usefulness of this technique. Sometimes attention is directed to the wrong object. A baby may notice the pointing finger rather than the nose when the word "nose" is uttered. Or the baby may suppose that the whole face or the whole person is meant by "nose." A general term, such as "eye," can be defined ostensively only by pointing to particular eyes, and there is always the danger that some special feature of the particular eyes, such as their color, will be mistakenly attached to the general term "eye."

The technique of ostensive definition is further limited because there may be no objects in the vicinity of the type for which a definition is required. A New Yorker can offer ostensive definitions of skyscrapers in midtown Manhattan— but not in the New Guinea highlands, unless some appropriate pictures are available. Moreover, the technique of ostensive definition is not suitable for abstract objects, such as numbers, the gross national product, or the average worker. Abstract objects cannot be pointed to or displayed. Nevertheless, despite these limitations, ostensive definition is useful in many circumstances because it provides a crucial connection between language and nonlinguistic aspects of the world.

2. Verbal Extensional Definition

Ostensive definition is sometimes called *nonverbal extensional definition*. The *extension* of a term is the set of individuals, objects, or events to which the term can be correctly applied. The extension of "boat" is the set of all boats; the extension of "dog" is the set of all dogs; the extension of "prizefighter" is the set of all prizefighters. In ostensive definition, as we have seen, some member or members of the set to which the term applies are pointed to, pictured, or displayed in some way.

Verbal extensional definitions also select members of the set to which the term applies, but the selection is accomplished verbally by naming members of the set. For example, "prizefighter" might be defined by naming some prize-fighters, such as Muhammad Ali, Joe Louis, and Sonny Liston; "President of the United States" might be defined by naming Washington, Adams, Jefferson, Lincoln, Roosevelt, Carter, and Reagan.

Verbal extensional definitions are similar to ostensive definitions in their limitations. Terms such as "prizefighter" refer not only to all present and past prizefighters but also to future prizefighters. In such cases, it is impossible to provide a complete verbal extensional definition that lists all members of the class. When only a partial listing is given, misunderstanding can occur because it is possible to focus on some property shared by all members of the list that is not the same as the term being defined. For example, Ali, Louis, and Liston are not only all prizefighters, they are also all heavyweights, all world champions, and all blacks.

Another limitation of the technique of verbal extensional definition is the difficulty of listing members of sets when the members have no names. Sometimes *subsets* (rather than *members*) of the set that is the extension of a term can be listed, and this may suffice to convey the meaning of the term. For example, we could define "marsupial" extensionally by naming various kinds of marsupials, such as opossums, kangaroos, and wallabies. But it would be very difficult to formulate a verbal extensional definition of "kangaroo." Individual kangaroos are not the sort of things that ordinarily have names, and various types of kangaroos are not known by familiar enough terms to convey their meanings to someone who did not know what a kangaroo was.

3. Intensional Definition

The *intension* of a term is the set of *all and only* those properties that a thing must possess for that term to apply to it. For example, a person must possess the property of being a professional boxer for the term "prizefighter" to be correctly applicable. When a term is given an *explicit intensional definition*, a phrase equivalent in meaning to the term is stated, as in

"Prizefighter" means "a professional boxer."

All intensional definitions are verbal. We can distinguish several types of explicit intensional definitions by recognizing that definitions have various purposes.

i. Definitions That Show How a Word Is Commonly Used

Most dictionary definitions, such as the definition of "prizefighter" just given, are of this type. They are sometimes called *lexical definitions*. To do its job properly, a lexical definition should be neither too narrow nor too broad. The definition should state the set of properties possessed by all things to which the term applies, and only to those things. For example, the definition of "knife"

"Knife" means "an instrument for cutting"

is too broad; some instruments for cutting, namely scissors, are not knives. The definition of "table"

"Table" means "a piece of furniture consisting of a flat top set horizontally on four legs"

is too narrow; some tables have fewer and some tables have more than four legs.
A definition can be both too broad and too narrow. For example

"Cat" means "domestic animal"

is too *broad,* since "domestic animal" applies to livestock, dogs, and various other pets as well. The definition is also too *narrow,* since many wild animals belong to the cat family.

In addition to being neither too broad nor too narrow, lexical definitions should not be circular. A *circular definition* incorporates the term being defined, or some variant of that term, in the definition. For example

"Full-time student" means "a person who devotes full time to his or her studies"

is a circular definition. Such definitions are not helpful in conveying the meaning of a word. Sometimes, circularity is not as apparent as it is in this example, because there are several definitions in the circle. Consider the following set of definitions taken from a recently published dictionary:

"Grazing" means "feeding on growing grass."

"Grass" means "any of various green plants that are eaten by grazing animals."

What we learn from these definitions is little more than grazing animals feed on growing grass and grass is what is eaten by grazing animals. This pair of definitions comes quite close to being circular.

ii. Definitions That Introduce a New Word into the Language

Occasionally, new situations arise or our interests shift to features not previously noted as important, and it is useful to introduce a new word into the language. Such definitions are called *stipulative definitions.* For example, the term "astronaut" is a recent introduction to the language. At the time it was introduced, its meaning was stipulated to be

"Astronaut" means "a person trained to make rocket flights to outer space."

Before the middle of this century, there were no rocket flights to outer space and no persons were trained to make these flights. Thus, there was no reason to have a special term to refer to such persons. New words can always be introduced into a language when salient features of the world make them applicable.

The *conventional* nature of language is most apparent in stipulative definitions. Expressions in a language do not acquire their meanings as a result of some *natural* connection between the words and the things in the world that the words denote. The connection between the word "thunder" and the meteorological phenomenon of thunder is *conventional,* unlike the *natural* connection between thunder and lightening. Words have the meanings they do as a result of the widespread acceptance of proposals to use them in certain ways. This is not to say that the first humans who used language stipulated the meanings of all of the original expressions in a manner similar to the stipulation of the meaning of "astronaut." Although the origins of language are a complete mystery, such a scenario seems highly unlikely. Nevertheless, given what we do know about the development of languages—the ways in which new words are added and words that are no longer useful are discarded—the conventional nature of language seems indisputable. Different human languages use different words to refer to many of the same features of the world (the development of different languages involved the adoption of different conventions), but no language is more correct or "true to the world" than another language.

Although new words can be introduced into language and their meanings can be stipulated by whoever introduces them, stipulative definitions must meet two requirements if they are to be acceptable:

1. A term that is stipulatively defined should not already have a widely accepted standard meaning. When Alice objects to Humpty Dumpty's claim that he is the master of words—words mean what he wants them to mean—she is complaining that he is stipulating new meanings for words with established senses. Confusion obviously results from Humpty Dumpty's attitude toward words with established usages.
2. A term that is stipulatively defined should be a useful addition to the language. Making up new words and offering stipulative definitions for them may be an amusing pastime, but unless the new words serve some useful purpose, it is unlikely that the proposed definitions will be incorporated into the language. Special interests or studies often require the stipulation of a new vocabulary; space technology, which has prompted the introduction of many new terms besides "astronaut," is a case in point. There is, however, the danger that mere *jargon*—terminology that is incomprehensible to those outside a special-interest group—may be substituted for ordinary language, even though the special interest requires no new concepts and could be expressed in terms with accepted standard meanings. Stipulative definitions of this type are unfortunate because they tend to result in the failure rather than the improvement of communication.

iii. Definitions That Reduce Vagueness

Sometimes, it is important to clarify the meaning of a vague term and make it more precise. Such definitions are called *precising definitions*. "Full-time university student" is a vague term in ordinary usage that means roughly "a person who devotes a major part of his or her energies to acquiring some type of knowledge or skill through university courses." However, the vagueness of the term poses a problem for universities that assign fees and benefits on the basis of whether students are full-time or part-time. Universities typically solve this problem by offering a precising definition of "full-time student" in their catalogs. One university lists the following definition of "full-time student":

> "Full-time student" means "student who is carrying a course load of at least 12 units a semester."

Note that this is not the same as a stipulative definition. No new term is being introduced, and a term already in use is not being given a completely different new meaning. In this precising definition, all borderline cases of the vague expression "full-time student" are simply eliminated by making a course load of at least 12 hours per semester the criterion for being a full-time student (at that university). This definition can be used to sort students at the university into two categories: those who are full-time, and those who are not full-time.

Not all cases of reducing vagueness are as simple as this. When terms like "religion" are vague because there are a number of different criteria for applying the term, it is frequently difficult to specify in a reasonable way just which criteria are most important or how many criteria must be met in order to apply the term. Recent debates concerning the definition of the "death of a person" and the "beginning of life of a person" make us aware of the complexity of the problem. Even when such definitions are proposed in judicial rulings that take into account public debates and studies by experts, they do not go unchallenged, for the definitions have grave and far-reaching social consequences. The definitions that are offered in these cases not only reduce vagueness but also involve a *theoretical* account of what it means to be a person. In such cases, definitions are appropriately classed as theoretical.

iv. Definitions for Theoretical Purposes

The term *theory* has several meanings, two of which will concern us here. In its first sense, "theory" refers to a general approach to or a belief about some subject matter that is expressed in a set of interrelated statements concerning the nature of the subject. In this sense, we might speak of a theory of justice involving such statements as "Justice requires that all persons be treated similarly under similar circumstances," "Justice requires that individuals in a society be given equal opportunities and access to the good things in that society," "Justice demands that punishments should be tailored to the nature of the offense," and other such claims. The definition

> "Death of a person" means "cessation of that person's brain functions"

involves such a theory, or set of interrelated claims, concerning the special character of human life. The theory is committed to the view that the body that has totally and irreversibly lost the use of its brain but that may have its circulatory, respiratory, and other systems maintained by machine is no longer a person. The term "vegetable" is sometimes applied in such situations to mark the transformation of the body from the time that it was the body of a person, capable of thought and feeling, to its passive state after loss of brain function. One who holds such a theory would, for example, probably agree that it is not immoral to remove a body that has lost all brain function from machines designed to maintain respiration and also that no harm was being done to the *person* if vital organs from that body were removed for transplanting, provided proper permissions had been obtained from the person before he or she died, or from relatives.

Another sense of "theory" refers to a set of general but precise claims about the nature of society or the physical world. Such theories often involve appeals to unobservable entities that form the basis for many other statements that can be confirmed or disconfirmed by observing the behavior of relevant features of the world. Theories in the physical sciences often assume this form. Examples from physics are the theory of relativity, the theory of atomic physics, and the theory of classical mechanics.

Frequently, physicists take a term from ordinary language and redefine it for some theoretical purpose. For example, in classical mechanics, "work" is defined as "the product of force and distance" and "momentum" is defined as "the product of mass and velocity." In such a theory, many of the terms are defined explicitly by means of other terms in the theory.

However, some terms, such as "force," are not explicitly defined. No expression synonymous with "force" is presented in the theory of classical mechanics. The meanings of such terms are given implicitly in the fundamental generalizations (or *laws*) of the theory. Newton's three laws of motion and his law of universal gravitation all say something about how forces behave (the effects of forces on bodies with respect to such other theoretical features as mass, acceleration, momentum, and distance). In a sense, we can say that the theory tells us what force is only insofar as it tells us how forces operate under various circumstances.

Theoretical definitions are similar to precising definitions in that both reduce vagueness. However, in addition to reducing vagueness, theoretical definitions connect the term being defined with other terms in the theory. A complete understanding of the theoretical meanings of both explicitly defined terms such as "work" and implicitly defined terms, such as "force," is gained only through an understanding of the entire theory.

v. Definitions Designed to Transfer Emotive Force

Definitions designed to transfer emotive force, such as feelings of approval or disapproval, are called *persuasive definitions*. Like other explicit intensional definitions, a persuasive definition should state the properties a thing must possess for the term to apply. However, persuasive definitions also convey an *attitude* toward what is being defined. For example, the definition

> "Homosexual" means "one who has an *unnatural* desire for those of the same sex"

is designed to convey a negative or disapproving attitude toward homosexuals through the use of the term "unnatural."

An attitude of approval—although it is a bit more subtle than the disapproving attitude in the definition of "homosexual"—is conveyed by the definition

> "Democracy" means "the acceptance and practice of the principle of equality of rights, opportunities, and treatment; lack of snobbery."

An attitude of approval is present in this definition because most people are generally considered to approve of such things as equality of rights and lack of snobbery. Perhaps the emotive force of this definition of "democracy" can best be seen if we contrast it with the definition

> "Democracy" means "rule by majority."

Most people would not regard this definition as persuasive. Its emotive force is probably quite neutral. "Rule by majority" does not engender the same degree of approval as appeals to equality of rights and lack of snobbery do.

If, however, there are some people who associate "rule by majority" with "mob rule," then the definition of "democracy" that equates it with "rule by majority" may convey negative emotive force to those persons.

As is often the case in various definitions of the same term, these two definitions of "democracy" differ in their statement of intension as well as in their emotive force. "Rule by majority" and "the acceptance and practice of the principle of equality of rights, opportunities, and treatment; lack of snobbery" do not refer to the same properties of a democracy.

Whether or not persuasive definitions are appropriate depends on the context in which a definition is offered. There is nothing intrinsically wrong with trying to persuade others to share our attitudes. Persuasive definitions are often presented in a humorous context. For example, "philosophy" has been defined as "a doubt which lives in one like a hookworm, causing pallor and lack of appetite." In this persuasive definition, as in many definitions proposed for humorous purposes, the intension of the term—the properties a thing must have if the term is to apply—is partially or completely ignored. When the purpose of a definition is entertainment, this may be perfectly acceptable. But if we are seeking the definition of an emotionally neutral term for the purpose of making its standard use known, then a persuasive definition is probably inappropriate and may be deceptive or misleading.

Familiarity with the technique of persuasive definitions increases our awareness that words that refer to the same objects may differ sharply in emotive force. It doesn't require much sensitivity to recognize the difference in attitudes carried or conveyed by the terms "woman" and "broad" or "black" and "nigger." Objectionable slang terms that are disrespectful to various segments of the population, such as ethnic, racial, and religious groups, are regrettably all too common.

Other expressions, however, can carry a similar negative emotive force in less obvious ways. Calling an airplane race in which the pilots are women a "powder-puff derby" conveys the attitude that such races are to be taken less seriously than races in which men are the pilots.

We should be especially sensitive to the emotive force of any expressions used in arguments, for emotively charged terms may lead us to accept or reject conclusions when this is not warranted by the evidence.

4. Contextual Definition

Thus far, with the exception of implicit theoretical definitions, we have confined our discussion to defining terms by giving their intensions or extensions in an *explicit* manner. For the most part, the terms we have defined in this way have been common nouns and adjectives. Some words, however, such as prepositions, articles, and conjunctions, do *not* have an intension or an extension—they do not refer to things, events, persons, or activities, although they do have meanings and play an essential role in language.

These terms have primarily grammatical or *syntactic* meanings. Examples of such words are "and," "or," and "if . . . then." Sometimes, these terms are defined *explicitly,* by presenting synonyms that have the same grammatical function ("and" means "also; in addition to; moreover; as well as"). More often, however, these terms are defined *implicitly,* by stating their grammatical functions and then giving examples (*contexts*) in which the term occurs. Such definitions are called *contextual definitions.* For example, "or" can be defined as a *coordinating conjunction* that introduces an alternative, as in "I'll offer him beer or wine." "Or" may also be defined as a word that connects sentences in such a way that the complex sentence that is formed is true whenever either of the sentences it connects is true and is false otherwise. Our truth-table definitions of the logical connectives are implicit definitions of this type.

Another kind of implicit contextual definition presents an expression (context) equivalent in meaning to an expression in which the term to be defined occurs. For example, "unless" is contextually defined in the following:

"We'll have a picnic unless it rains" means the same as "If it doesn't rain, then we'll have a picnic."

In this definition, no single expression *synonymous* with "unless" is explicitly presented. Instead, the defining expression is synonymous with the whole expression in which "unless" occurs and it does not contain "unless."

Exercises

1. Classify each of the following definitions as to type:
    a. "Communism" means "an economic theory or system of ownership of all property by the community as a whole."

b. "Communism" means "a form of government characterized by rigid state planning and control of the economy, ruthless suppression of all opposing political parties, suppression of individual liberties under a dictatorship, and expansion by military action and subversion."

c. "Nucleus" means "the central part of an atom, the fundamental parts of which are the proton and the neutron. It carries a positive charge and constitutes all the mass of the atom. It is what remains after the orbital electrons have been stripped away."

d. "The Big Ten" means "Indiana University, Ohio State, Michigan, Michigan State, Northwestern, Illinois, Wisconsin, Purdue, Minnesota, and Iowa."

e. "Monotreme" means "platypuses and echidnas."

f. "Naturalistic" means "glorifying all the meanness of human nature and the sordidness of human existence, emphasizing the disgusting, crude, animal part of human nature."

g. "Overweight" means "exceeds the U.S. Government standard chart's recommended weight per height by at least 10 percent."

h. In order to save space in the written reports of the curriculum committee, we will let "FLC" mean "first-year logic course."

i. It's just as "I believe in God" often means "I prefer not to think," so does "I love you" often mean "I want to own you."

—John Fowles, *Daniel Martin*

j. "Water freezes *only if* it has a temperature of 32°F or lower" means "*If* water freezes, *then* it has a temperature of 32°F or lower."

k. "Living ex-President of the USA" means Richard Nixon, Gerald Ford, Jimmy Carter.

l. "Superfluous" means "unnecessary."

m. "The" is a definite article that is used to refer to a particular person, place, or thing.

n. "Lecturing" means "a boring way of teaching in which the teacher drones on for nearly an hour while the students try to stay awake."

o. "Properly dressed for dining at local restaurants" means "wearing shoes and a shirt."

p. "The best age of a person" means "the age at which the person is old enough to know what's what and not old enough to show it."

q. Some anthropologists define "culture" as "a set of attributes and products of human societies, and therewith of mankind, that are extrasomatic and transmissible by mechanisms other than biological heredity."

r. "State university" means "an institution of higher learning that grants advanced degrees and is supported by taxes."

2. What is wrong with each of the following *lexical definitions*?

   a. "Politically" means "in a politic manner."

   b. "Hamster" means "a small animal."

   c. "Fork" means "a utensil for eating foods."

   d. "Whale" means "a mammal that swims."

3. At most state universities, residents and nonresidents of the state are charged different tuition fees for the same educational programs. Suppose you are a state

legislator assigned to a committee to define "resident" for the purpose of charging tuition fees. What type of definition is required here? What considerations would guide your attempt to define "resident"? What definition would you propose?

4. Provide an *implicit contextual definition* of "neither . . . nor."

5. Discuss the different *emotive force* (if any) for each of the following pairs of terms. If you ignore emotive force, do both members of each pair have the same intensional and extensional meaning (does each member of the pair refer to the same objects)?

    a. Fragile–weak
    b. Public servant–bureaucrat
    c. Mexican-American–Chicano
    d. Sweat–perspiration
    e. Chairman–chairperson
    f. Cop–police officer

5. Operational Definition

In addition to ostensive definition, another type of nonverbal definition has been of special importance to scientific studies. The technique of *operational definition* was first proposed by Nobel physicist P.W. Bridgman (*The Logic of Modern Physics,* 1927). Bridgman was aware of the different emotive and referential aspects of meaning and of the way words can mean different things to different persons as a result of varying associations and contexts of use. He wanted to establish the meanings of scientifically important terms in such a way that all of the scientists who used these terms would employ them in exactly the same way. Bridgman proposed specifying public and repeatable *operations,* such as measurement, to serve as criteria for the application of scientifically important terms.

Consider the following example of an operational definition:

"Each side of my table is three feet long" means that when a standard yardstick is lined up with a side of my table, the ends of the yardstick coincide with the ends of my table.

The technique of operational definition is not intended to apply to abstract terms, such as "length." Instead, a public and repeatable physical operation (such as measurement with a standard yardstick) is specified for determining whether or not a sentence containing expressions such as "is three feet long" can be applied correctly to a situation. Nothing is lost by refusing to consider "length" in the abstract, since scientists use the concept of length only in specific contexts. Once we understand how to use sentences in which expressions like "three feet long" occur, then we understand what such expressions mean. Since the operation of measuring with a standard yardstick is public and repeatable, this operational definition guarantees that scientists will all use the expression "three feet long" in exactly the same way.

With suitable instruments for measuring, many of the terms used by scientists can be defined in this way. For example, "This flame is blue" can be operationally defined as meaning that when subjected to analysis by a spectrometer, the flame registers between 4240 angstrom units and 4912 angstrom units. Operations other than measurement can also be used. For example, "The liquid in this jar is acid" means that when a piece of litmus paper is placed in this liquid, the litmus paper turns pink. All that is required is that there is a high degree of agreement among various observers as to the outcome of the operation and that the operation be repeatable.

The technique of operational definition is not without problematic features. For example, there may be several different types of operations for measuring a phenomenon such as temperature and no operation for coordinating the various results. In such cases, we could not, strictly speaking, refer to "the temperature" of a particular object, but only, for example, to "the Fahrenheit thermometer temperature." This introduces some awkwardness into scientific discourse. However, many scientists are willing to pay this price in order to specify the meanings of terms by tying them to observations and measurements.

Additional, more serious problems arise in trying to define some of the more highly theoretical terms used by scientists, such as "electron," that refer to things that are not directly observable. Attempts to *reduce* these terms to terms that can be operationally defined have not been very successful. At this point, this program of operational definition seems to offer little hope for providing such definitions for *all* of the important terms used by physical scientists. Nevertheless, this form of definition is regarded as important in standardizing meanings of some words by establishing operational criteria for the application of those words.

Even though operational definitions were first proposed for the physical sciences and despite the difficulties encountered there, many social scientists have become enthusiastic about the possibility of constructing such definitions for the terms that occur in their own disciplines. Behavioral psychologists, for example, believe that operational definitions are the best way to handle so-called mental terms, such as "intelligence," "belief," "anxiety," and "fear." They have tried to specify publicly observable features of behavior or physiology in order to define particular concrete uses of such terms. Some examples are

"John Jones is afraid of the dark" means that whenever Jones is in a dark place, he breaks out in a cold sweat and begins to tremble.

"María Garcia is very intelligent" means that Garcia scored above 135 on the Stanford–Binet (IQ) test.

Operationalistic attempts to define mental terms are highly controversial and have been dismissed as completely inadequate by many persons. There are two major types of objections. One has to do with the obvious difficulty of trying to handle concepts such as "intelligence" in a quantitative manner. Measuring someone's intelligence is much less straightforward than measuring that person's height. The tests that have been proposed as measurements have been criticized for being tied to specific cultural backgrounds and for measuring only some of the broad group of features that make up intelligence in a human being. Similarly, physiological manifestations of fear, anxiety, and other mental states vary from person to person and culture to culture, making the specification of publicly observable criteria for determining the presence of such states highly problematic.

The second objection cuts a bit deeper across the program of operational definition. An operational definition of a mental property is intended to equate that property with the outcome of some operation. However, many people claim that even if we devised satisfactory tests for measuring intelligence, what we would measure could not be the same thing as the score on the test. The test score, these objectors say, might be a good *indicator* of the degree of intelligence possessed by a person, but it would not be the *same thing* as intelligence. In other words, they hold that the meaning of someone's being in a particular mental state cannot be equated with techniques for measuring the presence of that mental state.

Despite these difficulties, some strong supporters of operational definition claim that a term is scientifically meaningful only if it is susceptible to operational definition. They hold that terms that cannot be defined operationally are of no use to science, or that only insofar as the terms are amenable to operational definition are the things they refer to suitable objects for scientific study. Others take the more moderate view that although operational definitions play an important role in any science, there are limits to their usefulness, and that it is inappropriate to try to define *every* term used in a discipline in this way.

III. REVIEW

If we want to be able to state our beliefs, opinions, and judgments clearly, so that others can understand us, and if we want to be able to assess ordinary-language arguments, we must recognize that there are many aspects of meaning—*extensional, intensional, grammatical* (also called *syntactic*), *emotive,* and *operational.* Various types of definitions are designed to capture these aspects of meaning, and it is important to know how to use definitions to achieve the type of clarity that is required in a given context. A review of the terminology introduced in this chapter follows.

Ambiguous: An expression is *ambiguous* when it has several distinct, *non-overlapping* meanings. Words with more than one distinct meaning are ambiguous, and *ambiguities* can also arise in larger units of language as a result of their grammatical structure or of the possible changes in meaning due to changes in emphasis.

Contextual Definition: A form of implicit definition in which terms are defined by showing how they are used in a given situation or situations. *Truth tables* provide implicit contextual definitions of logical connectives. Other examples are implicit definitions of theoretical terms and definitions presenting an expression in which the defined term occurs along with a synonymous expression in which it does not.

Equivocation: The use of an ambiguous expression in more than one of its senses in a single context. When an argument depends on equivocation to establish a conclusion, the *fallacy of equivocation* is committed.

Extension: The set of objects to which a term refers.

Intension: The set of *all and only* those properties a thing must possess for the term to apply to it.

Intensional Definition: Defining a term by stating the properties a thing must possess for the term to apply to it. All intensional definitions are verbal. Further distinctions can be made among intensional definitions by considering the purposes of definition:

>   **Lexical Definition:** To present the accepted standard use of a term.
>
>   **Stipulative Definition:** To introduce a new term into the language.
>
>   **Precising Definition:** To reduce the vagueness of a term.
>
>   **Persuasive Definition:** To express or evoke an attitude, such as approval or disapproval, toward things referred to by the term.
>
>   **Theoretical Definition:** To construct a theory. Theoretical definitions may be *explicit,* in which case terms are defined by giving *synonymous expressions* formulated in the vocabulary of the theory, or *implicit* (or *contextual*), in which case terms are defined according to their use in the laws or generalizations of the theory.

Operational Definition: Defining an expression by describing a publicly observable and repeatable operation that can be performed to determine whether or not a sentence containing the expression is correctly applicable to a given situation.

Ostensive Definition (*nonverbal extensional definition*): A nonverbal form of definition in which pointing or some other way of indicating the extension of a term is used to give the meaning of the term.

Syntactic Definition (*grammatical definition*): Terms that have no intension or extension are sometimes defined by indicating their *syntactic* or *grammatical* role in a language. These definitions are often supplemented by presenting a context in which the term occurs. (*Example*: "A" is an indefinite article, used in such expressions as "A dog ran out in the road.")

Vague: A term is *vague* if there are borderline areas in which it is unclear whether or not the term applies. *Vagueness* is a useful feature of language, but definitions that reduce vagueness are required in some circumstances.

Verbal Extensional Definition: Defining a term by listing or naming members of its extension.

IV. EXERCISES

1. Try to formulate *operational definitions* for each of the following:
    a. The term "sour" in "This lemon tastes sour."
    b. The expression "weighs 120 pounds" in "Joan weighs 120 pounds."

    c. The expression "believes that he will win a scholarship next year" in "Frank believes that he (Frank) will win a scholarship next year."

2. Social scientists often use questionnaires to formulate operational definitions. For example, they might be interested in arriving at an operational definition for the term "alcoholic" if they wanted to correlate alcoholism with some other social phenomenon, such as working in a particular profession or being subjected to the stresses of student life. Try to formulate a questionnaire that would operationally define whether or not the person who answers the questionnaire is an alcoholic. Mention any difficulties involved in devising such a questionnaire.

PROOF METHOD FOR TRUTH-FUNCTIONAL LOGIC

I. INTRODUCTION

Truth tables may be used to demonstrate the validity or the invalidity of any truth-functional argument form. However, these tables become unwieldy when an argument form contains more than four distinct sentence letters. An argument form with five distinct letters requires a truth table with 32 rows to show all of the possible combinations of truth values. Six sentence letters require a 64-row truth table, and adding just one more sentence letter requires an additional 64 rows. The chief advantage of applying other *proof methods* to truth-functional logic is their brevity compared to truth tables. The proof method presented here is a *tree method* modeled on a simplified version of proof methods developed by Gerhard Gentzen.*

We will use the logical symbols already introduced for negation ($\sim$), conjunction ($\cdot$), disjunction (v), material conditional ($\rightarrow$), and material biconditional ($\leftrightarrow$). In addition, we will use the gate symbol ($\vdash$) to indicate the relationship of *logical consequence,* or *following from.* The conclusion in a deductively valid argument is a logical consequence of, or follows from, the premises of that argument. Instead of writing an argument form, such as *modus ponens,* in the standard form

$$p \rightarrow q$$
$$p$$
$$\overline{}$$
$$q$$

we have used thus far, we will now write argument forms in the following way:

$$p \rightarrow q, p \vdash q$$

Premises, separated from one another by commas, are written to the left of the gate; the conclusion is written to the right of the gate. The preceding expression, which is called a *sequent,* may be read "*q* follows from the premises *p* $\rightarrow$ *q* and *p.*"

The strings of sentence forms on the left and the right sides of the gate in a sequent are called *sequences.* In our example, the sequence on the left has two members (*p* $\rightarrow$ *q* and *p*); it is a sequence of "length two." The sequence on the right has one member (*q*); it is a sequence of "length one." Sequences may be of "length zero," in which case they are called *empty sequences,* or their length may be equal to any positive integer. All sequences are finite in length.

We have seen that when the length of a sequence on the left side of the gate is greater than one, the members of the sequence are separated by commas and each comma on the left is read as "and." When more than one member of the

---

*See Stig Kanger, "A Simplified Proof Method for Elementary Logic," in *Computer Programming and Formal Systems,* edited by P. Braffort and D. Hirschberg.

sequence appears on the right side of the gate, these members are also separated by commas, but each comma on the right is read as "or." For example, we may read the sequent

$$p \vee q, p \rightarrow r, p \rightarrow s, \sim q \vdash r \bullet s, t \rightarrow p$$

as "Either $r \bullet s$ or $t \rightarrow p$ follows from the premisses $p \vee q$, and $p \rightarrow r$, and $p \rightarrow s$, and $\sim q$."

An empty sequence to the left of the gate indicates a true (although unspecified) premiss. An empty sequence to the right of the gate indicates a true conclusion.

Examples

(a) Read the sequent

$$\vdash p \rightarrow (q \vee \sim q)$$

as "$p \rightarrow (q \vee \sim q)$ follows from any true premiss."

(b) Read the sequent

$$p, p \rightarrow q, \sim p \vdash$$

as "Any true conclusion follows from p, and $p \rightarrow q$, and $\sim p$."

If a sentence form follows from any true premiss, then that sentence form must itself always be true. A sentence form that follows from any true premiss whatsoever is a *tautology*. Similarly, if a set of premisses deductively yields any true conclusion whatsoever, that set of premisses must be *contradictory*.

II. THE PROOF METHOD

In the following discussion, we will use the Roman capital letters "A" and "B" to refer to sentence forms. The sentence forms thus denoted may be either simple or complex. We will use the script capital letters "$\mathscr{D}$," "$\mathscr{E}$," "$\mathscr{F}$," and "$\mathscr{G}$" to denote finite and possibly empty sequences of sentence forms.

The proof method employs eleven postulates, which include one axiom and ten rules of inference. Postulates P.1–P.11 are presented schematically here, with brief comments.

P.1 $\mathscr{D}, A, \mathscr{E} \vdash \mathscr{F}, A, \mathscr{G}$ (axiom)

In this sequent, the same *sentence form* (A) occurs both to the left and to the right of the gate; on both sides, it is separated from the other *sequences of sentence forms* ($\mathscr{D}, \mathscr{E}, \mathscr{F}, \mathscr{G}$) by commas. This means that a *disjunction* that contains A is said to follow from a set of premisses that includes A. Such a disjunction could not fail to follow, for if A is a true premiss, then the disjunction contains a true disjunct and the disjunction is true also. Thus, all the premisses cannot be true while the conclusion is false. In our proof method, this instance of the *consequence relationship* is considered to be a fundamentally valid argument form (an *axiom scheme*).

The rules of inference in this proof method are used to eliminate connectives, with the goal of "reducing" the original argument form to a series of simpler forms that are instances of the axiom. Each of the rules of inference (P.2–P.11) allows us to eliminate a main connective in a sentence form on either the left or the right side of the gate:

P.2
$$\frac{\mathcal{D} \vdash \mathcal{F}, \sim A, \mathcal{G}}{A, \mathcal{D} \vdash \mathcal{F}, \mathcal{G}}$$
(eliminates $\sim$ on right)

P.3
$$\frac{\mathcal{D}, \sim A, \mathcal{E} \vdash \mathcal{F}}{\mathcal{D}, \mathcal{E} \vdash A, \mathcal{F}}$$
(eliminates $\sim$ on left)

P.4
$$\frac{\mathcal{D} \vdash \mathcal{F}, A \cdot B, \mathcal{G}}{\mathcal{D} \vdash \mathcal{F}, A, \mathcal{G} \qquad \mathcal{D} \vdash \mathcal{F}, B, \mathcal{G}}$$
(eliminates $\cdot$ on right)

P.5
$$\frac{\mathcal{D}, A \cdot B, \mathcal{E} \vdash \mathcal{F}}{\mathcal{D}, A, B, \mathcal{E} \vdash \mathcal{F}}$$
(eliminates $\cdot$ on left)

P.6
$$\frac{\mathcal{D} \vdash \mathcal{F}, A \vee B, \mathcal{G}}{\mathcal{D} \vdash \mathcal{F}, A, B, \mathcal{G}}$$
(eliminates $\vee$ on right)

P.7
$$\frac{\mathcal{D}, A \vee B, \mathcal{E} \vdash \mathcal{F}}{\mathcal{D}, A, \mathcal{E} \vdash \mathcal{F} \qquad \mathcal{D}, B, \mathcal{E} \vdash \mathcal{F}}$$
(eliminates $\vee$ on left)

P.8
$$\frac{\mathcal{D} \vdash \mathcal{F}, A \to B, \mathcal{G}}{A, \mathcal{D} \vdash \mathcal{F}, B, \mathcal{G}}$$
(eliminates $\to$ on right)

P.9
$$\frac{\mathcal{D}, A \to B, \mathcal{E} \vdash \mathcal{F}}{\mathcal{D}, \mathcal{E} \vdash A, \mathcal{F} \qquad \mathcal{D}, B, \mathcal{E} \vdash \mathcal{F}}$$
(eliminates $\to$ on left)

P.10
$$\frac{\mathcal{D} \vdash \mathcal{F}, A \leftrightarrow B, \mathcal{G}}{A, \mathcal{D} \vdash \mathcal{F}, B, \mathcal{G} \qquad B, \mathcal{D} \vdash \mathcal{F}, A, \mathcal{G}}$$
(eliminates $\leftrightarrow$ on right)

P.11
$$\frac{\mathcal{D}, A \leftrightarrow B, \mathcal{E} \vdash \mathcal{F}}{\mathcal{D}, \mathcal{E} \vdash A, B, \mathcal{F} \qquad A, B, \mathcal{D}, \mathcal{E} \vdash \mathcal{F}}$$
(eliminates $\leftrightarrow$ on left)

When we want to show that one sequence follows from another, we write the premiss sequence, followed by a gate, followed by the conclusion. Then we draw a line below that sequent and construct a "tree" of sequents below it, using the rules of inference (P.2–P.11). If we are able to construct a tree with an instance of P.1 (the axiom) at the bottom of every branch, then the proof has succeeded. If the sequence on the right is a logical consequence of the sequence on the left, we will always be able to construct such a tree.

In addition to the axiom and rules of inference of the proof method, one strategic rule for constructing proofs should be noted. Frequently, we may be able to continue a branch of the tree in more than one way, since we may have more than one main connective to eliminate. When this happens, we always prefer applications of P.2, P.3, P.5, P.6, and P.8 to applications of the other rules. Our preference for these rules will minimize tree branching, because these rules themselves do not branch. Before we focus on considering the justification of inference rules, we will consider some examples of proofs.

Examples

(a) To show that p v q follows from p, we construct the following tree:

$$\frac{p \vdash p \vee q \quad \text{(apply P.6)}}{p \vdash p, q \quad \text{(axiom)}}$$

Here, only one main connective (the v on the right) can be eliminated. Thus, P.6 is the appropriate rule. In applying P.6 to the sequent on the top line, A represents p, the sentence form to the left of the connective, and B represents q, the sentence form to the right of the connective. $\mathcal{D}$ represents the sequence that is left of the gate (p). $\mathcal{F}$ and $\mathcal{G}$ are the sequences to the right and the left of the sentence form A v B, respectively; in this example, $\mathcal{F}$ and $\mathcal{G}$ are empty sequences. In the sequent below the line, the same sequence $\mathcal{D}$ (p) is to the left of the gate. On the right of the gate, the v has been eliminated and replaced by a comma. The sequent below the line is an instance of the axiom, for the same sentence form (namely, p) occurs, separated from other sentence forms by commas, on the right of the gate and also on the left. Thus, we have shown that p v q follows deductively from p.

(b) To show that q follows from $p \rightarrow q$, $\sim p \rightarrow r$, and $\sim q \rightarrow \sim r$, we construct the following tree:

(1)
$$\overline{ p \rightarrow q, \sim p \rightarrow r, \sim q \rightarrow \sim r \vdash q }$$

(2) $\quad \sim p \rightarrow r, \sim q \rightarrow \sim r \vdash p, q \qquad \overline{q, \sim p \rightarrow r, \sim q \rightarrow \sim r \vdash q^*}$

(3) $\quad \sim q \rightarrow \sim r \vdash \sim p, p, q \qquad\qquad r, \sim q \rightarrow \sim r \vdash p, q$

(4) $\quad p, \sim q \rightarrow \sim r \vdash p, q^* \qquad \overline{r \vdash \sim q, p, q} \qquad \overline{r, \sim r \vdash p, q}$

(5) $\qquad\qquad\qquad\qquad\qquad q, r \vdash p, q^* \qquad r \vdash r, p, q^*$

Line (1) contains the sequent, with the premises on the left and the conclusion on the right of the gate. The only main connectives are →s to the left of the gate, so the only applicable rule is a branching one, P.9, which could be applied to any of the three sentence forms that make up the sequence on the left.

In this proof, P.9 is applied to the first conditional, $p \to q$. Thus, A is p, and B is q. $\mathcal{D}$, which refers to any sequence to the left of A → B, is empty, and $\mathcal{E}$ denotes the sequence $\sim p \to r$, $\sim q \to \sim r$. $\mathcal{F}$ refers to everything to the right of the gate (in this case, q).

Line (2) is the result of applying P.9 to $p \to q$ in line (1). The right-hand branch ends in an axiom (indicated by the *), with an occurrence of the sentence form q on both the right and the left sides of the gate. That branch is now complete. The left branch is not an instance of the axiom but contains further connectives that may be removed. Again, the only main connectives are the →s on the left, so P.9 is applicable.

Line (3) is the result of applying P.9 to $\sim p \to r$ in line (2). Here, A is $\sim p$ and B is r. $\mathcal{D}$ is empty, $\mathcal{E}$ is $\sim q \to \sim r$, and $\mathcal{F}$ is the sequence p, q. Neither of these branches is an instance of the axiom, but connectives remain, so each branch is continued.

In the left branch of the tree, a main connective on the right is a negation sign. Our strategy rule tells us to prefer the application of P.2 over any of the branching rules. Applying P.2 gives us p as A and $\sim q \to \sim r$ as $\mathcal{D}$. $\mathcal{F}$ is empty, and $\mathcal{G}$ is the sequence p, q to the right of $\sim$A. After applying P.2, this branch ends in an instance of the axiom on the left branch of line (4).

In the right branch of the tree, the only main connective is once more a → on the left side of the gate, so that P.9 is applicable. Line (4) on the right gives the result of applying this branching rule. Neither branch ends in an axiom at this stage, so both branches continue.

In the left branch, a negation on the right is eliminated by applying P.2, which results in the branch ending in an axiom on line (5). In the right branch, there is a negation on the left, which is eliminated by applying P.3; that branch also ends in an axiom on line (5).

Thus, each branch of the tree ends in an axiom, and we have succeeded in proving that q is a consequence of $p \to q$, $\sim p \to r$, and $\sim q \to \sim r$.

(c) To show that $\sim q$ is *not* a consequence of $p \to q$ and $\sim p$, we construct the following tree:

(1) $\qquad p \to q,\ \sim p \vdash \sim q$

$\qquad\qquad$ ------------------------ (P.3 applied to $\sim p$)

(2) $\qquad\qquad p \to q \vdash p,\ \sim q$

$\qquad\qquad$ ------------------------ (P.2 applied to $\sim q$)

(3) $\qquad\qquad q,\ p \to q \vdash p$

$\qquad\qquad$ ------------------------ (P.9 applied to $p \to q$)

(4) $\qquad q \vdash p,\ p \qquad q,\ q \vdash p$

In this case, we see two branches on line (4) that do not end in axioms. Whenever at least one branch does not end in an axiom and cannot be extended because no more connectives can be removed, we have a proof that the alleged conclusion does not follow from these premises—that the argument form is invalid.

(d) To show that $\sim(p \cdot q) \leftrightarrow (\sim p \vee \sim q)$ is a tautology, we construct the following tree:

(1) $\quad\quad\quad\quad\quad \vdash \sim(p \cdot q) \leftrightarrow (\sim p \vee \sim q)$

(P.10)

(2) $\quad \sim(p \cdot q) \vdash \sim p \vee \sim q \quad$ (P.3) $\quad\quad \sim p \vee \sim q \vdash \sim(p \cdot q) \quad$ (P.2)

(3) $\quad \vdash p \cdot q, \sim p \vee \sim q \quad$ (P.6) $\quad\quad p \cdot q, \sim p \vee \sim q \vdash \quad$ (P.5)

(4) $\quad \vdash p \cdot q, \sim p, \sim q \quad$ (P.2) $\quad\quad p, q \sim p \vee \sim q \vdash \quad$ (P.7)

(5) $\quad p \vdash p \cdot q, \sim q \quad$ (P.2) $\quad p, q, \sim p \vdash \quad$ (P.3) $\quad p, q, \sim q \vdash \quad$ (P.3)

(6) $\quad q, p \vdash p \cdot q \quad$ (P.7) $\quad\quad p, q \vdash p^* \quad\quad\quad\quad p, q \vdash q^*$

(7) $\quad p, q \vdash p^* \quad p, q \vdash q^*$

Note that each branch of this tree ends in an axiom. To prove that a sentence form is a tautology, it is sufficient to show that the sentence form follows from any true premiss. Thus, we set up the proof by placing an empty sequence to the left of the gate and the supposed tautology to the right of the gate. If every branch does end in an axiom, we have shown that the sentence follows from any true premiss and that it must itself be true. If some branch fails to end in an axiom and cannot be continued, then the sentence form is not a tautology.

Exercises

1. Use the proof method to determine the validity or the invalidity of each of the following argument forms:

a. $\dfrac{p \rightarrow q}{p \rightarrow (p \cdot q)}$

b. $\dfrac{p \vee q}{\sim p \vee \sim q}$

c. $\dfrac{p \rightarrow (q \rightarrow r)}{(p \rightarrow q) \rightarrow r}$ d. $\dfrac{p \rightarrow (q \rightarrow r)}{(p \cdot q) \rightarrow r}$

e. $\begin{array}{c} p \rightarrow (q \rightarrow r) \\ (q \rightarrow r) \rightarrow s \\ \hline p \rightarrow s \end{array}$ f. $\begin{array}{c} p \rightarrow (q \rightarrow r) \\ q \rightarrow (r \rightarrow s) \\ \hline p \rightarrow s \end{array}$

g. $\begin{array}{c} (p \vee q) \rightarrow (p \cdot q) \\ p \cdot q \\ \hline p \vee q \end{array}$

2. Use the proof method to determine whether or not the following sentence form is *tautologous*:

$$(p \rightarrow (q \rightarrow r)) \rightarrow ((p \rightarrow q) \rightarrow (p \rightarrow r))$$

How many rows would a truth table require to show this? How many lines would it take you to construct a truth table for this sentence form?

3. Use the proof method to show whether or not the following sentence form is a *self-contradiction*:

$$(p \rightarrow q) \cdot (q \rightarrow r) \cdot p \cdot {\sim} r$$

III. JUSTIFYING THE RULES OF INFERENCE (P.2–P.11)

A deductive rule of inference is *justified* when it can be shown that the use of the rule will never lead from true premises to a false conclusion—or, in other words, when it can be shown that the rule is *truth-preserving*.

When we remov connectives by using the rules of inference in this proof method, we reduce a complicated sequent (argument form) to a series of *less complicated* sequents, in the sense that each of the sequents below the lines has fewer truth-functional connectives than the sequents above the lines. What we want to show is that the use of any of the rules P.2–P.11 for eliminating connectives will result in sequents below the line with right-hand sequences that are the logical consequences of their left-hand sequences if and only if the right-hand sequence above the line is a logical consequence of its left-hand sequence.

The rules of inference used in this proof method depend for their justification on:

1. The definition of *logical consequence,* which states that a sentence (or sentence form) A is a logical consequence of a set of sentences (or sentence forms) $\mathcal{D}$ if it is impossible for all of the sentences (sentence forms) in the set $\mathcal{D}$ to be true while the sentence (sentence form) A is false.

2. The definitions of the *truth-functional connectives* ($\sim$, v, •, $\rightarrow$, $\leftrightarrow$).
3. The understanding that commas to the left of the gate represent "and" and that commas to the right of the gate represent "or."

In each rule, we note that the sequences $\mathcal{D}$, $\mathcal{E}$, $\mathcal{F}$, and $\mathcal{G}$ simply reappear unchanged in sequents below the line. They are never dropped or modified in any way. For this reason, we can ignore their content in justifying rules P.2–P.11. In other words, we can simply regard these sequences as *empty sequences* and focus on how the removal of the connectives that relate A and B affects the consequence relationship.

Justification of P.2

P.2
$$\frac{\mathcal{D} \vdash \mathcal{F}, \sim A, \mathcal{G}}{A, \mathcal{D} \vdash \mathcal{F}, \mathcal{G}} \quad \text{(eliminates } \sim \text{ on right)}$$

If we regard the sequences $\mathcal{D}$, $\mathcal{F}$, and $\mathcal{G}$ as empty, then the sequent above the line says that $\sim A$ is a consequence of an empty sequence. This means that $\sim A$ must be a tautology. Then A itself must be a self-contradiction, since A is equivalent to the denial of $\sim A$, and the denial of a sentence form that must be true is a sentence form that must be false. But if A is a self-contradiction, then any conclusion, including an empty sequence, follows from it. The sequent below the line says that an empty sequence follows from A, and this is so if and only if $\sim A$ follows from an empty sequence.

Justification of P.3

P.3
$$\frac{\mathcal{D}, \sim A, \mathcal{E} \vdash \mathcal{F}}{\mathcal{D}, \mathcal{E} \vdash A, \mathcal{F}} \quad \text{(eliminates } \sim \text{ on left)}$$

Again, we assume that $\mathcal{D}$, $\mathcal{E}$, and $\mathcal{F}$ are empty. Then the sequent above the line in P.3 says that an empty sequence follows from $\sim A$. Thus, $\sim A$ is a self-contradiction. But this means that A is a tautology, and a tautology follows from an empty sequence. So the consequence relationship holds in the sequent below the line in P.3 if and only if it holds in the sequent above the line.

Justification of P.4

P.4
$$\frac{\mathcal{D} \vdash \mathcal{F}, A \cdot B, \mathcal{G}}{\mathcal{D} \vdash \mathcal{F}, A, \mathcal{G} \qquad \mathcal{D} \vdash \mathcal{F}, B, \mathcal{G}} \quad \text{(eliminates • on right)}$$

P.4 allows us to eliminate a conjunction (•) on the right side of the gate. If a conjunction follows from any premises—including the *empty set* of premisses—then each of the conjuncts separately follows from those same premises. Thus, there are two sequents below the line, and each of these sequents contains one conjunct on the right side of the gate. Conversely, if each of two sentence forms follows from identical sets of premises, then their conjunction follows from that set of premises.

Justification of P.5

P.5
$$\frac{\mathcal{D}, A \bullet B, \mathcal{E} \vdash \mathcal{F}}{\mathcal{D}, A, B, \mathcal{E} \vdash \mathcal{F}}$$ (eliminates • on left)

P.5 allows us to eliminate a conjunction (•) on the left side of the gate. Consider an argument form with a conjunction with two members (A and B) as its only premiss. A conjunction is true if and only if both of its conjuncts are true. If the conclusion follows from this premiss, then the conclusion clearly follows from the two premises A and B. If the conclusion does not follow from A • B, then it will not follow from the two separate premises A and B. In P.5, a conjunctive premiss above the line is simply split into two separate premises below the line. (Remember that the comma on the left side of the gate is read as "and.") All other sequences ($\mathcal{D}$, $\mathcal{E}$, and $\mathcal{F}$) are simply carried along without alteration.

Justification of P.6

P.6
$$\frac{\mathcal{D} \vdash \mathcal{F}, A \vee B, \mathcal{G}}{\mathcal{D} \vdash \mathcal{F}, A, B, \mathcal{G}}$$ (eliminates v on right)

The justification of P.6 is quite obvious if we consider that commas on the right side of the gate are read as "or." To apply P.6, a wedge (v) on the right side of the gate is replaced by a comma. If the disjunction A v B follows from the premises on the left, then either A follows from those premises or B does. If the disjunction does not follow, then it is not true that either A or B follows from the premises.

Justification of P.7

P.7
$$\frac{\mathcal{D}, A \vee B, \mathcal{E} \vdash \mathcal{F}}{\mathcal{D}, A, \mathcal{E} \vdash \mathcal{F} \qquad \mathcal{D}, B, \mathcal{E} \vdash \mathcal{F}}$$ (eliminates v on left)

To apply P.7, a wedge on the left side of the gate is replaced with a comma. If a conclusion follows from a disjunction (A v B), the conclusion must be true if either A is true or B is true. However, this is equivalent to saying that the conclusion follows from A and also from B. Thus, there are two sequents below the line, and each sequent contains one disjunct as a premiss. Also, if a conclusion follows from either of two premises considered separately, then it clearly follows from the disjunction of those same premises.

Justification of P.8

P.8
$$\frac{\mathcal{D} \vdash \mathcal{F}, A \rightarrow B, \mathcal{G}}{A, \mathcal{D} \vdash \mathcal{F}, B, \mathcal{G}}$$ (eliminates → on right)

If a material conditional follows from some premises, this means that if all of the premises are true, then the conditional is also true. But if the conditional is true, then it cannot be the case that its antecedent is true and its consequent is false. Thus, if the antecedent of the conditional is added to the premises, then the consequent must follow from those premises supplemented by its antecedent. Similarly, if B follows from premises that include A, then the sentence form A → B will be true if those premises (excluding A) are all true. This justifies the application of P.8.

Justification of P.9

P.9
$$\frac{\mathscr{D}, A \to B, \mathscr{E} \vdash \mathscr{F}}{\mathscr{D}, \mathscr{E} \vdash A, \mathscr{F} \qquad \mathscr{D}, B, \mathscr{E} \vdash \mathscr{F}} \quad \text{(eliminates} \to \text{on left)}$$

Consider that A → B is logically equivalent to ~A v B. If we apply P.7 to the sequent $\mathscr{D}, \sim A \vee B, \mathscr{E} \vdash \mathscr{F}$, we obtain sequents $\mathscr{D}, \sim A, \mathscr{E} \vdash \mathscr{F}$ and $\mathscr{D}, B, \mathscr{E} \vdash \mathscr{F}$ below the line. If we then apply P.3 to $\mathscr{D}, \sim A, \mathscr{E} \vdash \mathscr{F}$, we obtain $\mathscr{D}, \mathscr{E} \vdash A, \mathscr{F}$. This sequent and the sequent $\mathscr{D}, B, \mathscr{E} \vdash \mathscr{F}$ occur below the line in the application of P.9.

Justifications of P.10 and P.11

P.10
$$\frac{\mathscr{D} \vdash \mathscr{F}, A \leftrightarrow B, \mathscr{G}}{A, \mathscr{D} \vdash \mathscr{F}, B, \mathscr{G} \qquad B, \mathscr{D} \vdash \mathscr{F}, A, \mathscr{G}} \quad \text{(eliminates} \leftrightarrow \text{on right)}$$

P.11
$$\frac{\mathscr{D}, A \leftrightarrow B, \mathscr{E} \vdash \mathscr{F}}{\mathscr{D}, \mathscr{E} \vdash A, B, \mathscr{F} \qquad A, B, \mathscr{D}, \mathscr{E} \vdash \mathscr{F}} \quad \text{(eliminates} \leftrightarrow \text{on left)}$$

These justifications are left as exercises. In each case, consider that A ↔ B is logically equivalent to (A → B) • (B → A).

It is interesting to note that this proof method may be used effectively even when the user does not understand the justifications of the rules of inference or why they work. The rules work in such a way that machines may be designed to test the validity of argument forms as well as to test whether sentence forms are tautologous or self-contradictory. If you have some computer experience, you might try to write a program for generating proofs using this proof method.

IV. EXERCISES

Use the proof method to decide whether the last sentence form is a logical consequence of the remaining sentence forms:

a. $p \to q$
    $\sim p \to r$
    $\sim q \to r$
    $\sim q$

b. $p \to q$
    $r \to \sim s$
    $q \to r$
    $p \to \sim s$

c. $(p \cdot q) \rightarrow (r \cdot s)$
   $\sim(q \vee s)$
   $t \rightarrow (\sim q \rightarrow (p \cdot r))$
   $\sim t$

d. $p \rightarrow q$
   $r \rightarrow s$
   $\sim s \rightarrow p$
   $q \rightarrow r$
   $\sim s \rightarrow t$

e. $(p \rightarrow q) \vee (r \rightarrow s)$
   $(p \rightarrow s) \vee (r \rightarrow q)$

f. $(p \leftrightarrow q) \rightarrow r$
   $\sim r$
   $\sim p \cdot q$
   s

2. Use the proof method to determine which of the following are tautologies. Take care to identify the main connectives correctly.
   a. $(p \rightarrow q) \vee (\sim p \rightarrow q)$
   b. $(p \rightarrow q) \rightarrow ((r \rightarrow (q \rightarrow s)) \rightarrow (r \rightarrow (p \rightarrow s)))$
   c. $((p \rightarrow q) \rightarrow (q \rightarrow r)) \leftrightarrow (q \rightarrow r)$
   d. $((p \rightarrow q) \rightarrow r) \rightarrow ((p \rightarrow r) \rightarrow r)$
   e. $(\sim p \rightarrow r) \rightarrow ((q \rightarrow r) \rightarrow ((p \rightarrow q) \rightarrow r))$
   f. $\sim(p \rightarrow q) \leftrightarrow (p \rightarrow \sim q)$

3. Using sentence letters to represent simple sentences, translate each of the following English arguments into argument forms. Then use the proof method to determine the validity or the invalidity of each argument form.
   a. Either the economy will improve or the stock market will crash. If the stock market crashes, banks will fail. But banks will not fail. So it is not the case that if the economy improves, the banks will fail.
   b. The President is happy if and only if his favorite bills are passed by Congress. If the President is happy, his staff feels good. But if the staff members feel good, they are in no condition to work for the bills, and if that is the case, the President's favorite bills will not be passed by Congress. Therefore, the President is unhappy.
   c. If the Republicans choose a good candidate, they will win the election unless there is a split in the party. It is not true that if the Republicans meet in Chicago, there will be a split in the party. But if they meet in Chicago, they will choose a good candidate. So they will choose a good candidate, and they will win the election.
   d. If some archaeologists are correct, then the first humans entered North America across the Bering Strait 30,000 years ago. If they crossed the Bering Strait 30,000 years ago, they must have spent time in what is now Alaska. If they spent time in what is now Alaska, they must have left artifacts with radiocarbon dates of about 30,000 years old. If such artifacts are there, they will be uncovered if the archaeologists excavate. So if the archaeologists excavate and if some archaeologists are correct, then they will uncover 30,000 year-old artifacts in Alaska.

Bibliography

Allen, Gary. *None Dare Call It Conspiracy,* 1972, Council Press, Rossmoor, California.

Anscombe, G.E.M. *An Introduction to Wittgenstein's Tractatus,* 2nd ed., 1959, Harper & Row, New York.

Aristotle. *The Works of Aristotle,* ed. W.D. Ross, 1921, Oxford University Press, New York.

Arnauld, Antoine. *The Art of Thinking,* trans. J. Dickoff and P. James, 1964, Bobbs-Merrill, Indianapolis.

Asimov, Isaac. *The Intelligent Man's Guide to the Biological Sciences,* 1960, Basic Books, New York.

Asimov, Isaac. *The Intelligent Man's Guide to the Physical Sciences,* 1960, Basic Books, New York.

Augustine, Saint. *The Confessions of St. Augustine,* trans. E.B. Pusey, 1951, Pocket Books, Inc., New York.

Binford, Lewis. *Bones,* 1981, Academic Press, New York.

Boswell, James. *Boswell for the Defense,* ed. W.K. Wimsatt, Jr. and F.A. Pottle, 1959, McGraw-Hill, New York.

Boswell, James. *Boswell on the Grand Tour,* ed. F. Brady and F.A. Pottle, 1955, McGraw-Hill, New York.

Boswell, James. *In Search of a Wife,* ed. F. Brady and F.A. Pottle, 1956, McGraw-Hill, New York.

Boswell, James. *Life of Johnson,* ed. C.B. Osgood, 1917, Scribner's Book Companies, New York.

Boswell, James. *The Ominous Years,* ed. C. Ryekamp and F.A. Pottle, 1963, McGraw-Hill, New York.

Braffort, P., and D. Hirschberg. *Computer Programming and Formal Systems,* 1967, North-Holland, Amsterdam.

Bridgman, P.W. *The Logic of Modern Physics,* 1927, Macmillan, New York.

Campbell, Keith. *Body and Mind,* 1970, Doubleday, Garden City, New York.

Carroll, Lewis. *Alice's Adventures in Wonderland,* 1962, Macmillan, New York.

Carroll, Lewis. *Symbolic Logic,* 1958, Dover Publications, Inc., New York.

Chesterfield, Lord (Philip Dormer Stanhope). *Lord Chesterfield's Letters,* A. L. Burt Co., New York.

Culbertson, James T. *Mathematics and Logic for Digital Devices,* 1958, Van Nostrand Sons, New York.

Darwin, Charles. *The Origin of Species,* 1903, Hurst and Co., New York.

De Beauvoir, Simone. *The Ethics of Ambiguity,* trans. B. Frechtman, 1964, The Citadel Press, New York.

Deetz, James. *Invitation to Archaeology,* 1967, The Natural History Press, Garden City, New York.

Descartes, René. *Discourse on Method and Meditations on First Philosophy,* trans. Donald A. Cress, 1980, Hackett Publishing Co., Indianapolis.

Devlin, Patrick Lord. *The Enforcement of Morals,* 1965, Oxford University Press, New York.

Dickens, Charles. *Our Mutual Friend,* 1894, Houghton Mifflin, Boston.

Doyle, Sir Arthur Conan. *The Annotated Sherlock Holmes,* ed. W.S. Baring-Gould, 1967, Clarkson N. Potter, Inc., New York.

Dunn, L.C., and T.H. Dobshansky. *Heredity, Race, and Society,* 1946, Penguin Books, New York.

Durrell, Lawrence. *Prospero's Cell and Reflections on a Marine Venus,* 1960, E.P. Dutton, New York.

Ehrlich, Paul. *The Population Bomb,* 1968, Ballantine Books, New York.

Eliot, George. *Felix Holt,* John W. Lovell Co., New York.

Eliot, George. *Middlemarch,* John W. Lovell Co., New York.

Firestone, Shulamith. *The Dialectic of Sex,* 1971, Jonathan Cape, New York.

Fowles, John. *Daniel Martin,* 1977, Little, Brown, Boston.

Frankfurt, Harry. *Demons, Dreamers, and Madmen,* 1970, Bobbs-Merrill, Indianapolis.

Freud, Sigmund. *The Basic Writings of Sigmund Freud,* trans. and ed. A.A. Brill, Modern Library, New York.

Galbraith, John Kenneth. *The Affluent Society,* 1976, Houghton Mifflin, Boston.

Gissing, George. *The Odd Woman,* 1971, W.W. Norton, New York.

Glob, P.V. *The Bog People,* 1971, Ballantine Books, New York.

Gould, R.A. *Living Archaeology,* 1980, Cambridge University Press, Cambridge, U.K.

Gould, S.J. *The Mismeasure of Man,* 1981, W.W. Norton, New York.

Greene, Graham. *The Human Factor,* 1978, Avon Books, New York.

Greene, T.M. *The Arts and the Art of Criticism,* 1973, Gordian Press, New York.

Harris, Marvin. *The Rise of Anthropological Theory,* 1968, Thomas Y. Crowell, New York.

Hume, David. *Dialogues Concerning Natural Religion,* ed. N. Pike, 1970, Bobbs-Merrill, Indianapolis.

Hume, David. *A Treatise of Human Nature,* ed. L.A. Selby-Bigge, 1888, Oxford University Press, New York.

Huxley, Julian. *New Bottles for Old Wine,* 1957, Harper & Row, New York.

Irving, Washington. *Bracebridge Hall,* H.M. Caldwell Co., New York.

Jochim, M.A. *Strategies for Survival,* 1981, Academic Press, New York.

Jolly, C., and F. Plog. *Physical Anthropology and Archaeology,* 2nd ed., 1979, Alfred A. Knopf, New York.

Koestler, Arthur. *The Invisible Writing,* 1954, Macmillan, New York.

Laclos, C. de. *Les Liaisons Dangereuses,* trans. P.W.K. Stone, 1961, Penguin Books, Baltimore.

Lenin, V.I. *Collected Works,* Vol. XIV, 1927, V.I. Lenin Institute, Moscow.

Levi, E.H. *An Introduction to Legal Reasoning,* 1970, University of Chicago Press, Chicago.

Lucretius. *On the Nature of the Universe,* trans. E.E. Latham, 1951, Penguin Books, Baltimore.

Maalfjit, A. de W. *Images of Man,* 1974, Alfred A. Knopf, New York.

MacMahon, B., and T.F. Pugh. *Epidemiology,* 1978, Little, Brown, Boston.

MacMahon, B., T.F. Pugh, and J. Ipsen. *Epidemiologic Methods,* 1960, Little, Brown, Boston.

Mates, Benson. *Elementary Logic,* 2nd ed., 1972, Oxford University Press, New York.

Mill, John Stuart. *A System of Logic,* 8th ed., 1874, Harper & Row, New York.

Millett, Kate. *Sexual Politics,* 1970, Doubleday, Garden City, New York.

Morris, Herbert. *On Guilt and Innocence,* 1976, University of California Press, Berkeley.

Mumford, Lewis. *Technics and Human Development,* 1966, Harcourt Brace Jovanovich, Inc., New York.

Murphy, J.G. *Civil Disobedience and Violence,* 1971, Wadsworth Publishing Co., Belmont, California.

Murray, Gilbert. *The Literature of Ancient Greece,* 1956, University of Chicago Press, Chicago.

Newman, J.R. *The World of Mathematics,* 1956, Simon & Schuster, New York.

Nietzsche, Friedrich. *The Philosophy of Nietzsche,* Modern Library, New York.

Nisbett, R., and L. Ross. *Human Inference: Strategies and Shortcomings of Social Judgment,* 1980, Prentice-Hall, Englewood Cliffs, New Jersey.

O'Connor, D.J., ed. *A Critical History of Western Philosophy,* 1964, The Free Press, New York.

Pepys, Samuel. *The Diary of Samuel Pepys, 1660–1669,* 9 vols., eds. Robert Latham and William Matthews, 1970, University of California Press, Berkeley.

Pliny the Elder. *The Natural History of Pliny,* trans. John Bostock, 1855, H.G. Bohn, London.

Reid, Thomas. *Works,* 6th ed., ed. W. Hamilton, 1863, Edinburgh.

Rousseau, Jean-Jacques. *The Social Contract,* ed. C.M. Sherover, 1974, New American Library, New York.

Russell, Bertrand. *My Philosophical Development,* 1959, Simon & Schuster, New York.

Russell, Bertrand. *Religion and Science,* 1961, Oxford University Press, New York.

Russell, Bertrand. *Skeptical Essays,* 1928, W.W. Norton, New York.

Salmon, W.C. *The Foundations of Scientific Inference,* 1967, University of Pittsburgh Press, Pittsburgh.

Salmon, W.C. *Logic,* 3rd ed., 1984, Prentice-Hall, Englewood Cliffs, New Jersey.

Shakespeare, William. *King Lear,* 1966, Airmont Publishing Co., New York.

Shakespeare, William. *Merchant of Venice,* 1965, Airmont Publishing Co., New York.

Shrader-Frechette, K.S. *Nuclear Power and Public Policy,* 1980, D. Reidel, Dordrecht, Holland.

Smith, Adam. *The Wealth of Nations,* 1863, Adam and Charles Black, Edinburgh.

Smith, A.H. *The Mushroom Hunter's Field Guide,* 1958, University of Michigan Press, Ann Arbor.

Storr, Anthony. *The Psychodynamics of Creativity,* 1977, Geigy Pharmaceuticals, Ardsley, New York.

Suppes, Patrick. *A Probabilistic Theory of Causality,* 1970, North-Holland, Amsterdam.

Swartz, Robert J. *Perceiving, Sensing, and Knowing,* 1965, Anchor Books, Garden City, New York.

Thompson, J. Eric S. *Maya Archaeologist,* 1963, University of Oklahoma Press, Norman.

Tolstoy, Leo. *The Death of Ivan Ilych and Other Stories,* 1960, New American Library, New York.

Tolstoy, Leo. *What Is Art?,* 1960, Liberal Arts Press, Indianapolis.

Twain, Mark. *The Writings of Mark Twain,* 1899–1922, F. Collier and Sons Co., New York.

Wesley, John. *The Journal of John Wesley,* ed. P.L. Parker, 1974, Moody, Northbrook, Ill.

Westfall, Richard S. *The Construction of Modern Science: Mechanisms and Mechanics,* 1971, Cambridge University Press, Cambridge, U.K.

Wharton, Edith. *The Custom of the Country,* 1913, Scribner's Book Companies, New York.

Wilde, Oscar. *The Plays of Oscar Wilde,* Modern Library, New York.

Wootton, Barbara. *Crime and the Criminal Law,* 1963, Stevens, London.

Young, Agatha. *The Men Who Made Surgery,* 1961, Hillman Books, New York.

Index

modus ponens (affirming the antecedent), 158–59, 225
modus tollens (denying the consequent), 159–61, 205
mood of a syllogism, 260
moral principles, 35
moral reasoning, analogy in, 69
morality, natural, 16
Morris, Herbert, 28–29
Morton, Peggy, 14
Mumford, Lewis, 45
Murphy, J. G., 11
Murray, Gilbert, 45
The Mushroom Hunter's Field Guide (Smith), 4, 75
mutually exclusive events, 129, 146
My Philosophical Development (Russell), 35

Natural History (Pliny the Elder), 44
natural morality, 16
necessary causal condition, 109, 110, 120
negation, 208, 209, 228, 229, 231, 234
negative particular generalization. *See* O sentence
negative universal generalization. *See* E sentence
New Bottles for Old Wine (Huxley), 22
The New York Times, 70, 102–103, 180, 189
Newburn, E., 104, 105
Newman, J. R., 145
Newton, Isaac, 114, 176, 182, 305
Nietzsche, Friedrich, 51, 71, 122
Nisbett, Richard, 60, 92
Nixon, Richard, 11
None Dare Call It Conspiracy (Allen), 5
nonreflexive relations, 280, 292
nonsymmetric relations, 280, 292
nontransitive relations, 279, 292
Notebook (Twain), 41
Nuclear Power and Public Policy (Shrader-Frechette), 132, 222
numerals, systems of, 226–28

O sentence, 238, 239, 240, 241, 242, 243, 244, 245, 250–51, 258, 260, 262, 272, 273, 274
observable prediction, 171, 177, 197, 198
observation, 93, 118
obversion, 247, 250, 251, 266, 273
O'Connor, D. J., 290n
The Odd Woman (Gissing), 20
The Ominous Years (Boswell), 81
On Liberty (Mill), 93
On the Nature of the Universe (Lucretius), 259
On the Subjection of Women (Mill), 93
operational definitions, 309–11, 312
ordered pairs, 285
ordinary-language arguments, 296–312
The Origin of Species (Darwin), 8, 40
ostensive definitions, 300, 312
Our Mutual Friend (Dickens), 9

Parade Magazine, 42, 60, 87
Pascal, Blaise, 148

Pasteur, Louis, 42–43
Pepys, Samuel, 99
Perceiving, Sensing, and Knowing (Swartz), 27
Personal Finance (Cole), 50
persuasive definitions, 305–307, 312
"Petersburg Paradox," 143–45
Physical Anthropology and Archaeology (Jolly and Plog), 71
Physics (Aristotle), 166
Physics Today, 52
Pierce, H., 181
Pittsburgh Post-Gazette, 26, 44, 50, 181
Pittsburgh Press, 88, 166
placebos, 107
Pliny the Elder, 44
Plog, F., 70–71
Politics (Aristotle), 45
polls, 41, 55, 58
Pope, Alexander, 71
Popper, Karl, 184
The Population Bomb (Ehrlich), 6–7
Port-Royal Logic (Arnauld), 267–68
post hoc, 115–16, 120
posterior probability, 193, 198
precising definitions, 304
predicate letters, 283, 285
predicates, 284–85
premisses, 8–10, 24, 32
  in arguments of confirmation, 177
  missing, 15–17, 37, 83, 161–62
  strength of, 58, 61, 85
  in syllogisms, 71, 83
prior probability, 176–77, 190, 191–93, 198
"Prisoner's Dilemma," 141–43
probabilistic cause, 110–11, 113, 114, 115, 120
A Probabilistic Theory of Causality (Suppes), 44
probability, 124–47
  inductive logic and, 124–27
  inverse, 192
  posterior, 193, 198
  prior, 176–77, 190, 191–93, 198
  rules of, 127–33, 145
  total, 192
probability calculus, 125, 190, 191
probability values, 127
proof
  indirect, 36, 49
  mathematical, 34
proof by cases, 262–63
proof by contradiction, 218–19
proof methods
  using rules for valid syllogisms, 260–64
  using tree method, 319–21
  using truth tables, 209–10, 212, 215–20, 223–25, 233–35
  using Venn diagrams, 252–56, 260, 261–63, 274
propositional logic. *See* truth-functional logic
Prospero's Cell (Durrell), 4
proximate cause, 108–109, 120
pseudo-scientific theories, 183
The Psychodynamics of Creativity (Storr), 22
psychological influences, 107, 119

A 3
B 4
C 5
D 6
E 7
F 8
G 9
H 0
I 1
J 2